BASIC *Second Edition*

AN INTRODUCTION TO COMPUTER PROGRAMMING

Robert J. Bent
George C. Sethares
Bridgewater State College

D1305099

Brooks/Cole Publishing Company
Monterey, California

To Eleanor and Anita

Brooks/Cole Publishing Company
A Division of Wadsworth, Inc.

Printed in the United States of America

15   14   13   12   11   10   9

Library of Congress Cataloging in Publication Data

Bent, Robert J., date
   BASIC : an introduction to computer
programming.

   Includes index.
   1. Basic (Computer program language)
I. Sethares, George C., date   II. Title.
QA76.73.B3B46   1982   001.64'24   81–17033
ISBN 0-5340-1101-2   AACR2

Subject Editor: *James F. Leisy, Jr.*
Project Initiation: *John Moroney*
Manuscript Editor: *Dex Ott*
Production Editor: *Marlene Thom*
Interior and Cover Design: *Stan Rice*
Illustrations: *John Foster*
Typesetting: *Graphic Typesetting Service, Los Angeles, California*

Cover photo courtesy of pda Engineering, Santa Ana, California.

Preface

This book was written with two principal goals in mind. First, we felt it important to present the elements of BASIC so that meaningful computer programs could be written at the earliest possible time. We adhere to the notion that one learns by doing. As a result, problem solving is emphasized from the beginning, and the various aspects of the BASIC language are introduced only as needed. Our second goal was to write a book that would serve as a general introduction to computer programming, not just to a programming language. Simply describing a variety of computer applications and ways to go about writing BASIC programs for these applications does not constitute an introduction to programming. What is required is a consideration of the entire programming process.

The approach we have taken toward this objective is to introduce programming principles only as they can be understood and appreciated in the context of the applications being considered. For example, a beginner can easily appreciate the necessity of choosing variable names and determining how they are related. Hence, this step is introduced and discussed very early. On the other hand, the value of modularization—that is, breaking down a long and possibly complex task into more manageable subtasks—is not so easily grasped in the context of the straightforward programming problems first encountered. As natural as modularization may appear to an experienced programmer, a beginner must "see" its usefulness before being convinced of its value. Therefore, this programming principle, although illustrated in the early examples, is not discussed as a programming principle until later in the book.

A working knowledge of elementary algebra is the only mathematics needed to understand most of the material and to complete the assignments successfully. The examples and problems involving more advanced topics in mathematics, such as the trigonometric functions, may be omitted with no loss in continuity. Both the examples and the numerous problem sets are drawn from a wide range of application areas, including business, economics, personal finance, the natural and social sciences, and mathematics.

Throughout the text we have attempted to conform to the most common BASIC usage. In most cases, our presentation of BASIC conforms to the most recent American National Standards Institute (ANSI) standard for BASIC. Phrases such as "Your system may allow you to . . ." indicate that the BASIC feature being introduced is not included in the BASIC standard. The material contained in this text, including the problem sets, has been carefully organized so that topics that are not a part of standard BASIC may be omitted with no loss in continuity.

A few remarks are appropriate concerning the order in which we have introduced the elements of BASIC. The INPUT statement is introduced early and before the READ and DATA statements to emphasize the interactive nature of BASIC. The GO TO statement is presented with the INPUT statement so that the nature of the computer as a fast and sophisticated calculator can be shown early. The IF statement is introduced in the very next chapter so that certain difficulties arising from the use of GO TO statements can quickly be resolved. Selecting an order in which to present the remaining BASIC statements was not so simple. So that a person using this text will not be tied down to the order we have chosen, the introductory material for the remaining BASIC statements is presented in such a way that these statements can easily be taken up in some other order. Specifically, FOR/NEXT loops (Section 10.1), BCD Files (Section 13.1), Binary Files (Section 13.3), Subroutines (Section 14.1), and Multi-line Functions (Section 14.3) can be taken up any time after Chapter 8 (More on the PRINT Statement), and in any order. Also, Section 9.1, which introduces the READ and DATA statements, is written so that it can be taken up any time after the IF statement is introduced in Chapter 6.

Since the publication of the first edition of this text, there have been many changes in BASIC language computing systems. These, together with the general improvement in the teaching of computer programming, dictate certain changes in this second edition. The following list describes several of these new features.

An earlier introduction of string variables. String variables are introduced with the numerical variables, and their use is illustrated throughout the text.

A complete chapter on data files. The most commonly used BASIC statements for input/output processing with files are described. Programming techniques that can be used in file processing, and major differences in how BASIC systems handle files, are discussed and illustrated by example. A separate section on file maintenance has also been included.

An introductory chapter on problem solving. In this chapter (Chapter 2), the terms *algorithm* and *variable* are defined, and the sense in which computer programs and algorithms are equivalent is explained. Also, the steps leading to the discovery of algorithms to carry out specified tasks (that is, the steps involved in problem solving), are discussed and illustrated by example.

An earlier introduction to top-down programming. The method of top-down programming is used from the very beginning. It is introduced in Chapter 2 (without giving the method a name) and illustrated in many of the worked out examples throughout the text. In addition, the separate section (Section 9.4) that summarizes the method of top-down programming appears earlier in the text—just after the READ and DATA statements are introduced.

A separate section (Section 6.8) on structured programming. The flowchart constructs used in structured programming are described, and the terms *structured algorithm* and *structured program* are defined. A sequence of short examples shows how the structured programming constructs are easily coded in the BASIC language. Also, the benefits to be gained by writing structured programs are discussed.

A new section on external sorting. Methods of sorting data that do not fit in the computer's main memory at the same time are described.

While preparing this revision, we were fortunate to have at hand the comments of many users of the first edition and the feedback from a national survey of over 1000 BASIC instructors. Their thoughtful criticisms and suggestions were carefully considered and, in many instances, incorporated as changes in this edition. We are grateful for this assistance. So that we can continue to make improvements for future readers, we would welcome hearing of your experiences with this second edition. A cutout page for this purpose is provided at the end of the book.

We wish to take this opportunity to acknowledge the helpful comments of our reviewers: Wayne Bishop, California State University, Los Angeles; John L. Callaghan; Shirley Fedorovich, Embry-Riddle University; D. L. Muench, St. John Fisher College; and Larry E. Thomas, St. Peter's College. We feel that their many thoughtful suggestions have led to a greatly improved text.

A very special thanks goes to Patricia Shea, our typist, proofreader, debugger, and general assistant. Her five years of cheerful cooperation are greatly appreciated. Finally, we are happy to acknowledge the fine cooperation of the staff at Brooks/Cole Publishing Company.

Robert J. Bent
George C. Sethares

Contents

Interacting with the Computer 41

The Computer as a Decision Maker 55

Functions 93

More on the PRINT Statement 111

Entering Large Quantities of Data 129

Loops Made Easier 151

Arrays 177

Processing String Data 203

Data Files 227

Subroutines 253

Random Numbers and Their Application 271

Sorting and Searching 295

17 Matrices 311

BASIC

AN INTRODUCTION TO COMPUTER PROGRAMMING

Second Edition

1

Computer Systems

An electronic computer has the ability to store large quantities of data, to process these data at very fast rates, and to present the results of this processing in ways that are meaningful to the task at hand. Thus, if the task is to prepare a payroll, employee data will be stored in the computer, the computer will process these data to calculate relevant wage statistics, and the results will be presented in printed form, possibly including paychecks. This payroll example illustrates the three principal tasks involved in any computer application: data must be presented to the computer **(INPUT)**, data must be processed **(PROCESS)**, and results must be presented in a meaningful way **(OUTPUT).** (See Figure 1.1.)

Figure 1.1
An INPUT–PROCESS–
OUTPUT diagram.

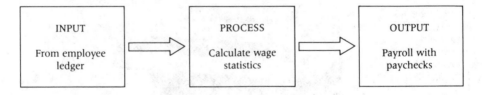

The purpose of this chapter is not to convince you that a computer can "do" many things, nor even to indicate the computer applications you will be able to carry out after completing this text. Rather, the objectives of this chapter are to introduce you to the types of computer equipment you may encounter, to describe what a computer program is, and to introduce certain terminology that is helpful when talking about computers.

1.1 Computer hardware

Central to every computer system is an electronic computer whose principal function is to process data. The computer component that does this is called the **central processing unit (CPU).** The CPU contains an **arithmetic unit,** consisting of circuitry that performs a variety of arithmetic and logical operations, and a **control unit,** which controls all electrical signals passing through the computer. In addition to the CPU, every computer has a **memory unit** that can store data, and from which data can be retrieved for processing. Fortunately, you need not understand how a computer processes data to make a computer work for you. The circuitry in a computer is not unlike that in an ordinary pocket calculator, and all who have used calculators know that no knowledge of their circuitry is needed to use them.

Data must be transmitted to the computer (*Input*), and results of the processing must be returned (*Output*). Devices meeting these two requirements are called **input** and **output (I/O) devices.** The I/O devices you are most likely to encounter in your introduction to computer programming are as follows.

Teletypewriter and Video Terminals: These serve as both input and output devices. On a teletypewriter (Figure 1.2) you transmit information to the computer simply by typing it at the teletypewriter keyboard and the computer transmits the results back to the teletypewriter, which produces a printed copy for you. A video terminal (Figure 1.3) works the same way except that the results are displayed on a video screen.

Line Printers: A line printer (Figure 1.4) serves only as an output device. As indicated by its name, an entire line of output is printed simultaneously.

Most modern computer systems are equipped with storage devices other than the memory unit. They are called *external* (or *secondary*) storage devices because they are not a part of the computer as is the memory unit. The most common external storage devices are as follows.

Magnetic-tape units: Information is stored on magnetic tapes as sequences of magnetized "spots." Although tape units can be rather "large" (Figure 1.5), some computer systems (especially microcomputer systems) use ordinary cassette tape recorders. Data are "read" from a tape by reading through the tape sequentially until the desired data are found. For this reason, tape units are called sequential access devices.

Disk-storage units: Information is stored on rotating disks that resemble phonograph records. However, the disks have no grooves; the data are stored as sequences of magnetized spots appearing on concentric circles. A disk unit will contain one or more disks, each with one or more read/write heads. Disk units are called random access devices. The term *random access* indicates

Figure 1.2
(far right) ASR Model 43 Data Terminal with paper tape unit. (*Courtesy of Teletype Corporation.*) (right) DECwriter LA-36 Terminal. (*Courtesy of Digital Equipment Corporation.*)

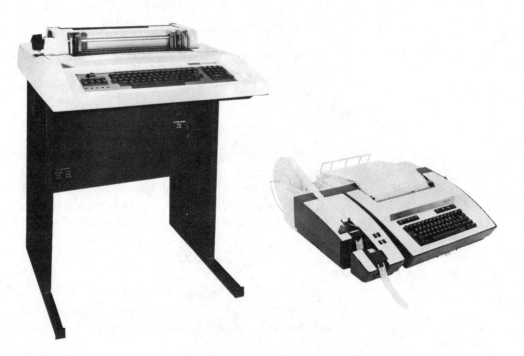

Figure 1.3
Digital VT100 Video display with keyboard. (*Courtesy of Digital Equipment Corporation.*)

Figure 1.4
Dataproducts' B-Series band printer. (*Courtesy of Dataproducts Corporation.*)

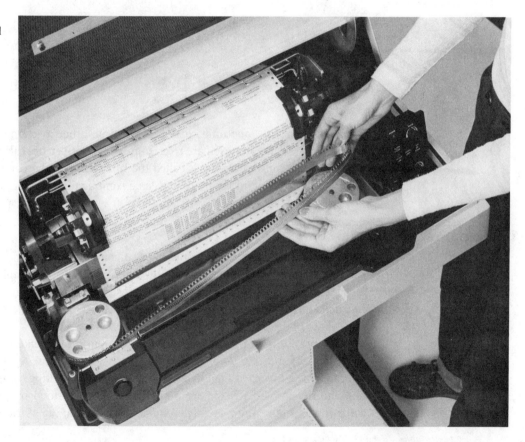

that data stored on any part of a disk can be accessed directly without having to read through the entire disk to find the desired data. Figure 1.6a shows a small floppy-disk unit. The term "floppy" is used because the disk is flexible. Figure 1.6b shows a disk pack containing several individual hard disks—that is, disks that are rigid and not flexible.

Figure 1.5
Magnetic tape unit. (*Courtesy of Honeywell Information Systems.*)

Data terminals, tape units, disk units, and all other mechanical and electrical devices other than the computer itself are referred to as **computer peripherals.** The computer and all peripherals constitute what is called the **hardware** of the computer system. Figure 1.7 illustrates the flow of information between a computer and its peripherals.

1.2 Computer software

The physical components, or hardware, of a computer system are inanimate objects. They cannot prepare a payroll or perform any other task, however simple, without human assistance. This assistance is given in the form of instructions to the computer. A sequence of such instructions is called a **computer program,** and a person who determines what these instructions should be is called a **programmer.**

The precise form that instructions to a computer must take depends on the particular computer system being used. **BASIC** (Beginner's All-purpose Symbolic Instruction Code)[1] is a carefully constructed English-like language used for writing computer programs. Instructions in the BASIC language are designed to be understood by people as well as by the computer. Even the uninitiated will understand the meaning of this simple BASIC program:

```
1 LET A=3
2 LET B=A+5
3 PRINT B
4 END
```

[1] BASIC was developed at Dartmouth College under the direction of John G. Kemeny and Thomas E. Kurtz.

Figure 1.6a
TRS-80 Mini-Disk System.
(*Courtesy of Radio Shack, a Division of Tandy Corporation.*)

Figure 1.6b
IBM 5445 Removable Disk Pack and Drive. (*Courtesy of IBM Corporation.*)

A computer is an electronic device and understands an instruction such as LET A = 3 in a very special way. An electronic device can distinguish between two distinct electrical states. Consider, for instance, an ordinary on/off switch for a light fixture. When the switch is in the "on" position, current is allowed to flow and the light bulb glows. If we denote the "on" position by the number 1 and the "off" position by the number 0, we can say that the instruction 1 causes the bulb to glow and the instruction 0 causes it not to glow. In like manner, we could envision a machine with two switches whose positions are denoted by the four codes 00, 01, 10, and 11 such that each of these four codes causes a different event to occur. It is this ability to distinguish between two distinct electrical states that has led to the

Figure 1.7
Flow of information through
a computer system.

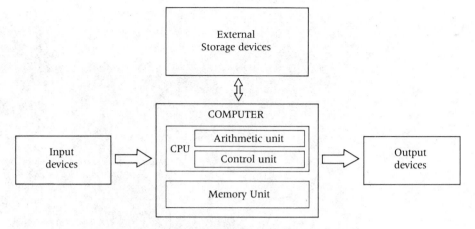

development of modern computers. Indeed, modern computers are still based on this principle. Each computer is designed to "understand" a certain set of primitive instructions. On some computers these instructions take the form of sequences of 0s and 1s, but their precise form is not important to the beginner. All such primitive instructions that are meaningful to a particular computer are together called the **machine language** for that computer.

You will not be required to write programs in machine language. The computer you use will contain an **interpreter** or a **compiler,** which automatically translates your BASIC instructions into equivalent machine-language instructions that are then executed by the computer. An *interpreter* translates a BASIC instruction into machine code each time it is to be carried out. As indicated in Figure 1.8, a *compiler* translates an entire program into machine code only once. For this reason, a BASIC program will execute much more rapidly on computers that use compilers than on computers that use interpreters. The difference can be significant!

BASIC compilers and interpreters are themselves computer programs. They are called **systems programs** because they are an integral part of the computer system being used. The BASIC programs appearing in this text, as well as the programs you will write, are called **applications programs.** They are not an integral part of the computer system, so they are not called systems programs. All computer programs, both systems programs and applications programs, are called **computer software.** The term *software* refers not only to computer programs, but also to any documentation, such as manuals and circuit diagrams, concerned with the operation of computers.

In addition to a BASIC interpreter or compiler, your system will include other systems programs. These will be programs that produce printed listings of your programs, that "save" your programs on secondary storage devices for later use, that assist you in finding errors in the programs you write, and, most important of all, a program that exercises general control over the entire system. This last program is called the **operating system.** It allows you to issue commands to the computer to "call up" and execute any of the other systems programs provided.

Figure 1.8
INPUT–PROCESS–OUTPUT
diagram for a BASIC
compiler.

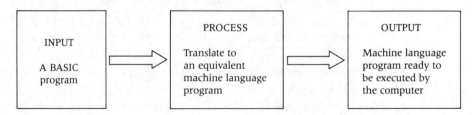

A computer system that accepts BASIC programs will be called a **BASIC system.** Figure 1.9 shows a complete BASIC system that contains a special cassette tape-storage unit. Figure 1.10 depicts a more elaborate BASIC system that includes several video displays. Such a system is called a **time-sharing system** because it provides for the simultaneous use of a computer by more than one user.

The emergence of computer science as a new discipline has been accompanied by a proliferation of new words and expressions. They are useful for talking about computers but

Figure 1.9
Radio Shack TRS-80
Microcomputer System.
(*Courtesy of Radio Shack, a
Division of Tandy
Corporation.*)

Figure 1.10.
Wang MVP Computer
System. (*Photo courtesy of
Wang Laboratories, Inc.,
Lowell, Mass.*)

are, for the most part, absolutely unnecessary if your objective is to learn a computer language such as BASIC to assist you in solving problems. In our discussion of computer hardware and software, we have attempted to introduce only fundamental concepts and frequently used terminology. If this is your first exposure to computers, you may feel lost in this terminology. Don't be disheartened: much of the new vocabulary has already been introduced. You will become more familiar with it and recognize its usefulness as you study the subsequent chapters. You will also find it helpful to reread this chapter after you have written a few computer programs.

1.3 Review true-or-false quiz

1. The principal function of a computer is to process data.   T   F
2. The term *arithmetic unit* is another name for the CPU.   T   F
3. I/O devices, external storage devices, and the central processing unit are called computer peripherals.   T   F
4. The function of a BASIC compiler is to translate BASIC programs into machine language.   T   F
5. The terms *compiler* and *interpreter* are used synonymously.   T   F
6. To solve problems using the BASIC language, you must know and understand what a compiler is or what an interpreter is.   T   F
7. A BASIC program written to solve a particular problem may accurately be called a systems program.   T   F
8. The expressions *computer software* and *computer program* are synonymous.   T   F
9. A computer system must contain at least one teletypewriter.   T   F
10. Disk storage units are called *random access devices* because information stored on a disk is accessed by randomly searching portions of the disk until the desired data are found.   T   F
11. Tape units are called *sequential access devices* because information is read from a tape by reading through the tape until the desired data are found.   T   F
12. An operating system is a computer system.   T   F

2

Problem Solving

A computer program consists of a sequence of instructions to the computer. These instructions describe a step-by-step process for carrying out a specified task. Such a process is called an *algorithm*. Algorithms have been with us since antiquity: the familiar division algorithm was known and used in ancient Greece; the activities of bookkeepers have always been guided by algorithms (an algorithm to determine a tax assessment, an algorithm to calculate a depletion allowance, and so on); even the instructions for assembling a child's new toy are often given as an algorithm.

Since a computer program describes an algorithm, the process of writing computer programs can be equated to the process of discovering algorithms. For this reason, an understanding of what is, and what is not, an algorithm is indispensable to a programmer.

2.1 Algorithms

An algorithm is a prescribed set of well-defined rules and processes for solving a problem in a finite number of steps. Here is an algorithm giving instructions for completing a financial transaction at a drive-in teller port.

    a. Press the call button.
    b. Remove the carrier from the tray.
    c. Place your transaction inside the carrier.
    d. Replace the carrier.
    e. When the carrier returns, remove the transaction.
    f. Replace the carrier.

To see that these six steps describe an algorithm, we must verify that each step is well defined and that the process stops in a finite number of steps. For example, step (a) requires that there be only one call button, and step (b) requires that there be but one tray containing a single carrier. Having verified that each step is well defined, and noting that the process is obviously finite, we are assured that the process does indeed describe an algorithm. In addition, it should be clear that the algorithm "does" what is claimed.

The previous example illustrates the following three properties of any algorithm.

1. Each step must be well defined—that is, unambiguous.
2. The process must halt in a finite number of steps.
3. The process must "do" what is claimed.

Following are two additional examples to help you gain an understanding of what an algorithm is and some practice with the process of discovering algorithms.

EXAMPLE 1. Let's find an algorithm to calculate the year-end bonus for all salaried employees in a firm. Employees are to be paid 3% of their annual salary or $400, whichever is larger.

To carry out this task, a payroll clerk might proceed as follows.

a. Open the employee ledger.
b. Turn to the next employee's account.
c. Determine the employee's bonus.
d. Write the employee's name and bonus amount on the bonus sheet.
e. If all bonuses have not been determined, return to step (b).
f. Close the ledger.

It is not difficult to see that these six instructions constitute an algorithm. Each step is well defined, and, since a business can employ only a finite number of people, the algorithm will terminate in a finite number of steps. Moreover, if this algorithm is followed, all employee bonuses will be determined as specified.

Although the algorithm "does" what was asked, the process could be made more specific by including more detail in step (c). Recalling the method specified for calculating bonus amounts, we can substitute the following for step (c).

c1. Multiply the employee's salary by .03 to obtain a tentative bonus.
c2. If the tentative bonus is at least $400, go to step (d).
c3. Set the bonus to $400.

Making this change, or *refinement*, we obtain the following more detailed algorithm.

a. Open the employee ledger.
b. Turn to the next employee's account.
c1. Multiply the employee's salary by .03 to obtain a tentative bonus.
c2. If the tentative bonus is at least $400, go to step (d).
c3. Set the bonus to $400.
d. Write the employee's name and bonus amount on the bonus sheet.
e. If all bonuses have not been determined, return to step (b).
f. Close the ledger.

Remark 1

The first algorithm is more general than the second. It describes a process one might follow to determine employee bonuses, however they are to be calculated. The second algorithm can be used only if bonuses are calculated as specified in the problem statement.

Remark 2

It is somewhat easier to verify that the first algorithm "does" what was asked. This is because of, and not in spite of, the detail not present in the algorithm. Having verified that the first algorithm is correct, all that is required to verify that the second algorithm is also correct is to check that steps (c1), (c2), and (c3) describe the same task as step (c) of the first algorithm.

EXAMPLE 2. Let's find an algorithm to determine the largest number in a list of ten numbers.

One way to determine the largest number in a list of ten numbers is to read them one at a time, remembering only the largest of those already read. To help us give a precise description of this process, let's use two symbols as follows:

L to denote the largest of those numbers already read.
N to denote the number currently being read.

The following algorithm can now be written.

a. Read the first number and denote it by L.
b. Read the next number and denote it by N.
c. If L is at least as large as N, skip the next step.
d. Assign the number N to L.
e. If all ten numbers have not been read, go to step (b).
f. Print the value of L and stop.

To verify this algorithm for the list of numbers

4, 5, 3, 6, 6, 2, 1, 8, 7, 3

we simply proceed step-by-step through the algorithm, always keeping track of the latest values of L and N. An orderly way to do this is to complete an assignment table as follows.

Algorithm step	L	N
a	4	
b		5
d	5	
b		3
b		6
d	6	
b		6
b		2
b		1
b		8
d	8	
b		7
b		3

Note that after all ten numbers have been processed the largest number in the list is the last value of L.

Remark

If the ten numbers are written on a sheet of paper, a person could simply look them over and select the largest. However, this process is heuristic and does not constitute an algorithm.[1] To see that this is so, imagine many hundreds of numbers written on a large sheet of paper. In this case, selecting the largest simply by looking over the numbers can easily result in an error. What is needed is an orderly process that will ensure that the largest number is selected. Examining numbers one at a time, as was done in the algorithm, is such an orderly process.

2.2 Variables

Algorithms can often be easily and clearly stated if symbols are used to denote certain quantities. Symbols are especially helpful when used to denote quantities that may change during the process of performing the steps in an algorithm. The symbols L and N used in Example 2 are illustrations of this practice.

A quantity that can change during a process is called a **variable quantity,** or simply a **variable.** A symbol used to denote such a variable quantity is the name of the variable. Thus, L and N, in Example 2, are names of variables. However, it is a common practice to refer to the *symbol* as being the variable itself, rather than just its name. For instance, step (f) of the algorithm for Example 2 says to print the value of L. Certainly, this is less confusing than saying "Print the value of the variable whose name is L."

Each of the examples in Section 2.1 concerns an algorithm describing a process to be carried out by people. A computer programmer must be concerned with algorithms describing processes to be carried out by a computer. This means that each step must describe an action that a computer can perform. This constraint is not so restrictive as it may appear. Computer languages, such as BASIC, contain instructions to assign numerical values to variables, to perform arithmetic operations, to compare numerical quantities and transfer control to different instructions depending on the result of this comparison, and to print numerical values. Each step in the algorithm of Example 2 represents one of those four types of action, which means that the algorithm does indeed describe a process that can be carried out by a computer.

Even instructions that appear to have nothing at all to do with computers can sometimes describe meaningful computer operations. As you progress through your study of BASIC, you will find that statements such as "Open the employee ledger," as found in the algorithm of Example 1, can indeed correspond to actions a computer can carry out.

The problems at the end of this chapter are designed to give you practice with the process of discovering algorithms. At this point it is not important that the individual steps in an algorithm correspond to actions that a computer can perform. A knowledge of what constitutes an admissible instruction to a computer will come as you gain experience in working with the BASIC language. What is important is that the individual steps are easy to understand and that the process described is an algorithm that, when carried out, does what is asked.

We conclude this chapter with a third example illustrating the process of discovering algorithms.

---

[1] A *heuristic process* is one involving exploratory methods. Solutions to problems are discovered by a continual evaluation of the progress made toward the final result. For instance, suppose you come upon an old map indicating that a treasure is buried in the Black Hills. You may be able to work out a plan that you know will lead to the location shown on the map. *That's an algorithm.* However, suppose you can find no such plan. Determined to find the location, or to verify that the map is a fake, you decide upon a first step in your search, with no idea of what the next step will be. *That's exploratory.* Carrying out this first step may suggest a second step, or it may lead you nowhere, in which case you would try something else. Continuing in this manner, you may eventually find the location, or you may determine that the map is a fake. But, it is also possible that the search will end only when you quit. Whatever the outcome, the process used is heuristic. Someone else using this process will undoubtedly carry out entirely different steps and perhaps reach a different conclusion.

EXAMPLE 3

Find an algorithm to prepare a depreciation schedule for a delivery van whose cost is $10,000, whose salvage value is $2,000, and whose useful life is 5 years. Use the straight-line method. (The straight-line method assumes that the value of the van will decrease by one-fifth of $8,000 (cost − salvage value) during each of the 5 years).

For each year, let's agree to write one line showing the year, the depreciation allowance for that year, the cumulative depreciation (sum of yearly depreciations to that point), and the book value (cost − cumulative depreciation) at the end of the year. A person carrying out this task might proceed as follows:

a. Look up the cost ($10,000), the salvage value ($2,000), and the useful life (5 years).
b. Determine the depreciation allowance for 1 year.
c. Subtract the depreciation allowance from the book value (initially the cost).
d. Add the depreciation amount to the cumulative depreciation (initially zero).
e. Write one line showing the year, the depreciation allowance for that year, the cumulative depreciation, and the book value at the end of the year.
f. If the schedule is not complete, go to step (c).
g. Stop.

Let's modify this algorithm to apply to any capital item whose cost, salvage value, and useful life are known but are not necessarily equal to those given in the problem statement.

To help describe this more general algorithm, let's first choose variable names to denote the various quantities of interest.

B = book value. (The initial book value is the cost.)
S = salvage value.
Y = useful life in years.
D = depreciation allowance for one year. ($D = (B − S)/Y$.)
C = cumulative depreciation (initially zero).

The following algorithm describes one way to carry out the specified task.

a. Assign values to B, S, and Y.
b. Assign the value $0.00 to C.
c. Calculate $D = (B − S)/Y$.
d. Subtract D from B.
e. Add D to C.
f. Write one line showing the year and the values D, C, and B.
g. If the schedule is not complete, go to step (d).
h. Stop.

This algorithm leads to the following depreciation schedule.

Year	Depreciation allowance	Cumulative depreciation	Book value
1	1600	1600	8400
2	1600	3200	6800
3	1600	4800	5200
4	1600	6400	3600
5	1600	8000	2000

Remark   It is not often that a problem statement exactly describes the problem to be resolved. Problem statements are usually written in a natural language, such as English, and thus are subject to the ambiguities inherent in natural languages. Moreover, they are written by people, which means that they are subject to human oversight and error. An algorithm describes a precise, unambiguous process for carrying out a task. Thus the task to be performed must be clearly understood. If it appears ambiguous, the ambiguities must be resolved. If it appears that one thing is being asked where another is actually desired, the difference must be resolved. For example, the problem statement in the present example asks for only a very limited algorithm (a book value of $10,000, a salvage value of $2000, and a useful life of 5 years) when what is really desired is the more general algorithm that has a wider application.

Skill in algorithm discovery must be developed by practice. The problem-solving methods begun in this chapter will be emphasized throughout the text. If you study the examples carefully and work a good selection of the problems at the end of each section, you will have ample opportunity to improve your problem-solving ability.

2.3 Problems

Problems 1–4 refer to the following algorithm, which is intended for completing an invoice:

a. Let AMOUNT = 0.
b. Read QUANTITY and PRICE of an item.
c. Add the product QUANTITY × PRICE to AMOUNT.
d. If there is another item, go to step (b). Otherwise, continue with step (e).
e. If AMOUNT is not greater than $500, go to step (h). Otherwise, continue with step (f).
f. Evaluate the product .05 × AMOUNT.
g. Subtract this product from AMOUNT.
h. Record the value AMOUNT and stop.

1. What interpretation could be given to the product appearing in step (f)?
2. What purpose would you say is served by step (e)?
3. If the values (10, $3.00), (50, $8.00), and (25, $12.00) are read by step (b), what value will be recorded by step (h)?
4. If the values (100, $2.00) and (50, $1.00) are read by step (b), what value will be recorded by step (h)?

Problems 5–8 refer to the following algorithm, which is intended for use by a payroll clerk as a preliminary step in the preparation of a payroll:

a. Read the next time card.
b. Let H = number of hours worked.
c. If H is not greater than 32, let G = B = 0 and go to step (f). Otherwise, continue with the next step.
d. Evaluate 6 × (H − 32) and assign this value to both G and B.
e. Let H = 32.
f. Evaluate 4 × H and add this value to G.
g. Write the values G and B on the time card.
h. If there is another time card, go to step (a). Otherwise, stop.

5. If the numbers of hours shown on the first four time cards are 20, 32, 40, and 45, respectively, what amounts will be written on these cards?
6. What is the base hourly rate for each employee?
7. What is the overtime rate?
8. Explain step (c).

What will be printed when each algorithm shown in Problems 9–12 is carried out?

9. a. Let SUM = 0 and N = 1.
   b. Add N to SUM.
   c. If N < 6, increase N by 1 and return to step (b). Otherwise, continue with step (d).
   d. Print the value SUM and stop.

10. a. Let PROD = N = 1.
   b. Print the values N and PROD on one line.
   c. Increase N by 1.
   d. If N exceeds 6, stop. Otherwise, continue with the next step.
   e. Multiply PROD by N and go to step (b).

11. a. Let A = B = 1 and NUM = 3.
   b. Evaluate A + B and assign this value to F.
   c. If NUM does not exceed 9, increase NUM by 1 and proceed to step (d). Otherwise, print the value F and stop.
   d. Assign the values of B and F to A and B, respectively, and go to step (b).

12. a. Let NUM = 56, SUM = 1, and D = 2.
   b. If D is a factor of NUM, add D to SUM and print D.
   c. If D $\geq$ NUM/2, print SUM and stop.
   d. Increase D by 1, and go to step (b).

Write an algorithm to carry out each task specified in Problems 13–19.

13. A retail store's monthly sales report shows, for each item, the fixed cost, the sale price, and the number sold. Prepare a three-column report with the column headings ITEM, GROSS SALES, and INCOME.

14. Each of several three-by-five cards contains an employee's name, Social Security number, job classification, and date hired. Prepare a report showing the names, job classifications, and complete years of service for employees who have been with the company for more than ten years.

15. A summary sheet of an investor's stock portfolio shows, for each stock, the corporation name, the number of shares owned, the current price, and the earnings as reported for the most recent year. Prepare a six-column report with the column headings CORP. NAME, NO. OF SHARES, PRICE, EARNINGS, EQUITY, and PRICE/EARNINGS. Use this formula:
$$\text{Equity} = \text{No. of Shares} \times \text{Price}$$

16. Each of several cards contains a single number. Determine the sum and the average of all of the numbers. (Use a variable N to count how many cards are read and a variable SUM to keep track of the sum of the numbers already read.)

17. Each of several cards contains a single number. On each card, write the letter G if the number is greater than the average of all of the numbers. Otherwise, write the letter L on the card. (You must read through the cards twice: once to find the average, and a second time to determine whether to write the letter G or the letter L on the cards.)

18. A local supermarket has installed a check-validation machine. To use this service, a customer must have previously obtained an identification card containing a magnetic strip and also a four-digit code. Instructions showing how to insert the identification card into a special magnetic-strip reader appear on the front panel. To validate a check, a customer must present the identification card to the machine, enter the four-digit code, enter the amount of the check, and place the check, blank side toward the customer, in a special clearly labeled punch unit. To begin this process, the CLEAR key must be depressed, and, after each of the two entries has been made, the ENTER key must be depressed. Prepare an algorithm giving instructions for validating a check.

19. Write an algorithm describing the steps to be taken to cast a ballot in a national election. Assume that a person using this algorithm is a registered voter and has just entered the building in which voting is to take place. While in the voting booth, the voter should simply be instructed to vote. No instructions concerning the actual filling out of a ballot are to be given.

2.4 Review true-or-false quiz

1. The terms *algorithm* and *process* are synonymous.   T F
2. The following steps describe an algorithm.
   a. Let N = 0.
   b. Increase N by 10.
   c. Divide N by 2.
   d. If N<10, go to step (b).
   e. Stop.   T F
3. A computer program should describe an algorithm.   T F
4. Every algorithm can be translated into a computer program.   T F
5. The expression *heuristic process* refers to an algorithm.   T F
6. It is always easier to verify the correctness of an algorithm that describes a very
   specific task than the correctness of a more general algorithm.   T F
7. The expressions *variable quantity* and *variable* are used synonymously. Both refer to
   a quantity that can change during a process.   T F

A First Look at BASIC

We must communicate with a computer before it will perform any service for us. The vehicle for such communication is the computer program, which, for our purposes, will be a sequence of instructions in the English-like language BASIC. Here is a BASIC program whose purpose is described in the first line.

```
100 REM PROGRAM TO AVERAGE THREE NUMBERS
110 REM   X, Y, AND Z DENOTE THE NUMBERS
120 REM   A DENOTES THE AVERAGE
130 LET X=43
140 LET Y=27
150 LET Z=23
160 LET A=(X+Y+Z)/3
170 PRINT "AVERAGE IS", A
180 END
```

If a computer carries out the instructions appearing in this program, it will produce the following output.

```
AVERAGE IS     31
```

The lines in this program are labeled with *line numbers* that determine the order in which the instructions are carried out by the computer. The program uses four words, called **keywords,** from the BASIC language: REM, to include remarks or comments as part of the program; LET, to associate certain numerical values with certain symbols (for example, line 130 associates 43 with the symbol X); PRINT, to print the results; and END, to indicate the last line of the program.

Unlike a natural language, such as English, a programming language must not allow ambiguities. The computer must do precisely what it is instructed to do. For this reason, great care must be taken to write BASIC instructions precisely according to the BASIC **syntax** (BASIC rules of grammar). The following sections describe how the keywords REM, LET, PRINT, and END can be used to form admissible BASIC programs. A complete treatment of these topics is not intended at this time; our immediate goal is to provide you with the minimal information needed to understand and to write some BASIC programs.

3.1 Numerical constants and variables

Three types of numerical constants are allowed in BASIC.

Type	Examples
Integer	726 99234 -726 $+423$ -16023 0
Decimal	726. -133.50 $+10.001$ $-99234.$ 0.201
Floating-point (exponential)	1E4 $-13.6E-2$ .12345E03 $+2.345E-01$

Integers are numbers with no decimal point, and decimals are numbers in which a decimal point appears. The use of commas and dollar signs in numbers is not allowed; using 99,234 to represent 99234 will result in an error. The third type of numerical constant may be new to you. The general form for a floating-point constant, together with its meaning, is

$$n\text{E}m = n \times 10^m$$

Here n may be any integer or decimal, but m must be an integer. E stands for "exponent." The values of the four floating-point numbers shown above are:

$$
\begin{aligned}
1\text{E}4 &= 1 \times 10^4 & &= 1 \times 10000 & &= 10000 \\
-13.6\text{E}-2 &= -13.6 \times 10^{-2} & &= -13.6 \times .01 & &= -0.136 \\
.12345\text{E}03 &= .12345 \times 10^3 & &= .12345 \times 1000 & &= 123.45 \\
+2.345\text{E}-01 &= 2.345 \times 10^{-1} & &= 2.345 \times .1 & &= 0.2345
\end{aligned}
$$

Note that 1E4 represents 10000, but E4 is meaningless.

Although in some programming languages the programmer must exhibit caution concerning the representation of numbers in these three forms, the BASIC programmer is free to use any form desired.

BASIC allows the following as numerical variable names.

$$A, B, C, \ldots, Z$$
$$A0, A1, A2, \ldots, A9$$
$$B0, B1, B2, \ldots, B9$$
$$\cdot \quad \cdot$$
$$\cdot \quad \cdot$$
$$Z0, Z1, Z2, \ldots, Z9$$

(Some, but not all, systems allow numerical variable names containing many characters—for example, SUM, PRICE1, and A135.)

3.2 String constants and variables

A **string constant** is a sequence, or **string,** of BASIC characters enclosed in quotation marks. The following are string constants.

```
"INCOME"              "NANCY JONES"
"X="                  "567"
"19 APRIL 1775"       "*****"
```

The value of a string constant is the sequence of all BASIC characters, including blanks, appearing between the quotes. Thus, the value of the string constant "NANCY JONES" is the string NANCY JONES. A string may contain as many characters as will fit on a line.

Variables whose values are strings are called **string variables.** A string variable is denoted by a single letter followed by a dollar sign: A$, B$, . . . , Z$. (As with numerical variables, some, but not all, systems allow string variable names containing many characters—for example, NAME$, COLOR$, and LETTER$.)

3.3 Arithmetic operations and expressions

BASIC uses the following symbols to denote arithmetic operations.

BASIC symbol	Meaning	Priority
∧ or ↑ or **	Exponentiation	1
*	Multiplication	2
/	Division	2
+	Addition	3
−	Subtraction	3

Any meaningful combination of BASIC constants, variable names, and operation symbols is called a BASIC **expression.** In any BASIC expression the order in which the operations are performed is determined first by the indicated priority and then, in any priority class, from left to right. This is in agreement with the usual meaning of arithmetic expressions.

EXAMPLE 1. In the following expressions the circled numbers indicate the order in which the operations will be performed by the computer.

```
    ①  ②
a. 5 − 4 + 3 =
   1   + 3 =
       4
```

Since + and − have the same priority, they are performed from left to right. Note that performing the + first gives the incorrect value −2.

```
    ③  ①  ②
b. 2 + 6 / 2 * 3 =
   2 +  3  * 3 =
   2 + 9 =
   11
```

Since / and * have the same priority, they are performed from left to right. Note that performing the * first gives the incorrect value 3.

```
    ③  ①  ④  ②
c. 5 * 2 ↑ 2 + 3 ↑ 2
```

Performing these operations one at a time, we obtain

```
5 * 2 ↑ 2 + 3 ↑ 2 =
5 *   4   + 3 ↑ 2 =
5 *   4   + 9     =
  20 + 9 =
     29
```

Parentheses may be used in BASIC expressions just as in ordinary algebra. They are used to override the normal order in which operations are performed and also to help clarify the meaning of numerical expressions. For example, 5/2*3 and (5/2)*3 have the same meaning in BASIC, but the second form is less likely to be misinterpreted. A third use of parentheses in BASIC is explained in Example 3.

EXAMPLE 2. In the following, P = 14, Q = −5, and R = 7.

BASIC expression	Value of expression
P+(Q−R)	2
P/(4*R)	0.5
(Q+P)/(R−4)	3
Q+P/R−4	−7
(Q+R)↑2+P	18
3↑(R+Q)	9
R*(R*(R+1)+1)	399

Expressions such as +5, −1.2, +A, and −B are also allowed in BASIC. Both +A and A have the same meaning, and −B denotes the negative of B. When + and − are used in this manner, they are called **unary operations.** It is unlikely that you will ever have cause to use the unary operation +, but you may often find it convenient to use the unary operation −. For example, if you need the negative of the sum of A and B, you can use the expression

    −(A+B)

Also, if you wish to raise the value of the expression X + Y*Z to the power −2, you can use

    (X+Y*Z)↑(−2)

rather than the equivalent but somewhat more complicated expression

    (1/(X+Y*Z))↑2

Unfortunately, BASIC systems differ in how numerical expressions containing the unary operation − are evaluated. In particular, on some systems the expression −5 ↑ 2 is evaluated as − (5 ↑ 2) to give −25, and on others it is evaluated as (−5) ↑ 2 to give 25. Following are the two methods used by computers to evaluate expressions containing unary operations.

Method 1: The unary operations + and − have the same priority as addition (+) and subtraction (−), but are performed prior to all other + and − operations (but not before ↑, *, and /). If your computer uses this method, $-5 \uparrow 2$ will be evaluated as $-(5 \uparrow 2)$ to give -25.

Method 2: The unary operations $+$ and $-$ are assigned the highest priority, hence they are performed prior to any of the other operations. If your computer uses this method, $-5 \uparrow 2$ will be evaluated as $(-5) \uparrow 2$ to give 25.

Although you should determine which method your computer uses, the best, and safest, policy is to use parentheses so that no confusion can arise.

EXAMPLE 3. In the following, A = 3, B = −2, and C = 4.

BASIC expression	Value of expression
−A	−3
+B	−2
−B	2
−A + B	−5
−5*A+4	−11
1−3↑C	−80
4−3+2/4+A	4.5
A↑2+B↑2	13
A/B*C	−6 (not −.375)
(C−5)↑(−2)	1
−2↑4	system dependent (−16 or 16)
(−2)↑4	16
−(2↑4)	−16
B↑C	16

Remark

The parentheses surrounding −2 in the expression (C − 5) ↑ (−2) are necessary so that two operation symbols do not appear adjacent to each other. Failure to observe this rule will result in an error on many BASIC systems.

Roots of numbers are indicated in BASIC by using the exponentiation operator ↑. Recall from algebra that

$$\sqrt{9} = 9^{1/2} = 3.$$

In BASIC, we write this as

$$9 \uparrow (1/2) \quad \text{or} \quad 9 \uparrow 0.5$$

EXAMPLE 4. In the following, M = 4 and N = 5.

Algebraic expression	Equivalent BASIC expression	Value
$\sqrt{M}$	M↑(1/2)	2
$\sqrt{M + N}$	(M+N)↑0.5	3
$\sqrt[3]{2M}$	(2*M)↑(1/3)	2
$\sqrt[3]{7 + MN}$	(7 + M*N)↑(1/3)	3
$6\sqrt{5 + M - N}$	6*(5 + M − N)↑0.5	12

Caution

BASIC systems are not designed to take roots of negative numbers. For example, the cube root of -8 is -2, but the BASIC expression $(-8) \uparrow (1/3)$ will not give this value. BASIC expressions such as A $\uparrow$ B will result in an error if the exponent B is not an integer and A is negative.

3.4 Problems

1. Evaluate the following.
   a. 2+3*5
   b. 5*7-2
   c. -4+2
   d. -(4+2)
   e. -3*5
   f. -3↑2
   g. 1+2↑3*2
   h. 6/2*3
   i. 1/2/2
   j. -2*3/2*3
   k. 2↑2↑3
   l. (2+(3*4-5))↑0.5

2. For A = 2, B = 3, and X = 2, evaluate each of the following.
   a. A+B/X
   b. (A+B)/2*X
   c. B/A/X
   d. B/(A*X)
   e. A+X↑3
   f. (A+B)↑X
   g. B↑A/X
   h. B+A/B-A
   i. A↑B+X
   j. B↑(X/A)
   k. -A↑B
   l. (-A)↑B

3. Some of the following are not admissible BASIC expressions. Explain why.
   a. (Y+Z)X
   b. X2*36
   c. A*(2.1-7B)
   d. X↑-2
   e. A+-B
   f. -(A+2B)
   g. 2X↑2
   h. X2↑2
   i. X-2↑2
   j. A12+B3
   k. A+(+B)
   l. A2-(-A2)

4. Some of the following are admissible BASIC expressions and some are not. Rewrite those that are not and evaluate all of them.
   a. -3*(4+.1)
   b. 2+(2)
   c. 4*-3
   d. (5/4)*8
   e. -2↑2*3
   f. 5E1.0
   g. (-3)↑2
   h. -3↑2
   i. 7/-14
   j. -3+(-3+1)
   k. 9↑1/2
   l. -9↑(1/2)

5. Write BASIC expressions for these arithmetic expressions.
   a. $0.06P$
   b. $5x + 5y$
   c. $a^2 + b^2$
   d. $\dfrac{6}{5a}$
   e. $\dfrac{a}{b} + \dfrac{c}{d}$
   f. $\dfrac{a + b}{c + d}$
   g. $ax^2 + bx + c$
   h. $\sqrt{b^2 - 4ac}$
   i. $(x^2 + 4xy)/(x + 2y)$

6. Write equivalent BASIC expressions without using parentheses.
   a. ((X+1)+Y)
   b. (A+B)*(A-B)
   c. A*(A*(A+B)+1)
   d. (A*B)/C
   e. A/(B*C)
   f. X*(X*(X*(X+D)+C)+B)+A
   g. P↑(Q*R)
   h. 1/(A*B*C*D)

3.5 The LET statement: Assigning values to variables

In Section 3.3 you saw how to write arithmetic expressions in a form acceptable to the computer. You will now learn how to instruct the computer to evaluate such expressions.

A BASIC **program statement,** also called a **programming line,** consists of an instruction to the computer preceded by an unsigned integer called the **line number.** The general form is

line number   BASIC instruction

For example,

100 LET A = 2 + 5

is a BASIC statement with line number 100. This statement, called a LET statement, will cause the computer to evaluate the sum 2 + 5 and then assign this value to A.

A BASIC **program** is a collection of BASIC program statements. The instructions are executed by the computer in the order determined by increasing line numbers, unless some instruction overrides this order.

The general form of our first BASIC statement, the LET statement, is

$$\textbf{ln} \text{ LET } \textbf{a} = \textbf{e}$$

where **ln** stands for line number, **a** denotes a variable name, and **e** denotes a BASIC expression that may simply be a constant. This statement directs the computer to evaluate the expression **e** and then assign this value to the variable **a.** Only numerical values may be assigned to numerical variables and only strings to string variables.

EXAMPLE 5. In the following, A = 2, B = −2, C = 3, and A$ = "ABC".

BASIC statement	After execution
30 LET S = A+B+C	S has the value 3.
55 LET X = A+1	X has the value 3.
90 LET Y = 4	Y has the value 4.
20 LET X = (1+A)↑C*(B+5)	X has the value 81.
40 LET M$ = "PQR"	M$ has the value PQR
85 LET R$ = A$	R$ has the value ABC

The next two examples contain BASIC programs ready to be typed into the computer and run. (The procedure for doing so will be described in the next chapter.) The columns to the right of each program show how the values of the variables are changed during program execution.

EXAMPLE 6. Assignment of numerical values.

	After execution of each statement	
The program	Value of P	Value of Q
100 LET P=12	12	
110 LET Q=P/2+1	12	7
120 LET P=Q/2+1	4.5	7
130 LET Q=P/2+1	4.5	3.25
140 END		

Remark 1   An **END** statement as shown in line 140 should terminate every program. There must be only one END statement, and its line number must be greater than all other line numbers in the program.

Remark 2   Note that no value is shown for Q following execution of line 100. Some, but not all, BASIC systems assign an initial value of zero to all numerical variables.

Remark 3   The practice of incrementing line numbers by something other than 1 is a good one (10 is very popular). It allows you to insert additional instructions, which may have been forgotten, in their proper place.

Remark 4   Newly written programs seldom do what they were meant to do. The programmer must find and correct all errors. (The errors are called **bugs,** and making the correction is referred to as **debugging** the program.) A very useful debugging technique is to pretend that you are the computer and prepare a table of successive values of program variables, as was done in this example.

EXAMPLE 7. Assignment of string values.

	After execution of each statement		
The program	Value of A$	Value of B$	Value of C$
200 LET A$ = "AND"	AND		
210 LET B$ = "SO"	AND	SO	
220 LET C$ = B$	AND	SO	SO
230 LET B$ = A$	AND	AND	SO
240 LET A$ = C$	SO	AND	SO
250 END			

Remark 1   Strings appearing in LET statements *must* be quoted. However, note that it is the *string* and not the *quoted string* that is assigned to the variable.

Remark 2   Note that no values are shown for B$ and C$ prior to the assignment of values to these variables in lines 210 and 220, respectively. Some systems assign an initial blank (" ") to each string variable, some assign an initial *empty string* (written " "), while on others, the initial value is unpredictable.

Remark 3   The maximum length of a string that may be assigned to a string variable varies from system to system. Although the BASIC standard specifies 18 as this maximum length, many systems allow as many characters as will fit on a programming line. (Experiment!)

The BASIC statement

    40 LET N = N+1

does not mean that N is equal to $N + 1$ (since that is impossible). It means that the expression $N + 1$ is *evaluated* and this value is *assigned* to the variable N. For example, the effect of the two programming lines

    30 LET N = 5
    40 LET N = N+1

is that the value 6 is assigned to N. Similarly, the statement

    70 LET S = S+Y

evaluates $S + Y$ and then assigns this new value to S. Thus, line 40 increases the value of N by 1 and line 70 increases the value of S by Y.

EXAMPLE 8. In the following, S = 3, Y = −2, H = −4, Z = 6, and M = 10.

BASIC statement	After execution
35 LET S = S+Y	S has the value 1.
90 LET H = H+2*Z	H has the value 8.
40 LET M = 2*M−Z	M has the value 14.

3.6 The PRINT statement

Every computer language must be designed so that the results can be made available in a usable form. In BASIC, the PRINT statement meets this requirement. The simplest form of this statement is

ln PRINT **a**

where **ln** denotes a line number and **a** denotes any one of the BASIC variables listed in Sections 3.1 and 3.2. The effect of this instruction is that the value of **a** is printed and then the teletypewriter carriage moves to the left margin of the next print line. If your system uses a video display screen, the *cursor* is positioned at the left margin of the next display line.

EXAMPLE 9

If the two lines

```
125 PRINT P
135 PRINT Q
```

are added to the program of Example 6,

```
100 LET P=12
110 LET Q=P/2+1
120 LET P=Q/2+1
130 LET Q=P/2+1
140 END
```

and the program is run, the computer will cause the following printout to occur.

```
4.5
3.25
```

It should be noted that the value of a variable, such as P in this program, is not altered after it is printed.

BASIC allows you to have messages printed during program execution. These messages can serve as headings or as identifying labels for printed results. The following example illustrates how this can be done.

EXAMPLE 10. Here is a program to calculate the sales tax (5%) on an automobile listing at $7,295.00.

```
100 PRINT "TAX COMPUTATION PROGRAM"
110 LET L=7295
120 LET R=0.05
130 LET T=L*R
140 PRINT "SALES TAX IS", T
150 END
```

When this program is executed it will produce the following output.

```
TAX COMPUTATION PROGRAM
SALES TAX IS 364.75
```

In this example, there are two messages, one each in lines 100 and 140, and each message is enclosed (as it must be) in quotation marks.

The following modification of the SALES TAX program illustrates that string variables, as well as numerical variables and string constants, can be included in PRINT statements.

EXAMPLE 11

```
100 LET H$="TAX COMPUTATION PROGRAM"
105 LET S$="SALES TAX IS"
110 LET L=7295
120 LET R=0.05
130 LET T=L*R
140 PRINT H$
150 PRINT S$,T
160 END
RUN

TAX COMPUTATION PROGRAM
SALES TAX IS     364.75
READY
```

The forms of the PRINT statement described in this section are adequate for many programming tasks. However, BASIC allows many other useful forms of the PRINT statement and these will be described as the need arises in the context of the applications being considered.

3.7 The REM statement: Remarks as part of a program

In the program shown at the outset of this chapter, certain comments are included (lines 100–120) to indicate the purpose of the program and to identify what quantities the variables X, Y, Z, and A represent. The BASIC statement that allows you to insert such comments is the REM (REMARK) statement. The general form is

ln REM comment

where **comment** denotes any comment or remark you may wish to include.

EXAMPLE 12

```
100 REM PROGRAM TO DETERMINE THE RATE OF RETURN
110 REM GIVEN THE CURRENT PRICE AND EARNINGS
120 REM    P DENOTES THE CURRENT PRICE OF A SECURITY
130 REM    E DENOTES THE RECENT ANNUAL EARNINGS
140 REM    R DENOTES THE RATE OF RETURN
150 LET P=80.00
160 LET E=6.00
170 REM CALCULATE THE RATE OF RETURN AND
180 REM PRINT SUMMARY RESULTS
190 LET R=100*E/P
200 PRINT "PRICE",P
210 PRINT "EARNINGS",E
220 PRINT "RATE OF RETURN",R
230 END
```

If this program is executed, the output will be as follows.

```
PRICE           80
EARNINGS        6
RATE OF RETURN  7.5
```

Remark 1   In this program, REM statements are used for three different purposes: to give a brief description of the program (lines 100 and 110), to describe the quantities represented by the variables used (lines 120, 130, and 140), and to describe the action of certain groups of programming lines (lines 170 and 180). Using REM statements in this manner is an excellent programming practice. Your programs will be easier to read and understand, easier to modify at some later date (should that be required), and easier to debug.

Remark 2   Comments appearing in REM statements need not be enclosed in quotation marks.

Remark 3   Unlike quoted messages appearing in PRINT statements, comments included in REM statements cause nothing to be printed when the program is executed by a computer. Their sole purpose is to document a program.

3.8 Problems

1. Write LET statements to perform the indicated tasks.
   a. Assign the value 7 to M.
   b. Increase the value assigned to B by 7.
   c. Double the value assigned to H.
   d. Assign the value of the expression $(A - B)/2$ to C2.
   e. Assign the tenth power of $1 + R$ to A.
   f. Decrease the value assigned to X by twice the value assigned to Y.
   g. Assign the string COST to C$.
   h. Replace the value of A$ by the string DOE, JANE.
   i. Store the contents of P$ in Q$.
   j. Assign the string ***** to S$.

2. Which of these are incorrect BASIC statements? Explain!
   a. 50 LET X = (A+B)C   b. 60 LET M = A1-A2
   c. 100 LET RJ = M-N   d. 103 LET M3 = A*A*A
   e. 15 LET X13 = 2+3*X   f. 100 LET A+B = S
   g. 20 LET X = 2.3E-05   h. 40 LET Y = 4E0.5
   i. 5 PRINT SUMMING PROGRAM   j. 8 PRINT "5+13=",S

```
k. 70 LET A$=DISCOUNT          l. 35 LET B$=B+B+B
m. 40 LET "AREA"=A$            n. 50 PRINT S$,A
o. 42 LET D$="A+B"             p. 80 REM "THE DISCOUNT IS D."
q. 60 LET M="MONTHLY RENT"     r. 90 PRINT "NAME:",N$
```

3. What will be printed when each program is run?

```
a. 100 LET A=5                 b. 10 LET P=100
   110 LET B=A+2                  20 LET R=8
   120 LET C=A+B                  30 LET I=R/100
   130 PRINT C                    40 LET A=P+I*P
   140 END                        50 PRINT "AMOUNT=",A
                                  60 END

c. 500 LET X=0                 d. 10 LET A=2
   510 LET X=X-1                  20 LET B=6
   520 LET Y=X↑2+3*X              30 LET A=2*A
   530 PRINT Y                    40 LET B=B/2
   540 END                        50 LET C=(A↑2+B↑2)↑(1/2)
                                  60 PRINT C
                                  70 END

e. 10 LET A = 1                f. 10 LET L$="LIST PRICE"
   20 LET B = 3                   20 LET D$="DISCOUNT"
   30 LET C = 2                   30 LET S$="SELLING PRICE"
   40 LET D = B↑2-4*A*C           40 LET L=45
   50 LET X = (-B+D↑.5)/(2*A)     50 LET D=(10/100)*L
   60 PRINT X                     60 LET S=L-D
   70 END                         70 PRINT L$,L
                                  80 PRINT D$,D
                                  90 PRINT S$,S
                                  99 END

g. 10 PRINT "BOBBY LOVES"
   20 LET M$="MARY"
   30 LET B$="BARB"
   40 LET B$=M$
   50 LET M$=B$
   60 PRINT M$
   70 END
```

4. Complete the following table as was done in Examples 6 and 7.

	A	B	C
a. 100 LET A = 1			
110 LET B = 2			
120 LET C = 1			
130 LET C = C+B			
140 LET A = B↑2			
150 LET B = C-B+A			
160 LET C = C-1			
170 LET B = A*B			
180 LET A = A/C			
190 LET C = B/A+1			
200 END			

	N	Output
b. 100 LET N = 1		
110 PRINT N		
120 LET N = N*(N+1)		
130 PRINT N		
140 LET N = N*(N+1)		
150 PRINT N		
160 LET N = N*(N+1)		
170 PRINT N		
180 END		

	X	Y	Z	Output
c. 100 LET X = 0				
110 LET Y = X + 7				
120 LET Z = Y+X↑2				
130 PRINT Z				
140 LET X = Z				
150 LET Y = X*Y*Z				
160 PRINT Y				
170 END				

5. Prepare tables showing the successive values of all variables and what will be printed.

```
a. 100 LET S=0
   110 LET A=25
   120 LET S=S+A
   130 PRINT S
   140 LET S=S+A
   150 PRINT S
   160 LET S=S/2
   170 PRINT S
   180 END
```

```
b. 100 LET X=1.5
   110 LET Y=3/(2*X+2)
   120 PRINT Y
   130 LET X=-X
   140 PRINT X
   150 PRINT Y
   160 END
```

```
c. 100 LET N=130
   110 LET C=3.00
   120 REM N=COUNT
   130 REM C=COST
   140 REM S=PRICE
   150 LET S=1.2*C
   160 LET G=N*S
   170 LET P=G-N*C
   180 PRINT "SALES",G
   190 PRINT "PROFIT",P
   200 END
```

```
d. 100 PRINT "NTH POWERS OF 7"
   110 LET A=7
   120 LET P=7
   130 LET P=A*P
   140 PRINT "FOR N=2",P
   150 LET P=A*P
   160 PRINT "FOR N=3",P
   170 LET P=A*P
   180 PRINT "FOR N=4",P
   190 REM "END OF TABLE"
   200 END
```

3.9 Review true-or-false quiz

1. Parentheses may be used only to override the normal order in which operations are performed by the computer.   T F

2. A BASIC program is a collection of BASIC programming lines.   T F

3. The terms *program statement* and *programming line* are used synonymously.   T F

4. $(A+B)↑.5$ and $(A+B)↑1/2$ have the same meaning.   T F

5. 2/3 is a numerical constant in BASIC.   T F

6. If A = 3, the statement   43 LET 1+A↑2=B1   assigns the value 10 to the variable B1.   T F

7. 150 LET A3 = A3*A3 is a valid BASIC statement.   T F

8. 1.0E1 = 10.   T F

9. 300 LET M = "1984" is a valid BASIC statement.   T F

10. REM statements are often used to explain the purpose of groups of programming lines.   T F

11. REM statements can be used to print messages during program execution.   T F

12. Comments appearing in REM statements must be enclosed in quotation marks.   T F

13. The BASIC statement LET X = X + 1 is a valid BASIC statement but will result in an error because there is no value X for which X = X + 1.   T F

14. Quotation marks are always necessary when we assign a string constant to a string variable with a LET statement.   T F

Entering and Running a Program

Chapter 3 presented examples of BASIC programs ready to be transmitted to the computer. There are several devices used for this purpose, but the most common are the teletypewriter and video display terminals (Figures 1.2 and 1.3). Such devices, which serve as the principal link between you and the computer, are called the **computer terminal,** the **remote terminal,** or simply the **terminal.** The use of the word *remote* indicates that the terminal need not be situated next to the computer; it may in fact be located many miles away. In this case, communication between terminal and computer is established by telephone.

Your terminal will have a keyboard, which is much like an ordinary typewriter keyboard (Figure 4.1). It consists of keys for the 26 uppercase letters of the English alphabet, the digits 0 through 9, and certain other familiar characters, such as $#,.;:=()-/$. In addition, there is a space bar, a carriage-return key, and several other keys whose functions will be explained as the need arises.

Communication must be established between you and the computer before you can begin typing in a program. When this has been accomplished, you are *on line.* Going *on line* can be as simple as pushing a button or turning a knob, or it may require a slightly more complicated *log-in procedure.* A typical log-in procedure is described in Appendix A. In what follows, we will assume that you are *on line.*

4.1 Entering a programming line: The RETURN key

Here is a program ready to be entered at the terminal.

```
100 REM SUM AND DIFFERENCE PROGRAM
110 LET P=5
120 LET Q=8
130 LET S=P+Q
140 LET D=Q-P
150 END
```

Figure 4.1
Keyboard of the HP9835A
BASIC language desktop
computing system. (*Courtesy
of Hewlett Packard.*)

To enter this program, you first type

```
100 REM SUM AND DIFFERENCE PROGRAM ®
```

where ® denotes the RETURN key on your keyboard. (On some systems this key is labeled
ENTER.) Depressing the return key ® causes two things to happen:

1. The line just typed is entered as part of the program.
2. The teletypewriter carriage (cursor, if you are using a video terminal) moves to the
   beginning of the next line.

You would then continue typing:

```
110 LET  P=5
120 LET  Q=8
130 LET  S=P+Q
140 LET  D=Q-P
150 END
```

At the end of each line, you must type ® to enter the line. This program contains no PRINT
statement, so, if it is executed, there will be no output—that is, the computer will give no
results. To rectify this situation, you could add PRINT lines simply by typing the following:

```
135 PRINT "SUM IS",S
145 PRINT "DIFFERENCE IS",D
```

BASIC allows you to enter these lines out of their natural numerical order; the program will still be executed according to the sequence of line numbers from smallest to largest. Thus, if a line is omitted in the initial typing of a program, it can be inserted at any time before execution simply by typing it in.

4.2 Spacing

Spaces may be used to improve the appearance and readability of BASIC programs. During program execution, the computer will ignore all spaces other than those appearing in quoted messages. (Other exceptions to this rule will be described as the need arises.) Thus, the three programming lines

```
130 LET  S=P+Q
130 LET     S = P + Q
130        LET S=P+Q
```

are equivalent BASIC statements.

Good programming practice dictates that this freedom of spacing be used to advantage; a program listing should be easily readable. Here are two rules you should follow. (On many systems, these rules must be observed.)

1. Insert at least one space before and after each BASIC keyword such as LET, PRINT, REM, and END. Thus, write 130 LET $S = P + Q$, but not 130LETS $= P + Q$.
2. Do not insert spaces within BASIC keywords, variables, line numbers, or constants. Thus, write 250 LET $S = X1 + 24.75$, but not 2 50 L E T S $=$ X 1 $+$ 24 . 75.

4.3 The system commands LIST and RUN

A printed list of all program statements already transmitted to the computer can be obtained by typing LIST. This is the first of several commands referred to as **system commands**. A system command has no line number and is not part of a BASIC program. It is an instruction to the computer to do a specific task at the time the command is issued. We illustrate for the program entered in Section 4.1.

```
LIST ®                                          (You type this.)

100 REM SUM AND DIFFERENCE PROGRAM    (This is printed by the computer.)
110 LET P=5
120 LET Q=8
130 LET S=P+Q
135 PRINT "SUM IS", S
140 LET D=Q-P
145 PRINT "DIFFERENCE IS", D
150 END
READY
```

Note that lines 135 and 145 have been inserted in their proper places even though they were actually typed after line 150. READY is the computer's signal that it is ready for you to make another entry (your system may use something other than READY.)

When you are reasonably certain that the program has been typed correctly, you can cause it to be executed (run) with the system command RUN. This command will cause the program instructions to be processed according to the sequence of their line numbers. We illustrate for the program just entered.

```
RUN ®                                        (You type this.)

SUM IS            13                          (This is printed by the computer.)
DIFFERENCE IS    3
READY
```

4.4 Making corrections

During a session at the terminal it is almost inevitable that typing errors will occur. Two methods for correcting such errors will now be described.

The simpler way to correct an error is to retype the entire line. This method must be used if the error is not noticed until after the line has been entered. Retyping the line will replace the incorrect line with the latest version entered.

EXAMPLE 1

```
210 LET X=5                                  (You type this.)
220 PRENT X
230 END
220 PRINT X
LIST ®

210 LET X=5                                  (This is printed by the computer.)
220 PRINT X
230 END
READY
```

Some systems will not allow a typing error such as

```
220 PRENT S
```

to go undetected. If such a line is entered, the computer will immediately print a message indicating that this is not a BASIC statement.

An entire line may be deleted from a program simply by typing its line number followed by the RETURN key.

EXAMPLE 2

```
30 LET Z=5                                   (You type this.)
40 PRINT X
50 LET Z−7=X
60 PRINT X
70 END
40
50 LET X=Z−7
LIST ®
```

```
30 LET Z=5
50 LET X=Z-7
60 PRINT X
70 END
READY
```

(This is printed by the computer.)

The second method of correcting typing errors can be used if an error is noticed before the line being typed has been entered—that is, before the return key ® has been depressed. For example, while typing in the line

```
55 LET S=35.2
```

you notice that you have typed

```
55 LRT
```

At this point you should depress the BACKSPACE key two times to erase the characters T and R.[1] You then type the correct characters E and T and continue typing to the end of the line. Using this method, you can erase as many characters as is required. For example, depressing the BACKSPACE key four times will erase the last four characters typed.

What is actually printed at your terminal when you erase characters in this manner depends on the system you are using. (Experiment!)

4.5 Error messages

You may not always be fortunate enough to detect *syntax errors* (violations of BASIC rules of grammar) before attempting to "run" your program. Should you issue the RUN command for such an incorrect program, appropriate *error messages* will be printed. These messages will indicate the type of error and, on many systems, the line number on which the error occurs. The exact form of such messages depends on the BASIC system being used. The following example illustrates how such error messages can be of help in correcting a program.

EXAMPLE 3

```
10 LET X=7
20 LET X+9=Z
30 PRINT "ANSWER IS,Z
40 END
99 END
RUN ®
```

(You type this.)

```
ILLEGAL STATEMENT AT 20
ILLEGAL STATEMENT AT 30
END NOT LAST AT 40
READY
```

(This is printed by the computer.)

---

[1] The BACKSPACE key is not standard; your system may instead require you to depress the RUBOUT key or to type some other combination of keys, such as SHIFT/0 or CTRL/H.

```
20 LET Z=X+9
30 PRINT "ANSWER IS",Z
40
RUN ®

ANSWER IS        16
READY
```

(You type this.)

(This is printed by the computer.)

As illustrated in the following example, error messages are sometimes printed even though a program contains no syntax errors.

EXAMPLE 4

Here is a program to compute the ratio

$$\frac{COST + MARKUP}{COST - MARKUP}$$

```
10 REM C DENOTES THE COST
20 LET C=100
30 REM M DENOTES THE MARKUP
40 LET M=100
50 LET R=(C+M)/(C-M)
60 PRINT "RATIO =",R
70 END
RUN ®

DIVISION BY ZERO AT 50
READY
```

Each line in this program is an admissible BASIC program statement; hence the program is syntactically correct. When run, the computer assigns 100 to C (line 20), assigns 100 to M (line 40), and then attempts to evaluate the expression in line 50. The error message tells you that the computer does not "know" how to divide by zero.

Normally, error messages will not be printed if syntax errors are not present—even if the program is incorrect. The following example illustrates such a situation.

EXAMPLE 5

```
10 REM COMPUTE THE AVERAGE OF X AND Y
20 REM THIS PROGRAM IS SYNTACTICALLY CORRECT
30 REM BUT PRODUCES INCORRECT RESULTS
40 LET X=10
50 LET Y=5
60 LET A=X+Y/2
70 PRINT "AVERAGE IS",A
80 END
RUN

AVERAGE IS       12.5
READY
```

The computer does precisely what you instruct it to do; it does not do what you meant it to do. The programming error in line 60 is an error in the logic of the program and is not a syntax error. Such errors are often very difficult to find.

If a system command (rather than a programming line) is typed incorrectly, the system will respond with a message indicating that the command is unrecognizable. Thus, you needn't worry about harming the system with novice mistakes.

4.6 On writing your first program

You are now ready to write your first program. Even for very simple problems, certain steps should be followed. Experience has shown that the following approach to problem solving is applicable both to simple and complex problems.

1. Be sure you thoroughly understand what is being asked in the problem statement. A good way to do this is to identify the following items:
   Input: Data to be presented to the computer for processing.
   Output: The results called for in the problem statement. This may involve identifying both output values and the form in which they are to be printed.
2. Identify what, if any, mathematical equations will be needed. For example, to convert degrees Celsius to degrees Fahrenheit, you could use the equation $F = (9/5)C + 32$.
3. Find and describe a step-by-step process (algorithm) that, if carried out, will result in a correct solution. For simple programming tasks, this step usually is not difficult. For example, to convert degrees Celsius to degrees Fahrenheit you could use the following algorithm:
   a. Assign a value to C (degrees Celsius).
   b. Calculate $F = (9/5)C + 32$.
   c. Print the result F and stop.
4. Write the program statements to carry out the algorithm you have described. This is called *coding the program.* Be sure to include adequate and meaningful comment statements.
5. Debug the program. This means running it to test for syntax errors and also to convince yourself that the program produces correct results.

EXAMPLE 6. Write a program to calculate the simple interest and the amount due for a loan of P dollars, at an annual interest rate R, for a time of T years. Use the program to find the interest and amount due when P = \$600, R = 0.1575, and T = 2.

A quick reading of this problem statement shows that the input and output values are as follows:

Input: P, R, and T.
Output: Simple interest and the amount due.

We should all recognize the familiar formulas that govern this situation.

Simple interest: $I = P \times R \times T$
Amount due: $A = P + I$

Knowing these formulas, we can write the following algorithm:

a. Assign values to P, R, and T.

b. Calculate the interest I and the amount due A.

c. Print the results (I and A) and stop.

The program

```
100 REM SIMPLE INTEREST PROGRAM
110 REM    P DENOTES AMOUNT OF LOAN
120 REM    R DENOTES ANNUAL INTEREST RATE
130 REM    T DENOTES TERM OF LOAN IN YEARS
140 REM ASSIGN VALUES TO P,R, AND T
150 LET P=600
160 LET R=0.1575
170 LET T=2
180 REM COMPUTE THE INTEREST I AND AMOUNT DUE A
190 LET I=P*R*T
200 LET A=P+I
210 REM PRINT THE RESULTS
220 PRINT "INTEREST",I
230 PRINT "AMOUNT DUE",A
240 END
RUN ®

INTEREST     189
AMOUNT DUE   789
READY
```

Remark 1

To find the interest and amount due for other loans, it is necessary only to retype the given conditions at lines 150, 160, and 170. (In Chapter 5 you will see how different values can be assigned to P, R, and T without having to retype programming lines.)

Remark 2

Notice that the REM statements in lines 140, 180, and 210 correspond to the three steps in the algorithm written for this example. Not only does this emphasize how the coding process follows from the algorithm, but also it suggests that each step in an algorithm should contain enough detail so that it can be easily coded. Writing your algorithms according to this principle and using the individual steps as REM statements are excellent programming practices.

The development of programming habits, both good and bad, begins with your first program. At the end of this chapter you will be asked to write some programs. To learn good habits from the start, you should follow the steps suggested in this section. *Coding should almost never be your first step.*

4.7 Problems

In Problems 1–4, assume that the lines shown are typed immediately after communication with your BASIC system has been established. What will be printed if the LIST command is entered? The RUN command?

1.
```
100 LET A=14
110 LET B=20
120 LET S=A+B
130 PRINT "SUM IS S"
140 END
110 LET B=30
130 PRINT "SUM IS",S
```

2.
```
100 LET X=5
110 LET X=10
120 LET Y=20
130 PRINT "X+Y"=S
110
125 LET S=X+Y
130 PRINT "X+Y=",S
140 END
150 RUN
150
```

3.
```
100 PRINT "DISCOUNT CALCULATION"
100 REM DISCOUNT PROGRAM
100
110 LET P=120
120 LET D=0.1*P
130 LET P=P-D
140 PRINT "DISCOUNT",D
150 PRINT "COST",C
130 LET C=P-D
160 END
```

4.
```
100 LET L$=AVERAGE
110 LET A=5
120 LET B=7
130 LET M=A+B/2
140 PRINT L$,M
150 END
110 LET A=9
130 LET M=(A+B)/2
100 LET L$="AVERAGE"
```

The programs in Problems 5–10 contain one or more bugs—either syntax errors (violations in the BASIC rules of grammar) or programming errors (errors in the logic of a program). Find each bug, tell which type of error it is, correct the programs, and show what will be printed if the corrected programs are run.

5.
```
10 REM PROGRAM TO COMPUTE
20 REM SIX PERCENT OF $23,000
30 LET D=23,000
40 LET R=6
50 LET R*D=A
60 PRINT "ANSWER IS",A
70 END
```

6.
```
10 REM PROGRAM TO AVERAGE
20 REM TWO NUMBERS
30 LET N1=24
40 LET N2=15
50 LET A=N1+N2/2
60 PRINT AVERAGE IS,A
70 END
```

7.
```
10 REM SALES TAX PROGRAM
20 REM    T=TAX RATE
30 REM    P=PRICE
40 LET 5=T
50 LET P=120.00
60 LET S=P+T*P
70 PRINT "TOTAL COST"=S
80 END
```

8.
```
10 REM PROGRAM TO FIND A SOLUTION X
20 REM TO THE FOLLOWING EQUATION
30 REM    35X+220=0
40 LET A=35
50 LET B=220
60 LET A*X+B=0
70 PRINT "SOLUTION IS",X
80 END
```

9.
```
100 REM PROGRAM TO SWAP THE
110 REM VALUES OF A AND B
120 LET A=5
130 LET B=8
140 PRINT "A=",A
150 PRINT "B=",B
160 REM INTERCHANGE A AND B
170 LET A=B
180 LET B=A
190 PRINT "A=",A
200 PRINT "B=",B
210 END
```

10.
```
100 REM "PROGRAM TO COMPUTE THE"
110 REM "EXCISE TAX T ON TWO CARS"
120 REM "VALUED AT V DOLLARS,IF THE"
130 REM "RATE IS 66 DOLLARS PER 1000."
140 LET V=4500
150 LET R=66/1000
160 LET T=V*R
170 PRINT TAX ON FIRST CAR IS T
180 LET V=5700
190 PRINT TAX ON SECOND CAR IS T
200 END
```

Listed below are a number of tasks to be performed. Write a BASIC program for each. Be sure to follow the guidelines suggested in Section 4.6. Use PRINT statements to label all output values and be sure to include adequate REM statements.

11. Compute the selling price S for an article whose list price is L if the rate of discount is D%.
12. Compute the original price if an article is now selling at S dollars after a discount of D%.
13. Compute the state gasoline tax in dollars paid by a driver who travels M miles per year if the car averages G miles per gallon and the tax is T cents per gallon.
14. Find the commission C on sales of S dollars if the rate of commission is R%.
15. Find the principal P that, if invested at a rate of interest R for time T years, yields the simple interest I. (Recall that I = PRT.)
16. Compute the weekly salary, both gross G and net N, for a person who works H hours a week for D dollars an hour (no overtime). Deductions are S% for state taxes and F% for federal taxes.
17. Convert degrees Celsius C to degrees Fahrenheit F (F = (9/5)C + 32). Run the program for several values of C, including C = 0 and C = 100.
18. Convert degrees Fahrenheit F to degrees Celsius C. Run the program for several values of F, including F = 0, F = 32, and F = 212.
19. Convert pounds L to grams G (1 oz = 28.3495 g).
20. Convert grams G to pounds L.
21. Convert yards Y to meters M. Run for several values of Y, including 1760 (1 in. = 2.54 cm).
22. Convert meters M to yards Y. Run for several values of M, including 1 and 1000.
23. Compute the area of a triangle of base B and height H.
24. Compute both the circumference and the area of a circle given the radius. Use π = 3.14159. (Your system may allow you to use PI for the value of π.)
25. Solve the equation AX + B = 0. Run the program for several values of A and B, including the case A = 0.
26. Compute the batting average A of a baseball player who has S singles, D doubles, T triples, and H home runs in B times at bat. (A = number of hits/B.)
27. Compute the slugging percentage P of the baseball player who was described in Problem 26. (P = total bases/B.)
28. Find the total cost C of four tires if the list price of each is L dollars, the federal excise tax is E dollars per tire, and the sales tax is S%.
29. Compute the total cost C of a table listed at L dollars selling at a discount of D% if the sales tax is S%.
30. Find the total taxes T on the McCormick property assessed at D dollars if the rate is R dollars per 1000. In addition, if the community uses X% of all taxes for schools, find how much of the McCormick tax is spent for schools.
31. The market value of a home is M dollars, the assessment rate is A% of the market value, and the tax rate is R dollars per 1000. Compute the property tax.
32. Compute the volume and surface area of a rectangular solid.
33. Compute the area of a triangle whose sides are a, b, and c. (Heron's formula for such a triangle is A = $\sqrt{s(s - a)(s - b)(s - c)}$, where $s = (a + b + c)/2$.)
34. A tin can is H inches high and the radius of its circular base is R inches. Calculate the volume and surface area. (Volume = area of base × height. Curved surface area = circumference of base × height.)

4.8 Review true-or-false quiz

1. System commands are carried out as soon as they are entered.   T   F
2. To correct an error committed while typing a program, you must retype the entire line.   T   F
3. A line may be deleted from a program simply by typing its line number and then depressing the RETURN key.   T   F
4. The program statement   20 PRINT "13(2 + 3) = 500"   contains a syntax error.   T   F
5. A program containing syntax errors will cause error messages to be printed when it is run.   T   F
6. A program containing no syntax errors can cause error messages to be printed.   T   F
7. Each step in an algorithm for a computer program should correspond to a single program statement.   T   F
8. A good programming practice is to choose REM statements to correspond to the individual steps of an algorithm.   T   F
9. Coding a BASIC program involves determining the programming lines to carry out a known algorithm.   T   F
10. The identification of what input values are required in a program should be made before an algorithm has been written, whereas the identification of what output values are required is best made after the algorithm has been described.   T   F

Interacting with the Computer

In this chapter we discuss two BASIC statements. The first is the INPUT statement, which allows you to type in values for variables during program execution and thus interact with the computer while your program is running. To help you make this two-way communication more meaningful, we will describe a more general form of the PRINT statement. The second BASIC statement that we will discuss is the GO TO statement, which allows you to override the normal sequential order in which programming lines are executed.

5.1 The INPUT statement

This new BASIC instruction is best illustrated by example.

EXAMPLE 1

```
10  INPUT T
20  LET A=T↑2
30  PRINT A
40  END
```

When line 10 is executed, a "?" will be printed and nothing further will take place until you type a BASIC constant and enter it by depressing ®. This value will be assigned to T, and only then will program execution continue. Let's run this program.

RUN®

? 13®

169

READY

(Underlined characters are printed by the computer.)

More than one value may be assigned by an INPUT statement. The program statement

```
90 INPUT X,Y
```

causes "?" to be printed, and two values, separated by a comma, should be typed. Thus, if you type 5,3 after this "?" and then depress ®, the value 5 will be assigned to X and 3 to Y. The general form of the INPUT statement is

ln INPUT input list

where **ln** denotes a line number and **input list** denotes a list of variables separated by commas. When an INPUT statement is executed, the computer prints the prompt "?" and you must respond by typing a value for each variable in the **input list.** The values you type must be separated by commas.

EXAMPLE 2. Here is a program to compute the cost C of renting a car for D days and driving it M miles. The rental rate is 12 dollars per day and 11 cents per mile.

```
10 INPUT D,M
20 LET C=12*D+0.11*M
30 PRINT "TOTAL COST IS",C
40 END
RUN®

? 3,253®                    (Underlined characters are printed by the computer.)
TOTAL COST IS    63.83
READY
```

PRINT statements can be used in conjunction with INPUT statements to instruct a user about how INPUT values should be entered. We illustrate by modifying the car-rental program of Example 2.

EXAMPLE 3

```
10 PRINT "ENTER NUMBER OF DAYS AND NUMBER"
20 PRINT "OF MILES, SEPARATED BY A COMMA."
30 INPUT D,M
40 LET C=12*D+0.11*M
50 PRINT "TOTAL COST IS",C
60 END
RUN®

ENTER NUMBER OF DAYS AND NUMBER        (Underlined characters are printed
OF MILES,SEPARATED BY A COMMA.                by the computer.)
?
```

At this point you simply follow the instructions and type two numbers separated by a comma. Let's complete this run as follows.

```
? 3,253®
TOTAL COST IS    63.83
READY
```

EXAMPLE 4. This example shows that the INPUT statement can be used to input string values for string variables.

```
10 PRINT "ENTER A NAME"
20 INPUT N$
30 PRINT "ENTER THE DATE"
40 INPUT D$
50 PRINT
60 PRINT N$
70 PRINT "INITIATION DATE:",D$
80 END
RUN
```

```
ENTER A NAME                          (Underlined characters are printed
? "MARTIN,STEVE"                              by the computer.)
ENTER THE DATE
? "MAY 1982"

MARTIN,STEVE
INITIATION DATE:              MAY 1982
READY
```

On most BASIC systems, the second input string MAY 1982 could have been typed without quotes. On all BASIC systems, the first input string MARTIN,STEVE must be enclosed in quotation marks—the comma is used as a separator for input values. Rules concerning the use of quotes on input strings differ among systems. The most common situation is that quotes are required only in the following cases.

1. Significant blanks begin or terminate a string. If such a string is not enclosed in quotation marks, the leading and trailing blanks are ignored.
2. A comma appears in the string.

However, it is always correct to enclose input strings in quotation marks.

Remark   The PRINT statement in line 50 causes a carriage return as shown by the blank line in the printout.

The readability of an output document can often be enhanced by having an input value appear on the same line as the message identifying this value. This can be accomplished by placing a semicolon after the quoted message in a PRINT statement. If this is done, the carriage return normally occurring after execution of the PRINT statement is suppressed. Thus, if you type 345 in response to the following INPUT statement,

```
200 PRINT "NUMBER OF MILES ";
210 INPUT M
```

the computer printout will be

<u>NUMBER OF MILES ?</u> 345   *(Underlined characters are printed by the computer.)*

EXAMPLE 5. Determine the yearly income and savings of a person whose weekly income and average monthly expenses are given.

Two values must be specified (weekly income and monthly expenses), and two values must be determined (yearly income and savings). Let's agree to use the following variable names.

I = weekly income
E = monthly expenses
Y = yearly income (note that Y = 52I).
S = yearly savings (note that S = Y − 12E).

An algorithm for solving this problem can now be written.

a. Assign values to I and E.
b. Determine yearly income and savings.
c. Print results.

Before this algorithm can be coded, you must decide how to assign values to I and E. Available are the LET and INPUT statements. Since we may use this program for different weekly incomes and monthly expenses, the decision is easy: use an INPUT statement.

The program

```
100 REM PROGRAM TO FIND YEARLY INCOME AND SAVINGS
110 REM GIVEN THE WEEKLY INCOME AND MONTHLY EXPENSES
120 REM
130 PRINT "WEEKLY INCOME";
140 INPUT I
150 PRINT "MONTHLY EXPENSES";
160 INPUT E
170 REM COMPUTE YEARLY INCOME AND SAVINGS
180 LET Y=52*I
190 LET S=Y-12*E
200 PRINT "YEARLY INCOME",Y
210 PRINT "YEARLY SAVINGS",S
220 END
RUN
```

<u>WEEKLY INCOME?</u> 250   *(Underlined characters are printed by the computer.)*
<u>MONTHLY EXPENSES?</u> 840
<u>YEARLY INCOME   13000</u>
<u>YEARLY SAVINGS   2920</u>
<u>READY</u>

Remark 1

The short discussion appearing just before the algorithm is called a **problem analysis.** It may simply contain a description of variables and how they are interrelated, as is the case here, or it may include a thorough analysis of alternative approaches to a solution. In any case, a problem analysis is the process of discovering a suitable algorithm.

Remark 2   Some BASIC systems allow you to include messages to be printed as part of an INPUT statement. For example, your system may allow you to replace the two lines

```
130 PRINT "WEEKLY INCOME";
140 INPUT I
```

with the single equivalent line

```
130 INPUT "WEEKLY INCOME"; I
```

5.2 Problems

Complete the following partial program so that it will perform the tasks specified in Problems 1–14. Be sure that messages printed by line numbers 100 and 130 are appropriate to the particular problem being solved. No references to the variable names X and A should be made in these messages.

```
100 PRINT "          "
110 INPUT X
120 LET A=
130 PRINT "          ",A
140 END
```

1. Determine how much $100 earning 6% interest compounded annually will be worth in X years (value after X years is $100(1 + .06)^x$).
2. Determine the commission earned by a salesperson who sells a $625 television set if the rate of commission is X%.
3. Determine the total cost of an article whose selling price is X dollars if the sales tax is 4.5%.
4. Determine the weekly salary of a part-time employee working X hours at $4.47 per hour (no overtime).
5. Determine the cost per driving mile for a car that averages 19.2 miles per gallon if gasoline costs X cents per gallon.
6. Determine the average of the four grades for a student who has received grades of 73, 91, 62, and X on four exams.
7. Determine the equivalent hourly salary, assuming a 40-hour week, for a worker whose annual salary is X dollars.
8. Determine the area of a circle given its diameter.
9. Determine the diameter of a circle given its area.
10. Convert inches to centimeters (1 in. = 2.54 cm).
11. Convert centimeters to inches.
12. Convert degrees to radians (1 degree = $\pi/180$ radians; use $\pi = 3.14159$).
13. Convert radians to degrees.
14. Determine the distance A to the horizon as viewed over a smooth ocean from a vantage point X feet above sea level. (Consider the right triangle in the following diagram.)

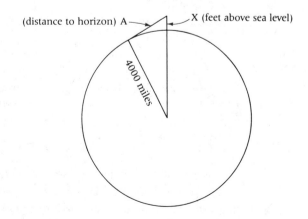

(distance to horizon) A ⟶   ⟵ X (feet above sea level)

4000 miles

Write a program to perform each task specified in Problems 15–21. Use PRINT statements to label results and to instruct a user concerning what values are to be entered.

15. For any three numbers A, B, and C, determine the three sums A + B, A + C, and B + C, and find the average of these sums.
16. For any three numbers P, Q, and R, determine the mean M, the differences P − M, Q − M, and R − M, and the sum of these differences.
17. Semester grades are based on three one-hour tests and a two-hour final examination. The one-hour tests are weighted equally, but the final counts as two one-hour tests. (All exams are graded from 0 to 100.) Determine the semester average for a student whose grades are G1, G2, G3, and F (F for final).
18. Janet and Jim are bricklayers. In one hour Janet can lay J1 bricks and Jim can lay J2. Determine how long it will take both of them to complete a job if the number of bricks required is known.
19. A baseball player is to be paid P dollars the first year of a 3-year contract. Find the total dollar value of the contract over 3 years if the contract calls for an increase of I% the second year and J% the third year.
20. Determine the yearly gross pay, net pay, combined tax deductions, and retirement deductions for a person whose monthly salary is given. The combined tax rate is R%, and 6% of the gross salary is withheld for retirement.
21. A manufacturer produces three items that sell for $550, $620, and $1750. A profit of 10% is realized on items selling below $1000, and 15% is realized on all other items. Determine the profit before and after taxes for a particular year, given the quantity of each item sold. The current tax rate on profits is R%.

5.3 The GO TO statement: A first look at loops

As we mentioned at the beginning of this chapter, the GO TO statement allows you to override the normal sequential order in which programming lines are executed. This means that you can direct the computer to execute sections of your program repeatedly and thus to perform many hundreds of calculations with only a few programming lines. Using only the LET, INPUT, GO TO, and PRINT statements, the computer is transformed into a very fast and useful calculator.

The general form of the GO TO statement is as follows.

$$\mathbf{ln}_1 \text{ GO TO } \mathbf{ln}_2$$

When executed, the statement transfers control to line number $\mathbf{ln}_2$; that is, the next instruction to be executed is the one whose line number is $\mathbf{ln}_2$.

EXAMPLE 6

The program

```
100 LET I=0
110 PRINT I
120 LET I=I+1
130 GO TO 110
140 END
```

will cause the numbers 0, 1, 2, 3, . . . to be printed one number per line. Each time the GO TO instruction at line 130 is executed, control is transferred back to line 110. This is what is meant by a loop. The loop consists of the three program statements 110, 120, and 130.

If the program in Example 6 is run, it will not halt of its own accord. You must stop it manually. How you do this depends on your system. You may be required to depress the S, I, ESC, or BREAK key, or some combination of keys such as CTRL/C or CTRL/S. In this text we will indicate that a program run has been terminated manually by including the following in the printout.

```
*TERMINATED*
READY
```

Thus, a run of the program of Example 6 would be shown as follows.

```
RUN
 0
 1
 2
 3
   *TERMINATED*
READY
```

EXAMPLE 7

The program

```
100 LET X=0
110 LET X=X+1
120 GO TO 110
130 END
```

will cause the variable X to take on the successive values 0, 1, 2, 3, . . . but will not print or do anything else. Again, the program must be stopped manually.

EXAMPLE 8. Here is a program to do multiplication.

```
100 PRINT "AFTER EACH '?' ENTER TWO NUMBERS"
110 INPUT A,B
120 LET P=A*B
130 PRINT "PRODUCT IS",P
140 PRINT
150 GO TO 110
160 END
RUN

AFTER EACH '?' ENTER TWO NUMBERS
? 5,3
PRODUCT IS         15

? 14,11
PRODUCT IS         154

? 9,13.69
PRODUCT IS         123.21

?
   *TERMINATED*
READY
```

Remark 1   The PRINT statement at line 140 causes nothing to be printed but does advance the print mechanism one line, as seen in the output.

Remark 2   The program run was halted manually while the computer was waiting for a response to the INPUT statement at line 110.

Programming tasks often call for output documents in tabular form. Normally, these will consist of one or more columns of data, each with a descriptive column heading. The following form of the PRINT statement can be used to print both column headings and the values appearing in the body of the table.

$$\textbf{ln } PRINT \ \textbf{a,b,c,...}$$

Here, **a, b,** and **c** denote string constants or variable names. This form of the PRINT statement can be used to print up to five messages or numerical values on a single line (four on some systems).

EXAMPLE 9. Prepare a table showing the weekly and annual salaries for persons working 40 hours a week if their hourly rates are $4.50, $4.60, $4.70, . . . , $5.50.

Problem analysis   The weekly pay W for a person working 40 hours a week at H dollars an hour is W = 40H dollars; the annual salary A for this person is A = 52W dollars.

We will evaluate W and A for each value of H, beginning with H = 4.50 and increasing to 5.50 in increments of 0.10. The following is one way to do this.

a. Print column headings.
b. Let H = 4.50.
c. Evaluate W = 40H and then A = 52W.
d. Print H, W, and A on one line.
e. Add 0.10 to H and go to step (c).

The program

```
100 REM SALARY TABLE PROGRAM
110 REM    H DENOTES HOURLY RATE
120 REM    W DENOTES EQUIVALENT 40 HOUR WEEK SALARY
130 REM    A DENOTES EQUIVALENT YEARLY SALARY
140 PRINT "HOURLY RATE","WEEKLY SALARY","ANNUAL SALARY"
150 LET H=4.50
160 LET W=40*H
170 LET A=52*W
180 PRINT H,W,A
190 LET H=H+0.10
200 GO TO 160
210 END
RUN
```

```
HOURLY RATE    WEEKLY SALARY  ANNUAL SALARY
   4.5            180.           9360.
   4.6            184.           9568.
   4.7            188.           9776.
   4.8            192.           9984.
```

```
4.9              196.              10192.
5.               200.              10400.
5.1              204.              10608.
5.2              208.              10816.
5.3              212.              11024.
5.4              216.              11232.
5.5              220.              11440.
5.6              224.
     *TERMINATED*
READY
```

Remark 1   Lines 160–200 constitute the loop used to print the table values. Since the column headings must be printed first, and only once, the statement that does this (line 140) must appear before the loop is entered.

Remark 2   Again, the program run must be terminated manually. Not only does this clutter the output, but it means that you must be present to stop the program when the desired output has been printed. This awkward situation can be avoided. In the next chapter you will learn how to program an automatic exit from a loop when the desired output has been printed.

We conclude this section with two examples illustrating the following programming practices stressed to this point.

1. To discover a correct algorithm, carefully analyze the problem statement and record this analysis in writing.
2. Use PRINT statements to identify what numbers are to be entered during program execution and also to label results clearly. The precise form of such PRINT statements is normally not determined until the algorithm has been described.
3. Use REM statements to make your program more readable and to clarify what is being done at any particular point.

EXAMPLE 10

A man lives in a large house with many rooms. He wants to paint the walls and ceiling of each room, but, before buying paint, he naturally needs to know how much paint is necessary. On the average, each window and door covers 20 sq ft. According to the label, each quart of paint covers 110 sq ft. Write a program that will allow the man to enter the dimensions of each room and the number of doors and windows in each room and then determine how many quarts of wall paint and how many quarts of ceiling paint are needed for that room.

Problem analysis   Although this problem statement is somewhat lengthy, it should not be difficult to identify the following input and output quantities.

Input: Name of each room.
          Length, width, and height of each room.
          Number of doors and windows in each room.
Output: Quarts of wall paint and quarts of ceiling paint needed for each room.

To determine how many quarts of wall paint are needed for a particular room we must determine the wall area (in sq. ft.) to be covered and divide this value by 110 since one quart of paint covers 110 sq. ft. Similarly, the amount of ceiling paint is obtained by dividing the ceiling area by 110.

Before attempting to write down an algorithm for carrying out this task, let's choose variable names for the quantities of interest. Doing this will allow us to write a concise algorithm by using variable names, rather than verbal descriptions for these quantities.

> N$ = the name of the room in question.
> L,W,H = the length, width, and height of N$ (in feet).
> T = the total number of windows and doors in N$.
> S = the area of all walls in N$ including door and window space (S = 2(L + W)H).
> B = the area of the T doors and windows (B = 20T).
> C = the area of a ceiling (C = LW).
> S1 = quarts of wall paint needed (S1 = (S − B)/110).
> C1 = quarts of ceiling paint needed (C1 = C/110).

Using these variable names, we can write the following algorithm. Note that the order in which the steps are to be taken is just how you might carry out this task with tape measure, pencil, and paper.

a. Enter values for N$, L, W, H, and T.
b. Determine the areas S, B, and C.
c. Determine the number of quarts of paint needed (S1 and C1).
d. Print the values of S1 and C1.
e. Go to step (a) and repeat the process for the next room.

The program

```
100 REM PAINT CALCULATION PROBLEM
110 PRINT "ROOM";
120 INPUT N$
130 PRINT "LENGTH, WIDTH, HEIGHT";
140 INPUT L,W,H
150 PRINT "TOTAL NUMBER OF WINDOWS AND DOORS";
160 INPUT T
170 REM CALCULATE AREAS
180 REM
190 LET S=2*(L+W)*H
200 LET B=20*T
210 LET C=L*W
220 REM QUARTS OF WALL AND CEILING PAINT
230 REM
240 LET S1=(S-B)/110
250 LET C1=C/110
260 REM PRINT RESULTS
270 REM
280 PRINT "QUARTS OF WALL PAINT",S1
290 PRINT "QUARTS OF CEILING PAINT",C1
300 PRINT
310 GO TO 110
320 END
RUN
```

```
ROOM? KITCHEN
LENGTH, WIDTH, HEIGHT? 13,13,9
TOTAL NUMBER OF WINDOWS AND DOORS? 5
QUARTS OF WALL PAINT          3.34545
QUARTS OF CEILING PAINT       1.53636

ROOM? FRONT BEDROOM
LENGTH, WIDTH, HEIGHT? 12,9,9
TOTAL NUMBER OF WINDOWS AND DOORS? 4
QUARTS OF WALL PAINT          2.70909
QUARTS OF CEILING PAINT        .981818

ROOM?
  *TERMINATED*
READY
```

EXAMPLE 11

A manufacturer uses the following method to determine the selling price for an item. First, the cost of materials is doubled to cover labor expenses. Then, this figure is increased by 20% to cover overhead. Finally, this last figure is increased by X% or Y% depending on whether or not it is over $500. (The programmer is not told the values of X and Y.) This last increase is to cover research-and-development (R & D) costs as well as profits. Write a program to assist in this task.

Problem analysis

According to the problem statement, the input and output values for each item are as follows.

Input: Cost of materials and percentage increase for R & D.
Output: Selling price.

To allow us to write a concise algorithm for the task to be carried out by the computer, let's choose variable names as follows.

C = cost of materials.
E = expenses, including cost of materials and labor ($E = 2C$).
T = total expenses, including overhead ($T = E + 0.2E$).
P = percentage to be added for R & D and for profit.
S = selling price ($S = T + (P/100)T$).

So that the correct value (X or Y) can be typed for P, the total expenses T must be shown to the manufacturer. That is, C must be entered and T printed before the computer requests (INPUT statement) a value for P. This analysis suggests the following algorithm.

a. Input C (cost of materials).
b. Compute E.
c. Compute and print T (cost of materials, labor, overhead).
d. Input P (percentage for profit and for R & D).
e. Compute and print S (selling price).
f. Go to step (a) for next item.

The program

```
100 REM PROGRAM TO DETERMINE SELLING PRICE
110 REM
120 PRINT "COST OF MATERIALS";
130 INPUT C
140 LET E=2*C
150 LET T=E+0.2*E
160 PRINT "COST OF MATERIALS,LABOR,OVERHEAD",T
170 PRINT "R & D - PROFIT PERCENTAGE";
180 INPUT P
190 LET S=T+P/100*T
200 PRINT "SELLING PRICE",S
210 PRINT
220 GO TO 120
230 END
RUN

COST OF MATERIALS?  248
COST OF MATERIALS,LABOR,OVERHEAD            595.2
R & D - PROFIT PERCENTAGE?  30
SELLING PRICE    773.76

COST OF MATERIALS?  163.50
COST OF MATERIALS,LABOR,OVERHEAD            392.4
R & D - PROFIT PERCENTAGE?  20
SELLING PRICE    470.88

COST OF MATERIALS ?
  *TERMINATED*
READY
```

5.4 Problems

1. What is printed by each program?

a.
```
100 LET A=1
110 PRINT A
120 LET B=1
130 PRINT B
140 LET C=A+B
150 PRINT C
160 LET A=B
170 LET B=C
180 GO TO 140
190 END
```

b.
```
100 LET A$="A"
110 LET B$="B"
120 LET C$="C"
130 PRINT A$,B$,C$
140 LET T$=B$
150 LET B$=A$
160 LET A$=T$
170 PRINT A$,B$,C$
180 LET T$=C$
190 LET C$=A$
200 LET A$=T$
210 GO TO 130
220 END
```

c.
```
10 LET X=1
20 LET P=1
30 LET P=P*X
40 PRINT X,P
50 LET X=X+1
60 GO TO 30
70 END
```

d.
```
10 LET S=0
20 LET A=5
30 LET S=S+A
40 PRINT S
50 LET A=-(A+1)
60 GO TO 30
70 END
```

2. Correct the following programs.

a.
```
10 REM PROGRAM TO PRINT THE
20 REM ODD WHOLE NUMBERS
30 LET N=1
40 PRINT N
50 LET N=N+2
60 GO TO 30
70 END
```

b.
```
10 REM PROGRAM TO DO SUBTRACTION
20 PRINT "TYPE TWO NUMBERS";
30 INPUT A,B
40 LET D=A-B
50 GO TO 20
60 PRINT "SECOND - FIRST =",D
70 END
```

c.
```
10 REM PROGRAM TO PRINT AN
20 REM 8 PERCENT TAX TABLE
30 LET X=100
40 LET T=8*X
50 PRINT "PRICE","TAX"
60 PRINT X,T
70 LET X=X+1
80 GO TO 40
90 END
```

d.
```
10 REM PROGRAM TO PRINT A
20 REM TABLE OF SQUARE ROOTS
30 LET N=2
40 PRINT "NUMBER","SQUARE ROOT"
50 LET R=N↑1/2
60 PRINT N,R
70 LET N=N+1
80 GO TO 60
90 END
```

Write a program to print each table described in Problems 3–16. Begin each program with a PRINT statement describing the table. If a table has more than one column, column headings should be printed.

3. The first column contains the number of miles (1, 2, 3, . . .), and the second column gives the corresponding number of kilometers (1 mile = 1.6093 kilometers).

4. The first column contains the temperature in degrees Celsius from -20 to 40 in increments of 2, and the second column gives the corresponding temperature in degrees Fahrenheit ($F = (9/5)C + 32$).

5. A one-column table (list) containing the terms of the arithmetic progression a, $a + d$, $a + 2d$, $a + 3d$, ... Values for a and d are to be assigned by the user.

6. A one-column table (list) of the terms of the geometric progression a, ar, ar^2, ar^3, ... Values for a and r are to be assigned by the user.

7. The first column gives the amount of sales (500, 1000, 1500, . . .), and the second gives the commission at a rate of R%.

8. The first column contains the principal (50, 100, 150, . . .), and the second column gives the corresponding simple interest for 6 months at an annual interest rate of R%.

9. The first column contains the annual interest rate (7.0%, 7.25%, 7.5%, . . .), and the second column gives the simple interest on a principal of $1000 for 9 months.

10. The first column gives the list price of an article ($25, $50, $75, . . .), the second gives the amount of discount at 25%, and the third gives the corresponding selling price.

11. Ucall Taxi charges 45 cents for a ride plus 13 cents for each tenth of a mile. The first column gives the number of miles (0.1, 0.2, 0.3, . . .), and the second gives the total charges.

12. The first column contains the number of years ($n = 1, 2, 3, . . .$), the second the amount in the account, and the third the interest earned at the end of n years on a principal of $1000 at 6.5% compounded annually ($a = p(1 + r)^n$).

13. The first column contains the radius of a circle in inches (1, 2, 3, . . .), and the remaining columns give the corresponding diameter, circumference, and area of the circle.

14. A three-column table showing the values of n, n^2, and $\sqrt{n}$ for $n = 1, 2, 3, ...$

15. A three-column table showing the values of n, 2^n and $\sqrt[n]{2}$ for $n = 1, 2, 3, ...$

16. An accurate sketch of the graph of $y = \sqrt{1.09}x^3 - \sqrt[3]{8.51}x^2 + (1.314/1.426)x - 0.8$ on the interval $1 \leq x \leq 3$ is required. To make this task easier, produce a table of the y values where the x's are in increments of 0.1.

Write a program to perform each task specified in Problems 17–20.

17. A list of numbers is to be typed at the terminal. After each number is typed, the program should cause two values to be printed: a count of how many numbers have been typed and the average of all numbers entered to that time.

18. A program should continually request two numbers of the user. After each pair of numbers is entered, the program should cause two values to be printed: the product of the two numbers just typed and the average of all products printed to that point.

19. A person wishes to determine the dollar amount of any collection of U.S. coins simply by specifying how many of each type of coin is included.

20. A philanthropist, having decided to donate to a cause, uses the following method to determine an amount to give. The figure asked for is decreased by 20%, and this value is compared with the average of last year's actual donation and this year's request. If it is less than this average, it is reduced by P%; otherwise it is reduced by Q%. (Only the philanthropist knows P and Q.) Your program is to assist with these calculations. (You may wish to refer to the problem analysis in Example 11.)

5.5 Review true-or-false quiz

1. The PRINT and INPUT statements provide the means for two-way communication between a user and a running program.   T F

2. Using a PRINT statement immediately following an INPUT statement is a very useful method of identifying what values should be typed at the terminal.   T F

3. A single PRINT statement may be used to print headings for more than one column.   T F

4. If the statements

```
149 PRINT "FIRST","SECOND","THIRD"
150 PRINT A, B, C
```

appear in a loop, all A, B, and C values will be printed in columns with the headings FIRST, SECOND, and THIRD.   T F

5. If the statement 50 PRINT X,Y appears in a loop, the column of X values and the column of Y values that are printed will "line up" according to decimal points.   T F

6. If a program contains the line 100 GO TO 130, the lines 110 and 120 will never be executed.   T F

7. A program is written using only LET, PRINT, and GO TO statements. If, during execution, any one line of this program is executed twice, the program will not stop of its own accord. (You are to assume that the program contains no errors and that it does include a proper END statement.)   T F

8. A *problem analysis* is the process of discovering a correct algorithm.   T F

9. It is never correct to type THORPE,JIM in response to an INPUT statement.   T F

The Computer as a Decision Maker

BASIC contains several statements, called control statements, that allow you to control the order in which program statements are executed. In this chapter we introduce the IF statement, whose purpose is to override the normal sequential execution of the statements in a program—but only if a certain condition, specified by the programmer, is satisfied. It is with this ability to make decisions that the full potential of the computer is realized.

6.1 The IF statement

The simplicity and usefulness of the IF statement are best illustrated by example.

EXAMPLE 1. Here is a program to print 6 percent of any input value, but only if the input value is not negative.

```
100 INPUT X
110 IF X<0 THEN 140
120 LET T=.06*X
130 PRINT "TAX IS",T
140 END
RUN

? 43
TAX IS          2.58
READY
```

After a value is INPUT, the condition X<0 in line 110 is tested. If it is true, control passes to line 140 and the program stops without printing anything. If the condition is false, the normal sequential execution of the program is not interrupted and control passes to line 120. T is assigned the value of .06*X and line 130 causes the output shown.

EXAMPLE 2. Here is a program to print 6 percent of each of many input values and to stop when a negative number is typed.

```
100  INPUT X
110  IF X<0 THEN 160
120      LET T=.06*X
130      PRINT "TAX IS",T
140      INPUT X
150  GO TO 110
160  END
RUN

?  43
TAX IS           2.58
?  100
TAX IS           6.
?  -1
READY
```

As in Example 1, an input value X is compared with 0. If X is not less than zero, control passes to the line following the IF statement, the computer calculates and prints the tax T, another value is input for X, and then the GO TO statement in line 150 transfers control back to line 110. This process is repeated until an input value X<0 is typed. When this happens, the IF statement transfers control to line 160 and program execution terminates.

Remark
The IF and GO TO statements in this program are used to set up a loop in which the group of statements

```
LET T=.06*X
PRINT "TAX IS",T
INPUT X
```

is executed repeatedly. Indenting this group as shown in the program listing enhances the readability of the entire program. The practice of indenting program statements is not new to us. In several of the examples considered thus far, REM statements describing the meanings of variable names used in a program are indented. Other situations in which indentations should be used to improve the readability of your programs will be mentioned as they arise.

These two examples illustrate the two very different uses of IF statements: *to construct loops* (Example 2) and *to make decisions* (Example 1). When used to construct loops, certain difficulties encountered with the GO TO statement are easily avoided.

Loops using only the GO TO statement	*Loops using the IF statement*
1. The only way out of a loop is to stop the program manually.	1. An exit from a loop can be made under program control.
2. Results obtained in a loop can be printed only by using PRINT statements within the loop. This often results in the printing of unwanted intermediate results.	2. Results can be printed after completing a loop.
3. A program can contain only one loop.	3. More than one loop can be included in a program.

As a *decision maker* the IF statement has many applications. As illustrated in Example 1, it can be used to "examine" a value typed at the terminal and then take a course of action that depends on this value.

The form of the IF statement illustrated in these two examples is

$$\mathbf{ln_1} \text{ IF } \textit{condition} \text{ THEN } \mathbf{ln_2}$$

If the condition is satisfied (that is, true), transfer is made to $\mathbf{ln_2}$; if the condition is not satisfied, program execution continues with the next sequential line number following $\mathbf{ln_1}$. The precise form that the condition in an IF statement can take is the subject of the next section.

Many BASIC systems allow other more general forms of the IF statement. Two particularly useful and widely implemented forms are as follows.

$$\mathbf{ln} \text{ IF } \textit{condition} \text{ THEN } \mathbf{s}$$
$$\mathbf{ln} \text{ IF } \textit{condition} \text{ THEN } \mathbf{s_1} \text{ ELSE } \mathbf{s_2}$$

where $\mathbf{s}$, $\mathbf{s_1}$, and $\mathbf{s_2}$ denote any BASIC statements. The action of the first form (the IF-THEN statement) is as follows. If the condition is true, the statement $\mathbf{s}$ is executed and control then passes to the next line unless $\mathbf{s}$ causes a jump to another line. If the condition is false, $\mathbf{s}$ is not executed and control simply passes to the next line. In the second form (the IF-THEN-ELSE statement) $\mathbf{s_1}$ is executed if the condition is true and $\mathbf{s_2}$ is executed if the condition is false. Thus, exactly one of the statements $\mathbf{s_1}$ and $\mathbf{s_2}$ will be executed. Control then passes to the next line unless the statement executed ($\mathbf{s_1}$ or $\mathbf{s_2}$) causes a jump to another line.

EXAMPLE 3. Here is a program to count how many of three input values are less than the average of all three.

```
100 REM***A COUNTING PROGRAM***
110 REM N DENOTES THE COUNT
120 REM X,Y,AND Z DENOTE THE INPUT VALUES
130 REM A DENOTES THEIR AVERAGE
140 LET N=0
150 INPUT X,Y,Z
160 LET A=(X+Y+Z)/3
170 REM***BEGIN COUNTING***
180 IF X<A THEN LET N=N+1
190 IF Y<A THEN LET N=N+1
200 IF Z<A THEN LET N=N+1
210 PRINT "NUMBERS LESS THAN THE AVERAGE:",N
220 END
RUN

? 70,90,74
NUMBERS LESS THAN THE AVERAGE:      2
READY
```

Lines 140–160 set the counter N to 0, accept input values for X, Y, and Z, and assign their average to A. For the input values shown, $(70 + 90 + 74)/3 = 78$ is assigned to A. The condition X<A in the first IF statement is true so the statement LET N = N + 1 is executed and N becomes 1. The condition Y<A is false so the statement LET N = N + 1 in line 190 is skipped. The condition Z<A is true, so the statement LET N = N + 1 in the third IF statement is executed to give N = 2. Finally, the PRINT statement causes the output shown.

Remark   The first time the statement LET N = N + 1 is executed, it increases the value of N from 0 to 1; the second time from 1 to 2. Thus, the statement LET N = N + 1 actually does the counting. The use of such "counting" statements is widespread in computer programming.

EXAMPLE 4. Here is an illustration of the IF-THEN-ELSE statement.

```
10 INPUT X
20 IF X=0 THEN 10
30 IF X>0 THEN PRINT "POSITIVE" ELSE PRINT "NEGATIVE"
40 END
```

If the input value X is 0, line 20 transfers control back to the INPUT statement and you must type another value for X. Thus, this program "ignores" any zeroes that are input.

If X is not zero, control passes to the IF-THEN-ELSE statement in line 30. If X is positive, the statement following the keyword THEN is executed causing POSITIVE to be printed. If the condition X>0 is false, the statement following the keyword ELSE is executed causing the word NEGATIVE to be printed.

Remark 1   The statement in line 20 can also be written as

```
20 IF X=0 THEN GO TO 10
```

Some programmers prefer this more descriptive form.

Remark 2   If your system does not allow the IF-THEN-ELSE statement, you can write line 30 by using two lines as follows.

```
30 IF X>0 THEN PRINT "POSITIVE"
35 IF X<0 THEN PRINT "NEGATIVE"
```

If your system allows only the form IF *condition* THEN *line number,* you can code line 30 by using four lines as follows.

```
30 IF X>0 THEN 36
32 PRINT "NEGATIVE"
34 GO TO 40
36 PRINT "POSITIVE"
```

6.2 Relational expressions

The condition in an IF statement involves the comparison of two BASIC expressions. The BASIC symbols used to make such comparisons, together with their arithmetic counterparts, are shown in Table 6.1.

Any two BASIC expressions can be compared using these BASIC symbols. Some examples of correctly written conditions are as follows.

$$X > 200 \qquad 13 = B - C$$
$$M <> N \qquad (A + B)/2 < A$$
$$17 <= 13 \qquad Y1 - Z1 >= 45$$

TABLE 6.1   Relational symbols used in IF statements.

BASIC symbol	Arithmetic symbol	Meaning
=	=	Equal
<	<	Less than
>	>	Greater than
<>	≠	Not equal to
<=	≤	Less than or equal to
>=	≥	Greater than or equal to

Expressions such as these are called **relational expressions** and may be used as the condition in an IF statement. Their use in such statements is illustrated in the following examples.

EXAMPLE 5. In each part of this example we are given values for certain variables and an IF statement. We are to tell what happens when the IF statement is executed.

a. With X = 5000, consider

```
40 IF .07*X>300 THEN 70
```

Since .07*X has the value 350, the condition .07*X>300 is satisfied. Transfer is made to line 70.

b. With A = 2, B = 3, and C = 1, consider

```
50 IF A-B<=C THEN LET C=A-B
```

Since A − B has the value − 1 and C has the value 1, the relational expression A − B <= C is true. The LET statement is executed assigning the value − 1 to C.

c. With M = 2 and N = 4, consider

```
120 IF N<>2*M THEN GO TO 200
```

Both N and 2*M have the value 4; hence, the condition N<>2*M is false. No transfer is made to line 200, and control passes to the statement immediately following the IF statement.

EXAMPLE 6. Let's write a program to input two numbers A and B and print the message BOTH if both are negative and the message NOT BOTH otherwise.

Problem analysis   The logic of this problem is slightly complicated. First, the number A must be tested to determine if it is negative. If it is, then B must be tested. But, as soon as a number being tested is not negative, the message NOT BOTH should be printed. An algorithm for doing this is as follows.

a. Input values for A and B.
b. If A is not negative, print NOT BOTH and stop.
c. If B is not negative, print NOT BOTH and stop.
d. Print BOTH and stop.

The program

```
10 INPUT A,B
20 IF A>=0 THEN 60
30 IF B>=0 THEN 60
40 PRINT "BOTH"
50 GO TO 70
60 PRINT "NOT BOTH"
70 END
RUN

? -5,-4
BOTH
READY
```

Remark 1

The GO TO at line 50 simply serves to terminate this program. The BASIC statement

```
50 STOP
```

does the same thing. You may include a STOP statement anywhere in your program and use as many as you wish.

Remark 2

Beginning programmers are often tempted to begin coding a program without first describing an algorithm to be followed. If this practice were followed for the problem at hand, we could easily be led into making the tests $A < 0$ and $B < 0$ rather than the tests $A >= 0$ and $B >= 0$ as was done in lines 20 and 30. The result would be a program similar to the following.

```
10 INPUT A,B
20 IF A<0 THEN 40
30 GO TO 50
40 IF B<0 THEN 70
50 PRINT "NOT BOTH"
60 GO TO 80
70 PRINT "BOTH"
80 END
```

This is a correct but rather poor program. It contains an extra GO TO statement that makes it more difficult to follow than the first program. There are no hard and fast rules for choosing between the two tests $<$ and $>=$. The "best" choice will be dictated by a carefully prepared algorithm.

EXAMPLE 7. Here is a program segment to allow a user to instruct the computer to halt execution of a program.

```
300 PRINT "ARE YOU FINISHED";
310 INPUT C$
320 IF C$="NO" THEN 350
330 PRINT "GOODBYE"
340 STOP
350 (Next statement to be executed.)
```

If you type NO in response to the statement INPUT C$, the string NO is assigned to C$ and the condition in line 320 is true. Thus, control transfers to line 350 and program execution continues. If YES is typed, the condition C$ = "NO" is false so the transfer to line 350 is not made. The computer then prints GOODBYE and program execution halts.

Remark   Strings appearing in relational expressions must always be enclosed in quotation marks. Failure to observe this rule will result in an error message. Recall that using quotes for strings typed in response to an INPUT statement is usually optional. Situations where they are required were described in Chapter 5.

6.3 Compound logical expressions

A **logical expression** is an expression that is either *true* or *false*. The relational expressions encountered in the preceding section are either true or false, hence they are logical expressions. BASIC allows you to write *compound* logical expressions by using the logical operators AND, OR, and NOT. These are best illustrated by example.

EXAMPLE 8. Here is an illustration of the logical operators AND, OR, and NOT.

a. The logical expression

(A<B) AND (B<C)

is true if both of the relational expressions A<B and B<C are true; otherwise, it is false. Thus, the given expression is true only if A, B, and C satisfy the double inequality A<B<C. It should be noted that the expression A<B<C is not allowed in BASIC. A relational expression must contain only one of the relational operators =, <>, >, >=, <, and <=.

b. The logical expression

(A<B) OR (A<C)

is true if either or both of the relational expressions are true. Thus, the given expression is true if A is less than B, or C, or both; otherwise it is false. Note that this expression is false only if the expression

(A>=B) AND (A>=C)

is true.

c. The logical expression

NOT (A<B)

is true if the relational expression A<B is not true; otherwise it is false. Note that the given expression NOT (A<B) is equivalent to the relational expression A>=B. By equivalent, we mean that for any values of A and B, the expressions are both true or both false.

We now give precise definitions of the logical operators AND, OR, and NOT.

If **le₁** and **le₂** are logical expressions, the truth values (*true* or *false*) of the three logical expressions (**le₁**) AND (**le₂**), (**le₁**) OR (**le₂**), and NOT (**le₁**) are as shown in Tables 6.2, 6.3, and 6.4.

TABLE 6.2   The AND operator.

le_1	le_2	(le_1) AND (le_2)
true	true	true
true	false	false
false	true	false
false	false	false

TABLE 6.3   The OR operator.

le_1	le_2	(le_1) OR (le_2)
true	true	true
true	false	true
false	true	true
false	false	false

TABLE 6.4   The NOT operator.

le_1	NOT (le_1)
true	false
false	true

EXAMPLE 9. The following illustrate typical uses of logical expressions containing the AND and OR operators.

---

a. The statement

```
IF (A>0) AND (B>0) THEN 200
```

will transfer control to line 200 if both A and B are positive. Otherwise, control passes to the line following the IF statement.

b. The statement

```
IF (G>=80) AND (G<=89) THEN PRINT "B"
```

will cause the letter B to be printed only if the value of G is between 80 and 89, inclusive.

c. The statement

```
IF (G<80) OR (G>89) THEN 300
```

will cause a transfer to line 300 only if G is not between 80 and 89, inclusive.

Remark   The logical expression in part (b) is true only when G satisfies the double inequality $80 \leq G \leq 89$, whereas the logical expression in part (c) is true only when $G<80$ or $G>89$—that is, only when the double inequality $80 \leq G \leq 89$ is false. Thus, the two logical expressions (G >= 80) AND (G <= 89) and NOT ((G<80) OR (G>89)) are equivalent—that is, for any value of G, they are both true or both false.

EXAMPLE 10

In Example 6, the following program was written to determine if two input values A and B are both negative.

```
10 INPUT A,B
20 IF (A>=0) THEN 60
30 IF (B>=0) THEN 60
40 PRINT "BOTH"
50 STOP
60 PRINT "NOT BOTH"
70 END
```

By using the AND operator, this program can be rewritten in the following slightly more readable form.

```
10 INPUT A,B
20 IF (A<0) AND (B<0) THEN 50
30 PRINT "NOT BOTH"
40 STOP
50 PRINT "BOTH"
60 END
```

Moreover, if your system allows the IF-THEN-ELSE statement, you can write

```
10 INPUT A,B
20 IF (A<0) AND (B<0) THEN PRINT "BOTH" ELSE PRINT "NOT BOTH"
30 END
```

A logical expression may contain more than one of the operators NOT, AND, and OR. An expression such as

```
(M=0) OR (A<B) AND (A<C)
```

is admissible. However, the order in which the OR and AND operators are carried out matters. In BASIC, the following priorities are used:

Logical operator	Priority
NOT	highest
AND	intermediate
OR	lowest

In any logical expression, the order in which the logical operators are performed is determined first by the indicated priority and then, in any priority class, from left to right. As with arithmetic expressions, parentheses may be used to override this order or simply to clarify what order is intended. Thus, the logical expression

```
(M=0) OR (A<B) AND (A<C)
```

is equivalent to the expression

```
(M=0) OR ((A<B) AND (A<C))
```

If you want the OR to be performed first, you must use parentheses and write

```
((M=0) OR (A<B)) AND (A<C)
```

EXAMPLE 11. Here is a program to input four numbers and print IN ORDER if they are in increasing order, and NOT IN ORDER if they are not.

```
10  INPUT A,B,C,D
20  IF NOT ((A<B) AND (B<C) AND (C<D)) THEN PRINT "NOT ";
30  PRINT "IN ORDER"
40  END
```

6.4 Problems

1. If $A = 1$, $B = 2$, and $C = 3$, which of the following relational expressions are true?
   a. A+B<=C
   b. A+B>=C
   c. 3<>C
   d. 7.0>=7
   e. A/C*B<=.5
   f. 3-(C/B)=3-C/B
   g. A/B/C>A
   h. -A-B-C<=-(A+B+C)*B
   i. (A<C) AND (A+B=C)
   j. NOT ((A>B) OR (C>A))
   k. ((A>B) OR (B>C)) AND (A-B+C<0)
   l. NOT (A>B) AND NOT (C>A)

2. Each of the following contains an error (not necessarily a syntax error). Find it, and explain what will happen if a program containing the given line is run.
   a. 57 IF (A-B)*(A+B) THEN 47
   b. 60 IF M-N<27, THEN 13
   c. 90 IF 2<Y<4 THEN 27
   d. 70 IF A<B THEN 70
   e. 50 IF X<X-B THEN 51
   f. 40 IF A1>A2 PRINT A1
   g. 85 IF NOT (K/3) THEN LET K=K+1
   h. 90 IF (A OR B) THEN PRINT "OK"
   i. 40 IF J=K THEN 60 ELSE 40
   j. 35 IF K=4 OR 7 THEN PRINT K

3. Correct the following programs.
   a.
   ```
   10 REM PROGRAM TO PRINT THE ODD
   20 REM WHOLE NUMBERS THROUGH 15
   30 LET N=1
   40 PRINT N
   50 LET N=N+2
   60 IF N<15 THEN 30
   70 END
   ```

   b.
   ```
   100 REM TELL WHETHER ANY NON-ZERO
   110 REM INTEGER IS POSITIVE OR NEGATIVE
   120 INPUT N
   130 IF N=0 THEN 120
   140 IF N>0 THEN PRINT N,"IS POSITIVE"
   150 STOP
   160 IF N<0 THEN PRINT N,"IS NEGATIVE"
   170 END
   ```

4. What will be printed when each of the following is run?
   a.
   ```
   10 LET A=3
   20 LET B=3
   30 LET C=(A+B)/B
   40 LET D=B/A-C
   50 IF D>=0 THEN LET D=13
   60 PRINT D
   70 END
   ```

   b.
   ```
   10 LET A=5
   20 LET B=-A
   30 IF A+B<>0 THEN 70
   40 LET A=-B
   50 PRINT A
   60 GO TO 80
   70 PRINT B
   80 END
   ```

   c.
   ```
   1 LET S=0
   2 LET S=S+2
   3 IF S<13 THEN 2 ELSE PRINT S
   4 LET S=S/2
   5 IF S>3.3 THEN 4 ELSE PRINT S
   6 END
   ```

   d.
   ```
   100 LET B=0
   110 LET I=0
   120 LET A=11
   130    LET B=B+I+2
   140    IF A<B THEN 180
   150    LET I=I+1
   160    LET A=A-1
   170 IF B<A THEN 130
   180 PRINT I
   190 END
   ```

```
e. 10 LET S=5
   20 LET J=3
   30 IF S<7 AND J>10 THEN PRINT J
   40 LET J=S+J
   50 IF S+J<15 THEN PRINT S ELSE PRINT J
   60 PRINT "THAT'S ALL"
   70 END
```

```
f. 10 LET L=22
   20 IF NOT (L<40 OR L>60) THEN 60
   30    IF L<40 THEN LET L=L+50
   40    IF L>60 THEN LET L=L-10
   50 GO TO 20
   60 PRINT L
   70 END
```

5. Write programs that are equivalent to the following but contain no GO TO statements. (Use IF statements of the form IF *condition* THEN *line number* only if absolutely necessary.)

```
a. 10 INPUT N
   20 IF N>=50 THEN 40
   30 GO TO 50
   40 LET N=N/2
   50 IF N>=25 THEN 70
   60 LET N=N/2
   70 PRINT N
   80 END
```

```
b. 10 LET S=10
   20 INPUT A
   30 IF A>0 THEN 50
   40 GO TO 60
   50 LET S=20
   60 PRINT S
   70 END
```

```
c. 10 INPUT X,Y
   20 IF X>0 THEN 40
   30 GO TO 10
   40 IF Y>0 THEN 60
   50 GO TO 10
   60 LET S=X+Y
   70 PRINT S
   80 END
```

```
d. 10 INPUT A,B
   20 IF A>B THEN 60
   30 PRINT "SMALLEST IS",A
   40 PRINT "LARGEST IS",B
   50 STOP
   60 LET T=A
   70 LET A=B
   80 LET B=T
   90 GO TO 30
   99 END
```

Write a program to perform each task specified in Problems 6–21. Appropriate messages should be printed (keep them short) that give instructions to the user concerning values to be entered.

6. Two numbers A and B are to be typed. If the first is larger, print A IS LARGER. Otherwise, print A IS NOT LARGER.

7. Two numbers M and N are to be typed. If the sum equals 5, print 5. Otherwise, print NOT 5.

8. Two numbers X and Y are to be typed. If the product is less than or equal to the quotient, print PRODUCT. Otherwise, print QUOTIENT.

9. Three numbers are to be typed. If the second is less than the sum of the first and third, print LESS. Otherwise, print NOT LESS.

10. For any two numbers M and N, print POSITIVE if both are positive and NEGATIVE if both are negative. Otherwise, print NEITHER.

11. A person earns R dollars an hour with time-and-a-half for all hours over 32. Determine the gross pay for a T-hour week. (R and T are to be entered during program execution.)

12. The cost of sending a telegram is $1.35 for the first ten words and 9¢ for each additional word. Find the cost if the number of words is input at the terminal.

13. If the wholesale cost of an item is under $100, the markup is 20%. Otherwise, the markup is 30%. Determine the retail price for an item whose wholesale cost is entered during program execution.

14. Two numbers X and Y are to be typed. If the sum of X and Y is greater than 42, print 42. If not, increase X by 10 and Y by 3, print the new X and Y, and again check to see if the sum is greater than 42. Continue until the sum is greater than 42.

15. One number is to be typed. If it is between 7 and 35, inclusive, print BETWEEN and stop. If it is less than 7, increase it by 5; if it is greater than 35, decrease it by 5. In either case, print the value obtained. The program should continue with this new value until it is between 7 and 35.

16. For any three numbers typed at the terminal, print ALL if all three are negative; otherwise, print NOT ALL.

17. For any three numbers input, print ALL NEGATIVE if all are negative, ALL POSITIVE if all are positive, and NEITHER in all other cases.
18. Input a positive integer N, and determine the first positive integer I whose cube is greater than N.
19. Find the first positive integer N for which $33N - 28 > 24N + 200$ and $5N - 63 \geqslant 2N + 21$.
20. Division of one positive integer A by another positive integer B is often presented in elementary school as repeated subtraction. Write a program to input two positive integers A and B, and determine the quotient Q and the remainder R by this method.
21. Input two positive integers A and B, and compute $A \uparrow B$ without using $\uparrow$.

6.5 Flowcharts and flowcharting

The following diagram is a pictorial representation of a simple algorithm to recognize whether or not an input value is 5.

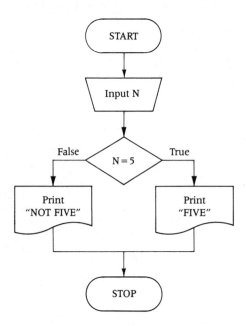

Such a pictorial representation of the sequence of steps in an algorithm or a program is called a **programming flowchart,** or simply a **flowchart.** Flowcharts are useful for program documentation. In addition, it is often easier to prepare a pictorial description of a process to be followed than to attempt a detailed description in words. The flowchart is an excellent way to do this. Some of the components used to construct flowcharts can be seen in the following examples.

EXAMPLE 12. Here are two equivalent flowcharts for a program to print the numbers 100, 110, 120, . . . , 200:

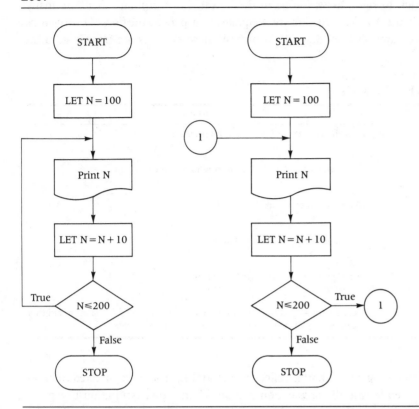

EXAMPLE 13. Here is a flowchart displaying the process of adding the integers from 1 to 10:

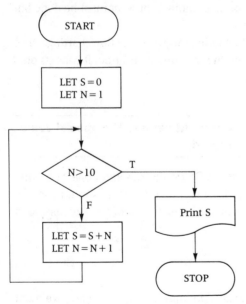

Remark 1   When two or more assignment statements are included in a single box they are evaluated from top to bottom.

Remark 2   Note that we have labeled the flow lines from the diamond-shaped decision symbol with the letters T and F for true and false, respectively.

In these examples, arrows connecting six different types of symbols are used to describe the sequence of steps in an algorithm. When possible, the flow should be directed from top to bottom or from left to right, as was done in these examples. Although there are many flowchart symbols [1] in use, the six used here are adequate for displaying the flow of instructions for many BASIC programs. A brief description of how these symbols are used is given in Table 6.5.

TABLE 6.5 Flowchart symbols.

The symbol	Its use
	To designate the start and end of a program.
	To describe data to be INPUT during program execution.
	To describe the output.
	To describe any processing of data.
	To designate a decision that is to be made.
	A connector—used so that flow from one segment of a flowchart to another can be displayed and also to avoid drawing long lines.

The process of preparing a flowchart is called **flowcharting.** There are no fixed rules on how one should proceed toward the preparation of a flowchart; flowcharting must be practiced. However, it is helpful to determine *what* must be done before attempting to describe *how* to do it (a flowchart is concerned principally with *how* to carry out a task). If you don't do this, you will be confronted with the problem of determining not *what* must be done but what must be done *first*. This can be very difficult.

We conclude this section with two examples illustrating the process of flowcharting. Once a flowchart is prepared, the task of writing the program is reasonably routine; it consists only of coding the steps indicated in the flowchart.

EXAMPLE 14. Construct a flowchart to find the largest number in a list of input values. The special value 9999 is to be typed to indicate that all numbers in the list have been entered.

Problem analysis

One way to determine the largest number in a list is to read the numbers one at a time, remembering only the largest of those already read. (This method was illustrated and discussed in Chapter 2, Example 2.) To help us give a precise description of this process, let's use the following variable names:

L = largest of those numbers already read.
N = the number currently being read.

It is not difficult to construct a flowchart describing an algorithm for this task. First, we must input the first number and assign it to L. Thus, we can begin with the following flowchart segment:

---

[1] Flowchart symbols as proposed by the American National Standards Institute (ANSI) are described in "Flowcharting with the ANSI Standard: A Tutorial," by Ned Chapin, *Computing Surveys*, Vol. 2, No. 2, June 1970.

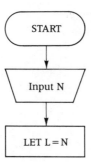

The next step is to input another value and compare it with 9999, to determine if the end of the input list has been reached. To display this step, we can add the following to our partial flowchart:

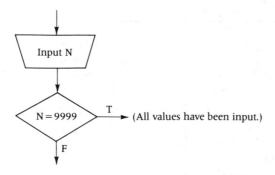

If N = 9999 (the *True* branch), we simply print L, the largest number, and stop. Thus, we can complete the T (*True*) branch by adding the following to our partial flowchart.

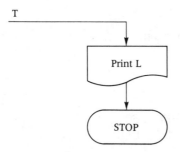

Note that while constructing the flowchart (that is, while discovering an algorithm), we always have a partial flowchart in front of us to help us decide what the next step should be. Continuing this process of flowchart construction, a flowchart such as the following will emerge:

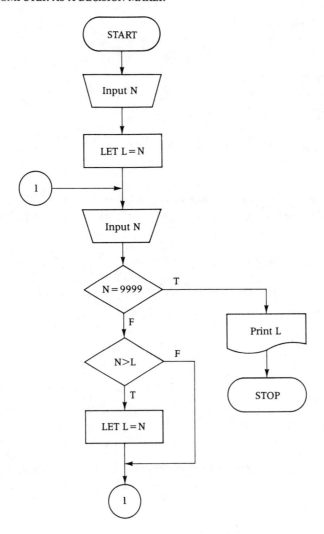

Here is one way to code this flowchart:

```
100 INPUT N
110 LET L=N
120     INPUT N
130      IF N=9999 THEN 160
140       IF N>L THEN LET L=N
150 GO TO 120
160 PRINT L
170 END
```

The following table summarizes the values of the variables when this program is run with the input list

8, 3, 9, 2, 9999

Line number	N	L	Output
100	8	—	
110	8	8	
120	3	8	
120	9	8	
140	9	9	
120	2	9	
120	9999	9	
160	9999	9	9

Remark

The value 9999 used as a final input value to indicate that all numbers in the list have been entered is called an EOD (end of data) tag.

EXAMPLE 15. Construct a flowchart for a program to determine the number of years required for an investment of $1000 earning 7.5% compounded annually to double in value.

Problem analysis

The compound interest formula is

$$A = P(1 + R)^N,$$

in which

P denotes the principal (P = 1000);
R denotes the rate per period (R = 0.075);
N denotes the number of periods; and
A denotes the value after N periods.

We can begin our flowchart construction by assigning initial values to P, R, and N.

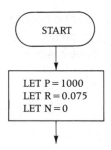

Next, we must compare the value of A after one year with 2P. Since N denotes the number of years that have passed, we can add the following to our partial flowchart.

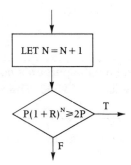

If the condition is true, we simply print N and stop. If it is false, we increase N by 1 and repeat the comparison. Adding these two steps to the partial flowchart we obtain the following complete algorithm.

The flowchart

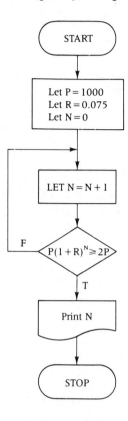

If this flowchart is coded, a GO TO statement will be needed following the IF statement. This can be avoided by using $<$ rather than $\geq$ in the decision box. The flowchart will have exactly the same structure, but the program will be easier to read.

The program

```
100 LET P=1000
110 LET R=0.075
120 LET N=0
130     LET N=N+1
140 IF P*(1+R)↑N<2*P THEN 130
150 PRINT "NUMBER OF YEARS TO DOUBLE",N
160 END
RUN

NUMBER OF YEARS TO DOUBLE          10
READY
```

EXAMPLE 16. Construct a flowchart for a program to determine a salesperson's commission if the schedule is 4% on any sales up to $500 and 6% on all sales in excess of $500. The total sales are to be input at the terminal.

Problem analysis

Let's denote the total sales by S and the commission by C. The following formulas govern this situation.

If S $\leq$ 500, C = .04S

If S $>$ 500, C = .04(500) + .06(S − 500)

For any amount S, we must determine the commission C as indicated by these formulas. Having identified what must be done, we must show how to do it. First, we must input a value for S. Let's assume that a sales amount of 0 means that all commissions have been determined and printed. (As mentioned previously, this input value 0 is called an EOD [end of data] tag.) This suggests the following flowchart segment to get us started:

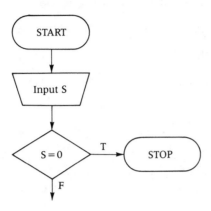

Next, we must compare S with 500 to determine which of the commission formulas to use. This immediately gives rise to the following complete flowchart for the given problem statement. Note that including 0 as an EOD-tag allows many commissions to be calculated during a single program run. Although this was not specified in the problem statement, it is certainly a desirable feature to include in the program.

The flowchart

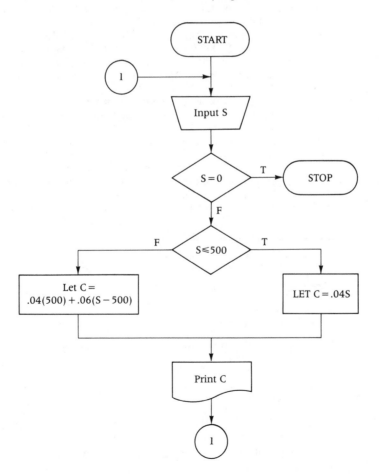

6.6 Problems

Prepare a flowchart and then a program to accomplish each task specified in Problems 1–14. Try to avoid GO TO statements in your programs.

1. Input one number. If it is between 3 and 21, print BETWEEN. Otherwise, print NOT BETWEEN.
2. Input two numbers. If either one is positive, print EITHER. Otherwise, print NEITHER.
3. Input three distinct numbers. If the first is the largest, print LARGEST. Otherwise, print NOT LARGEST.
4. Input three distinct numbers. If the second is the largest, print LARGEST. If it is the smallest, print SMALLEST. Otherwise, print NEITHER.
5. Input two values A and B. Print the value 1 if A = B = 0 or A = B = 1. Print the value 0 in all other cases.
6. Input a list of numbers whose last value is 9999. Print the smallest and largest values in the list excluding the 9999.
7. Input a list of numbers terminated with 9999. Print the largest number and also a count of how many numbers are included in the list.
8. (This is more difficult.) Input a list of numbers as in Problem 7. Print the largest number in the list and also a count of how many numbers appear in the list before the first occurrence of this largest number. For example, if the list is 6, 9, 6, 12, 10, 5, 12, 7, 5, the largest value is 12 and the count is three. (*Hint:* To determine the specified count you will need a variable to count the input values and another to "remember" the number of input values appearing before the "current" largest value.)
9. For any input list, determine how many times a number is strictly larger than the one just before it. For example, if the list is 17, 3, 19, 27, 23, 25, the answer will be three, because 19 > 3, 27 > 19, and 25 > 23.
10. A list of numbers, terminated with the special value 9999, is to be typed. Two counts, N and P, are required as follows. P is a count of how many times a number typed is greater than the number typed just before it; N is a count of how many times a number typed is less than the number typed just before it. (For example, if 1, 5, 3, 3, 7 are typed, then P = 2 and N = 1, whereas if 5, 4, 3, 4, 8, 9 are typed, then P = 3 and N = 2.)
11. Several pairs (X, Y) of numbers are to be input. Any pair with X = Y serves as the EOD-tag. Determine and print counts of how many pairs satisfy X < Y and how many pairs satisfy X > Y.
12. Each salesperson earns a base weekly salary of $185.00. In addition, if a salesperson's total weekly sales exceed $1000.00, a commission of 5.3% is earned on any amount up to $5000.00 and 7.8% is earned on any amount in excess of $5000.00. Determine the weekly pay, before deductions, for any salesperson whose total weekly sales amount is input. Use an EOD-tag to effect an orderly exit from the program.
13. A company payroll clerk needs a computer program to assist in preparing the weekly payroll. For each employee the clerk is to enter the hours worked H, the hourly pay rate R, the federal tax rate F, the state tax rate S, and the Social Security rate T. The clerk needs to know the gross pay, the net pay, and the amount of each deduction. Employees receive time-and-a-half for each hour worked over 40 hours. (The algorithm should not be too detailed. For example, after H, R, F, S, and T have been called for, a single line might read "Determine the gross pay, the three deductions, and the net pay." The details for doing this would then be worked out during the flowchart construction.)
14. A salesperson's monthly commission is determined according to the following schedule.

Net sales	Commission rate
Up to $10,000	6%
Next $4000	7%
Next $6000	8%
Additional amounts	10%

Determine the monthly commission given the total monthly sales.

6.7 Summing with the IF statement

As a programmer you will often encounter problems whose solutions require finding the sum of many numbers. Since summing is a repetitive process, it can be accomplished very nicely with a loop. In this case it is important that an exit be made from the loop only after the required sum has been obtained. The examples in this section illustrate the following three ways to exit from a loop:

1. Before the loop is initiated, specify the exact number of terms to be added (Example 17).
2. Program the computer to terminate the loop upon recognition of a special value, such as 9999 (Example 18).
3. Cause an exit from the loop when some prescribed condition has been satisfied (Example 19).

EXAMPLE 17

Construct a flowchart and write a program to evaluate the sum

$$S = 1^2 + 2^2 + 3^2 + \cdots + N^2$$

where N is to be specified by the user. If the input value N is less than 1, print the sum $S = 0$.

Problem analysis

A simple algorithm for this task is as follows.

a. Input N
b. Calculate the sum $S = 1^2 + 2^2 + \cdots + N^2$.
c. Print S and stop.

To carry out step (b), you can start with a sum S of zero and add the squares of the numbers 1, 2, 3, . . . , N to S, one at a time. The following flowchart describes this process.

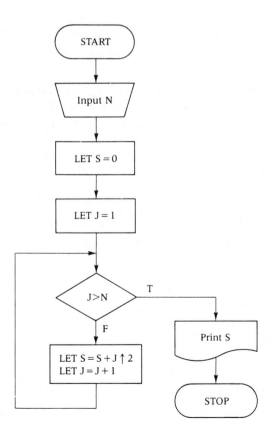

The program

```
10 INPUT N
20 LET S=0
30 LET J=1
40 IF J>N THEN 80
50    LET S=S+J↑2
60    LET J=J+1
70 GO TO 40
80 PRINT "SUM IS",S
90 END
RUN

? 5
SUM IS          55
READY
```

The following table traces the values of N, S, and J as this program is executed with the input value N = 5.

Line number	N	S	J	Output
10	5	—	—	
20	5	0	—	
30	5	0	1	
50	5	1	1	
60	5	1	2	
50	5	5	2	
60	5	5	3	
50	5	14	3	
60	5	14	4	
50	5	30	4	
60	5	30	5	
50	5	55	5	
60	5	55	6	
80	5	55	6	SUM IS 55

EXAMPLE 18. Construct a flowchart for a program to find the averages of several sets of numbers typed in at the terminal. The value 9999, when typed, means that all entries for that particular set of numbers have been made. After each set of numbers has been processed, the user should be asked if there is another set to be processed.

Problem analysis

The input and output values for this task are as follows:

Input: Several sets of numbers, each set terminated with 9999.
Output: The average of each set of numbers input.

To input one set of numbers and determine their average, you will need the following variables.

N = the value being typed at the terminal.
S = the sum at any time (initially zero).
K = the number of values entered (initially zero).
A = the average (A = S/K).

Before any numbers in a set have been entered, S and K must be set equal to 0. When a number N is typed, we must determine if N is 9999. If it is not, the sum S is increased by

N, the counter K is increased by 1, and a new value is entered for N. If N is 9999, all numbers in the set have been entered, so the average A = S/K is printed. The computer must then ask if there is another set to be processed. The following flowchart displays this process.

The flowchart

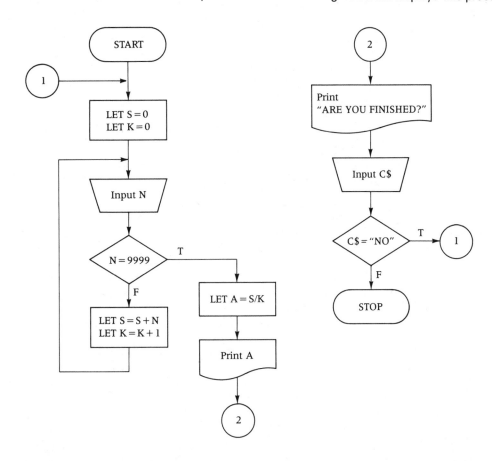

EXAMPLE 19. A person wishes to borrow $1000 but can only afford to pay back $40 per month. A loan officer at the bank states that such a loan is possible at an interest rate of 1.2% per month on the unpaid balance. Write a program to compute the total number of payments, the amount of the final payment, and the total amount the borrower must pay to the bank. (Assume that the first $40 payment is to be made one month after the date of the loan.)

Problem analysis

So that the program will be applicable to any problem of this type, let's assign the variables as follows.

R = the monthly rate of interest (R = .012).
P = the monthly payment (P = 40).
B = the balance still owed to the bank at any time (initially 1000).
I = the interest due for the previous month (I = B*R).
N = the number of payments made to date (initially zero).
T = the total amount paid to date (initially zero).

Whenever a payment is made, the bank calculates the new balance as follows. The interest I = B*R for the previous month is added to the old balance (LET B = B + I). If this balance B is not greater than P, a final payment of B dollars will be made. If B is greater than P, then the current payment of P dollars is subtracted from B (LET B = B − P) and this is the new balance. In either case the current payment must be added to the total amount T, and N, which counts the number of payments made, must be increased by 1.

The flowchart

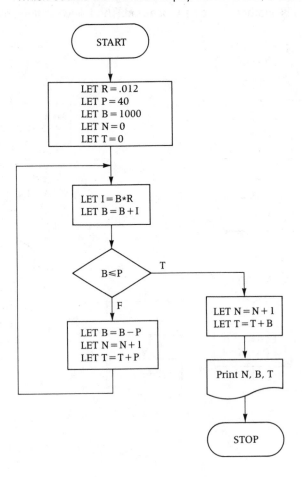

The program

```
100 REM INITIALIZE VARIABLES
110 LET R = .012
120 LET P = 40
130 LET B = 1000
140 LET T = 0
150 LET N = 0
160 REM CALCULATE INTEREST AND NEW BALANCE
170     LET I = B*R
180     LET B = B+I
190     REM CHECK FOR LAST PAYMENT
200     IF B<=P THEN 270
210     REM MAKE A PAYMENT OF P DOLLARS
220     LET B = B-P
230     LET N = N+1
240     LET T = T+P
250 GO TO 170
260 REM MAKE FINAL PAYMENT AND PRINT RESULTS
270 LET N = N+1
280 LET T = T+B
290 PRINT "NO. OF PAYMENTS IS",N
300 PRINT "FINAL PAYMENT IS",B
```

```
310 PRINT "TOTAL AMT. PAID ON LOAN IS",T
320 END
RUN

NO. OF PAYMENTS IS          30
FINAL PAYMENT IS            36.0571
TOTAL AMT. PAID ON LOAN IS  1196.06
READY
```

6.8 Structured programming

The importance of preparing an algorithm before beginning the coding process cannot be overemphasized. However, just as unreadable programs are often written by people who begin a programming task while seated at a computer terminal, so too unreadable algorithms can be written if certain guidelines are not followed. The algorithms we have presented in this text take one of two forms:

1. An English-like step-by-step process describing how to carry out a specific task.
2. A flowchart displaying the steps to be followed.

When using the first form, the individual steps often correspond to program segments rather than to single program statements. For instance, the following algorithm was written for the task given in Example 17.

a. Input N.
b. Calculate the sum $S = 1^2 + 2^2 + \cdots + N^2$.
c. Print S and stop.

If you can see how to code step (b), there is no need to include more detail in this algorithm. However, if it is not obvious to you how to code step (b), you can attempt to rewrite the step in more detail. Here is one way to do this.

b1. Let S = 0.
b2. For J = 1, 2, 3, . . . , N, add J ↑ 2 to S.

This process of refining the steps in an algorithm is called the **method of stepwise refinement** and has been illustrated in several of the worked out examples, beginning with those in Chapter 2. A more complete discussion of this programming method is given in Section 9.4.

When using flowcharts to display the steps in an algorithm, the same process of refinement can be used. For the example cited, you could have begun by writing the following flowchart.

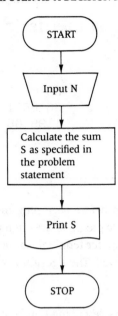

As before, if coding this flowchart is easy for you, there is no need to include more detail. However, if it is not clear how to code the box that calculates S, you should attempt to rewrite this step by including more detail. In Example 17, we displayed this detail by using the following flowchart segment.

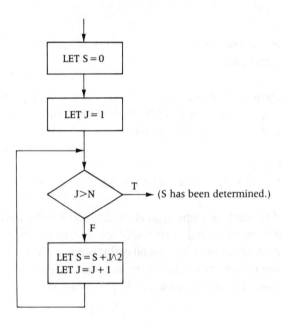

When writing an algorithm, whether in English, as a flowchart, or in BASIC, the following situations arise:

1. Two or more tasks are to be carried out in sequence. (Figure 6.1)
2. One of two tasks is to be selected depending on a specified condition. It may be that one of the two tasks is to do nothing. (Figure 6.2)
3. A task is to be carried out repeatedly. (Figure 6.3)

Figure 6.1
Sequence.

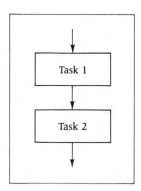

Figure 6.2
Selection.

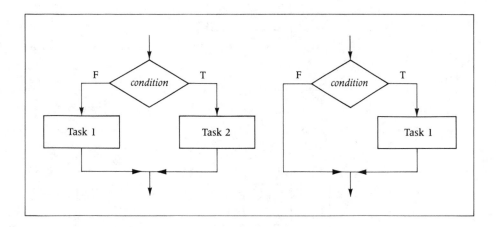

Figure 6.3
Repetition.

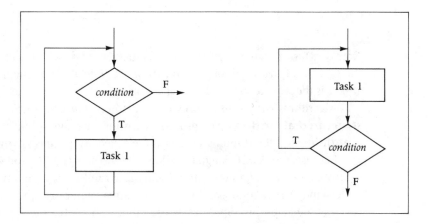

These three control structures are referred to as **structured programming constructs.** It has been shown[2] that any algorithm can be written using only these constructs. The following diagram shows how two of these constructs (*sequence* and *repetition*) are used in the algorithm, shown in Example 17, to calculate the sum $S = 1^2 + 2^2 + 3^2 + \cdots + N^2$.

[2] "Flow Diagrams, Turing Machines and Languages with only Two Formation Rules," by Corrado Bohm and Guiseppe Jacopini, *Comm. A.C.M.*, **9** (May 1966), pp. 366–371.

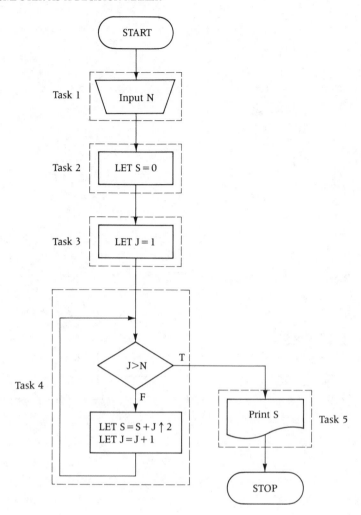

Note that Task 4 is an instance of the construct *repetition,* whereas the entire program is simply the *sequence* of Tasks 1 through 5 in that order. Note also that the task being repeated within Task 4 is the *sequence* of two LET statements.

Algorithms written using only the constructs *sequence, selection,* and *repetition* are called **structured algorithms.** The process of writing such algorithms is called **structured programming** and the resulting programs are called **structured programs.**

Because the BASIC language allows you to use GO TO and IF statements to transfer control to any line in a program, it is easy to write BASIC programs that are very difficult to understand. The time to avoid writing an unreadable program is during the process of discovering the algorithm. Specifically, each time you are tempted to write a step such as *Go to step (b),* or *If N<5, go to step (b),* you should ask if this transfer of control is part of a selection or repetition structure. If it is not, you should try something else.

Even with great care in algorithm construction, BASIC programmers often encounter the following control structure in their algorithms.

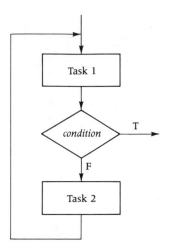

Although this is not one of the structured constructs (sequence, selection, and repetition), it can always be replaced by the following structured flowchart segment.

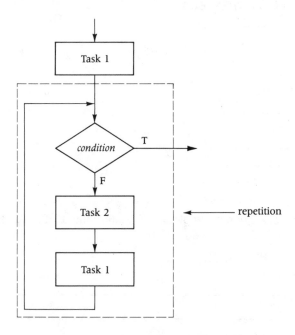

However, it is debatable whether writing the BASIC code for Task 1 twice in the program is worth the effort. The usual practice among BASIC programmers is to allow this construct as one of the building blocks for programs. (It was used in Example 19 of Section 6.7.)

If you use only the programming constructs described in this section, your final product, the program, will have a simpler structure and hence will be easier to read, to debug, and to modify, should that be required. For instance, note that each of the suggested constructs has exactly one entry point and exactly one exit point. This means that an entire program can be broken down into blocks of code, each block having but one entry point and one exit point. Since each of these blocks will perform a known task, the individual blocks can be debugged separately, thus greatly simplifying the task of verifying the correctness of the entire program. As you write larger and larger programs, you will find this method of debugging not only useful, but essential.

Once you have written an algorithm using the suggested constructs, the task of coding it as a BASIC program is routine, as we now show.

EXAMPLE 20

To code the selection construct

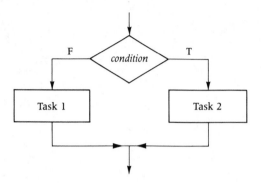

you can write (the line numbers are for illustration only):

500 IF *condition* THEN 600

$$\left.\begin{array}{l} \rule{3cm}{0.4pt} \\ \rule{3cm}{0.4pt} \\ \rule{3cm}{0.4pt} \\ \rule{3cm}{0.4pt} \end{array}\right\}\text{ code for Task 1}$$

590 GO TO 700
600

$$\left.\begin{array}{l} \rule{3cm}{0.4pt} \\ \rule{3cm}{0.4pt} \\ \rule{3cm}{0.4pt} \\ \rule{3cm}{0.4pt} \end{array}\right\}\text{ code for Task 2}$$

700 (next statement)

If Task 1 and Task 2 denote single BASIC statements s_1 and s_2, respectively, you can write

IF *condition* THEN s_2 ELSE s_1

EXAMPLE 21

To code the selection construct

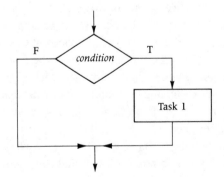

you can write

500 IF NOT *condition* THEN 600

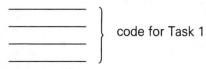

600 (next statement)

If Task 1 denotes a single BASIC statement **s₁**, you can write

IF *condition* THEN **s₁**

EXAMPLE 22

To code the repetition construct

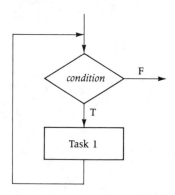

you can write

500 IF NOT *condition* THEN 600

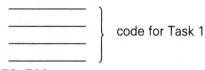

590 GO TO 500
600 (next statement)

Remark 1   Note that the code for Task 1 must contain a statement that changes some variable appearing in the *condition*. Indeed, the *condition* must eventually become *false*, otherwise you have an infinite loop.

Remark 2   This control structure says to *do* the given task *while* the *condition* is true. For this reason, it is called the DOWHILE structure and is often represented in algorithms as follows:

DOWHILE *condition*
        Description of task
        being repeated.

DOWHILE is not in the BASIC language. It simply suggests BASIC code.

EXAMPLE 23

To code the repetition construct

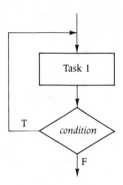

you can write

```
500  REM  (description of Task 1)
510        _____
           _____  }  code for Task 1
           _____
           _____
600  IF condition THEN 510
610  (next statement)
```

EXAMPLE 24

To code the construct

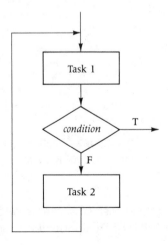

you can write

```
500        _____
           _____  }  code for Task 1
           _____
           _____
```

```
600 IF condition THEN 700
    _____
    _____  } code for Task 2
    _____
    _____

690 GO TO 500
700 (next statement)
```

6.9 Problems

1. Write programs to compute the following sums S or products P. N, if present, is to be assigned with an INPUT statement.
   a. $S = 1 + 2 + 3 + \cdots + N$
   b. $S = 5 + 7 + 9 + \cdots + 91$
   c. $S = 3 + 8 + 13 + 18 + \cdots + 93$
   d. $S = (-10)^7 + (-8)^5 + (-6)^3 + (-4)^1 + (-2)^{-1}$
   e. $S = 1 + 1/2 + 1/3 + 1/4 + \cdots + 1/N$
   f. $S = 1 - 1/2 + 1/3 - 1/4 + \cdots + (-1)^{N+1}/N$
   g. $S = 1 - 1/3 + 1/5 - 1/7 + \cdots + (-1)^{N+1}/(2N - 1)$
   h. $S = 2^2 + 4^2 + 6^2 + \cdots + (2N)^2$
   i. $S = 1 + 1/4 + 1/9 + \cdots + 1/N^2$
   j. $P = (1/2)(2/3)(3/4)(4/5) \cdots (N/(N + 1))$
   k. $P = (1 - 1/2)(1 - 1/3)(1 - 1/4) \cdots (1 - 1/N)$

Write a program to perform each task specified in Problems 2–13.

2. Calculate the sum and average of any 20 input values.
3. Input a list of numbers whose last value is 999. Calculate the sum and average of all input values excluding 999.
4. Many numbers are to be input. The number 0 is used as the EOD-tag. Determine the sum of all positive numbers and the sum of all negative numbers. Both sums are to be printed.
5. A list of numbers is to be input as in Problem 4. Determine and print the average of all positive numbers and the average of all negative numbers.
6. A young man agrees to begin working for a company at the very modest salary of a penny per week, with the stipulation that his salary will double each week. What is his weekly salary and how much has he earned at the end of six months?
7. N numbers are to be typed. Numbers less than 50 are to be doubled and those greater than 50 halved. However, if 50 is typed, no more numbers are to be entered. Calculate the average of these modified numbers, but exclude 50 if it is typed.
8. Find the total amount credited to an account after four years if $25 is deposited each month at an annual interest rate of 5.5% compounded monthly.
9. Mary deposits $25 in a bank at the annual interest rate of 6% compounded monthly. After how many months will her account first exceed $27.50?
10. On the first of each month other than January, a person deposits $100 into an account earning 6% interest compounded monthly. The account is opened on February 1st. How much will the account be worth in 5 years just prior to the February deposit?
11. Andrew's parents deposit $500 in a savings account on the day of his birth. The bank pays 6.5% compounded annually. Construct a table showing how this deposit grows in value from the date of deposit to his 21st birthday.
12. Sally receives a graduation present of $1000 and invests it in a long-term certificate that pays 8% compounded annually. Construct a table showing how this investment grows to a value of $1500.
13. Find the averages of several sets of numbers typed at the terminal. The value 999, when typed, means that all entries for the set being typed have been made. The input value -999 means that all input sets have been processed.

Construct a flowchart for each algorithm shown in Problems 14–19. In each case use only the sequence, selection, and repetition constructs presented in Section 6.8.

14. a. Input values for N, R, and T.
    b. If $N \leq 40$, let $S = N \times R$. Otherwise, let $S = 40R + (N - 40)(1.5)R$.
    c. Reduce S by the amount $S \times T$.
    d. Print S and stop.

15. a. Input a value for N.
    b. If N=0, print the message GOODBYE and stop.
    c. If N>0, print the integers from 1 up to N. Otherwise, print the integers from 0 down to N.
    d. Input another value for N and repeat step (b).

16. a. Input values for A and B.
    b. If A and B have the same sign (the condition for this is $A \times B > 0$), print POSITIVE or NEGATIVE according to whether A and B are positive or negative.
    c. If either A or B is zero, print "FINI" and stop. Otherwise, repeat step (a).

17. a. Input an integer N.
    b. If N = 0, stop.
    c. Print BETWEEN if N is between 70 and 80, exclusive; otherwise print NOT BETWEEN.
    d. Go to step (a).

18. a. Input values for X, Y, and Z.
    b. If $X < Y$, print $Y - X$ and go to step (d).
    c. Print $Z - X$ only if $X < Z$.
    d. Print X, Y, and Z.
    e. Stop.

19. a. Input a value for N.
    b. If N is less than or equal to 0, go to step (a).
    c. If $N > 100$, print VALUE IS TOO LARGE and go to step (g).
    d. If $N > 50$, calculate $SUM = 50 + 51 + 52 + \cdots + N$ and go to step (f).
    e. Calculate $SUM = 1 + 2 + 3 + \cdots + N$.
    f. Print the value of SUM.
    g. Print the message GOODBYE and stop.

Reconstruct the flowcharts shown in Problems 20–24 by using only the sequence, selection, and repetition constructs shown in Figures 6.1, 6.2, and 6.3. In the given flowcharts, C1, C2, and C3 denote logical expressions and S1, S2, S3, and S4 denote single statements or groups of statements. To illustrate, the unstructured flowchart

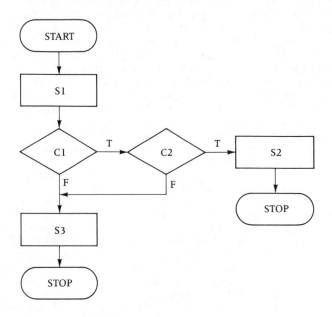

can be written in the equivalent form

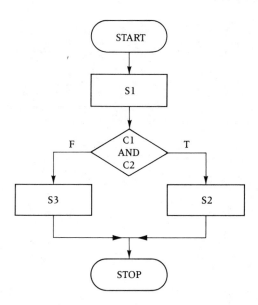

In this illustration, we had to combine two symbols. For the problems, you may also have to write a symbol *more* than once.

20.

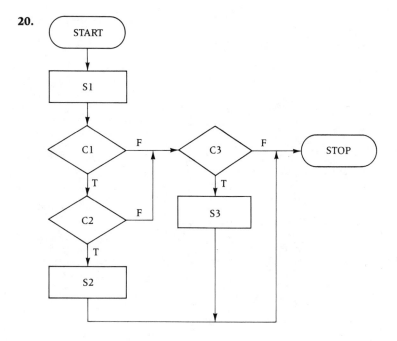

21.

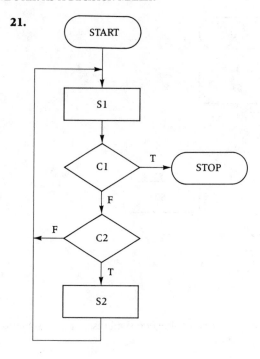

22.

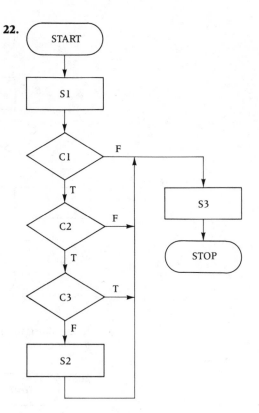

23.

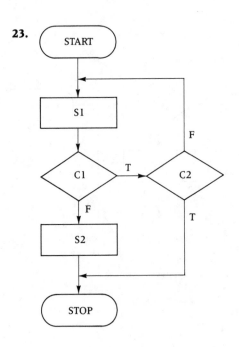

24.

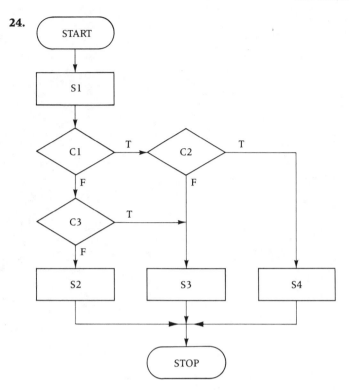

6.10 Review true-or-false quiz

1. In BASIC the IF statement is used for two fundamentally different purposes. T F
2. The IF statement makes it possible to write all BASIC programs so that they need not be terminated manually. T F
3. The IF statement should not be used to construct a loop within a loop. T F
4. If a program is to print results and terminate when $P < Q$, it is always best to use an IF statement with the condition $P < Q$. T F
5. If the END statement is at line 999, it is never necessary to include the statement GO TO 999 in your program. T F
6. At most, one STOP statement may be used in a BASIC program. T F
7. String constants appearing in relational expressions must be quoted. T F
8. A flowchart is a pictorial representation of the sequence of statements in a computer program. T F
9. A written algorithm will usually contain more detail than the corresponding flowchart. T F
10. A flowchart is an excellent way to display the logic of a program, but flowcharting is of little value while writing the program. T F
11. Once a flowchart has been constructed, the program is easily written. T F
12. The question that is asked in a decision box of a flowchart is the basis for the condition in an IF statement. T F
13. If the relational expression in an IF statement is false, the normal sequential execution of the program is interrupted. T F
14. A BASIC program containing only LET, PRINT, and INPUT statements, together with a proper END statement, is necessarily *structured*. T F
15. A program as described in (14), which also contains IF statements of the form IF *condition* THEN *statement*, where *statement* denotes a LET, PRINT, or INPUT statement, may or may not be structured. T F

7

Functions

Since BASIC is a problem-solving language, and since problems are often formulated in mathematical terms, two types of functions are included in the language. In Section 7.1 the so-called built-in functions, or functions supplied with your BASIC system, are described. Then, in Section 7.3, you will learn how to define other functions—ones that you may need but that are not included in your system.

7.1 BASIC functions

The *built-in functions*, also called *intrinsic functions* or **BASIC** *functions*, are an integral part of the BASIC language and may be used in any program. In this section we'll describe some of the more familiar of these and show by example how they are used. A list of the more common BASIC functions is provided at the end of this section. (See Table 7.1.)

The BASIC function ABS

Let **e** denote any BASIC numerical expression. If **ABS(e)** appears in a BASIC program, its value is the absolute value of the value of the expression **e.** For example, ABS(3) = 3, ABS(−3) = 3, and ABS(4 − 9) = 5. For this reason, ABS is called the absolute-value function. The following examples illustrate its use.

EXAMPLE 1. Here is a program to print the absolute value of the sum of any two numbers.

```
10 INPUT X,Y
20     IF X=0 THEN 60
30     LET Z=ABS(X+Y)
40     PRINT "ABSOLUTE VALUE OF SUM IS",Z
50 GO TO 10
60 END
RUN

? 7,3
ABSOLUTE VALUE OF SUM IS        10
? 5,-9
ABSOLUTE VALUE OF SUM IS        4
? 0,0
READY
```

Remark

This program could have been written without using the ABS function. For example, if line 30 were replaced by the three lines

```
30 LET Z=X+Y
32 IF Z>=0 THEN 40
34 LET Z=-Z
```

the resulting program would function in the same way as the original. Clearly the first version is more desirable; its logic is transparent, whereas the logic of the second version is somewhat obscure. As a general rule you should use the BASIC functions supplied with your system. Your programs will be not only easier to write but also easier to understand and hence easier to debug or modify.

EXAMPLE 2. Let's write a program to input 20 values and count how many of them are within 2.5 units of 7.

Problem analysis

We choose variable names as follows:

X = the value being input.
C = the number of values input.
N = the number of values within 2.5 units of 7.

To find how close a number X is to 7, we subtract X from 7 or 7 from X (depending on whether 7 is larger or smaller than X). Since we are interested only in how close X is to 7—not in which is larger—we simply examine the absolute value of X − 7. X will be within 2.5 units of 7 if ABS(X − 7) is less than or equal to 2.5.

The flowchart

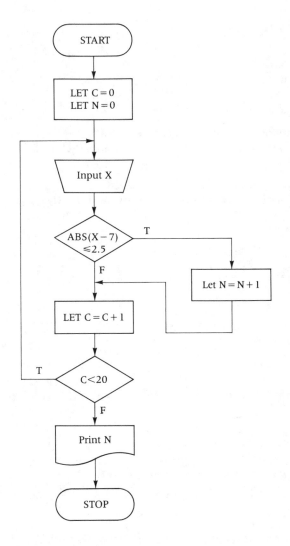

The program

```
110 LET  C=0
120 LET  N=0
130       INPUT X
140       IF ABS(X-7)<=2.5 THEN LET N=N+1
150       LET  C=C+1
160 IF C<20 THEN 130
170 PRINT "NUMBER WITHIN 2.5 UNITS OF 7 IS",N
180 END
```

The BASIC function INT

If INT(**e**) is used in a BASIC program, its value is the greatest integer less than or equal to the value of the expression **e.** For example, INT(2.6) = 2, INT(7) = 7, INT(7 − 3.2) = 3, and INT(−4.35) = −5. For this reason INT is called the **greatest-integer function.**

The INT function can be used to round off numbers. For example, suppose X satisfies the inequalities

$$36.5 \leq X < 37.5.$$

Then X + 0.5 satisfies the inequalities

$$37 \leq X + 0.5 < 38,$$

and we see that

$$\text{INT}(X + 0.5) = 37.$$

That is, to round a number X to the nearest integer, use the BASIC expression INT(X + 0.5). Problem 4 of Section 7.2 is concerned with rounding numbers.

EXAMPLE 3. Here is a program to tell whether or not a value input is an integer.

```
100 INPUT A
110 IF A=INT(A) THEN 130
120 PRINT "NOT ";
130 PRINT "AN INTEGER"
140 END
```

The condition A = INT(A) is true only when A is an integer. If it is, line 120 is skipped and the message AN INTEGER is printed.

EXAMPLE 4. This program tells whether a value typed is odd or even. If the value typed is not an integer, it is rejected.

```
100 INPUT N
110 IF N<>INT(N) THEN 100
120 PRINT "THE NUMBER IS"
130 IF N/2=INT(N/2) THEN PRINT "EVEN" ELSE PRINT "ODD"
140 END
```

If the value typed is not an integer, line 110 transfers control back to the INPUT statement so that another value can be typed. If an integer is typed, control passes to line 120 which prints the partial output THE NUMBER IS. Line 130 then tests the condition N/2 = INT(N/2). If N is even, N/2 is an integer and the condition is true. If N is odd, N/2 is not an integer and the condition is false. Thus, the partial output is completed with the word EVEN if N is even or ODD if N is odd.

In the preceding example, an IF statement with the condition N/2 = INT(N/2) was used to recognize when an integer N is divisible by 2. To test when an integer N is divisible by an integer D that is not necessarily 2, the condition

```
N/D = INT(N/D)
```

may be used in an IF statement, since N/D is an integer only if N is exactly divisible by D.

Relational expression	Truth value
63/7 = INT(63/7)	True
6/4 = INT(6/4)	False
INT(105/15) = 105/15	True
INT(100/8) <> 100/8	True

Caution: Using relational expressions of the form

```
N/D = INT(N/D)
```

can lead to unexpected difficulties. A computer stores numbers and does arithmetic in the binary number system. This means that a calculation involving a number that cannot be represented exactly as a binary number may be only approximate and, hence, exact comparisons may not be possible. The same situation occurs in the decimal number system. For instance, 1/3 cannot be represented exactly as a finite decimal. Thus, working with decimals, you could obtain

```
INT(6/3) = INT(6*0.3333333) = INT(1.9999998) = 1,
```

and not 2, which is the correct value. If your BASIC system does not behave as it should, you can always fudge things so that it will. For instance, you can choose a small number E, such as E = 1E − 10, and use the relational expression

```
N/D = INT(N/D + E).
```

EXAMPLE 5. Write a program to tell whether a number typed at the terminal is a prime.

Problem analysis

Let N denote the number to be tested. A number N is prime if it is an integer greater than 1 whose only factors are 1 and N. To determine if a number N is prime, you can divide it successively by 2, 3, . . . , N − 1. If N is divisible by none of these, then N is a prime. However, it is not necessary to check all the way to N − 1 but only to $\sqrt{N}$. Can you see why? We will use this fact.

Let's construct a flowchart to describe this process in detail. Since all primes are at least as large as 2, we will reject any input value that is less than 2. Thus, we can begin our flowchart as follows.

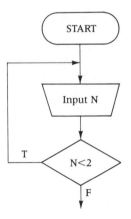

Next we must test all integers between 2 and $\sqrt{N}$, inclusive, as possible factors of N. If we test them in the order D = 2,3,4, and so on, we can stop testing when D>$\sqrt{N}$ or when D is a factor of N. Thus, we can add the following to our partial flowchart.

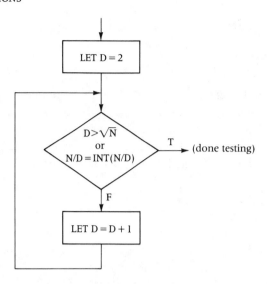

When we are done testing, we can be sure that N is prime if the last D value satisfies the condition $D>\sqrt{N}$, since this means that no factor less than or equal to $\sqrt{N}$ was found. On the other hand, if this last D value does not satisfy the condition $D>\sqrt{N}$, then it must satisfy the only other condition, $N/D=INT(N/D)$, that can get us out of the loop. This means that D is a factor of N that lies between 2 and $\sqrt{N}$, inclusive; that is, N is not prime. We can now complete the flowchart as shown on the next page.

Remark

It is tempting to say that N is not a prime if the last value of D is a factor of N—that is, if $N/D=INT(N/D)$ is true. If you use this condition (instead of the condition $D>\sqrt{N}$) to complete the flowchart, you will find that you have a bug. You should find it. *Suggestion:* When debugging a program, test it for *extreme* values of any input variables. In this problem, the smallest value that the program will actually test is $N=2$, so 2 is an extreme value here.

**Prime number
flowchart**

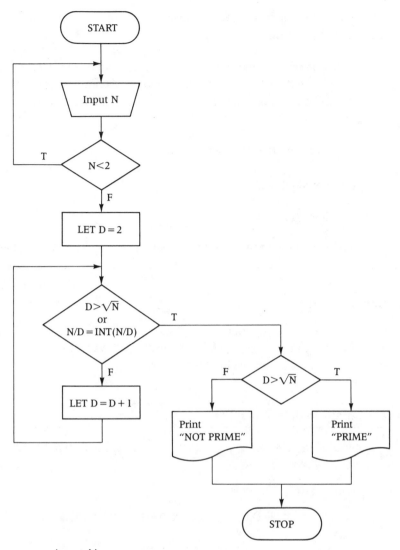

**Corresponding prime
number algorithm**

a. Input N.
b. If N<2 then repeat step (a).
c. Let D = 2.
d. If D>√N or N is divisible by D, skip the next step.
e. Increase D by 1 and repeat step (d).
f. If D>√N print PRIME; otherwise print NOT PRIME.
g. Stop

The program

```
100 INPUT N
110 IF N<2 THEN 100
120 LET D=2
130 IF D>SQR(N) OR N/D=INT(N/D) THEN 160
140     LET D=D+1
150 GO TO 130
160 IF D>SQR(N) THEN PRINT "PRIME" ELSE PRINT "NOT PRIME"
170 END
RUN

? 79
PRIME
READY
```

Remark 1   The BASIC function SQR used in lines 130 and 160 is simply another way to get the square root of a number.

Remark 2   If this program is run, there is no guarantee that the user will type an integer. Line 110 ensures that the prime number algorithm will not be carried out for N<2, but if 256.73 is input, the algorithm will be carried out producing a silly result. To avoid this, you can insert the line

```
115 IF N<>INT(N) THEN 100
```

Remark 3   By inserting the single line

```
165 GO TO 100,
```

many numbers can be tested without having to rerun the program each time.

The BASIC trigonometric functions

If **e** is a BASIC numerical expression, then SIN(**e**), COS(**e**), TAN(**e**), and ATN(**e**) evaluate the sine, cosine, tangent, and arctangent of the value of **e**. If the value of **e** denotes an angle, then this value must be in radian measure.

EXAMPLE 6. Here is a program to determine SIN(D) for D = 0°, 5°, 10°, . . . , 45°.

Since D denotes an angle in degrees, it must be changed to radian measure. Recalling the correspondence

1 degree = π/180 radians,

we must multiply D by π/180 to convert to radian measure.

```
100 PRINT "DEGREES","SINE"
110 PRINT "-------","----"
120 LET D=0
130     LET Y=SIN(3.14159/180*D)
140     PRINT D,Y
150     LET D=D+5
160 IF D<=45 THEN 130
170 END
RUN
```

DEGREES	SINE
0	0
5	.08716
10	.17365
15	.25882
20	.34202
25	.42262
30	.50000
35	.57358
40	.64279
45	.70711

READY

Remark

If your system allows you to use PI for π, the value 3.14159 in line 130 should be replaced by PI.

EXAMPLE 7. Given side *a* and angles A and B in degrees, use the Law of Sines to determine side *b* of the following triangle.

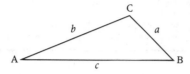

Problem analysis

The Law of Sines states that

$$\frac{a}{\sin A} = \frac{b}{\sin B}$$

Solving for *b*, we obtain

$$b = \frac{a \sin B}{\sin A}$$

Since the angles A and B will be given in degrees, they must be changed to radian measure as required by the BASIC function SIN. In the following program A1 and B1 denote the sides *a* and *b*, respectively.

The program

```
100 REM APPLICATION OF LAW OF SINES
110 PRINT "INPUT ANGLES A,B IN DEGREES"
120 INPUT A,B
130 PRINT "INPUT SIDE OPPOSITE ANGLE A"
140 INPUT A1
150 REM CONVERT TO RADIANS AND COMPUTE SIDE B1
160 LET A = 3.14159/180*A
170 LET B = 3.14159/180*B
180 LET B1 = A1*SIN(B)/SIN(A)
190 PRINT "SIDE OPPOSITE ANGLE B IS",B1
200 END
RUN

INPUT ANGLES A,B IN DEGREES
? 28,42
INPUT SIDE OPPOSITE ANGLE A
? 2
SIDE OPPOSITE ANGLE B IS        2.85057
READY
```

TABLE 7.1   The most common BASIC functions.

Function	Purpose
ABS(x)	Gives the absolute value of x.
INT(x)	Gives the greatest integer less than or equal to x.
SGN(x)	Returns the value 1 if x is positive, -1 if x is negative, and 0 if x is zero.
SQR(x)	Calculates the principal square root of x if $x \geq 0$. Results in an error if x is negative.
RND(x)	Returns a pseudo-random number between 0 and 1. (See Chapter 15.)
SIN(x)	Calculates the sine of x where x is in radian measure.
COS(x)	Calculates the cosine of x where x is in radian measure.
TAN(x)	Calculates the tangent of x where x is in radian measure.
ATN(x)	Calculates the arctangent of x; $-\pi/2 \leq \text{ATN}(x) < \pi/2$.
LOG(x)	Calculates the natural logarithm $\ln(x)$. x must be positive.
EXP(x)	Calculates the exponential e^x, where $e = 2.71828\ldots$ is the base of the natural logarithms.

7.2 Problems

1. Evaluate the following BASIC expressions.
   a. ABS(3*(2-5))
   b. ABS(-3*(-2))
   c. ABS(2-30/3*2)
   d. INT(26.1+0.5)
   e. INT(-43.2+0.5)
   f. INT(10*2.37+0.5)/10
   g. 100*INT(1235.7/100+0.5)
   h. ABS(INT(-3.2))
   i. INT(ABS(-3.2))

2. Evaluate the following with A = -4.32, B = 5.93, and C = 2864.7144.
   a. INT(ABS(A))
   b. ABS(INT(A))
   c. INT(B+0.5)
   d. INT(A+0.5)
   e. INT(C+0.5)
   f. 10*INT(C/10+0.5)
   g. 100*INT(C/100+0.5)
   h. 1000*INT(C/1000+0.5)
   i. INT(1000*C+0.5)/1000

3. What will be printed when each program is run?

   a.
   ```
   100 LET N=0
   110 IF N>4 THEN 170
   120    LET X=N*(N-1)
   130    LET Y=ABS(X-8)
   140    PRINT N,Y
   150    LET N=N+1
   160 GO TO 110
   170 END
   ```

   b.
   ```
   100 LET X=1.1
   110 LET Y=X
   120    LET Z=INT(Y)
   130    PRINT Y,Z
   140    LET Y=X*Y
   150 IF Y<=1.5 THEN 120
   160 END
   ```

   c.
   ```
   100 LET S=13.99
   110 IF S>14 THEN 160
   120    LET R=INT(100*S+0.5)/100
   130    PRINT S,R
   140    LET S=S+0.003
   150 GO TO 110
   160 END
   ```

   d.
   ```
   100 LET N=63
   110 LET D=1
   120    LET D=D+1
   130    IF D>N/2 THEN 170
   140    IF N/D<>INT(N/D) THEN 120
   150    PRINT D
   160 GO TO 120
   170 END
   ```

4. Using the INT function, write a programming line that will round off the value of X:
   a. to the nearest tenth.
   b. to the nearest hundredth.
   c. to the nearest thousandth.
   d. to the nearest hundred.
   e. to the nearest thousand.

Write a program to perform each task specified in Problems 5–11. Where appropriate, messages should be printed to identify values to be typed and also to label the output values. A user should be able to input several different sets of numbers without having to rerun the program.

5. Two positive integers are to be input to determine if the first is divisible by the second.
6. Two numbers are to be input to determine if the absolute value of their sum is equal to the sum of their absolute values.
7. Three positive integers are to be typed to determine whether the first is divisible only by the second, only by the third, by both the second and third, or by neither.
8. Determine and print all positive factors of a positive integer N input at the terminal. (Include the factors 1 and N.)
9. Determine and print all prime numbers between 10 and 78.
10. Determine and print all prime numbers between A and B. A and B are to be input and are to be rejected if either is not a positive integer or if B is not greater than A.
11. Print the exact change received from a purchase of P dollars if an amount D is presented to the salesclerk. Assume that D is at most $100. The change should be given using the largest possible denominations of bills and coins. For example, if P = 17.43 and D = 100, the change should be as follows.

> 1 $50 bill
> 1 $20 bill
> 1 $10 bill
> 1 $2 bill
> 1 50¢ coin
> 1 nickel
> 2 pennies

Write a program to perform each task specified in Problems 12–18. In each, a list of numbers is to be typed during program execution. Use an EOD-tag to indicate that the entire list has been typed.

12. A list of integers is to be input. Any integer less than 1 serves as the EOD-tag. Print the sum and a count of the even input values and also the sum and count of the odd ones.
13. Find the sum and the sum of the absolute values of any list of numbers input at the terminal. Print the number of values in the list as well as the two sums.
14. The deviation of a number N from a number M is defined to be ABS(M − N). Find the sum of the deviations of the numbers 2, 5, 3, 7, 12, −8, 43, −16 from M = 6. (All of these values are to be input during program execution.)
15. Find the sum of the deviations of numbers X from INT(X) where the Xs are input at the terminal.
16. Find the sum of all numbers in a list that are divisible by 5 or by 7.
17. Find the sum and average of all numbers in a list that are divisible by 3 or by 11.
18. A list of numbers is typed at the terminal. Two sums S1 and S2 are to be found. S1 is the sum of the numbers, and S2 is the sum of the numbers each rounded to the nearest integer. Print both sums and also the number of values in the list.

Write programs as required in Problems 19–26.

19. The distance d of a point (x, y) in the plane from the line $ax + by + c = 0$ is given by

$$d = \frac{|ax + by + c|}{\sqrt{a^2 + b^2}}$$

Write a program to input the coefficients a, b, and c, and compute the distance d for any number of points (x, y) typed at the terminal. Be sure that all input requests and all output values are labeled.
20. If a, b, and c are any three numbers with $a \neq 0$, the quadratic equation

$$ax^2 + bx + c = 0$$

can be solved for x by using the formula

$$x = \frac{-b \pm \sqrt{b^2 - 4ac}}{2a}$$

If $b^2 - 4ac > 0$, the formula gives two solutions; if $b^2 - 4ac = 0$, it gives one solution. However, if $b^2 - 4ac < 0$, there are no real solutions. Your program is to solve the quadratic equation for any input values a, b, and c, with $a \neq 0$.

21. Recall from arithmetic that, when you divide a positive integer A by a positive integer B, you get a quotient Q and a remainder R ($0 \leqslant R < B$) according to the equation

$$A/B = Q + R/B \quad \text{(or, equivalently, } A = BQ + R\text{)}.$$

For example, if A = 11 and B = 4, then Q = 2 and R = 3, since $11/4 = 2 + 3/4$. Determine Q and R for any positive integers A and B. (Use the INT function.)

22. Add the digits in any three-digit positive integer. For example, if 378 if input, then 18 ($3 + 7 + 8$) should be printed. The program should reject typed-in values that are not integers greater than 99 and less than 1000. (*Hint:* $8 = 378 - 10*\text{INT}(378/10)$.)

23. Add the digits in any positive integer. (See Problem 22.)

24. Produce a table of values for sine, cosine, and tangent for the values 0 to π in increments of 0.1.

25. Referring to the figure in Example 7, write a program to determine side c if sides a and b and angle C are given. (Use the Law of Cosines: $c^2 = a^2 + b^2 - 2ab\cos(C)$.)

26. An object moves so that its distance d from a fixed point P at time t is

$$d = \frac{1}{1 - .999\cos t}$$

Produce a table (with column headings) of the d values for t between 0 and 2π in increments of 0.1.

7.3 User-defined functions: The DEF statement

In addition to providing the built-in functions, BASIC allows you to define and name your own functions. These functions, called **user-defined functions,** can be referenced in any part of your program. There are several advantages in doing so: a function need be defined only once, even though it is used many times in a program; programs can be written so that they are easier to read and their logic is easier to follow; and a program containing a user-defined function is easily modified to treat different functions.

As many as 26 functions can be defined in a single program. The function names allowed are FNA, FNB, . . . , FNZ. The means for defining functions is the DEFINE statement (abbreviated DEF), which we will illustrate by example.

EXAMPLE 8

The statement

```
100 DEF FNA(X) = 1+X↑2
```

defines a function whose name is FNA (also called the function A, since the FN in FNA is an abbreviation for function). If the expression FNA(3) is used in the program, its value will be $1 + 3^2 = 10$. Similarly, if the variable Y has been assigned the value 3, then the expression FNA(Y) will again have the value 10. The following short program employs this user-defined function to produce a table of values for the function $1 + X^2$.

```
100 DEF FNA(X)=1+X↑2
110 PRINT " X","1+X↑2"
120 PRINT
130 LET Z=0
140     LET Y=FNA(Z)
150     PRINT Z,Y
160     LET Z=Z+0.5
```

```
170 IF Z<=2 THEN 140
180 END
RUN
```

X	1+X↑2
0	1
.5	1.25
1	2
1.5	3.25
2	5

```
READY
```

Remark

The variable name X used in the definition in line 100 could have been any simple numerical variable name.[1] It is called a "dummy" variable because it serves only to define the function; if used later in the program, it is treated the same as any other variable. For example, if the DEF statement in this program were changed to

```
100 DEF FNA(Z) = 1+Z↑2
```

the program would function just as before. No conflict would arise because of the appearance of the variable Z elsewhere in the program.

The general form of the DEF statement, illustrated in Example 8, is

$$\mathbf{ln}\ \text{DEF}\ \ \text{FN}\mathbf{a}(\mathbf{b}) = \mathbf{e}$$

where **a** denotes any letter of the English alphabet, **b** denotes a simple numerical variable, and **e** denotes a BASIC numerical expression defining a function of the variable **b.**

The following rules govern the use of the DEF statement and of the user-defined functions.

1. A function definition should be given in a lower-numbered line than any program statement that references the function.
2. The BASIC expression used in a DEF statement may involve built-in functions and user-defined functions. However, a function may not be defined in terms of itself. A statement such as DEF FNC(Y) = 2 + FNC(Y) is not allowed.
3. A function that has been defined by a DEF statement may be used anywhere in the program, in the same way that the built-in BASIC functions are used.
4. If **e** denotes any BASIC expression, and if a function such as FNA has been defined, then FNA(**e**) is a valid expression.
5. Good programming practice dictates that all function definitions should be placed near the beginning of the program to improve its clarity.

The following examples illustrate various uses of user-defined functions.

---

[1] All variable names considered to this point are called simple, to distinguish them from the subscripted variables yet to be discussed.

EXAMPLE 9. Here is a program to convert centimeters to inches and then to feet. The function FNR rounds values to two decimal places.

```
100 DEF FNR(X)=INT(100*X+0.5)/100
110 PRINT "CENTIMETERS","INCHES","FEET"
120 PRINT
130 LET C=10
140 REM CONVERT CENTIMETERS (C) TO INCHES (I)
150 REM AND INCHES (I) TO FEET (F)
160     LET I=C/2.54
170     LET F=I/12
180     LET I=FNR(I)
190     LET F=FNR(F)
200     PRINT C,I,F
210     LET C=C+10
220 IF C<=100 THEN 160
230 END
RUN
```

CENTIMETERS	INCHES	FEET
10	3.94	.33
20	7.87	.66
30	11.81	.98
40	15.75	1.31
50	19.69	1.64
60	23.62	1.97
70	27.56	2.3
80	31.5	2.62
90	35.43	2.95
100	39.37	3.28

```
READY
```

FNR rounds values to two decimal places. Since this must be done for both inches and feet, it makes sense to employ a user-defined function.

EXAMPLE 10. Salaried employees are to receive an end-of-year bonus of $100 plus 1% of their annual salaries. The following program calculates the bonus amounts for any salary figures entered at the terminal.

```
100 REM THE FUNCTION FNB DETERMINES THE BONUS AMOUNT
110 REM THE FUNCTION FNR ROUNDS TO THE NEAREST WHOLE DOLLAR
120     DEF FNB(S)=100+(0.01)*S
130     DEF FNR(X)=INT(X+0.5)
140 PRINT "TYPE 0 TO STOP"
```

```
150 REM DETERMINE BONUS B FOR ANY SALARY S
160     PRINT
170     PRINT "SALARY";
180     INPUT S
190     IF S=0 THEN STOP
200     LET B=FNB(S)
210     LET B=FNR(B)
220     PRINT "YEAR-END BONUS",B
230 GO TO 160
999 END
RUN

TYPE 0 TO STOP

SALARY? 13028
YEAR-END BONUS   230

SALARY? 12560
YEAR-END BONUS   226

SALARY? 0
READY
```

This program shows that more than one user-defined function can be included in a single program. Here FNB calculates the bonus amount and FNR is used to round this figure to the nearest whole-dollar amount.

Remark

Lines 200 and 210 can be replaced by the single line

```
200 LET B=FNR(FNB(S))
```

The program will behave exactly as before.

Your BASIC system may allow you to use the DEF statement to define functions of two variables. In this case the same function names, FNA, FNB, ..., FNZ, must be used. For example, the statement

```
10 DEF FNC(X,Y) = X↑2+Y↑2
```

defines a function whose value for any numbers x and y is $x^2 + y^2$. If the expression FNC(2,3) is used in the program, its value will be $2^2 + 3^2 = 13$. Similarly, if the variables A and B have the values 2 and 3, respectively, then FNC(A,B) will again have the value 13.

EXAMPLE 11. Here is a program to input four values A, B, C, and D and print the larger of $\sqrt{A^2 + B^2}$ and $\sqrt{C^2 + D^2}$.

```
100 DEF FNC(X,Y)=SQR(X↑2+Y↑2)
110 PRINT "ENTER 4 NUMBERS";
120 INPUT A,B,C,D
130 LET U=FNC(A,B)
140 LET V=FNC(C,D)
150 IF U>V THEN PRINT "FIRST TWO NUMBERS GIVE LARGER VALUE",U
160 IF U<V THEN PRINT "LAST TWO NUMBERS GIVE LARGER VALUE",V
170 IF U=V THEN PRINT "BOTH PAIRS GIVE THE VALUE",U
180 END
RUN

ENTER 4 NUMBERS? 2,6,3,5
FIRST TWO NUMBERS GIVE LARGER VALUE          6.32456
READY
```

7.4 Problems

1. Each of these short programs contains an error—either a syntax error that will cause an error message to be printed or a programming error that the computer will not recognize but that will cause incorrect results. In each case, find the error and tell which of the two types it is.

   a.
   ```
   10 REM PRINT 6 PERCENT
   20 REM OF ANY NUMBER
   30 DEF FNZ(U)=.06*U
   40 INPUT X
   50 LET V=FNZ(U)
   60 PRINT V
   70 END
   ```

   b.
   ```
   10 REM A TABLE OF SQUARES
   20 DEF FNS(I)=X↑2
   30 LET I=1
   40 IF I>9 THEN 90
   50    LET S=FNS(I)
   60    PRINT I,S
   70    LET I=I+1
   80 GO TO 40
   90 END
   ```

   c.
   ```
   10 REM BONUS CALCULATION
   20 DEF FCN(S)=200+0.02*S
   30 PRINT "SALARY";
   40 INPUT S
   50 LET B=FCN(S)
   60 PRINT "BONUS IS";B
   70 END
   ```

   d.
   ```
   10 DEF FNC(X,Y) = X+Y
   20 DEF FND(X) = X↑2
   30 INPUT I
   40 LET J = FND(I,FNC(I))
   50 PRINT J
   60 END
   ```

2. What will be printed when each program is run?

   a.
   ```
   10 DEF FNQ(A)=A+1
   20 DEF FNR(A)=A+2
   30 LET X=0
   40    LET A=FNR(FNQ(X))
   50    PRINT X,A
   60    LET X=X+1
   70 IF X<=3 THEN 40
   80 END
   ```

   b.
   ```
   110 DEF FNI(P,R,T)=P*R/100*T
   120 LET T=1/2
   130 LET P=1000
   140 LET R=10
   150 IF R>16 THEN 200
   160    LET I=FNI(P,R,T)
   170    PRINT I
   180    LET R=R+2
   190 GO TO 150
   200 END
   ```

3. Write a user-defined function that:
   a. converts degrees Celsius to degrees Fahrenheit (F = (9/5)C + 32).
   b. converts degrees Fahrenheit to degrees Celsius.
   c. converts feet to miles.
   d. converts kilometers to miles (1 mi = 1609.3 m).
   e. converts miles to kilometers.

  f. gives the average of two numbers.

  g. gives the average speed in miles per hour for a trip of D miles that takes T hours.

  h. gives the selling price if an article whose list price is X dollars is selling at a discount of Y%.

  i. gives the cost in dollars of a trip of X miles in a car that averages 15 miles per gallon if gasoline costs Y cents per gallon.

  j. gives the hypotenuse of a right triangle whose legs are A and B.

  k. gives the area of a circle of radius R.

  l. gives the volume of a sphere of radius R.

  m. gives the sine of an angle of A degrees.

Write a program to perform each task specified in Problems 4--10.

4. Produce a three-column table showing the conversions from feet F to miles, and then to kilometers, for the values F = 1000, 2000, 3000, . . . , 20,000. All output values are to be rounded to three decimal places. Write user-defined functions to perform the two conversions required and to do the rounding.

5. Produce a four-column table as follows. The first column is to contain the mileage figures 10 miles, 20 miles . . . , 200 miles. The second, third, and fourth columns are to give the time in minutes required to travel these distances at the respective speeds of 45 mph, 50 mph, and 55 mph. All output values are to be rounded to the nearest minute. Write user-defined functions to calculate the times and to do the rounding.

6. Produce a three-column table showing the conversions from grams G to ounces and then to pounds (1 oz = 28.3495 g) for G = 20, 40, 60, . . . , 400. All output values are to be rounded to three decimal places. Employ a user-defined function to do the rounding.

7. Produce a three-column table showing the values of t, x, and y for $t = 0, 1, 2, . . . , 10$, where $x = 5/(1 + t)$ and $y = \sqrt{x^2 + 1}$. Determine x and y with user-defined functions.

8. Determine the area in square centimeters of any rectangle whose length and width in inches are typed in by the user. Use a function FNC that converts inches to centimeters.

9. Write a user-defined function FNC whose value FNC(L) is the area of a circle with circumference L. Also write a function FNS whose value FNS(L) is the area of a square with perimeter L. Use these two functions in a program to produce a table of values of FNC(L) and FNS(L) for L = 1, 2, 3, . . . , 10.

10. A thin wire of length L is cut into two pieces of lengths L1 and L2. One piece is bent into the shape of a circle and the other into a square. Decide how the wire should be cut if the sum of the two enclosed areas is to be as small as possible. (Use the functions FNC and FNS of Problem 9.) How should the wire be cut if the sum of the areas is to be as large as possible?

7.5 Review true-or-false quiz

1. If there is a BASIC function that performs a needed task, you should use it even if it is a simple matter to write your own programming lines to perform this task. T F

2. To determine whether or not the positive integer M is divisible by the positive integer N, we must use an IF statement with the condition INT(M/N) = M/N and not the condition INT(M/N)<>M/N. T F

3. INT(5/2)<>5/2. T F

4. ABS(INT(−2.3)) = INT(ABS(−2.3)). T F

5. If A = ABS(INT(A)), then A is a positive integer. T F

6. It is a good practice to write our programs so that meaningless values typed in by a user will be rejected. T F

7. The relational expression INT(N) = N is true if N is either zero or a positive integer and is false in all other cases. T F

8. If the statement 1 DEF FNC(P) = 2*P ↑ 2 appears in a program, then the function FNC may be referenced as often as desired and in exactly the same way as any BASIC function is referenced. T F

9. If the variable Y is used as the dummy variable in a DEF statement, then Y may also be used as a variable in the program. T F

10. If FNF(X) is defined in a program, we may also define the function FNC(X) = 2 + FNF(X). T F

11. There is nothing wrong with the statement DEF FNA(Y) = 2 + FNA(Y). T F

12. If functions FNA and FNB have been defined, the statement PRINT FNA (I,FNB(I) will necessarily result in an error when the program is run. T F

13. The expression SIN(37*3.14159/180) may be used to find the sine of 37 degrees. T F

More on the PRINT Statement

Up to now we have been working with the restriction that at most five values can be printed on any one line and that, moreover, the spacing of these results is determined by the computer, not by us. In this chapter we will show how more than five values can be printed on a line and how, using the TAB function, you can prescribe the precise position on a line for each value being printed. These forms of the PRINT statement are acceptable to essentially all BASIC systems. In addition, we will describe the PRINT USING statement, an extended and very useful form of the PRINT statement that has been implemented on many BASIC systems.

8.1 Printing more numbers on a line

A teletypewriter will normally print up to 72 characters per line. It is common practice to number these print positions 1 through 72.[1] When programming in BASIC, we consider a line to be divided into five zones. One way of doing this is as follows:

zone 1	zone 2	zone 3	zone 4	zone 5
1–15	16–30	31–45	46–60	61–72

The statement PRINT A,B,C,D,E will cause the values of the five variables to be printed, one number per zone. If more than five variables appear in a PRINT statement, the sixth value is printed on the next line in zone 1, the seventh in zone 2, and so on.

[1] Some BASIC systems use the numbers 0 through 71.

EXAMPLE 1

```
100 LET A=20
110 LET B=-3
120 LET C=3.123
130 PRINT A,B,C,A,B,C
140 END
RUN
```

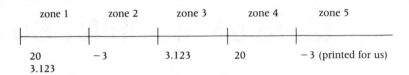

Remark   Normally, when the value of a variable is printed, the first position of the zone in which it is printed is reserved for the sign of the number. However, if the number is positive or zero, the sign is omitted and the first position is left blank.

In the same way, up to five **strings** can be printed on one line, provided that each string fits in its zone. Strings are printed beginning in the first position of a zone.

EXAMPLE 2

```
100 PRINT "FIRST COLUMN","THE SECOND COLUMN","THIRD COLUMN"
110 END
RUN
```

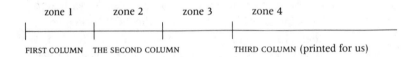

The second string uses all 15 positions in zone 2 and 2 positions from zone 3. This means that the third string must start in zone 4.

Remark   If the string variables A$, B$, and C$ have the values FIRST COLUMN, THE SECOND COLUMN, and THIRD COLUMN, respectively, the statement

```
100 PRINT A$,B$,C$
```

produces the same output.

More than five values can be printed per line if we use semicolons instead of commas to delimit (separate) the variables in a PRINT statement. If this is done, zones will be ignored and the numbers will be packed more closely. Normally, one space will separate numbers,[2] with a possible second space if a number is not negative (the sign position). As many numbers will be printed on a line as will fit. If line 130 of Example 1 is changed to

```
130 PRINT A;B;C;A;B;C
```

the output will be

```
20 -3  3.123  20 -3  3.123
```

If string constants or string variables are separated by semicolons in a PRINT statement, the output will be merged. For example, if A$ = "TO", B$ = "GET", and C$ = "HER!!!", the two statements

```
100 PRINT A$;B$;C$
```

and

```
100 PRINT "TO";"GET";"HER!!!"
```

will both produce the same output

```
TOGETHER!!!
```

If spaces are desired, they must be included as part of a string. Or, you can write

```
100 PRINT A$;" ";B$;" ";C$
```

EXAMPLE 3. Here are two programs showing that PRINT statements using semicolons as delimiters may contain both variables and string constants.

```
10 LET X=5                        10 LET X=5
20 LET Y=-3                       20 LET Y=-3
30 PRINT X;"IS POSITIVE"          30 PRINT "X=";X;"AND Y=";Y
40 PRINT Y;"IS NEGATIVE"          40 END
50 END                            RUN
RUN
                                  X= 5 AND Y=-3
 5 IS POSITIVE                    READY
-3 IS NEGATIVE
READY
```

[2]Some BASIC systems implemented on microcomputers leave no spaces between numbers when semicolons are used. On such a system the output would be 20−33.12320−33.123. If your system behaves in this way you must insert spaces between numerical values being printed as explained in what follows. In this book, we assume that numerical values are always separated in the output.

8.2 Suppressing the carriage return

It often happens that a program contains a loop in which a new value to be printed is determined each time the loop is executed. If the print instruction is of the form

```
PRINT T
```

successive values of T will be printed on separate lines (to the delight of paper manufacturers). However, if you terminate this print line with a comma or a semicolon, more than one value will be printed on each line: up to five if a comma is used and as many as will fit on the line if a semicolon is used.

EXAMPLE 4

```
100 LET N=1
110     LET T=2*N-1
120     PRINT T;
130     LET N=N+1
140 IF N<15 THEN 110
150 PRINT
160 PRINT "THAT'S ALL FOLKS!"
170 END
RUN

 1   3   5   7   9   11  13  15  17  19  21  23  25  27
THAT'S ALL FOLKS!
READY
```

Remark

When the last number (27) is printed by line 120, the semicolon prevents the print mechanism from being positioned at the beginning of the next line. The PRINT statement in line 150 causes a carriage return so that the subsequent printout will appear on a new line.

EXAMPLE 5

```
10 REM PROGRAM TO PRINT A ROW OF 50 DASHES
20 LET N=0
30     PRINT "-";
40     LET N=N+1
50 IF N<50 THEN 30
60 END
RUN

--------------------------------------------------

READY
```

8.3 Printing values of numerical expressions

BASIC allows you to include any arithmetic expression, not just variables, in a PRINT statement. For instance, if A has the value 4, the statement PRINT 3.1, 2*A + 1 will cause the two numbers 3.1 and 9 to be printed in zones 1 and 2 of the same line. The statement PRINT 3.1;2*A + 1 will cause these same two numbers to be printed closer together.

EXAMPLE 6

```
10 PRINT "2+3*5 =";2+3*5
20 END
RUN

2+3*5 = 17
READY
```

EXAMPLE 7

```
10 INPUT A
20 LET R=5
30     PRINT R;"PERCENT OF";A;"IS";A*R/100
40       LET R=R+1
50 IF R<9 THEN 30
60 END
RUN

? 500
 5 PERCENT OF 500 IS 25.
 6 PERCENT OF 500 IS 30.
 7 PERCENT OF 500 IS 35.
 8 PERCENT OF 500 IS 40.
READY
```

Remark

Variable names should be used in programs only if there is a good reason for doing so. For example, to print the value of R% of A, the single statement

```
PRINT A*R/100
```

can be used rather than the following two statements.

```
LET T=A*R/100
PRINT T
```

Similarly, if the average of three numbers A, B, and C is required, you can write

```
PRINT (A+B+C)/3
```

rather than

```
LET S=A+B+C
PRINT S/3
```

Variables such as T and S in these two illustrations are called **temporary variables,** since they are used to store values only temporarily. There are times when temporary variables are needed; there are also times when their use will lead to a "better" program even though they are not actually needed. However, it is generally a good programming practice to avoid them when possible. The resulting programs will be easier to understand.

8.4 Problems

1. Exactly what will be printed when each program is run?

a.
```
10 PRINT "BASEBALL'S HALL OF FAME",
20 PRINT "COOPERSTOWN, N.Y.","U.S.A."
30 END
```

b.
```
100 LET N=0
110     PRINT N,
120     LET N=N+5
130 IF N<38 THEN 110
140 PRINT "FINI"
150 END
```

c.
```
10 LET X=5
20 LET Y=X+3
30 PRINT X;"TIMES";Y;"=";X*Y
40 END
```

d.
```
10 PRINT "HAPPY"
20 PRINT "        HAPPY"
30 PRINT " ","HOLIDAY"
40 END
```

e.
```
10 LET N=1
20     PRINT N;
30     LET N=N+2
40 IF N<9 THEN 20
50 LET N=N-7
60 PRINT
70 IF N=2 THEN 20
80 END
```

f.
```
10 LET X=5
20     PRINT "IF A=";
30     PRINT X;
40     PRINT "A+2=";
50     PRINT X+2,
60     LET X=X+5
70     PRINT
80 IF X<=15 THEN 20
90 END
```

2. Assuming that X = 1 and Y = 2, write PRINT statements to print the following. No numbers are to appear in the PRINT statements. (The spacing need not be exactly as shown; BASIC systems do differ.)

a. 1/2 = .5　　　　　　b. X + Y = 3　　　　　　c. X − 2 = −1
d. SCORE: 2 TO 1　　e. DEPT. NO. 5　　　　　f. BLDG 4.25

3. The following programs do not do what is claimed. Correct them.

a.
```
100 REM A PROGRAM TO PRINT
101 REM      1   2   3
102 REM      4   5   6
110 LET X=1
120     PRINT X;
130     LET X=X+1
140 IF X<=3 THEN 120
150     LET X=X+1
160     PRINT X
170 IF X<=6 THEN 150
180 END
```

b.
```
100 REM A PROGRAM TO PRINT
101 REM      777777
110 LET X=1
120     PRINT 7;
130     LET X=X+1
140 IF X<=6 THEN 120
150 END
```

c.
```
100 REM A PROGRAM TO PRINT
101 REM      TEA FOR TWO
110 PRINT "TEA";"FOR";"TWO"
120 END
```

Write a program to perform each task specified in Problems 4–17.

4. Fifteen years ago the population of Easton was 3571; it is currently 7827. Find the average increase in population per year. The output should be

```
FIFTEEN YEAR POPULATION INCREASE IS _____ .
THIS REPRESENTS AN AVERAGE INCREASE OF _____ PER YEAR.
```

5. An item has a list price of L dollars but is on sale at a discount of D%. Find the selling price. The output should be

```
LIST PRICE $_____
DISCOUNT OF ____ PERCENT IS $_____
SELLING PRICE $_____
```

6. If the wholesale price of a car is under \$4300, the markup is 22%; otherwise the markup is 27%. Determine the retail price if the wholesale price is input at the terminal. The output should be

```
WHOLESALE PRICE IS _____ DOLLARS.
MARKUP IS _____ PERCENT.
RETAIL PRICE IS _____ DOLLARS.
```

7. A manufacturer produces an item at a cost of C dollars per unit and sells each unit for S dollars. In addition, a fixed yearly cost of F dollars must be absorbed in the manufacture of this item. The number of units that must be sold in one year to break even (breakeven volume) is given by the formula

$$\text{Breakeven volume} = \frac{F}{S - C} \text{ units.}$$

For any values of C, S, and F input, the printed output is to be

```
FIXED COST PER YEAR? _____
PRICE PER UNIT? _____
COST PER UNIT? _____
_____ UNITS MUST BE SOLD TO BREAK EVEN.
THIS REPRESENTS _____ DOLLARS IN SALES.
```

8. Print a row containing M dashes followed by the string THE END. M is to be input.
9. Print THE END beginning in column position N. N is to be input. (Use the statement PRINT " "; to print a space.)
10. Print a square array of asterisks with M rows and M columns. M is to be input.
11. Print a square array of # symbols with N rows and N columns. Printing is to begin in column position P. N and P are to be input.
12. Print a square array of asterisks with 12 rows and 12 columns. The design is to be centered on the page.
13. Print a rectangular array of + signs with R rows and C columns. The design is to be centered on the page. R and C are to be input.
14. Input 4 numbers for A, B, C, and D, and print the product $(AX+B)(CX+D)$. For example, if A = 2, B = 5, C = 3, and D = 4, the output should be as follows.

```
(2X+5)(3X+4) = 6X↑2 + 23X + 20
```

(The spacing need not be exactly as shown.)
15. Write a program to input a decimal constant, and print it as a quotient of two integers. For example, if 23.79 is input, the output should be 2379/100. (The arithmetic performed by a computer can be approximate when fractions are involved; see the discussion following Example 6 in Section 7.1. This situation will undoubtedly arise in this problem. Be sure to fix your program so that it works in all cases.)
16. Write a program to input a decimal constant, and print it as a quotient of two integers that have no common factors. For example, if 4.40 is input, the output should be 22/5.
17. Print the prime factorization of any positive integer greater than 1 typed at the terminal. For example, if 35 is input, the output should be 35 = 5*7; if 41 is input, the output should be 41 IS PRIME; if 90 is input, the output should be 90 = 2*3*3*5.

8.5 The TAB function

By using the semicolon in PRINT statements, you can specify the exact form of your output. However, as you probably found while writing the programs for the preceding problem set, this process can be cumbersome. To relieve you of this burden, BASIC includes the TAB function, which may be included in a PRINT statement to specify the column position at which printing is to commence.

EXAMPLE 8

```
10  PRINT TAB(7);"WET"
20  PRINT TAB(6);"PAINT"
30  END
RUN
```

```
12345678901234567890
      WET
      PAINT
READY
```

(For reference only)

EXAMPLE 9

```
10  LET I=1
20      PRINT TAB(I);3*I
30        LET I=I+1
40  IF I<6 THEN 20
50  END
RUN
```

```
1234567890123456789

 3
  6
   9
    12
     15
READY
```

(For reference only)

Each time line 20 is executed, the instruction PRINT TAB(I) will cause the value of 3*I to be printed beginning in column position I, as shown in the printout. The apparent discrepancy is due to the suppressed plus sign, which, if printed, would occupy column position I.

EXAMPLE 10

```
100 LET K=8
110     PRINT TAB(K);"*";TAB(22-K);"*"
120     LET K=K+1
130 IF K<=10 THEN 110
140 PRINT TAB(11);"*"
150 END
RUN
```

```
1234567890123456789012
```
(For reference only)

```
READY
```

Each time line 110 is executed, the expression TAB(K) will cause the string * to be printed in column position K and TAB(22-K) will cause the second asterisk to be printed in column position 22-K. Line 140 prints the final asterisk.

We conclude this section by giving the general form of the PRINT statement that includes the TAB function.

ln PRINT TAB(**a**); **e**; TAB(**b**); **f**; . . .

where

a, b, . . . are numerical expressions whose values are rounded to integers (truncated, on some systems) to determine the print positions for the values to be printed;

e, f, . . . are BASIC expressions (arithmetic or string) whose values are to be printed.

A semicolon or comma may terminate such a PRINT statement, in which case the carriage return will be suppressed.

8.6 Problems

1. Exactly what will be printed when each program is run?

a.
```
10 LET I=0
20     PRINT TAB(2*I+1);-I
30     LET I=I+1
40 IF I<=4 THEN 20
50 PRINT "THAT'S ENOUGH";
60 END
```

b.
```
10 PRINT " 7777777"
20 LET N=1
30 LET S=6
40     PRINT TAB(S);S+N
50     LET N=N+1
60     LET S=S-1
70 IF S>=1 THEN 40
80 END
```

c.
```
10 LET X=1
20     PRINT TAB(X↑2);"*"
30     LET X=X+1
40 IF X<=5 THEN 20
50 END
```

d.
```
10 LET X=0
20 PRINT TAB(5);"X";TAB(15);"X↑2"
30     PRINT
40     LET X=X+1
50     PRINT TAB(4);X;TAB(14);X↑2;
60 IF X<4    THEN 30
70 END
```

2. Write PRINT statements to do the following.
   a. Print the letter B in print position 6 and the digit 3 in print position 10.
   b. Print the values of X, .04X, .06X, and .08X on one line about equally spaced. Do not use commas.
   c. Print six zeros on one line equally spaced along the entire print line.
   d. Print your name centered on the page.

Write a program to perform each task specified in Problems 3–9. Use the TAB function.

3. Print your name on one line, street and number on the next line, and city or town and state on the third line. Your name should begin at the center of the paper, and successive lines should be indented.
4. Print a row of 15 As beginning in print position 21 and a row of 13 Bs centered under the As.
5. Print a rectangular array of asterisks with five rows and eight columns, centered on the page.
6. Print a square array of # symbols with M rows and M columns, centered on the page. M is to be input.
7. Produce a six-column tax table showing 5%, 6%, 7%, 8%, 9%, and 10% for the amounts $100 to $300 in increments of $25. The table should have a title centered on the page, and each column should be labeled appropriately.
8. A person earning H dollars an hour, with time-and-a-half for hours over 32, has the following deductions: F% for federal taxes, S% for state taxes, and R% for retirement. Prepare a table with an appropriate title and with each column appropriately labeled showing the hours worked T, the gross pay, the net pay, and the amounts of the three deductions. The values T = 20, 21, 22, . . . , 50 are to appear in the first column.
9. Produce the following designs.

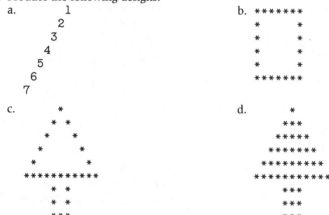

8.7 The PRINT USING statement

Consider the following simple program with output.

```
100 REM PRINT COLUMN HEADINGS
110 PRINT TAB(5);"N";TAB(14);"1/N↑2"
120 PRINT
130 REM PRINT TABLE VALUES
140 LET N=1
150     PRINT TAB(4);N;TAB(13);1/N↑2
160     LET N=N+1
170 IF N<=10 THEN 150
180 END
RUN
```

```
    N           1/N↑2

    1           1
    2           .25
    3           .111111
    4           .0625
    5           .04
    6           2.77778E-2
    7           2.04082E-2
    8           .015625
    9           1.23457E-2
   10           .01
READY
```

Even though the TAB function is used to control the output format, the second column appears rather cluttered. The PRINT USING statement provides a simple way to rectify this situation. BASIC systems differ in how this statement must be written. We present the most common forms to show how this extended version of the PRINT statement can be used to help you prepare improved output documents.

A PRINT USING statement includes not only the variables and expressions whose values are to be printed, but also specifies the format to be used in printing these values. The following example illustrates the three most common forms of the PRINT USING statement.

EXAMPLE 11. Each of parts (a), (b), and (c) contains a program segment to produce the output
ASSETS INCREASED BY 23.5 PERCENT.

```
a. 100 LET F$="ASSETS INCREASED BY ##.# PERCENT."
   110 LET A=23.487
   120 PRINT USING F$,A
```

The PRINT USING statement prints the value of A in the form specified by the contents of a string variable (F$ in this example). The specification ##.# included in F$ says to print the value of A by using two positions to the left and one to the right of the decimal point. The value 23.487 of A is rounded to fit the specification ##.#.

b. 110 LET A=23.487
   120 PRINT USING "ASSETS INCREASED BY ##.# PERCENT.",A

This equivalent form of the PRINT USING statement shown in part (a) does not require a separate statement to assign the form of the output to a string variable. The output format is simply enclosed in quotation marks and placed immediately after the keywords PRINT USING as shown.

c. 110 LET A=23.487
   120 PRINT USING 130,A
   130 :ASSETS INCREASED BY ##.# PERCENT.

The PRINT USING statement prints the value of A in the form specified in line 130.

The statement at line 130, whose keyword is the colon (:), is called an IMAGE statement since it displays an image of the output to be produced.

The three forms of the PRINT USING statement shown in Example 11 are included in the following general form.

$$\text{PRINT USING } \mathbf{s, a, b, c, \ldots}$$

a, b, c, . . . denote numerical or string expressions whose values are to be output.

s   denotes either a string variable [as in Example 11(a)], a string constant [as in Example 11(b)], or the line number of an IMAGE statement that contains a string [as in Example 11(c)].

The string referenced by **s** is called the output format. It is made up of format specifications (##.# in Example 11) and strings ("ASSETS INCREASED BY " and "PERCENT." in Example 11). Each format specification consists of pound (#) characters and possibly a decimal point. The pound symbol is used to specify a position for a possible digit or character to be printed. The strings included in the output format are printed exactly as they appear, including any blanks. They are not enclosed in quotes unless they contain the pound character.

In what follows, we will use the form of the PRINT USING statement in which **s** denotes a string variable. If your system requires one of the other forms, it is a simple matter to make the necessary changes as illustrated in Example 11.

EXAMPLE 12

If X = 453, the two lines

    100 LET M$="ITEM NUMBER #####"
    110 PRINT USING M$,X

will cause the printout

    ITEM NUMBER   453

The format specification ##### is used to specify how 453 is to appear in the output. Since 453 uses only three of the possible five positions, it is printed right justified; that is, it appears in the rightmost three positions reserved by the specification. (Notice that only one space precedes ##### in M$, whereas three spaces precede 453 in the output.)

EXAMPLE 13

If A = 42.237 and B = 25, the two lines

```
200 LET H$="####.## ####.##"
210 PRINT USING H$,A,B
```

will cause the printout

```
42.24   25.00
```

This example illustrates two points: numbers are rounded (not truncated) to fit a format specification (42.237 is rounded to 42.24) and all decimal positions included in a specification will be printed (25, the value of B, is printed as 25.00).

EXAMPLE 14

If N = 16, and B$ = "BLDG.", the two lines

```
70 LET Z$="######## ##"
80 PRINT USING Z$,B$,N
```

will cause the printout

```
BLDG.    16
```

Since BLDG., the value of B$, uses only five of the eight positions reserved by the specification ########, it is printed left justified; that is, it appears in the leftmost five positions reserved by the format specification. Thus, numerical values are printed right justified (see Example 12) and strings are printed left justified.

EXAMPLE 15

If N$ = "CARLTON", the two lines

```
120 LET F$="NAME: ####"
130 PRINT USING F$,N$
```

will cause the printout

```
NAME: CARL
```

If a format specification does not provide enough print positions to print an output string, the output string is truncated on the right to fit the specification. In the example, only four print positions are specified for the output variable N$; hence only the first four characters in N$ are printed.

The control over the output format that can be achieved with the PRINT USING statement is further illustrated in the following two examples.

EXAMPLE 16. Here is an improved version of the program shown at the beginning of this section.

```
100 REM ASSIGN OUTPUT FORMATS
110 LET A$="    N            1/N↑2"
120 LET B$="    ##         #.####"
130 REM PRINT COLUMN HEADINGS
140 PRINT USING A$
150 PRINT
160 REM PRINT TABLE VALUES
170 LET N=1
180     PRINT USING B$,N,1/N↑2
190     LET N=N+1
200 IF N<=10 THEN 180
210 END
RUN

      N          1/N↑2

      1        1.0000
      2         .2500
      3         .1111
      4         .0625
      5         .0400
      6         .0278
      7         .0204
      8         .0156
      9         .0123
     10         .0100
   READY
```

Notice that the second column in the output now lines up according to the decimal points and that the exponential forms of numbers are not printed. The format specification #.#### in B$ controls this.

The PRINT USING statement in line 140 uses the output format in A$ to print the column headings. Note that this PRINT USING statement specifies an output format string, as it must, but contains no other values to be printed.

The PRINT USING statement is especially useful when reports are to be printed in which the columns must line up according to the decimal points. The program in the following example illustrates another such application of the PRINT USING statement.

EXAMPLE 17

```
100 REM *********** PROGRAM TO PRINT PROPERTY TAX TABLES ***********
110 REM
120 REM PROPERTY IS ASSESSED AT P PERCENT OF MARKET VALUE.
130 REM LOWEST AND HIGHEST MARKET VALUES IN TABLE ARE TO BE INPUT. MARKET
140 REM VALUES ARE SHOWN FROM LOWEST TO HIGHEST IN INCREMENTS OF $100.
150 REM
160 REM ***** DATA ENTRY SECTION *****
170 PRINT "LOWEST AND HIGHEST MARKET VALUES";
180 INPUT L,H
190 PRINT "ASSESSMENT PERCENT";
200 INPUT P
210 PRINT "TAX RATE PER THOUSAND";
220 INPUT R
230 PRINT
240 REM ***** ASSIGN OUTPUT FORMATS *****
250 LET A$="   MARKET     ASSESSED     TOTAL    SEMIANNUAL   MONTHLY"
260 LET B$="   VALUE       VALUE        TAX         BILL       BILL"
270 LET C$=" ######.##   ######.##   #####.##   #####.##    ####.##"
280 REM
290 REM ***** PRINT COLUMN HEADINGS *****
300 PRINT USING A$
310 PRINT USING B$
320 PRINT
330 REM ***** CALCULATE AND PRINT TABLE VALUES *****
340 REM      L DENOTES MARKET VALUE
350 REM      A DENOTES ASSESSED VALUE
360 REM      T DENOTES TAX FOR ONE YEAR
370     LET A=L*P/100
380     LET T=A*R/1000
390     PRINT USING C$,L,A,T,T/2,T/12
400     LET L=L+100
410 IF L<=H THEN 370
420 END
RUN
```

```
            LOWEST AND HIGHEST MARKET VALUES? 12500,13400
            ASSESSMENT PERCENT? 87
            TAX RATE PER THOUSAND? 56.45

               MARKET      ASSESSED     TOTAL    SEMIANNUAL    MONTHLY
               VALUE        VALUE        TAX        BILL         BILL

              12500.00    10875.00     613.89     306.95        51.16
              12600.00    10962.00     618.80     309.40        51.57
              12700.00    11049.00     623.72     311.86        51.98
              12800.00    11136.00     628.63     314.31        52.39
              12900.00    11223.00     633.54     316.77        52.79
              13000.00    11310.00     638.45     319.22        53.20
              13100.00    11397.00     643.36     321.68        53.61
              13200.00    11484.00     648.27     324.14        54.02
              13300.00    11571.00     653.18     326.59        54.43
              13400.00    11658.00     658.09     329.05        54.84
            READY
```

Remark

The strings assigned to A$ and B$ in lines 250 and 260 contain no pound (#) characters. Because of this, the PRINT USING statements in lines 300 and 310 can be replaced by the statements PRINT A$ and PRINT B$, respectively. The output will be the same.

8.8 Problems

1. What will be printed when each program is run?

a.
```
10 REM STOCK FRACTION VALUES
20 LET F$="  #/#=##.# CENTS"
30 LET D=8
40 LET N=1
50     PRINT USING F$,N,D,N/D*100
60     LET N=N+2
70 IF N<=7 THEN 50
80 END
```

b.
```
10 LET J=1
20 LET Y$="TIME## A= #.##"
30     LET A=0.004*J
40     PRINT USING Y$,J,A
50     LET J=J+1
60 IF J<=3 THEN 30
70 END
```

c.
```
10 LET A=23.60
20 LET W$="1234567890"
30 LET X$="  ##.##"
40 PRINT USING W$
50 PRINT USING X$,A
60 PRINT TAB(3);A
70 END
```

d.
```
10 LET A$="RIVER#####"
20 LET B$="         ####SWAIN"
30 PRINT USING A$,"BOAT"
40 PRINT USING B$,"BOAT"
50 END
```

e.
```
10 LET A$="EYELIDS"
20 LET B$="POPULAR"
30 LET C$="###"
40 PRINT USING C$,B$;
50 PRINT USING C$,A$
60 END
```

f.
```
10 LET A$="BOBBY"
20 LET B$="JUDITH"
30 LET C$="######LOVES #######"
40 LET D$="#### LOVES ###"
50 PRINT USING C$,A$,B$
60 PRINT USING D$,B$,A$
70 END
```

Write a program to perform each task specified in Problems 2–5.

2. Print the numbers 1, 10, 100, 1000, 10000, 100000, and 1000000 in a column in the middle of the page so that they are "lined up" on the right.
3. Print the numbers .33333, 3.3333, 33.333, 333.33, and 3333.3 in a column so that the decimal points line up.
4. Produce a table showing 1%, 2%, 3%, . . . , 8% of the values from ten cents to two dollars in increments of ten cents. Your table should have nine columns, each with a column heading, and all columns are to line up according to the decimal points.
5. An employer is considering giving all employees a flat across-the-board raise R in addition to a percentage increase P. P and R are to be input at the terminal. A three-column table, with the column headings

```
PRESENT SALARY, AMOUNT OF RAISE, NEW SALARY,
```

is to be printed. The first column is to list the possible salaries from $10,000 to $15,000 in increments of $500. Columns must line up according to the decimal points.

8.9 Review true-or-false quiz

1. The use of a semicolon in a PRINT statement always causes a separation of at least one space between the items being printed.   T F
2. PRINT statements containing messages that are separated by commas may cause these messages to be merged in the output.   T F
3. If you want to suppress the carriage return following execution of a PRINT statement, a semicolon must be used to terminate the PRINT line.   T F
4. If commas are used to separate values to be printed, columns will "line up." However, this will generally not be the case when semicolons are used.   T F
5. If a message is to be centered in the printout, the TAB function must be used.   T F
6. The PRINT USING statement allows you to include in a program an "image" of how you wish an output line to be formatted.   T F
7. A PRINT USING statement containing no variables whose values are to be printed will cause a carriage return to occur, but nothing will be printed.   T F

Entering Large Quantities of Data

Many applications call for programs to process long lists of data values. BASIC includes two statements, the READ and DATA statements, that together allow you to include such lists as part of a program. The inconvenience of typing large quantities of data during program execution can thus be avoided. These two statements, along with the RESTORE statement, which is often used with them, are described in this chapter.

9.1 The READ and DATA statements

These two statements are best illustrated by example.

EXAMPLE 1. Here is a program to "read" two values and print their sum.

```
100 READ A
110 READ B
120 PRINT A+B
130 DATA 17,8
140 END
RUN

 25
READY
```

Line 130 contains the data to be added. Line 100 assigns the first of these values (17) to A, and line 110 assigns the next (8) to B. When line 130, the DATA line, is encountered, it is ignored and control passes to the next line, which in this program terminates the run.

The two READ statements in this program can be replaced by the single statement

```
READ A,B
```

as shown in the following equivalent program.

```
100 READ A,B
110 PRINT A+B
120 DATA 17,8
130 END
```

EXAMPLE 2. Here is a program to "read" and print a list of numbers.

```
100 READ X
110 PRINT X
120 GO TO 100
130 DATA 7,-123,40
140 END
RUN

 7
-123
 40

OUT OF DATA AT 100
READY
```

Line 130 contains the list of numbers. When line 100 is first executed, the first data value (7) is assigned to X and control passes to line 110, which prints this value. The GO TO statement transfers control back to line 100, which then assigns the next value (-123) to X. This process is repeated until the data list is exhausted. This will happen when the READ statement is executed for the fourth time. Since only three values are supplied in the DATA line, this attempt to read a fourth value causes the OUT OF DATA message to be printed, and program execution terminates.

EXAMPLE 3. Here is a program to average N sets of scores with each set containing three numbers.

```
100 REM      N DENOTES THE NUMBER OF SETS OF SCORES
110 REM      I COUNTS HOW MANY SETS HAVE BEEN READ
120 REM      A,B,C DENOTE THE THREE SCORES IN ONE SET
130 PRINT "SCORE 1","SCORE 2","SCORE 3","AVERAGE"
140 READ N
150 LET I=1
160    READ A,B,C
170    PRINT A,B,C,(A+B+C)/3
180    LET I=I+1
190 IF I<=N THEN 160
200 DATA 4
210 DATA 71,78,79,80,71,83
```

```
220 DATA 65,75,85,90,95,97
230 END
RUN
```

SCORE 1	SCORE 2	SCORE 3	AVERAGE
71	78	79	76
80	71	83	78
65	75	85	75
90	95	97	94

```
READY
```

The first READ statement (line 140) assigns the first data value (4) to the variable N. This N is then used to ensure that exactly four sets of scores are read and processed. By using one of the data values in this manner, you can ensure that a READ statement will not be executed after the data list is exhausted.

The general forms of the READ and DATA statements are as follows.

ln READ   (list of variables separated by commas)
ln DATA   (list of BASIC constants separated by commas)

The following rules govern the use of these two statements.

1. As many DATA lines as desired may be included in a program, and as many values as will fit may appear on each line.
2. All values appearing in the DATA lines constitute a single list, called the **data list.** The order in which data values appear in this list is precisely the order in which they appear in the DATA lines. When a READ statement is executed, the variable or variables appearing are assigned successive values from the data list.
3. It is not necessary that all data values be read. However, if a READ statement is executed after the data values have all been used, an OUT OF DATA message will be printed and program execution will terminate.
4. If a DATA statement is encountered during program execution, the statement is ignored and control passes to the next line. For this reason, DATA lines may appear anywhere in the program prior to the END statement. However, they should be positioned to enhance the readability of your programs. Placing them just before the END statement is a common practice.

The statements READ N and READ A, B, C in the previous example would appear in a flowchart as follows.

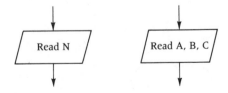

A different symbol is needed for the READ statement, because the symbol for the INPUT statement is used to signify that data are to be input *manually* during program execution. The READ statement requires no such action on the part of the user.

The first data value in Example 3 (the 4 in line 200) is used to indicate that four sets of numbers are to be processed. This same program can be used to process more than four sets of numbers. A user would simply retype the data lines, making sure that the first data value tells how many sets are included. However, a user should not be required to make this count without good reason. For long lists, the task is boring and errors are likely. To avoid these problems, you can use a special value to terminate the list rather than a count to start it. Such a value is called an **End of Data (EOD) tag.** Each time a READ statement is executed, the value or values read are checked for this EOD tag. This technique is illustrated in the following example.

EXAMPLE 4. Write a program to find the largest number in a data list and also to determine how many numbers are included in the list.

Problem analysis

Let's assign variable names as follows.

X = the most recent number read from the data list.
N = a count of how many numbers have been read.
L = the largest of the numbers read.

An algorithm for finding the largest number in a list is shown in Example 2 of Section 2.1. The following flowchart describes a slight modification of this algorithm that can be used in the present situation.

The flowchart

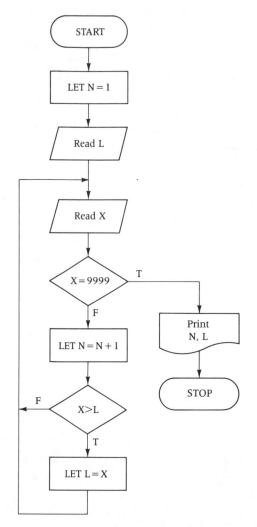

The program

```
100 REM FIND THE LARGEST DATA VALUE
110 REM    X=VALUE LAST READ
120 REM    N=NUMBER OF VALUES READ
130 REM    L=LARGEST OF ALL VALUES READ
140 REM
150 REM READ FIRST NUMBER INTO L AND SET COUNTER N TO 1
160 READ L
170 LET N=1
180 REM READ AND PROCESS THE REMAINING NUMBERS
190    READ X
200    IF X=9999 THEN 240
210    LET N=N+1
220    IF X>L THEN LET L=X
230 GO TO 190
240 PRINT "NUMBER OF DATA VALUES";N
250 PRINT "LARGEST DATA VALUE";L
900 DATA 88,72,64,89,93,72,65
910 DATA 84,92,69,73,91
998 DATA 9999
999 END
RUN

NUMBER OF DATA VALUES 12
LARGEST DATA VALUE 93
READY
```

Remark 1

The EOD tag is 9999. Each time a value is read for X (line 190) a comparison is made (line 200) to see if the list has been exhausted.

Remark 2

Note that there is no flowchart symbol for DATA statements. DATA statements simply provide a means of presenting data to the computer for processing. They cause nothing to happen during the actual execution of the program; hence, they have no place in a flowchart whose purpose is to describe the flow of activity in a program.

The READ and DATA statements can also be used to assign values to string variables, as we now illustrate.

EXAMPLE 5

```
100 READ A$,B$
110 PRINT B$,A$
120 DATA "FLIES", "TIME"
130 END
RUN

TIME            FLIES
READY
```

The READ statement assigns the first data value (FLIES) to A$ and the second (TIME) to B$. The PRINT statement then produces the output shown.

Although the strings in the DATA line of Example 5 are enclosed in quotation marks, the following rules indicate that quotations marks are not always required.

Rules governing the use of quotation marks in DATA statements:

1. When strings appear in DATA lines, the quotation marks are sometimes optional. The rules that apply to such strings may differ among systems. The most common situation is that quotes are required only in the following cases.
   a. Significant blanks begin or terminate the string. (If such a string is unquoted, the leading and trailing blanks are ignored.)
   b. A comma appears in the string. (The comma is used to delimit BASIC constants.)
   c. On some systems, any string beginning with a nonalphabetic character must be quoted. (Experiment with your system.)
2. It is always correct to enclose strings in quotation marks.

EXAMPLE 6. Here is a program to illustrate quoted and unquoted strings in DATA lines.

```
100 LET I=1
110     READ Z$
120     PRINT Z$
130     LET I=I+1
140 IF I<=5 THEN 110
150 DATA VI,"  AL","1234",TO GO,"RICE,JIM"
160 END
RUN

VI
  AL
1234
TO GO
RICE,JIM
READY
```

Quotes are needed for " AL" because of the leading blanks, for "1234" (on some systems) because the first character is nonalphabetic, and for "RICE,JIM" because of the comma.

Numerical and string constants appearing in DATA lines constitute a *single* data list; no special treatment is given to string constants. The execution of a READ statement will attempt to assign the "next" value in this list to the variable being assigned. If the variable and the data value are not of the same type, an error will result.

EXAMPLE 7

Each of several DATA lines contains a person's name, social security number, and the number of quarters earned toward social security benefits. The following program reads this information and prints the names and social security numbers of those people who have earned at least forty quarters. The last DATA line is used to indicate the end of data.

```
100 REM        N$=A PERSON'S NAME
110 REM        S$=THE PERSON'S S.S.NO.
120 REM        Q=NUMBER OF QUARTERS EARNED
130 PRINT "PERSONS WHO HAVE EARNED FORTY QUARTERS"
140 PRINT
150 REM READ AND PROCESS S.S.DATA
160    READ N$,S$,Q
170    IF N$="XXXX" THEN STOP
180    IF Q>=40 THEN PRINT N$;TAB(25);"SSN=";S$
190 GO TO 160
700 DATA HERBERT L. SAUNDERS,033-22-7174,8
710 DATA STEPHEN C. COE,031-19-7613,44
720 DATA ALICE T. TRUCCHI,026-24-4231,40
730 DATA SUSAN A. JACOBSON,019-26-1218,18
740 DATA MARY C. RIDGEWOOD,021-66-6235,46
998 DATA XXXX,XXXX,0
999 END
RUN

PERSONS WHO HAVE EARNED FORTY QUARTERS

STEPHEN C. COE          SSN=031-19-7613
ALICE T. TRUCCHI        SSN=026-24-4231
MARY C. RIDGEWOOD       SSN=021-66-6235
READY
```

Remark 1

The TAB function in line 180 ensures that the S.S. numbers will line up. Without using the TAB, the placement of the SSN on a line would depend on the length of the name N$.

Remark 2

If the social security numbers given in the DATA lines are written without the dashes, it will still be necessary to read these numbers into string variables rather than numerical variables. If you don't do this, the leading zeros will be lost. Moreover, many BASIC systems do not allow such large numbers.

9.2 Problems

1. What will be printed when each program is run?

a.
```
10 LET I=1
20    READ A,B,C
30    IF A=7 THEN 50
40    PRINT C
50    LET I=I+1
60 IF I<=4 THEN 20
70 DATA 2,7,4,3,4,7,7
80 DATA 6,9,12,7,1,6
90 END
```

b.
```
10 READ N
20 LET J=1
30    READ X
40    LET Y=X+1
50    PRINT Y
60    LET J=J+1
70 IF J<=N THEN 30
80 DATA 2,5,3,7,8,-4
90 END
```

c.
```
10 READ A,B$,M$
20 LET M$=B$
30 PRINT M$;
40 READ A,B$,M$
50 LET M$=B$
60 LET B$=M$
70 PRINT B$
80 DATA 6,CAT,MOUSE
90 DATA 8,"WOMAN","MAN"
99 END
```

d.
```
100 LET I=1
110    READ X
120    IF X=9999 THEN 180
130    PRINT X
140    LET I=I+1
150 IF I<=3 THEN 110
160 PRINT I
170 DATA 7,3,18,21,42,9999
180 END
```

2. Find and correct each error.

```
a. 10 READ X,X$
   20 PRINT X$;X
   30 DATA "1";A
   40 END
```

```
b. 10 READ Y;Z$
   20 PRINT Z$;" OF ";Y
   30 DATA "42",SUMMER
   40 END
```

```
c. 10 READ B$
   20 IF B$=HELLO THEN 10
   30 PRINT B$
   40 STOP
   50 DATA HELLO, GOODBYE
   60 END
```

```
d. 10 READ N$
   20 READ A,B,C
   30 PRINT "NAME: ";N$
   40 PRINT "SCORES: ";A,B,C
   50 DATA DOOLEY,TOM
   60 DATA 85,81,76
   70 END
```

3. The following programs do not do what they claim. Find and correct all errors.

```
a. 100 REM SUM 5 VALUES
   110 REM IN A DATA LINE
   120 LET S=0
   130 LET I=1
   140     READ I
   150     LET S=S+I
   160     LET I=I+1
   170 IF I<=5 THEN 140
   180 PRINT S
   190 DATA 7,12,14,-3,6
   200 END
```

```
b. 100 REM PRINT SQUARES OF
   110 REM 12,37,21,96
   120 LET N=1
   130     READ A↑2
   140     PRINT A↑2
   150     LET N=N+1
   160 IF N<4 THEN 130
   170 DATA 12,37,21,96
   180 END
```

```
c. 100 REM AVERAGE N DATA VALUES
   110 READ X
   120 IF X=1E-30 THEN 160
   130     LET S=0
   140     LET S=S+X
   150 GO TO 120
   160 PRINT "AVERAGE IS",S/N
   170 DATA 18,23,17,22
   180 DATA 1E-30
   190 END
```

```
d. 100 REM SUM MANY SETS OF NUMBERS
   110 REM 999 ENDS EACH SET.
   120 REM 9999 ENDS THE RUN.
   130 LET S=0
   140     READ X
   150     IF X=9999 THEN 999
   160     LET S=S+X
   170     IF X=999 THEN PRINT S
   180 GO TO 140
   500 DATA 5,9,4,2,6,999
   510 DATA 41,16,18,2,999
   998 DATA 9999
   999 END
```

Write a program to perform each task specified in Problems 4–13.

4. Read values from DATA lines two at a time. Print each pair of values, their sum, and their average on one line. Run your program using the following DATA lines. The last two values (0,0) are to be used to detect the end of the data.

```
800 DATA 70,80,90,65,75,85
810 DATA 50,40,65,80,78,76
820 DATA 62,60,65,50,60,85
830 DATA 35,45,60,90,96,92
890 DATA 0,0
```

5. Read values three at a time from DATA lines and print them only if the third is greater than the average of the first two. Run your program using the data given in Problem 4. A slight modification to line 890 is needed.

6. Read values three at a time from DATA lines and print them only if they are in ascending order. Use the data shown in Problem 4. A slight modification of line 890 is needed.

7. Find how many of the numbers appearing in DATA lines lie between 40 and 60, inclusive, and also determine the average of these numbers. Use the data given in Problem 4.

8. A list of scores in the range 0 to 100 is to be examined to determine the following counts.

$C1$ = number of scores less than 40.
$C2$ = number of scores between 40 and 60, inclusive.
$C3$ = number of scores greater than 60.

Determine these counts for any list appearing in DATA lines. Use the data given in Problem 4.

9. A list of scores in the range 0 to 100 is to be examined to determine the following counts.

C1 = number of scores less than 20.
C2 = number of scores less than 40 but at least 20.
C3 = number of scores less than 60 but at least 40.
C4 = number of scores less than 80 but at least 60.
C5 = number of scores not less than 80.

Determine these counts for any list appearing in DATA lines. Use the data given in Problem 4.

10. A list of numbers is to be examined to determine how many times a number is strictly larger than the one just before it. For example, if the list is 17, 3, 19, 27, 23, 25, the answer will be 3, since 19>3, 27>19, and 25>23. Use the data given in Problem 4.

11. A candidate for political office conducted a pre-election poll. Each voter polled was assigned a number from 1 to 3 as follows.

1 = will vote for the candidate.
2 = leans toward the candidate but still undecided.
3 = all other cases.

Tally the results of this poll. DATA lines are to be used to present the data to the computer.

12. Modify Problem 11 by assigning two values to each voter. The first is as stated, and the second is to designate whether the voter is female F or male M. There are now six counts to be determined. (Use READ A,S$ to read the two values, a number, and a string F or M, assigned to a voter.)

13. Values appearing in DATA lines are to be read three at a time to determine whether it is possible to construct a triangle using the three numbers as the lengths of the sides. If it is possible, print TRIANGLE POSSIBLE and the three values. If it is not possible, print TRIANGLE NOT POSSIBLE and the three values.

Write a program to produce a printed report as specified in Problems 14–20. Make sure that each report has a title, centered on the page, and that each column has an appropriate heading. All data are to be presented in DATA lines.

14. Given the employee number and monthly sales, print a three-column report showing the employee number, monthly sales, and commission if the commission rate for each person is 6%.

Employee number	Monthly sales
6234	$4,050
6551	6,500
7321	3,750
7718	3,640
8049	7,150

15. Given the employee name, monthly sales, and commission rate for each person, print a four-column report showing the employee name, the monthly sales, the commission rate, and the total commission.

Employee name	Monthly sales	Commission rate
Hart	$28,400	2%
Wilson	34,550	2.5%
Brown	19,600	3%
Ruiz	14,500	2%
Jensen	22,300	3.25%
Grogan	31,350	1.5%

16. Given the employee number, base salary, monthly sales, and commission rate, print a four-column report showing the employee number, base salary, commission, and total monthly earnings.

Employee number	Base salary	Monthly sales	Commission rate
2618	$400	$6,900	3%
3525	445	8,400	2.5%
4131	430	9,250	3%
4812	465	8,920	4%
5127	425	9,725	3.5%

17. Given the employee name, base salary, quota, commission rate, and monthly sales, print a four-column report showing the employee name, the base salary, the commission, and the total earnings. A salesperson receives a commission only on those sales that exceed the quota.

Employee name	Base salary	Quota	Commission rate	Sales
J. D. Flynn	$350	$7,000	5%	$10,900
A. R. Owens	400	9,000	5.5%	7,600
U. T. Best	390	6,500	6%	9,700
J. R. Ewing	425	3,500	5%	10,200
K. T. Olsen	450	7,500	4.7%	7,100

18. Given the item number, the quantity, and the unit value of each item, print a four-column report showing the item number, the quantity, the unit value, and the total value of each item. The total value of the entire inventory should be printed below the report.

Item number	Quantity	Unit value
3047	198	$ 2.43
3055	457	3.97
3068	237	1.96
3093	1047	5.47
3247	593	10.93
3346	1159	12.41
3469	243	.83
3947	2042	8.37

19. Using the following table, determine the batting average and slugging percentage for each player. In the table, 1B indicates a single, 2B a double, 3B a triple, HR a homerun, and AB the number of times a player has been at bat.

$$\text{batting average} = \frac{\text{number of hits}}{\text{AB}} \qquad \text{slugging percentage} = \frac{\text{total bases}}{\text{AB}}$$

Player	1B	2B	3B	HR	AB
Gomez	100	22	1	14	444
Boyd	68	20	0	3	301
Jackson	83	15	8	7	395
O'Neil	68	22	1	8	365
Struik	65	11	3	6	310
McDuffy	54	11	4	0	256
Vertullo	78	18	1	15	418
Ryan	25	1	1	0	104
Torgeson	49	15	0	11	301
Johnson	54	5	2	0	246

Print a table listing the players with their batting averages and slugging percentages in two adjacent columns.

20. (Electric Bill Problem) Given the customer number, the previous month's reading, and the current reading in kilowatt hours (KWH), print a report showing the customer number, the total number of KWHs used, and the total monthly bill. The charges are computed according to the following schedule: $1.41 for the first 14 KWH, the next 85 KWH at $.0389/KWH, the next 200 at $.0214/KWH, the next 300 at $.0134/KWH, and the excess at .0099/KWH. In addition, there is a fuel-adjustment charge of $.0322/KWH for all KWHs used.

Customer number	Previous month's reading	Current reading
2516	25,346	25,973
2634	47,947	48,851
2917	21,342	21,652
2853	893,462	894,258
3576	347,643	348,748
3943	41,241	41,783
3465	887,531	888,165

9.3 The RESTORE statement

We have described a *data list* as the list of all data values appearing in all DATA lines in a program. Associated with a data list is a conceptual *pointer* indicating the value to be read by the next READ statement. The pointer is initially set to the first value in the list, and, each time a value is read, the pointer moves to the next value. The BASIC statement

ln RESTORE

positions this pointer back to the beginning of the data list so that the values can be read again.

EXAMPLE 8. Here is a program to illustrate the RESTORE statement.

```
10 READ A,B
20 RESTORE
30 READ C
40 RESTORE
50 READ D,E,F
60 PRINT A;B;C;D;E;F
70 DATA 1,2,3,4,5,6
80 END
RUN

 1 2 1 1 2 3
READY
```

Line 10 assigns the first two data values (1 and 2) to A and B, respectively. The RESTORE statement at line 20 positions the pointer back to the beginning of the data list; hence, when line 30 is executed, the first data value is again assigned, this time to the variable C. Line 40 once again restores the pointer so that when line 50 is executed, the values 1, 2, and 3 are assigned to D, E, and F.

Many applications require that the values given in DATA lines be used more than once. For example, suppose the O'Halloran Shoe Company wants to know the average monthly income for its retail store and also the number of months in which the income exceeds this average. To determine this information, we must first find the average, a task that requires reading each number once, and then compare each number with this average, which requires a second look at each data value. In the following example this task is accomplished with the RESTORE statement.

EXAMPLE 9. Determine the average monthly income over a full year and the number of months in which the income exceeds this average.

Problem analysis   The input and output values for this problem statement are as follows:

Input: Twelve monthly income figures.
Output: The average monthly income for the year. A count of the number of months in which the income exceeds this average.

To count the number of months in which the income exceeds the average, we must first find the average. This suggests the following algorithm.

  a. Calculate the average monthly income for one year.
  b. Count the number of months in which the income exceeds the average.
  c. Print the results.

Before attempting to write the program segments that correspond to these three steps, we must decide how the 12 monthly income figures are to be presented to the computer for processing. If we use the INPUT statement, these 12 amounts must be typed *twice,* without error, during program execution. If a typing error is made, it may be necessary to begin over again. However, if we include these amounts in DATA lines, they can be read a second time by using a RESTORE statement. Moreover, a typing error can be corrected simply by retyping the line containing the error. Thus, we will use DATA lines.

Next, let's choose variable names. Since exactly 12 values (the 12 income figures) must be read in each of steps (a) and (b), we must keep a count of how many of these have been read. Let's use M (month) to denote this count and I (income) for the monthly income figure last read. Also, let's use S for the sum of the monthly income figures, A for their average, and C for the count to be found in step (b). (This choice of variable names is summarized in lines 100–140 of the program.) Using these variable names, we can rewrite the algorithm as follows. Steps (a1) through (a5) describe step (a), and steps (b1) through (b5) describe step (b).

Algorithm (refined)

  a1. Initialize the counters: S = 0, M = 1.
  a2. Read I.
  a3. Add I to S and 1 to M.
  a4. If M ≤ 12, go to step (a2).
  a5. Let A = S/12.
  b1. Restore the data pointer.
  b2. Initialize the counters: C = 0, M = 1.
  b3. Read I.
  b4. If I>A, add 1 to C.
  b5. Add 1 to M and if M ≤ 12, go to step (b3).
   c. Print the results.

Remark

In this problem analysis, we took considerable care to proceed in an orderly way toward an algorithm that would be easy to understand and whose correctness would be fairly obvious. We started by subdividing the task described in the problem statement into three simpler subtasks (steps (a), (b), and (c) in the first algorithm). Detailed algorithms for the first two of these subtasks were then written and inserted into the three-step algorithm to give us the final refined algorithm. This approach to problem solving is called the **method of step-wise refinement** and has been illustrated in several of the earlier worked out examples. The method is discussed and further described in the next section.

The program

```
100 REM    M DENOTES THE MONTH (M=1,2,3,...,12)
110 REM    I DENOTES INCOME FOR A SINGLE MONTH
120 REM    S DENOTES THE CUMULATIVE INCOME
130 REM    A DENOTES THE AVERAGE MONTHLY INCOME
140 REM    C COUNTS THE NUMBER OF TIMES I EXCEEDS A
150 REM CALCULATE THE AVERAGE MONTHLY INCOME FOR ONE YEAR
160 LET S=0
170 LET M=1
180     READ I
190     LET S=S+I
200     LET M=M+1
210 IF M<=12 THEN 180
220 LET A=S/12
230 REM COUNT THE NUMBER OF MONTHS IN WHICH
235 REM THE INCOME EXCEEDS THE AVERAGE
240 RESTORE
250 LET C=0
260 LET M=1
270     READ I
280     IF I>A THEN LET C=C+1
290     LET M=M+1
300 IF M<=12 THEN 270
310 REM PRINT THE RESULTS
320 PRINT "AVERAGE MONTHLY INCOME";A
330 PRINT "NUMBER OF MONTHS INCOME EXCEEDS AVERAGE";C
500 DATA 13200.57,11402.48,9248.23,9200.94
510 DATA 11825.50,12158.07,11028.40,22804.22
520 DATA 18009.40,12607.25,19423.36,24922.50
999 END
RUN

AVERAGE MONTHLY INCOME 14652.6
NUMBER OF MONTHS INCOME EXCEEDS AVERAGE 4
READY
```

Remark

Note that the REM statements in lines 150, 230–235, and 310 correspond exactly to the three steps of the original algorithm. Thus, the program is *segmented* into three parts just as the original problem was *segmented* into three subtasks.

9.4 Top-down programming

Programming is essentially a three-step process.

1. Carefully read the problem statement so that it is completely understood. If necessary, rewrite the problem statement to clarify what is being asked.
2. Discover and describe an algorithm that, when followed, will lead to a solution to the problem.
3. Using the algorithm described in step (2), write and debug the program.

For lengthy problem statements or for tasks that are intrinsically difficult, step (2) can be troublesome. When you are confronted with such a situation, it is natural to segment the problem into simpler, more manageable tasks.

> We understand complex things by systematically breaking them down into successively simpler parts and understanding how these parts fit together locally.[1]

As natural as the idea of problem segmentation may appear, choosing subtasks that actually simplify matters may not be easy. Unfortunately, a formula for identifying appropriate subtasks is not known. What is known is a method that will help in your attempts to find such subtasks. This method was illustrated in Example 9 of Section 9.3. The task to be performed in that example was as follows.

Problem statement   Determine the average monthly income over a full year and the number of months in which the income exceeds this average.

The approach taken was to begin with an algorithm containing as little detail as possible. The objective was to describe a procedure that would be easy to understand. The algorithm chosen was as follows.

    a. Calculate the average monthly income for one year.
    b. Count the number of months in which the income exceeds the average.
    c. Print the results.

That this algorithm describes a process for carrying out the stated task should be evident—in spite of the detail *not present*. For example, the algorithm contains no variable names (they were chosen later), and it does not tell "how" to find the average or "how" to determine the required count. Details of any kind should be introduced only as needed; each time a detail is introduced, the complexity of the algorithm increases. The algorithm was kept simple by considering "what" must be done, not "how" it should be done.

The next step was to introduce variable names and show "how" the steps in the algorithm could be carried out. The variable names chosen were as follows:

    M = the month (M = 1, 2, 3, . . . , 12).
    I = the income for a single month.
    S = the cumulative income.
    A = the average monthly income.
    C = a count of the number of times I exceeds A.

Step (a) was then broken down into steps (a1) through (a5), and step (b) was rewritten as steps (b1) through (b5). Replacing steps (a) and (b) with these refinements, we obtained the following more detailed algorithm.

    a1. Initialize the counters: S = 0, M = 1.
    a2. Read I.
    a3. Add I to S and 1 to M.
    a4. If M $\leq$ 12, go to step (a2).
    a5. Let A = S/12.
    b1. Restore the data pointer.
    b2. Initialize the counters: C = 0, M = 1.
    b3. Read I.
    b4. If I > A, add 1 to C.
    b5. Add 1 to M and if M $\leq$ 12, go to step (b3).
    c. Print the results.

---

[1] "Structured Programming with **go to** Statements," by Donald E. Knuth, *Computing Surveys*, **6**, No. 4 (December 1974).

This algorithm was then translated into a BASIC program. Knowing that the original three-step algorithm was correct, and also that the refinements of steps (a) and (b) correctly carry out these two tasks, we can be sure that this final 11-step algorithm is also correct.

We illustrate this process of step-wise refinement with another example.

EXAMPLE 10

At the end of each month, a wholesale firm makes an inventory that shows, for each item in stock, the item code, the quantity on hand, and the average cost per unit. Following is a portion of the most recent inventory.

Item code	Units on hand	Average cost/unit
AA13	844	1.63
MK21	182	5.93
.	.	.
.	.	.
.	.	.

We are asked to prepare an inventory report that contains the given information and also the total cost of the inventory by item. In addition, a second short report is to be printed identifying the item (or items) whose inventory represents the greatest cost to the company.

$$\text{Total Cost} = (\text{Units on hand}) \times (\text{Average cost per unit})$$

Problem analysis

Let's begin with the following simple algorithm.

a. Prepare the inventory report.
b. Determine the item (or items) whose inventory represents the greatest cost.

Writing a program segment to produce a printed report such as the one required in step (a) is not new to us. After printing a report title and appropriate column headings for the values to be printed, we will process the data, item by item, to determine and print these values.

To carry out step (b), we must first find the greatest total cost of all items in stock and then compare the total cost for each item with this largest value. Thus, step (b) can be broken down into the two simpler tasks (b1) and (b2) shown in the following refined algorithm.

 a. Prepare the inventory report.
b1. Determine the greatest total cost of all items in stock.
b2. Print a report identifying each item whose inventory represents this greatest cost figure.

The task of finding the largest number in a set of numbers is likewise not new to us (see Example 4 of Section 9.1). We simply calculate the total cost of the items in stock, one at a time, always keeping track of the largest of the amounts encountered. To carry out step (b2), we must again calculate the total cost amounts, item by item, and then compare each with the largest amount found in step (b1).

Having identified what tasks must be performed, we must consider how to carry them out using the BASIC language. As described above, the given inventory data must be examined more than once. If we include these data in DATA lines, the RESTORE statement will allow us to examine the inventory data as often as needed. Let's agree to use one DATA line for the three values (item code, units on hand, and average cost per unit) associated with each stock item. A last DATA line containing the values XXXX,0,0 will be used to indicate the end of data.

```
500 DATA AA13, 844, 1.63
510 DATA MK21, 182, 5.93
    .
    .
    .
998 DATA XXXX,0,0
```

The next task is to choose variable names. To carry out step (a), we will need variables for the three values in a DATA line and a fourth to calculate the cost amounts required in the inventory report. In addition, we need a variable for the largest amount to be found in step (b1). These variable names are shown in lines 110–150 of the program.

The program

```
100 REM------INVENTORY PROGRAM----------
110 REM    I$ = ITEM CODE
120 REM     Q = QUANTITY (IN UNITS) ON HAND
130 REM     C = AVERAGE COST PER UNIT
140 REM     T = TOTAL COST REPRESENTED BY ITEM I$
150 REM     L = LARGEST OF ALL COST FIGURES
160 REM PREPARE AND PRINT THE INVENTORY REPORT
170 PRINT  "              WAREHOUSE INVENTORY REPORT"
180 PRINT
190 PRINT "ITEM CODE","UNITS ON HAND","AV. COST/UNIT","TOTAL COST"
200 PRINT
210    READ I$,Q,C
220    IF I$="XXXX" THEN 260
230    LET T=Q*C
240    PRINT I$,Q,C,T
250 GO TO 210
260 PRINT
270 REM DETERMINE THE LARGEST (L) COST AMOUNT
280 LET L=0
290 RESTORE
300    READ I$,Q,C
310    IF I$="XXXX" THEN 340
320    IF Q*C>L THEN LET L=Q*C
330 GO TO 300
340 REM PRINT REPORT OF ITEM OR ITEMS WHOSE
350 REM INVENTORY REPRESENTS THE GREATEST COST
360 RESTORE
370    READ I$,Q,C
380    IF I$="XXXX" THEN 999
390    IF L=Q*C THEN PRINT "ITEM ";I$;" REPRESENTS THE MAXIMUM COST";L
400 GO TO 370
998 DATA XXXX,0,0
999 END
```

If this program is run with these DATA lines

```
500 DATA AA13,  844,  1.63
510 DATA MK21,  182,  5.93
520 DATA HJ43,  467,  4.37
530 DATA AC91,  764,  5.62
540 DATA YM15,  877,  4.73
550 DATA ST14,  636,  2.64
560 DATA LJ27,  292,  9.63
570 DATA LT51, 1067,  3.78
580 DATA WA19,  532,  7.41
590 DATA TK41,  103, 11.53
```

it will produce the following report.

```
                WAREHOUSE INVENTORY REPORT
   ITEM CODE    UNITS ON HAND    AV. COST/UNIT    TOTAL COST

    AA13            844              1.63           1375.72
    MK21            182              5.93           1079.26
    HF43            467              4.37           2040.79
    AC91            764              5.62           4293.68
    YM15            877              4.73           4148.21
    ST14            636              2.64           1679.04
    LJ27            292              9.63           2811.96
    LT51           1067              3.78           4033.26
    WA19            532              7.41           3942.12
    TK41            103             11.53           1187.59

   ITEM AC91 REPRESENTS MAXIMUM COST 4293.68
```

Remark   The job of finding the greatest cost L (lines 270–330) could have been accomplished by modifying the first program segment (lines 160–260). The resulting program would have been slightly shorter, but not necessarily better. Indeed, combining tasks during the coding process can easily lead to serious programming errors. The problem analysis we carried out led us to consider three separate tasks. The program is segmented into three parts corresponding to these tasks. They are identified in the REM statements in lines 160, 270, and 340. As a result, the program is easy to read and understand, even though it may be longer than necessary. In addition, because of the systematic way in which tasks were broken down into simpler tasks, we can be confident that the program is absolutely correct (barring syntax or typing errors).

The problem analysis carried out in the preceding example can be displayed in a diagram (on p. 146). At the "top" is the problem statement. It contains a complete description of what is to be done. The two tasks at the next "lower" level show how the problem was broken down into two slightly simpler tasks. The second of these, step (b), was broken down again, and it was then found that each of the terminal tasks, steps (a), (b1), and (b2), could easily be translated into a BASIC program. Hence, no further subdivision was carried out.

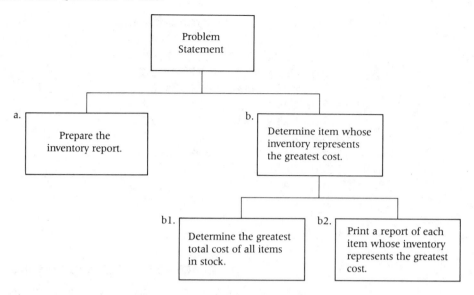

The **method of step-wise refinement,** illustrated in Examples 9 and 10, is also called **top-down programming.** You start at the top (the problem statement), break this task down into simpler tasks, then break these tasks into even simpler ones, and continue this process, all the while knowing how the tasks at each level combine, until the tasks at the lowest level contain whatever detail is desired.

Let's summarize some of the more relevant aspects of the method of top-down programming.

1. Each algorithm is obtained from the preceding one by subdividing one or more of the individual tasks into simpler ones. At each step, or *level of refinement,* more details emerge to bring you closer to a solution—that is, to the desired program.
2. At the upper levels of refinement, dependence on the particular computer being used is avoided; the objective is to determine "what" tasks must be performed, not "how" to carry them out.
3. At the lower levels of refinement, dependence on the computer language being used is unavoidable; the individual tasks in the final refinement correspond to actual program segments.
4. At each level, the algorithm obtained must be *debugged.* If the algorithm at one level is correct, it should be a simple matter to *debug* the algorithm at the next lower level. You need only check to ensure that each task broken down into simpler tasks is broken down correctly. It is this aspect of the top-down approach that increases the likelihood that the final program will be correct.

We don't mean to imply that the method of top-down programming will always lead directly to a "good" program. It may be that a level of refinement is reached that, for some reason, is undesirable. When this happens, you may either start over at the top or *back up* one or more levels and continue from that point with a different refinement. Difficult problems may require backing up in this manner several times before a satisfactory algorithm emerges.

The step-by-step process of segmenting complex tasks into simpler ones is not new; good programmers have always used such an approach. However, giving a name to the process has had two significant consequences. It has introduced the method of step-wise refinement to many people who previously programmed in a more or less haphazard fashion. As a result, better programs—that is, programs that are easier to read and more likely to be correct—are being written. The second consequence is that the method of problem segmentation has been carefully studied and formulated into an orderly process, as illustrated in the worked-out examples. Since the way in which tasks are broken down into subtasks depends on who is carrying out this process, top-down programming is not an algorithm that will always lead to the same program. Rather, it is a *process* that brings order to an otherwise disorderly human activity—namely, programming. We might say that some "structure" has been introduced into the process of designing programs.

As noted, one of the benefits of using a top-down approach is that the resulting programs are more likely to be correct. But to know that a program is correct is another matter. Any serious consideration of this topic must necessarily concern the structure of the program itself, not just the structure of the process that leads to the program. It is in this context that the expression **structured programming** has emerged. Section 6.8 contains a brief discussion of **structured programming,** including a description of what constitutes a **structured program.** Although some indication was given how the structure of a program relates to the task of verifying its correctness, a complete discussion of this topic is beyond the scope of an introductory text such as this one. The principal concern of a beginning programmer is to write good programs. The following guidelines should help.

Guidelines for writing good (structured) programs

1. Use the method of top-down programming. If you follow the rules of top-down programming described in this section, you should obtain correct algorithms that are easily translated into correct and easy-to-read programs.
2. While constructing an algorithm, keep in mind the programming structures *sequence, selection,* and *repetition* described in Section 6.8. In particular, each time you write a step that includes words such as *go to step (b)* or *repeat step (e),* ask yourself if this step is part of a selection or repetition structure. If it is not, try something else.
3. Code specific subtasks, using program segments with exactly one entry point and exactly one exit point. This means that a program segment should contain only one statement that initiates it and only one that gets you out. This is one of the basic rules of structured programming. Programs written in this way are said to be *block structured.*

We conclude this chapter by quoting Edsger W. Dijkstra, who gave structured programming its name[2] and who remains a central figure in the effort to discover the true nature of programs and the programming process.

> We understand walls in terms of bricks, bricks in terms of crystals, crystals in terms of molecules, etc.

> The only effective way to raise the confidence level of a program significantly is to give a convincing proof of its correctness. But one should not first make the program and then prove its correctness, because then the requirement of providing the proof would only increase the poor programmer's burden. On the contrary: the programmer should let the correctness proof and program grow hand in hand.[3]

---

[2] *Structured Programming, Software Engineering Techniques,* by E. W. Dijkstra (J. N. Buxton and B. Randell, Eds.), NATO Scientific Affairs Division, Brussels, Belgium, 1970, pp. 84–88.

[3] "The Humble Programmer" (1972 ACM Turing Award Lecture), by E. W. Dijkstra, *Communications of the ACM,* **15,** No. 10 (October 1972), pp. 859–866.

9.5 Problems

1. What will be printed when each program is run?

a.
```
10 LET I=2
20    READ Y
30    PRINT Y
40    LET I=I+2
50 IF I<=6 THEN 20
60 RESTORE
70 DATA 9,3,5,8,12
80 END
```

b.
```
100 LET I=1
110    READ X
120    IF X=5 THEN RESTORE
130    PRINT X
140    LET I=I+1
150 IF I<=4 THEN 110
160 DATA 3,5,8,9,6
170 END
```

c.
```
10 READ A$,B$,C$
20 RESTORE
30 READ D$
40 PRINT B$;C$;D$
50 DATA HEAD, ROB, IN, HOOD
60 END
```

d.
```
110 LET J=4
120    READ A$,S
130    IF A$<>"BURNS" THEN PRINT A$;S ELSE RESTORE
140    LET J=J+2
150 IF J<=9 THEN 120
170 DATA ALLEN,40,BURNS,36
180 DATA CASH,38,DOOR,40
190 DATA EVANS,39
200 END
```

2. The following programs do not do what they claim. Find and correct all errors.

a.
```
100 REM PROGRAM TO PRINT
110 REM 10 20 30
120 REM 30 20 10
130 READ A1,A2,A3
140 PRINT A1,A2,A3
150 RESTORE
160 READ A3,A2,A1
170 PRINT A3,A2,A1
180 DATA 10,20,30
190 END
```

b.
```
100 REM PROGRAM REQUESTS NUMBERS
110     UNTIL THE NUMBER TYPED
120     IS IN THE DATA LIST
130 LET I=0
140 INPUT N
150 LET I=I+1
160 IF I>4 THEN 140
170 READ A
180 IF A<>N THEN 150
190 PRINT "OK"
200 DATA 1,5,9,8
210 END
```

3. Write a program to allow a user to input several values to determine if they appear in the DATA lines. For each number input, the message IS IN THE LIST or IS NOT IN THE LIST, whichever is appropriate, is to be printed. The user should be able to terminate the run by typing 0. Try your program using the following DATA statements.

```
500 DATA 40, 83, 80, 65, 32, 91, 90, 41, 92, 86, 80, 70, 55
998 DATA 9999
```

(9999 is an EOD tag.)

4. Several pairs of numbers are included in DATA lines. The first of each pair represents an item code number, and the second represents the current selling price. Write a program to allow a user to type several code numbers to obtain the current selling prices. If an incorrect code is typed, an appropriate message should be printed. The user should be allowed to terminate the run by typing 0. Use the following data lines.

```
500 DATA 1235, 12.39, 2865, 17.99, 4020, 23.00, 3640, 20.50
510 DATA 4930, 43.50, 5641, 88.20, 6600, 94.55, 5020, 16.79
998 DATA 0,0
```

5. I.M. Good, a candidate for political office, conducted a preelection poll. Each voter polled was assigned a number from 1 to 5 as follows.

(1) Will vote for Good.
(2) Leaning toward Good but still undecided.

(3) Will vote for Shepherd, Good's only opponent.
(4) Leaning toward Shepherd but still undecided.
(5) All other cases.

The results of the poll are included in DATA lines as follows.

```
500 DATA 1, 1, 2, 5, 3, 3, 5, 1, 2
510 DATA 5, 5, 2, . . .
      .
      .
      .
998 DATA 9999
```

Write a program to print two tables as follows.

TABLE 1

	FOR	LEANING
GOOD	–	–
SHEPHERD	–	–

TABLE 2

	FOR OR LEANING	PERCENTAGE OF TOTAL NUMBER OF PEOPLE POLLED
GOOD	–	–
SHEPHERD	–	–
OTHERS	–	–

Write a program to perform each task described in Problems 6–10. In each case, be sure to begin by segmenting the given task into subtasks.

6. A list of words appears in DATA lines. A user should be allowed to type in a word. If the word appears in the list, all words in the list up to but not including it should be printed. If the word doesn't appear, a message to that effect should be printed. In either case the user should be allowed to enter another word. If END is typed, the run should terminate.
7. Print all numbers appearing in a data list, in the order in which they appear, up to but not including the largest value in the list. Nothing else is to be printed. Test your program using the data shown in Problem 3.
8. Print all numbers appearing in a data list that differ from the average of all numbers in the list by no more than D. (A value for D is to be input.) Test your program using the data shown in Problem 3.
9. A wholesale firm has two warehouses, designated A and B. During a recent inventory, the following data were compiled.

Item	Warehouse	Quantity on hand	Average cost per unit
6625	A	52000	1.954
6204	A	40000	3.126
3300	B	8500	19.532
5925	A	22000	6.884
2202	B	6200	88.724
2100	B	4350	43.612
4800	A	21500	2.741
7923	A	15000	1.605
1752	B	200	193.800

Prepare a separate inventory report for each warehouse. Each report is to contain the given information and also is to show the total cost represented by the inventory of each item.
10. Using the inventory data shown in Problem 9, prepare an inventory report for the warehouse whose entire stock represents the greatest cost to the company.

9.6 Review true-or-false quiz

1. The READ and DATA statements provide the means to present large quantities of data to the computer without having to type them in during program execution.   T   F
2. DATA statements must follow the READ statements that "read" the data values.   T   F
3. The line 90 DATA 5,-3E2,7 + 3,12 is a valid BASIC statement.   T   F
4. A *pointer* is a special value appearing in a data list.   T   F
5. More than five variables may appear in a READ statement.   T   F
6. It is not necessary to read an entire data list before the first value can be read for a second time.   T   F
7. At most, one RESTORE statement may be used in a BASIC program.   T   F
8. When large quantities of data are included in DATA lines, the first value must be a count of the number of values included.   T   F
9. The READ and DATA statements are often useful when no interaction between the computer and the user is required.   T   F
10. When we assign values to a string variable with the READ statement, quotation marks are sometimes necessary.   T   F
11. The EOD tag used in reading long lists of data must be a numeric constant, even though all other data values appearing in the DATA lines are string constants.   T   F
12. It is always correct to use quotes on string constants.   T   F
13. It is sometimes useful to assign values to both string variables and numeric variables using the same READ statement.   T   F
14. The method of top-down programming is an advanced and difficult programming technique.   T   F
15. When you are using the top-down approach, a good first step is to read the problem statement carefully to determine variable names to be used.   T   F
16. In the top-down approach, debugging is simply the process of checking to see that individual tasks are correctly broken down into simpler tasks.   T   F

10

Loops Made Easier

Loops occur in all but the most elementary computer programs. In addition to providing the IF and GO TO statements to construct loops, BASIC contains the FOR and NEXT statements, which in many situations can be used to simplify writing loops and also to produce more readable programs. In this chapter we describe the FOR and NEXT statements, and indicate those situations in which they should be used to construct loops. In addition, we discuss the FOR-WHILE and FOR-UNTIL statements that are also useful in loop construction but are available on only certain BASIC systems.

10.1 FOR/NEXT Loops

Following are two ways to print the integers from 1 to 5.

Program 1

```
100 LET I=1
110    PRINT I;
120    LET I=I+1
130 IF I<=5 THEN 110
140 END
RUN

 1  2  3  4  5
READY
```

Program 2

```
100 LET I=1
110 IF I>5 THEN 150
120    PRINT I;
130    LET I=I+1
140 GO TO 110
150 END
RUN

 1  2  3  4  5
READY
```

151

The same thing can be accomplished by the following program.

Program 3

```
100 FOR I=1 TO 5
110     PRINT I;
120 NEXT I
130 END
RUN

  1  2  3  4  5
READY
```

This program simply instructs the computer to execute line 110 five times, once for each integer I from 1 to 5. Just how the computer will accomplish this depends on the particular implementation of BASIC on your system. Our assumption in this text is that Program 3 is equivalent to Program 2. This assumption conforms to the BASIC standard. Thus, the action of Program 3 can be described as follows.

a. When line 100 (the FOR statement) is encountered, I is assigned the initial value 1.
b. I is compared with the terminal value 5.

   If I > 5, control passes to the line following the NEXT statement (line 130).
   The loop has been satisfied.
   If I ≤ 5, control passes to the line following the FOR statement (line 110).

c. Line 110 prints the current value of I.
d. When the NEXT statement, line 120, is encountered, I is incremented by 1 and the comparison in step (b) is repeated.

The following examples further illustrate the use of the FOR and NEXT statements to construct loops. To clarify the meaning of the FOR/NEXT loop, we have written each program in two ways, without and with the FOR and NEXT statements.

EXAMPLE 1. Here is a program to calculate and print the price of one, two, three, four, five, and six items selling at seven for $1.00.

```
100 REM U DENOTES THE        100 REM U DENOTES THE
105 REM UNIT PRICE           105 REM UNIT PRICE
110 LET U=1.00/7             110 LET U=1.00/7
120 LET I=1                  120 FOR I=1 TO 6
130 IF I>6 THEN 180          130     LET P=U*I
140     LET P=U*I            140     PRINT I,P
150     PRINT I,P            150 NEXT I
160     LET I=I+1            160 END
170 GO TO 130
180 END
```

The FOR/NEXT loop instructs the computer to execute the statements

```
LET P=U*I
PRINT I,P
```

six times, once for each integer I from 1 to 6. These two statements are called the *body* or *range* of the loop. It is an excellent programming practice to indent the body of each FOR/NEXT loop to improve program readability.

EXAMPLE 2. Here is a loop to print the numbers -4, -2, 0, 2, 4, 6.

```
100 LET J=-4              100 FOR J=-4 TO 6 STEP 2
110 IF J>6 THEN 150       110    PRINT J;
120    PRINT J;           120 NEXT J
130    LET J=J+2          130 END
140 GO TO 110             RUN
150 END
RUN                       -4 -2  0  2  4  6
                          READY
   -4 -2  0  2  4  6
   READY
```

The first program describes the action of the second as follows:

a. The FOR statement, line 100, assigns the initial value -4 to J.
b. J is compared with the terminal value 6.

   If J > 6, control passes to line 130, the line following the NEXT statement.
   If J ≤ 6, control passes to line 110, the line following the FOR statement.

c. Line 110 prints the current value of J.
d. When the NEXT statement, line 120, is encountered, J is incremented by 2 (STEP 2) and the comparison in step (b) is repeated.

EXAMPLE 3. Here is a loop to print 5, 4, 3, 2, 1.

```
100 LET N=5               100 FOR N=5 TO 1 STEP -1
110 IF N<1 THEN 150       110    PRINT N;
120    PRINT N;           120 NEXT N
130    LET N=N-1          130 END
140 GO TO 110             RUN
150 END
RUN                          5  4  3  2  1
                             READY
   5  4  3  2  1
   READY
```

This example illustrates that negative increments are acceptable. The initial value of N is 5, and, after each pass through the loop, N is decreased by 1 (STEP – 1). As soon as N attains a value less than 1 (as specified in the FOR statement), control passes out of the loop to the statement following the NEXT statement.

The general form of a FOR/NEXT loop is

```
FOR v = a TO b STEP c
    .
    .
    .
NEXT v
```

where **v** denotes a simple numerical variable name and **a, b,** and **c** denote arithmetic expressions. (If STEP **c** is omitted, **c** is assumed to have the value 1.) **v** is called the *control variable* and the values of **a, b,** and **c** are called the *initial, terminal,* and *step* values, respectively. The action of a FOR/NEXT loop is described by the following diagrams.

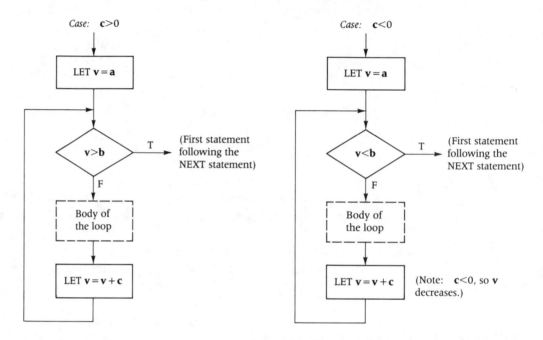

The following example shows that an exit from a FOR/NEXT loop can be caused by a statement in the body of the loop.

EXAMPLE 4. Here is a program to print a table showing the 5.5%, 6%, 6.5%, . . . , 10% discount on any amount A typed at the terminal. However, if for some percentage rate the discount exceeds $50, the printing is to terminate.

```
100 PRINT "AMOUNT";
110 INPUT A
120 PRINT
130 PRINT "PERCENT RATE","DISCOUNT"
140 FOR R=5.5 TO 10 STEP 0.5
150    LET D=(R/100)*A
160    IF D>50 THEN 200
170    PRINT R,D
180 NEXT R
190 STOP
200 PRINT "DISCOUNT FOR RATE";R;"PERCENT IS";D
210 END
RUN
```

```
AMOUNT? 700

PERCENT RATE    DISCOUNT
  5.5            38.5
  6.             42.
  6.5            45.5
  7.             49.
DISCOUNT FOR RATE 7.5 PERCENT IS 52.5
READY
```

This program illustrates the following points.

1. The body of a loop may contain any admissible BASIC statements and as many of these as you wish.
2. Exit from a loop may be caused by a statement within the loop. In this example, the discount D is 52.5 for the rate R = 7.5; hence, the IF statement at line 160 will transfer control to line 200 when R has this value.
3. The initial, terminal, and step values in a loop need not be integers. Here, the initial value is 5.5 and the step value is 0.5.

Remark

Most often, the FOR and NEXT statements are used to construct loops only if the number of times the loop is to be repeated is known before entering the loop. This is not the case here. However, since it is known that the loop is to be repeated at most for the values R = 5.5, 6, 6.5, . . . , 10, it makes sense to use a FOR/NEXT loop.

In each FOR/NEXT loop shown in Examples 1–4, the control variable appears in a statement in the body of the loop. The next example shows that you are not required to do this.

EXAMPLE 5. Here is a loop to print a row of N dashes.

```
200 FOR I=1 TO N
210    PRINT "-";
220 NEXT I
```

Of course, N must be assigned a value prior to execution of line 200. If N is 15, a row of 15 dashes will be printed.

If the terminal value N in Example 5 is 0, then the entire loop will be skipped, since the initial value, I = 1, will be greater than the terminal value, N = 0. However, as noted previously, the precise action caused by a FOR/NEXT loop may differ on your system. Some BASIC systems are designed so that execution of the FOR statement results in at least one pass through the loop (the comparison is made at the end of the loop rather than at the beginning). We restate this as a warning.

WARNING: On some BASIC systems, when the FOR statement beginning a FOR/NEXT loop is executed, at least one pass is made through the loop.

Following are some points concerning the use of FOR/NEXT loops that were not raised explicitly in this section.

1. The initial, terminal, and step values are determined once, when the FOR statement is executed, and cannot be altered within the body of the loop.
2. Although the control variable can be modified inside the loop, don't do it. The resulting program will be very difficult to read.
3. Entry into a loop should be made only by executing the FOR statement.
4. If an exit is made from a loop prior to its completion (an IF or GO TO statement), the current value of the control variable will be retained. (See Example 4.)
5. If an exit is made via the NEXT statement (that is, the loop is satisfied), the value of the control variable is the first value not used. (On systems not conforming to the BASIC standard, this may not be the case. Experiment!)
6. Although it is allowed, never transfer control out of a loop to perform some task and then back into the body so that looping can continue. Programs written in this way can be very difficult to understand.
7. Loops may contain loops. (This is the subject of Section 10.5.)

10.2 Loops containing READ statements

Here is a program to read and print a list of N values included in DATA lines.

```
100 REM N DENOTES THE NUMBER OF VALUES TO BE READ
110 READ N
120 REM READ AND PRINT N DATA VALUES
130 LET I=1
140 IF I>N THEN 999
150    READ V
160    PRINT V
170    LET I=I+1
180 GO TO 140
500 DATA 10
510 DATA 65,82,90,50,40
520 DATA 88,75,78,32,96
999 END
```

Line 110 reads the first datum (10) and the computer uses this value for N. Lines 130, 140, 170, and 180 serve only to set up a loop in which the two statements

```
READ V
PRINT V
```

are executed N times. Since we know exactly how many times these statements are to be repeated, a FOR/NEXT loop should be used to improve the readability of the program.

```
100 REM N DENOTES THE NUMBER OF VALUES TO BE READ
110 READ N
120 REM READ AND PRINT N DATA VALUES
130 FOR I=1 TO N
140    READ V
150    PRINT V
160 NEXT I
500 DATA 10
510 DATA 65,82,90,50,40
520 DATA 88,75,78,32,96
999 END
```

As noted previously (Example 4), it is sometimes advisable to use a FOR/NEXT loop even if the number of times the loop will be repeated is not known in advance. The following example of a FOR/NEXT loop containing a READ statement illustrates another instance of this practice.

EXAMPLE 6

A list containing fewer than 50 scores is included in DATA lines. The value 9999 is used as the end-of-data tag. The following program prints all scores that are less than 60, and also counts how many scores are included in the entire list.

```
100 PRINT "SCORES UNDER 60"
110 FOR N=1 TO 50
120    READ S
130    IF S=9999 THEN 180
140    IF S<60 THEN PRINT S
150 NEXT N
160 PRINT "I CAN HANDLE ONLY 49 SCORES"
170 STOP
180 LET N=N-1
190 PRINT "THE GIVEN LIST CONTAINS";N;"SCORES."
500 DATA 85,70,52,61,83
510 DATA 40,60,90,95,35
998 DATA 9999
999 END
RUN

SCORES UNDER 60
 52
 40
 35
THE GIVEN LIST CONTAINS 10 SCORES.
READY
```

First, N is set to 1 (the FOR statement) and a score S is read and processed by lines 120–140. When line 150 is encountered, N is increased by 1 and the next score is processed. This looping continues until 9999 is read. When this happens, line 130 transfers control to line 180. At this point, N tells how many numbers have been read, including 9999 which is not a score. Thus, line 180 subtracts 1 from N to give the correct count of scores read.

Remark 1

Using a FOR/NEXT loop in this program serves two purposes. First, as described above, the control variable N is used to count the scores as they are read. Second, since it is specified that fewer than 50 scores are included in DATA lines, the computer should not attempt to process more than 49 scores. If a 50th score (not 9999) is inadvertently included in the DATA lines, the loop will be executed a fiftieth time and then control will pass to line 160 which prints a message informing the user that the program is being used incorrectly.

Remark 2

In the next chapter, we describe other programming situations in which it is important to limit the number of times that a loop can be repeated. The program in this example shows a convenient way to do this.

10.3 Flowcharting FOR/NEXT loops

FOR/NEXT loops occur in many BASIC programs. For this reason, special flowchart symbols have been designed for representing such loops. The diagram we'll use has found wide acceptance and is one that can significantly improve the readability of flowcharts.

Using only the flowchart symbols given in Chapter 6 the loop

```
FOR I=1 TO N
      .
      .
      .
NEXT I
```

may be flowcharted as follows.

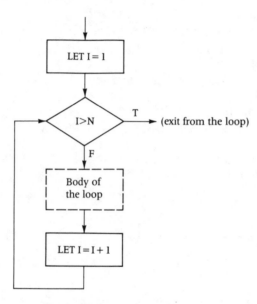

We'll represent this loop with the following diagram.

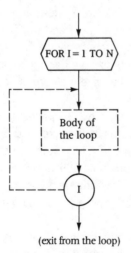

EXAMPLE 7. Here is a flowchart for a program to input ten numbers and print their average.

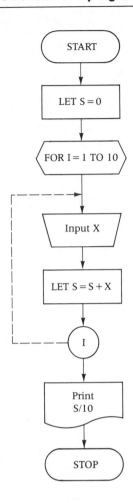

The flowchart symbol for a FOR statement is easily modified for loops with step values other than 1.

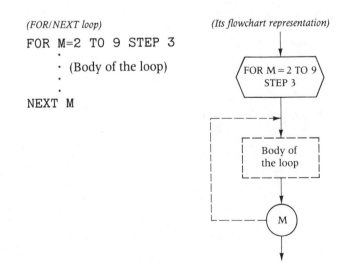

```
FOR X=10 TO 0 STEP -0.5
    .
    .    (Body of the loop)
    .
    .

NEXT X
```

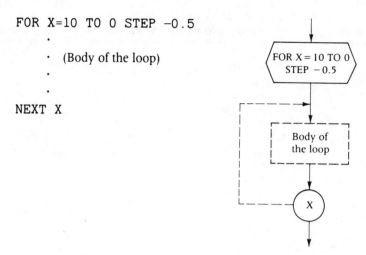

10.4 Problems

1. What will be printed when each program is run?

a.
```
10 FOR J=2 TO 4
20    PRINT J+2
30 NEXT J
40 END
```

b.
```
10 FOR N=5 TO -3 STEP -4
20    PRINT N
30 NEXT N
40 END
```

c.
```
10 LET C=0
20 LET X=1
30 FOR Q=1 TO 4.9 STEP 2
40    LET C=C+1
50    LET X=X*Q
60 NEXT Q
70 PRINT "TIMES THROUGH LOOP=";C
80 PRINT X
90 END
```

d.
```
10 FOR I=1 TO 3
20    PRINT "+";
30 NEXT I
40 FOR J=5 TO 7
50    PRINT "/";
60 NEXT J
70 END
```

e.
```
10 FOR J=2 TO 2
20    PRINT "LOOP"
30 NEXT J
40 END
```

f.
```
10 READ N
20 FOR J=1 TO N
30    READ X
40    PRINT X+1
50 NEXT J
60 DATA 2,5,3,7,8,-4
70 END
```

g.
```
10 FOR I=2 TO 6 STEP 3
20    READ Y
30    PRINT I;Y
40 NEXT I
50 RESTORE
60 DATA 9,3,5,8,12
70 END
```

h.
```
10 DEF FNA(X,Y)=X/Y
20 FOR J=1 TO 4
30    READ A,B
40    IF ABS(FNA(A,B))>1 THEN PRINT A;B
50 NEXT J
60 DATA 5,2,-3,4,-2
70 DATA -7,-9,-6,-2
80 END
```

2. Each of the following programs contains an error—either a syntax error that will cause an error message to be printed or a programming error that the computer will not recognize but that will cause incorrect results. In each case find the error and tell which of the two types it is.

```
a. 10 REM 6% PROGRAM
   20 FOR N=1 TO 6
   30    READ X
   40    PRINT X,.06*X
   50 NEXT X
   60 DATA 85,90,95
   70 DATA 70,75,85
   80 END
```

```
b. 10 REM COUNT THE POSITIVE
   20 REM NUMBERS TYPED
   30 FOR I=1 TO 10
   40    LET C=0
   50    INPUT N
   60    IF N<=0 THEN 80
   70    LET C=C+1
   80 NEXT I
   90 PRINT C;"ARE POSITIVE"
   99 END
```

```
c. 10 REM SUMMING PROGRAM
   20 LET S=0
   30 FOR X=1 TO 4
   40    READ X
   50    LET S=S+X
   60 NEXT X
   70 DATA 18,25,33,41
   80 END
```

```
d. 10 REM PRINT THE NUMBERS
   20 REM 1 3 6 10 15
   30 LET S=1
   40 FOR N=1 TO 15 STEP S
   50    PRINT N
   60    LET S=S+1
   70 NEXT N
   80 END
```

Write the programs called for in Problems 3–15. In each case, a single FOR/NEXT loop is to be used.

3. Twenty numbers are to be entered at the terminal. Determine how many of these numbers are negative, how many are positive, and how many are zero.

4. Print the integers from 1 to 72, eight to the line.

5. Print the integers from 1 to 72, eight to the line, equally spaced. (Use the TAB function.)

6. A program is desired to assist grade school students with their multiplication tables. After an initial greeting, the computer should ask the student to type a number from 2 to 12 so that products involving this number can be practiced. (Call this number N, but don't confuse the student with this information.) Next, the student should be asked to answer the questions $2 \times N = ?, 3 \times N = ?, \ldots, 12 \times N = ?$ Of course, the value of N should be printed, and not the letter N. If a question is answered correctly, the next question should be asked; if not, the question should be repeated. However, if the same question is answered incorrectly twice, the correct answer should be printed and then the next question should be asked. After all questions pertaining to N have been answered, the student should have the opportunity to try another multiplication table or to stop.

7. The following DATA lines show the salaries for all salaried employees in a small firm. (The first value (10) denotes how many salaries are listed.)

```
800 DATA 10
810 DATA 9923, 10240, 10275, 11390, 12560
820 DATA 12997, 13423, 14620, 19240, 22730
```

Prepare a report showing the effect of a flat across-the-board raise of I dollars in addition to a percentage increase of P%. I and P are to be input. Include three columns labeled PRESENT SALARY, RAISE, and NEW SALARY.

8. The following DATA lines show the annual salaries for all salaried employees in a firm. Each salary amount is followed by a count of the number of employees earning that amount. (This firm has a salary step schedule.)

```
800 DATA 8
810 DATA 9020, 4, 10250, 8, 12330, 16, 12940, 30
820 DATA 13570, 21, 14840, 86, 15920, 28, 16520, 7
```

Prepare a three-column report as in Problem 7. In addition, conclude the report by printing the total cost to the owners of the old salary package, the total cost of the new salary package, the total dollar amount of all raises (the difference of the previous two figures), and the overall percent increase this amount represents.

9. Produce each of the following designs. Use the TAB function.

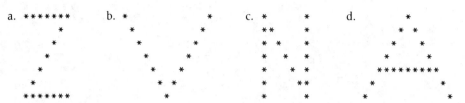

10. Evaluate the following sums. If a value for N is required, it is to be input and you may assume it is positive.

   a. $1 + 2 + 3 + \cdots + N$

   b. $1 + 3 + 5 + 7 \cdots + 51$

   c. $1 + 3 + 5 + 7 + \cdots + (2N - 1)$

   d. $2 + 5 + 8 + 11 + \cdots + K$, where $N - 3 < K \leq N$

   e. $(.06) + (.06)^2 + (.06)^3 + \cdots + (.06)^N$

   f. $1 + 1/2 + 1/3 + 1/4 + \cdots + 1/N$

   g. $1 + 1/4 + 1/9 + 1/16 + \cdots + 1/N^2$

   h. $1 + 1/2 + 1/4 + 1/8 + \cdots + 1/2^N$

   i. $1 - 1/2 + 1/3 - 1/4 + \cdots - 1/100$

   j. $4[1 - 1/3 + 1/5 - 1/7 + \cdots + (-1)^{N+1}/(2N - 1)]$

11. Find the sum of the odd integers between A and B, inclusive. A and B are to be input. If A and B are not integers, the program is to terminate.

12. Find the sum of the integers $A*J + B$ for J = 1, 2, . . . , N. A, B, and N are to be input, and the run is to be terminated if N is not a positive integer or if A and B are not integers.

13. The least common multiple of any two positive integers A and B is to be determined. A and B are to be entered during program execution. (*Hint:* If L is the larger of A and B, the least common multiple of A and B is between L and $A*B$, inclusive).

14. For any positive integer N, determine the product $1 \times 2 \times 3 \times 4 \times \cdots \times N$. This product is denoted by the symbol N! and is called N factorial. A value for N is to be input and the program is to terminate if N is not positive.

15. For positive integers N, N! is defined as in Problem 14. In addition, 0! is defined to be 1. (Thus, $0! = 1! = 1$.) Find and print N! for any nonnegative input value N. If $N < 0$, the program should terminate. N! is not defined for negative integers.

10.5 Nested loops

It is permissible, and often desirable, to have one FOR/NEXT loop contained in another. When nesting loops in this manner, there is one rule that must be observed:

If the body of one FOR/NEXT loop contains either the FOR or the NEXT statement of another loop, it must contain both of them (see Figure 10.1).

Figure 10.1
Correctly and incorrectly
nested loops.

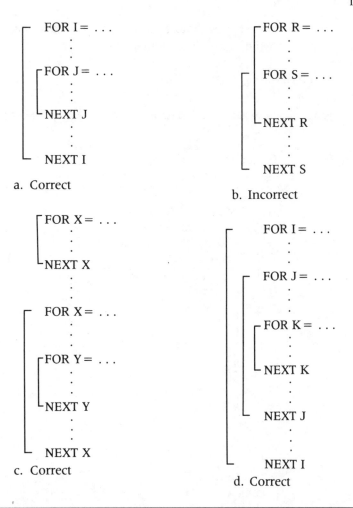

a. Correct

b. Incorrect

c. Correct

d. Correct

EXAMPLE 8. Let's write a program whose output is the following addition table for all possible sums of the integers 1 through 5.

```
2 3 4 5 6
3 4 5 6 7
4 5 6 7 8
5 6 7 8 9
6 7 8 9 10
```

Problem analysis

The sum 3 + 4 is to be printed in the third row and fourth column. More generally, the sum I + J is to be printed in the Ith row and Jth column. Since an entire row must be printed before we go on to the next row, the following algorithm is suggested.

a. Let I = 1.
b. Print I + J for J = 1, 2, . . . , 5.
c. Let I = I + 1 and, if I ≤ 5, go to step (b).
d. Stop.

Programming this algorithm will indeed print the sums in the order specified but not in the format shown. A semicolon following the PRINT statement

```
PRINT I + J;
```

will suppress the carriage return but will print too many numbers on one line. This problem can be rectified by using the statement

PRINT

each time a row is completed (that is, each time step (b) is completed).

The flowchart

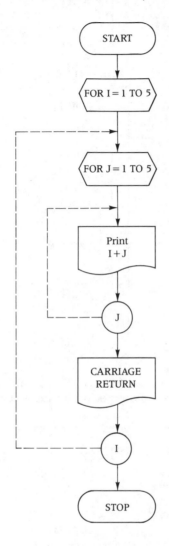

The program

```
100 REM I DENOTES A ROW; J A COLUMN
110 FOR I=1 TO 5
120    REM THE J LOOP PRINTS THE ITH ROW
130    FOR J=1 TO 5
140       PRINT I+J;
150    NEXT J
160    PRINT
170 NEXT I
180 END
RUN
```

```
 2  3  4  5  6
 3  4  5  6  7
 4  5  6  7  8
 5  6  7  8  9
 6  7  8  9 10
READY
```

The next two examples show how nested FOR/NEXT loops can be used to print designs.

EXAMPLE 9. Here is a program to print five rows of asterisks, one in the first row, two in the second, and so on.

```
10 REM I DENOTES THE ROW; J THE COLUMN
20 FOR I=1 TO 5
30    REM PRINT A ROW OF I *'S
40    FOR J=1 TO I
50       PRINT "*";
60    NEXT J
70    PRINT
80 NEXT I
90 END
RUN

*
**
***
****
*****
READY
```

To center this design on the page, you can use the TAB function. For example, to cause the printing of each row to begin in column position 20, simply include the statement

```
35 PRINT TAB(20);
```

This statement causes the print mechanism to move to print position 20 so that the loop in lines 40–60 will print I *'s beginning in this print position.

EXAMPLE 10

Let's write a program to produce the following design.

```
*       *
 *     *
  *   *
   *
  *   *
 *     *
*       *
```

Problem analysis   Although the TAB function can be used, we will illustrate another technique for accomplishing the same result. The print statement PRINT "*"; will be used to print an * and the statement PRINT " "; will be used when a blank is required. Notice that the design uses 7 rows and 7 columns. Let's superimpose the design on a diagram with numbered rows and columns.

Suppose, now, that the computer is ready to print the character in the Ith row and the Jth column. Examination of the design shows that an * should be printed if: (1) the row and column numbers are equal, $I = J$ (the line of asterisks sloping down to the right), or (2) the sum of the row and the column numbers is 8, $I + J = 8$ (the line of asterisks sloping up to the right). In all other cases, a blank should be printed.

Algorithm
a. Let $I = 1$ (to print the first row).
b. For $J = 1,2,\ldots,7$, print an * if $I = J$ or if $I+J=8$. Otherwise, print a blank. (This prints the Ith row.)
c. Increase I by 1 and repeat step (b) if $I \leqslant 7$.
d. Stop.

The program
```
100 FOR I=1 TO 7
110    REM J LOOP PRINTS ITH ROW
120    FOR J=1 TO 7
130       IF (I=J) OR (I+J=8) THEN 160
140       PRINT " ";
150       GO TO 170
160       PRINT "*";
170    NEXT J
180    PRINT
190 NEXT I
200 END
RUN

*         *
 *       *
  *     *
   *
  *     *
 *       *
*         *
READY
```

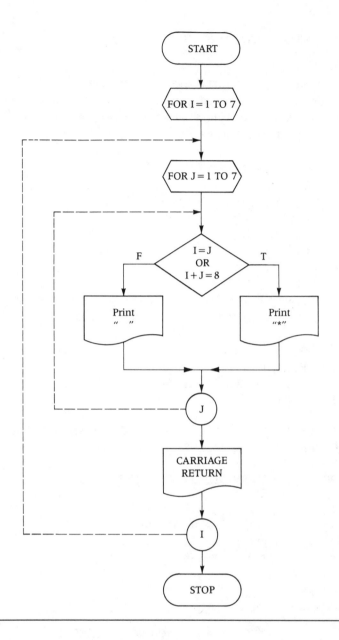

Nested FOR/NEXT loops are especially useful when tables must be prepared in which the rows and columns each correspond to equally spaced data values. The following is an example illustrating one such application of nested loops.

EXAMPLE 11. Prepare a table showing the possible raises for salaried employees whose salaries are $10000, $11000, $12000, . . . , $17000. A raise is to consist of a flat across-the-board increase of I dollars and a percentage increase of either 1%, 2%, 3%, or 4%.

Problem analysis   Let's agree on the following variable names.

S = Present salary ($10000, $11000, . . . , $17000).
I = Flat across-the-board increase (to be input).
P = Percentage increase (1%, 2%, 3%, 4%).
R = Amount of the raise for a given S, I, and P.

The formula governing this situation is

R = (P/100)*S + I

For each salary S, we must display four possible raises R, one for each of the indicated percentages P. Thus, a five-column table is appropriate, the first showing the present salary S and the other four showing the four possible raises. The following program segment can be used to print these values.

```
FOR S=10000 TO 17000 STEP 1000
   PRINT S,
   FOR P=1 TO 4
     LET R=(P/100)*S+I
     PRINT R,
   NEXT P
NEXT S
```

All that remains is to include an INPUT statement, so that a value can be typed for I, and the PRINT statements needed to print a title for the table and appropriate column headings.

The program

```
100 PRINT "               SALARY INCREASE SCHEDULE"
110 PRINT
120 PRINT "ACROSS THE BOARD INCREASE";
130 INPUT I
140 PRINT
150 PRINT "SALARY","-----ADDITIONAL PERCENTAGE INCREASE-----"
160 PRINT ,"1 PERCENT","2 PERCENT","3 PERCENT","4 PERCENT"
180 PRINT
190 FOR S=10000 TO 17000 STEP 1000
200    PRINT S,
210    FOR P=1 TO 4
220      LET R=(P/100)*S+I
230      PRINT R,
240    NEXT P
250 NEXT S
260 END
RUN
```

```
               SALARY INCREASE SCHEDULE
ACROSS THE BOARD INCREASE ? 550

SALARY        -----ADDITIONAL PERCENTAGE INCREASE-----
              1 PERCENT  2 PERCENT  3 PERCENT  4 PERCENT

    10000       650.       750.       850.       950.
    11000       660.       770.       880.       990.
    12000       670.       790.       910.      1030.
    13000       680.       810.       940.      1070.
    14000       690.       830.       970.      1110.
    15000       700.       850.      1000.      1150.
    16000       710.       870.      1030.      1190.
    17000       720.       890.      1060.      1230.
READY
```

10.6 The FOR-WHILE and FOR-UNTIL statements

The FOR-WHILE and FOR-UNTIL statements provide a convenient way to code loops in BASIC. These two statements are allowed on certain DEC[1] computers but have yet to be implemented on all BASIC systems. We include them here because they represent an important improvement in the BASIC language; they are designed to help you in writing structured programs. In addition, they can be used to simplify the coding of your algorithms while, at the same time, improving the readability of your programs.

The FOR/NEXT loop

```
FOR K=1 TO 20
        .
        .
        .

(body of loop)
        .
        .
        .

NEXT K
```

causes the statements in the body of the loop to be executed repeatedly until the value of the control variable K exceeds 20. This loop can also be written in the following two equivalent forms.

```
FOR K=1 UNTIL K>20          FOR K=1 WHILE K<=20
      .                             .
      .                             .
      .                             .
(body of loop)               (body of loop)
      .                             .
      .                             .
      .                             .
NEXT K                       NEXT K
```

In each of these loops, we specify the starting value 1 for K and also a condition. In the first loop the condition is (K>20) and the loop is repeated *until* this condition is true. In the second loop the condition is (K<=20) and the loop is repeated *while* this condition is true.

The condition specified after the keywords UNTIL and WHILE does not have to involve the control variable K; it can be any admissible logical expression as shown in the following example.

---

[1] Digital Equipment Corporation (DEC) is the world's largest manufacturer of minicomputer systems.

EXAMPLE 12. Here is a program to read values from a data list until the sum S of the values read exceeds 50 or until the EOD tag 999 is encountered.

```
10 LET S=0
20 READ X
30 FOR N=1 UNTIL (S>50) OR (X=999)
40    LET S=S+X
50    READ X
60 NEXT N
70 PRINT N;S
80 DATA 23,36,30,26,999
99 END
RUN

 2  59
READY
```

First, S is initialized to zero and the first datum 23 is assigned to X. When line 30 is encountered, the condition (S>50) OR (X = 999) is tested. Since it is *false*, N is assigned its initial value 1 and lines 40 and 50 are executed to give S = 23 and X = 36. When the statement NEXT N is encountered, the condition (S>50) OR (X = 999) is tested again (before the control variable N is changed). Since the condition again is *false*, 1 is added to N and lines 40 and 50 are executed a second time to give S = 59 and X = 30. This time the condition is *true* so control passes out of the loop to line 70 and the output shown is printed.

Remark 1

Note that the final value of the control variable N tells exactly how many times the body of the loop was executed. This is because the condition in line 30 is tested before the control variable is changed.

Remark 2

Line 30 can be changed to

```
30 FOR N=1 WHILE (S<=50) AND (X<>999)
```

and the program will behave exactly as described. In general, if *logexpr* denotes any logical expression, the following two statements are equivalent.

```
FOR N=1 UNTIL logexpr
FOR N=1 WHILE NOT (logexpr)
```

Remark 3

Here is a good way to code this program without using the FOR-WHILE statements.

```
10 LET S=0
20 LET N=0
30 READ X
40 IF (S>50) OR (X=999) THEN 90
50    LET N=N+1
60    LET S=S+X
70    READ X
80 GO TO 40
90 PRINT N;S
95 DATA 23,26,30,26,999
99 END
```

This program is equivalent to the program that uses the FOR-UNTIL statement but is slightly less readable. If indentations were not allowed—unfortunately, this is so on some BASIC systems—it would be even less readable.

In the preceding example, 1 was added to the control variable N each time the loop was repeated. You can specify step values other than 1 as shown in the next example.

EXAMPLE 13

The compound interest expression $(1+P/100) \uparrow 10$ gives the value of $1 after interest has been compounded for 10 periods at the rate of P% per period. This program evaluates the compound interest expression for the values P = 5, 5 1/8, 5 1/4, 5 3/8, and so on, to determine the smallest percentage (in increments of 1/8) that will double the value of an investment in 10 interest periods.

```
10 LET A=0
20 FOR P=5 STEP 1/8 WHILE A<2
30    LET A=(1+P/100)↑10
40 NEXT P
50 PRINT "PERCENT PER PERIOD:";P
60 PRINT "VALUE OF $1 AFTER 10 PERIODS: $";A
70 END
RUN

PERCENT PER PERIOD: 7.25
VALUE OF $1 AFTER 10 PERIODS: $ 2.0136
READY
```

When line 20 is encountered for the first time, the condition A<2 is *true* (that's why we initialized A to 0 in line 10), so the loop is entered. Since the body of the loop consists of the single statement LET A = $(1+P/100) \uparrow 10$, this statement is executed repeatedly for P = 5, 5 1/8, 5 1/4, and so on, provided that A<2. As soon as A≥2 (this occurs just after line 30 is executed with P = 7.25), control passes out of the loop to give the output shown.

Remark   Line 20 can be changed to

```
20 FOR P=5 STEP 1/8 UNTIL A>=2
```

without changing the action of the program.

The general form of FOR-WHILE and FOR-UNTIL loops is

```
                          WHILE
FOR  v = a  STEP  b    or    logexpr
                          UNTIL
             .
             .
             .

  (body of loop)
             .
             .
             .

NEXT  v
```

where **v** denotes a simple numerical variable name, **a** and **b** denote numerical expressions, and **logexpr** denotes a logical expression. (If STEP **b** is omitted, **b** has the default value 1.) **v** is called the control variable, **a** and **b** are called the *initial* and *step* values, respectively, and **logexpr** is called the *condition*. The action of a FOR-WHILE loop is as follows.

1. When a FOR-WHILE statement is first encountered, the *condition* is tested. If it is true, the initial value **a** is assigned to **v** and the body of the loop is executed. If the condition is false, control passes immediately to the statement following NEXT **v.**

2. Immediately after each pass through the loop, the *condition* is tested. If it is true, the step value **b** is added to **v** and the body of the loop is executed. If the condition is false, control passes out of the loop to the statement following NEXT **v.** When this happens the current values of the control variable **v** and of any other variables appearing in the body of the loop are retained.

Statements (1) and (2) also describe the action of a FOR-UNTIL loop provided that the words *true* and *false* are interchanged. Thus, the two statements

```
FOR  v = a STEP  b  UNTIL  logexpr
```

and

```
FOR  v = a  STEP  b  WHILE NOT (logexpr)
```

are equivalent. You should choose the form that makes your program easier to read.

When coding loops, you should use a FOR-NEXT loop when the exact number of times the loop will be repeated is known before the loop is entered. Otherwise, you should use a FOR-WHILE or FOR-UNTIL loop.

10.7 Problems

1. What will be printed when each program is run?

a.
```
10 FOR I=1 TO 3
20     FOR J=2 TO 3
30         PRINT J
40     NEXT J
50 NEXT I
60 END
```

b.
```
10 FOR J=9 TO 7 STEP -2
20     FOR K=4 TO 9 STEP 3
30         PRINT J+K;
40     NEXT K
50 NEXT J
60 END
```

c.
```
10 FOR X=1 TO 3
20     FOR Y=1 TO 5
30         PRINT X;
40     NEXT Y
50     PRINT
60 NEXT X
70 END
```

d.
```
10 FOR X=1 TO 4
20     FOR Y=X+1 TO 5
30         PRINT Y;
40     NEXT Y
50     PRINT
60 NEXT X
70 END
```

e.
```
10 LET X=0
20 FOR P=1 TO 6
30     FOR Q=2 TO 7
40         FOR R=2 TO 4
50             LET X=X+1
60         NEXT R
70     NEXT Q
80 NEXT P
90 PRINT X
99 END
```

f.
```
10 DEF FNA(X,Y)=ABS(X)+ABS(Y)
20 FOR X=-5 TO 5
30     FOR Y=-5 TO 5
40         IF FNA(X,Y)<=4 THEN PRINT "*";ELSE PRINT " ";
50     NEXT Y
60     PRINT
70 NEXT X
80 END
```

2. Each of the following programs contains an error—either a syntax error that will cause an error message to be printed or a programming error that the computer will not recognize but that will cause incorrect results. In each case, find the error and tell which of the two types it is.

a.
```
10 REM PRINT PRODUCTS
20 FOR I=1 TO 3
30 FOR J=2 TO 4
40 PRINT I;"TIMES";J;"=";I*J
50 NEXT I
60 NEXT J
70 END
```

b.
```
10 REM PRINT SUMS
20 FOR A=3 TO 1
30 FOR B=4 TO 1
40 PRINT A;"PLUS";B;"=";A+B
50 NEXT B
60 NEXT A
70 END
```

c. A program to print:
```
1   2
1   3
1   4
2   3
2   4
3   4
```
```
10 FOR I=1 TO 4
20 FOR J=2 TO 4
30 IF I=J THEN 50
40 PRINT I;J
50 NEXT J
60 NEXT I
70 END
```

d. A program to print:
```
XXXXX
 XXXX
  XXX
   XX
    X
```
```
10 FOR R=1 TO 5
20 FOR C=1 TO 5
30 IF R>=C THEN 60
40 PRINT " ";
50 GO TO 70
60 PRINT "X";
70 NEXT C
80 PRINT
90 NEXT R
99 END
```

3. Produce the following designs. Each time a PRINT statement is executed, no more than one character should be printed. (Do not use the TAB function.)

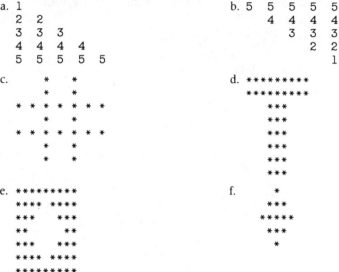

```
a.  1                                  b.  5   5   5   5   5
    2   2                                      4   4   4   4
    3   3   3                                      3   3   3
    4   4   4   4                                      2   2
    5   5   5   5   5                                      1

c.        *       *                    d.  * * * * * * * *
          *       *                        * * * * * * * *
    *   *   *   *   *   *   *                      * * *
          *       *                              * * *
    *   *   *   *   *   *   *                      * * *
          *       *                              * * *
          *       *                              * * *
                                                 * * *

e.  * * * * * * * *                    f.        *
    * * * *   * * * *                           * * *
    * * *       * * *                          * * * * *
    * *           * *                           * * *
    * * *       * * *                              *
    * * * *   * * * *
    * * * * * * * *
```

Write a program to perform each task specified in Problems 4–21.

4. Produce a tax-rate schedule showing the 4%, 5%, 6%, and 7% tax on the dollar amounts $1, $2, $3, . . . , $25.

5. Prepare a table showing the interest earned on a $100 deposit for the rates .05 to .08 in increments of .01 and for times 1, 2, . . . , 8 years. Interest is compounded annually $(I = P(1 + R)^N - P)$.

6. Prepare the table for Problem 5 except that rates are to be in increments of .005 instead of .01.

7. Present the information required in Problem 6 by producing seven short tables, one for each interest rate specified. Each of these tables should be labeled, as should the information contained in the tables.

8. For each of the tax rates 5%, 5⅛%, 5¼%, 5⅜%, and 5½%, produce a table showing the tax on the dollar amounts $1, $2, $3, . . . , $25. Each of the five tables is to have an appropriate title and is to contain two labeled columns, the first showing the dollar amounts $1, $2, $3, . . . , $25 and the second showing the corresponding tax amounts.

9. Five sets of numbers, with each set containing six integers, are to be read. The sum of the six numbers in each set is to be printed in the form.

SUM FOR SET NUMBER _____IS _____.

Your program should contain only one READ statement and it should read only one number at a time.

10. Thirty nonnegative integers are to be input as described in Problem 9. After printing the sum of each of the five sets as shown in Problem 9, the computer is to print the message

THE LARGEST OF THESE SUMS IS _____.

11. Modify the task described in Problem 10 so that the computer not only determines the largest of the five sums, but also the smallest.

12. Produce a listing of all three-digit numbers whose digits are 1, 2, or 3. Spaces are not to appear between the digits of the numbers. (*Hint:* Use triple-nested loops with control variables I, J, and K ranging from 1 to 3. If I, J, and K are the digits, the number is 100*I + 10*J + K.)

13. Produce a listing of all three-digit numbers as described in Problem 12. However, if no digit is repeated in a number, it is to be preceded by an *. Thus, a portion of your printout should be as follows:

> .
> .
> .
>
> 121
> 122
> * 123
> 131
> * 132
> 133
> .
> .
> .

14. Produce a multiplication table of all products of positive integers up to N*N, where N is to be supplied by the user and is to be less than 12. (Use the TAB function.)

15. Let's define an operation whose symbol is $\odot$ on the set A = {0, 1, 2, 3, 4, 5} as follows: The "product" of two integers i and j is given by

$i \odot j$ = the remainder when $i \times j$ is divided by 6

Write a program to print all possible "products" of numbers in the set A.

16. For each integer N from 1 to 20, determine the sum of all integers from 1 to N. The printout is to contain two columns with the following column headings:

> N   1+2+3+⋯+N

17. For each integer N from 0 to 10, determine N factorial. The printout is to contain two columns with the following column headings:

> N   N FACTORIAL

Recall that 0! = 1, and for N > 0, N! = 1 × 2 × 3 × ⋯ × N.

18. Determine the largest value the expression $XY^2 - X^2Y + X - Y$ can assume if X and Y can be any integers from 1 to 5, inclusive.

19. Find the maximum and minimum values of the expression $3X^2 - 2XY + Y^2$ if X and Y are subject to the following constraints.

$$X = -4, -3.5, -3, \ldots, 4$$
$$Y = -3, -2.5, -2, \ldots, 5$$

20. The expression $f(x, y) = x^3 - 4xy + x^2 + 10x$ is to be examined for all integers x and y between 1 and 5 to determine those pairs (x,y) for which $f(x,y)$ is negative. All such pairs are to be printed, together with the corresponding negative value of $f(x,y)$.

21. Find all pairs of integers (X, Y) that satisfy the following system of inequalities.

$$2X - Y < 3$$
$$X + 3Y \geqslant 1$$
$$-6 \leqslant X \leqslant 6$$
$$-10 \leqslant Y \leqslant 10$$

The solutions are to be printed as individual ordered pairs (X, Y). (*Hint:* The last two conditions give the initial and terminal values of FOR/NEXT loops.)

10.8 Review true-or-false quiz

1. If a group of statements is to be executed several times in a program, it is always a good practice to use a FOR/NEXT loop.   T F
2. In any one program the number of FOR statements and the number of NEXT statements must be equal.   T F
3. The IF statement often provides a convenient way to transfer control out of a FOR/NEXT loop.   T F
4. If a loop begins with the statement FOR I = 1 TO 35, the variable I must occur in some statement before the NEXT I statement is encountered.   T F

5. If an exit is made from a loop via an IF statement in the body of the loop, the current value of the control variable will be retained.   T   F

6. If an exit is made from a loop via the NEXT statement, the value of the control variable will be reset to zero.   T   F

7. The statement FOR J = X TO 10 STEP 3 is valid even though X may have a value that is not an integer.   T   F

8. In the statement FOR N = 15 TO 200 STEP C, C must be a positive integer.   T   F

9. The initial, terminal, and step values in a FOR/NEXT loop cannot be modified in the body of the loop.   T   F

10. The control variable in a FOR/NEXT loop can be modified in the body of the loop; moreover, doing so represents a good programming practice.   T   F

11. The control variable of a loop containing a loop may be used as the initial, terminal, or step value of the inner loop.   T   F

11

Arrays

If we wish to examine all numbers in a data list to determine counts of those less than 50 and those greater than 50, and then to perform some calculation on these counts, two variable names must be used to store the two counts. If more than two counts are involved, more than two variables must be used. This situation poses a real problem when only the simple BASIC variables considered to this point are available. Imagine the complexity of a program using as many as 100 different simple variables. To be useful, a programming language must provide the means for handling such problems efficiently. BASIC meets this requirement with the inclusion of **subscripted variables.** These variables may be referenced simply by specifying their numerical subscripts. They not only resolve the difficulty cited but also greatly simplify numerous programming tasks involving large quantities of data. In this chapter we consider the application of subscripted variables to programming tasks involving the processing of numbers. The use of subscripted *string* variables is described in Chapter 12.

11.1 One-dimensional arrays

A **one-dimensional array,** or **list,** is an ordered collection of items in the sense that there is a first item, a second item, and so on. For example, if you have taken five quizzes during a semester and received grades of 71, 83, 96, 77, and 92, you have a list in which the first grade is 71, the second grade is 83, and so forth. In mathematics we might use the following subscripted notation.

$$g_1 = 71$$
$$g_2 = 83$$
$$g_3 = 96$$
$$g_4 = 77$$
$$g_5 = 92$$

However, since the BASIC character set does not include subscripts, the notation is changed.

$$G(1) = 71$$
$$G(2) = 83$$
$$G(3) = 96$$
$$G(4) = 77$$
$$G(5) = 92$$

We say that the *name* of the array is G, that $G(1)$, $G(2)$, $G(3)$, $G(4)$, and $G(5)$ are *subscripted* variables, and that 1, 2, 3, 4, and 5 are the *subscripts* of G. $G(1)$ is read **G sub 1,** and in general $G(I)$ is read **G sub I.** $G(1)$, G1, and G are all different variables and can be used in the same program; the computer has no problem distinguishing among them, even though people often do.

The array G can be visualized as follows:

	1	2	3	4	5
G	71	83	96	77	92

The name of the array appears to the left, the subscripts above each entry, and the entries inside, just below their subscripts. Names that are acceptable for simple variables are also admissible array names.

The value of a subscripted variable—that is, an entry in an array—is referenced in a program just as values of simple variables are referenced. For example, the two LET statements

```
LET G(1)=71
LET G(6)=G(1)+12
```

assign 71 to the subscripted variable $G(1)$ and 83 to $G(6)$; that is, 71 and 83 are assigned as the first and sixth entries of array G.

Arrays provide one significant advantage over simple variables—namely, the subscripts may be variables or other numerical expressions rather than just integer constants. We illustrate by example.

EXAMPLE 1. Here is a program segment to assign values to G(1), G(2), G(3), G(4), and G(5).

```
100 FOR I=1 to 5
110    READ G(I)
120 NEXT I
130 DATA 71,83,96,77,92
```

On each pass through the loop, the index I of the loop serves as the subscript. The first time through the loop, I has the value 1; hence the statement in line 110 assigns the value 71 to G(1). Similarly, G(2) through G(5) are assigned their respective values during the remaining four passes through the loop.

EXAMPLE 2. Here is a program segment to calculate the sum S of the odd numbered entries in a list G that contains five entries. The sum is stored as the sixth entry of G.

```
200 LET S=0
210 FOR K=1 to 3
220    LET S=S+G(2*K-1)
230 NEXT K
240 LET G(6)=S
```

On the first pass through the loop the control variable K is 1, so the subscript $2*K-1$ has the value $2*(1)-1=1$. Thus, G($2*K-1$) refers to G(1), and this value is added to S. On the second pass, $2*K-1$ has the value $2*(2)-1=3$, so that G(3) is added to S. Similarly, G(5) is added to S on the third pass. After the loop has been satisfied, the value of S is assigned to G(6). At this point both S and G(6) have the same value.

The subscript that appears within the parentheses to indicate the position in an array (I in Example 1 and $2*K-1$ in Example 2) may be any BASIC numerical expression. Thus, the following are all admissible.

$$A(7) \qquad X(I+1)$$
$$B(7+3/2) \qquad Z(100-N)$$

When the computer encounters a subscript, the subscript is evaluated; if it is not an integer, it is rounded to the nearest integer (some systems truncate instead of rounding off). The smallest subscript allowed on your system will be either 0 or 1. In this text we will assume that it is 1 so that the programs presented will perform as indicated on all systems. If the computer encounters a subscript smaller than the smallest subscript allowed, an error diagnostic will be printed and the program run will terminate. The largest subscripts allowed will be discussed in the next section. For now, assume the top limit to be 10.

Subscripted variables may also be assigned values by INPUT statements, as well as by READ and LET statements. For example, the loop

```
FOR I=1 TO 5
   INPUT G(I)
NEXT I
```

can be used to input values for G(1) through G(5) during program execution.

Values assigned to subscripted variables are retained until changed in another programming line, just as is the case with simple variables.

EXAMPLE 3

```
100 FOR I=1 TO 5
110    READ G(I)
120 NEXT I
130 PRINT G(1),G(3)
140 LET G(3)=G(1)
150 PRINT G(1),G(3)
160 DATA 71,83,96,77,92
170 END
RUN

   71              96
   71              71
READY
```

When line 140 is executed, the value 71 of G(1) is assigned to G(3), but G(1) is not changed. After execution of this line, G(1) and G(3) have the same value 71 as shown in the output. Note that the previous value 96 of G(3) is lost.

The appearance of the same array name (G in the following example) in two FOR/NEXT loops, each using a different control variable (I and J in the example), often causes some difficulty for the beginning programmer.

EXAMPLE 4. Here is a program segment that increases each entry of the array G by 2 and then stores the resulting values in a second array M, but in the reverse order.

```
100 FOR I=1 TO 5
110    LET G(I)=G(I)+2
120 NEXT I
130 FOR J=1 TO 5
140    LET M(J)=G(6-J)
150 NEXT J
```

Let's assume that prior to execution of this program segment, the array G is read as in Example 1. Pictorially,

	1	2	3	4	5
G	71	83	96	77	92

The first loop (the I loop) adds 2 to each entry in G.

	1	2	3	4	5
G	73	85	98	79	94

The second loop (the J loop) creates a new array M. For J = 1, the assignment statement is LET M(1) = G(5); for J = 2, LET M(2) = G(4); and so on. Thus, after execution of this second loop, M is as follows:

	1	2	3	4	5
M	94	79	98	85	73

Remark 1

Creating new arrays that are modifications of existing arrays is a common programming task. In this example, the entries in the array M are a rearrangement of the entries in array G. Note that the creation of array M by the J loop in no way modifies the existing array G.

Remark 2

Although it is common practice to refer to the symbols G(I) and M(J) as variables, remember that the actual variable names are G(1), G(2), G(3), and so on. Each time the LET statements are executed, I and J have particular values indicating which of these variables is being referenced.

11.2 The DIM statement

Whenever a subscripted variable—say $Z(1)$—appears in a program, ten memory locations (11 if zero subscripts are allowed) are automatically reserved for the array Z. These locations are used to store values for $Z(1)$, $Z(2)$, ..., $Z(10)$. If subscripts larger than 10 are needed, you must see to it that more space is reserved in memory. This is accomplished with the DIM statement.

EXAMPLE 5. Here is a program segment to read values for the N variables B(1), B(2), . . . , B(N).

```
100 DIM B(35)
110 INPUT N
120 FOR I=1 TO N
130    READ B(I)
140 NEXT I
```

Line 100 reserves 35 memory locations for the array B. If 35 is input for N at line 110, the FOR/NEXT loop will read values from DATA lines for B(1), B(2), . . . , B(35). If 20 is input for N, the FOR/NEXT loop will assign values only to the variables B(1), B(2), . . . , B(20); the remaining variables, B(21), . . . , B(35), although available, are simply not used. However, if a value larger than 35 is input for N, the attempt to read a value for B(36) will cause an error message to be printed, indicating that a subscript is out of range, and the program run will terminate.

The DIM statement is also called the **dimension statement,** because it determines the dimension (that is, the length) of an array. When a program contains a DIM statement—for example, DIM B(35)—we say that the array B has been **dimensioned.**

When coding a program that will read input data into an array, you must see to it that the DIM statement specifies an array large enough to accommodate all of the input values. Thus, if you know in advance that your program will never be required to read more than 1,000 values into an array A, the statement

```
DIM A(1000)
```

will suffice. However, this statement actually reserves 1,000 locations in the computer's memory; that is, your program will tie up these 1,000 memory locations whether or not a particular run of the program uses them. This means that you must not only ensure that your array is large enough, but you should keep it as small as possible.

Although BASIC requires a DIM statement only for those arrays whose subscripts exceed 10, many programmers dimension every array appearing in their programs. This practice facilitates the debugging process since a DIM statement explicitly establishes which variables are arrays and what dimensions they have.

The program segment in Example 5 shows how data can be read into an array when the number of values to be read is known in advance; in the example, this number is the first input value. Many programming applications require that data terminated with an EOD-tag be read into an array. The following example shows how this can be done.

EXAMPLE 6. Here are two program segments to read a list of numbers into an array K.

Program segment 1

```
100 DIM K(100)
110 LET I=0
120 REM READ NEXT VALUE INTO ARRAY K
130    LET I=I+1
140    READ K(I)
150 IF K(I)<>9999 THEN 130
160 REM N DENOTES ACTUAL LENGTH OF LIST
170 LET N=I-1
```

Program segment 2

```
100 DIM K(100)
110 FOR I=1 TO 100
120    REM READ NEXT VALUE INTO ARRAY K
130    READ K(I)
140    IF K(I)=9999 THEN 180
150 NEXT I
160 PRINT "INADEQUATE DIM STATEMENT AT LINE 100."
170 STOP
180 REM N DENOTES ACTUAL LENGTH OF LIST
190 LET N=I-1
```

Each of these program segments uses I to keep track of the subscript. Each time a value is read for K(I) it is compared with the EOD-tag 9999. If K(I) does not equal 9999, the subscript I is increased by 1 and another value is read. When the EOD-tag is read, we have K(I) = 9999; that is, the EOD-tag is in the Ith position of the array. Control then passes to the statement LET N = I − 1 so that N specifies the number of values, exclusive of the EOD-tag, read into the array. In any further processing of this array we would use N to specify its length.

Each program segment will also cause program execution to terminate if an attempt is made to read more than 100 numbers. The first will halt with an error diagnostic indicating that a subscript is out of range. The second will halt after printing the more informative message INADEQUATE DIM STATEMENT AT LINE 100. The method used in Program Segment 2 is recommended when reading values into arrays. It allows you to specify precisely what messages are to be printed should a person use your program incorrectly.

More than one DIM statement may appear in a program, and each DIM statement may be used to dimension more than one array. The programming line

```
5 DIM A(100),X(50),Z(5)
```

is acceptable and will reserve 155 memory locations: 100 for the array A, 50 for the array X, and 5 for the array Z.

The general form of the DIM statement, as it applies to one-dimensional arrays (lists) is

ln DIM **a(e)**,**b(f)**, . . . , **c(g)**

where **a, b, c** denote array names and **e, f, g** are positive-integer *constants*. DIM statements must appear before any reference is made to the array being dimensioned. The customary practice (and a good one at that) is to place all DIM statements near the beginning of a program.

Remark

As noted in Chapter 1, every BASIC system uses either a compiler (an *entire* program is translated into machine code before it is executed), or an interpreter (each BASIC statement is translated into machine code each time it is executed). Many, if not all, systems that use interpreters allow *dynamic storage allocation* for arrays. This means that you can use numerical expressions other than constants to specify dimensions for arrays. For example, you can write

```
200 INPUT N
210 DIM A(N),B(2*N)
```

and then specify dimensions for the arrays A and B during program execution. This capability can be useful if the available memory space on your system is severely limited. Since compiler based systems do not allow dynamic storage allocation, we will use DIM statements with constants to specify array dimensions in all examples.

At the outset of this chapter we mentioned that subscripted variables can be used effectively in programming tasks that require us to determine many counts. The following example illustrates this use of subscripted variables.

EXAMPLE 7. A list of integers, all between 1 and 100, is contained in DATA lines. Let's write a program to determine how many of each integer are included. We assume that 9999 terminates the list.

Problem analysis

We must determine 100 counts: the number of 1s, the number of 2s, and so on. Let's use C(1), C(2), . . . , C(100) to store these counts. Now, each value appearing in the DATA lines must be read to determine which of the 100 integers it is. If it is 87, then C(87) must be increased by 1; if it is 24, then C(24) must be increased by 1. Using X to denote the value being read, we may write the following algorithm.

a. Initialize: C(I) = 0 for I = 1 to 100.
b. Read a value for X.
c. If X = 9999, print the results and stop.
d. Add 1 to C(X) and go to step (b).

Let's conserve paper by printing two columns, containing I and C(I), but suppressing the output whenever C(I) = 0 (that is, if I is not in the given list). The following flowchart segment shows how to cause this printout.

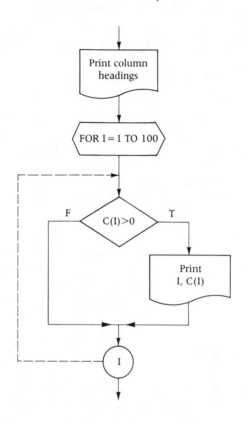

The program

```
100 REM INITIALIZE COUNTERS
110 DIM C(100)
120 FOR I=1 TO 100
130     LET C(I)=0
140 NEXT I
150 REM READ X AND ADD 1 TO C(X) UNTIL
160 REM THE EOD TAG 9999 IS ENCOUNTERED
170     READ X
180     IF X=9999 THEN 210
190     LET C(X)=C(X)+1
200 GO TO 170
210 REM PRINT THE FREQUENCY TABLE
220 PRINT "DATUM","FREQUENCY"
230 PRINT "-----","----------"
240 FOR I=1 TO 100
250     IF C(I)>0 THEN PRINT I,C(I)
260 NEXT I
500 DATA 80,80,80,80,80,60,60,50
510 DATA 50,50,45,45,50,50,50,32
998 DATA 9999
999 END
RUN
```

```
DATUM          FREQUENCY
-----          ---------
 32               1
 45               2
 50               6
 60               2
 80               5
READY
```

11.3 Problems

1. What will be printed when each program is run?

   a.
   ```
   10 LET I=2
   20 READ X(I),X(1)
   30 FOR I=1 TO 2
   40    PRINT X(I)
   50 NEXT I
   60 DATA 4,5,7,3
   70 END
   ```

   b.
   ```
   10 LET J=1
   20 READ X(J)
   30 FOR I=1 TO 3
   40    READ X(I+1)
   50    PRINT X(I);
   60 NEXT I
   70 DATA 3,1,5,6,8
   80 END
   ```

   c.
   ```
   110 READ J
   120 FOR J=5 TO 7
   130    READ M(J)
   140 NEXT J
   150 READ B,C
   160 FOR K=B TO C
   170    PRINT M(K);
   180 NEXT K
   190 DATA 2,9,8,4,6,6,3
   200 END
   ```

   d.
   ```
   10 FOR I=1 TO 3
   20    READ A(I)
   30 NEXT I
   40 FOR I=1 TO 2
   50    LET A(I)=A(I+1)
   60    LET A(I+1)=A(I)
   70    PRINT A(I),A(I+1)
   80 NEXT I
   90 DATA 7,8,3
   99 END
   ```

2. Explain what is wrong with each of the following.

   a.
   ```
   10 FOR A=9 TO 12
   20    READ M(A)
   30    PRINT M(A);
   40 NEXT A
   50 DATA 7,3,5,2,9,1,-3,-2
   60 END
   ```

   b.
   ```
   300 REM PROGRAM SEGMENT TO REVERSE THE
   310 REM ORDER IN AN ARRAY L OF LENGTH 10
   320 FOR K=1 TO 10
   330    LET L(11-K)=L(K)
   340 NEXT K
   ```

   c.
   ```
   400 REM PROGRAM SEGMENT TO FIND THE
   410 REM LARGEST NUMBER S IN AN ARRAY L
   420 REM OF LENGTH N
   430 FOR J=1 TO N
   440    IF S<L(J) THEN LET L(J)=S
   450 NEXT J
   ```

Write a program to perform each task specified in Problems 3–15. The RESTORE statement is not to be used in any of these problems.

3. Input an array A of undetermined length and print the values in reverse order. Use an EOD-tag to terminate the input list.

4. Five numbers are to be input into an array B as follows. The first value is to be assigned to B(1) and B(10), the second to B(2) and B(9), and so on. The array B is then to be printed, and five more values are to be input in the same manner. This process is to continue until all data values have been processed. Your program is to come to an orderly halt.

5. Ten values are to be read into an array Y. Then a new array X containing 20 values is to be created so that the odd-numbered entries in X contain zeros and the even-numbered entries are the entries of Y in the same order. Print both arrays. Do not assume that your BASIC system initializes all variables to zero.

6. Read 20 values into an array A, and print three columns as follows. Column 1 contains the 20 values in the original order; column 2 contains the 20 values in reverse order; column 3 contains the average of the corresponding elements in columns 1 and 2.

7. The following DATA lines show the annual salaries of all the employees in Division 72 of the Manley Corporation. The last value (72) is an EOD tag.

```
500 DATA 14000, 16200, 10195, 18432, 13360
510 DATA 19300, 16450, 12180, 25640,  8420
520 DATA  8900,  9270,  9620,  9940, 11200
530 DATA 72
```

Calculate and print the average salary of all employees in Division 72, and then print a list of those salaries exceeding this average.

8. Read the salary data shown in Problem 7 into array S. Then create a new array T as follows. T(I) is to be obtained by subtracting S(I) from the average of all the salaries. The arrays S and T are then to be printed as a two-column table with appropriate column headings.

9. Use the salary data shown in Problem 7 to create two arrays as follows. A is to contain all salaries less than $14,000, and B is to contain the rest. Arrays A and B are then to be printed as columns with appropriate column headings.

10. An undetermined number of values are to be input into arrays P and N so that array P contains those that are positive and N contains those that are negative. Zeros are to be ignored and 999 is to serve as the EOD-tag. When the EOD tag is encountered, the two lists are to be printed in adjacent columns with the headings POSITIVES and NEGATIVES.

11. A number of scores, each lying in the range from 0 to 100, are given in a collection of DATA lines. These scores are to be used to create an array C as follows.

C(1) = a count of those scores S satisfying $S \leqslant 20$
C(2) = a count of those scores S satisfying $20 < S \leqslant 40$
C(3) = a count of those scores S satisfying $40 < S \leqslant 60$
C(4) = a count of those scores S satisying $60 < S \leqslant 80$
C(5) = a count of those scores S satisfying $80 < S \leqslant 100$

The results should be printed in tabular form as follows.

Interval	Frequency	
0–20	C(1)	(actually the value of C(1))
20–40	C(2)	
40–60	C(3)	
60–80	C(4)	
80–100	C(5)	

12. Problem 11 asked for a count of the number of scores in each of five equal-length intervals between 0 and 100. Instead of using five intervals, allow a user to type a positive integer N to produce a similar frequency table using N equal-length intervals.

13. The mean M and standard deviation D of a set of numbers contained in data lines are desired. The following method should be used to compute D. If the numbers are $x_1, x_2, x_3, \ldots, x_n$, then $D = \sqrt{S1/(n-1)}$, where

$$S1 = (x_1 - M)^2 + (x_2 - M)^2 + \cdots + (x_n - M)^2.$$

14. Let any three consecutive entries of an array L be related to each other by the equation

$$L(J+2) = L(J+1) + L(J)$$

Input two integer values for L(1) and L(2) and generate L(J) for J = 3; ..., 100. Print these 100 integers in four columns; the first column is to display L(1) through L(25), the second is to display L(26) through L(50), and so on. Examine your output to be sure that the values printed are correct.

15. A correspondence between x and y is given by the following table. (Each y entry corresponds to the x entry just above it.)

x	0	2	4	6	8	10	12	14	16	18	20
y	−5	3	27	67	123	195	283	387	507	643	795

A program is desired that will allow a user to type two numbers, the first being a 0, 1, or 2 and the second being a value for x. The computer is to respond as follows.

0. If the first number typed is 0, the y value corresponding to x is to be printed. If the x value is not in the table, the message NOT FOUND should be printed. The user should then be allowed to type in two more numbers.
1. If the first number typed is 1, the y value corresponding to x should be printed. However, if x is not in the table, a linear interpolation should be performed to determine y. If x_1 and x_2 are successive values in the list with x lying between them, and if y_1 and y_2 are the corresponding y values, the value y to be printed is given by

$$y = y_1 + \frac{x - x_1}{x_2 - x_1}(y_2 - y_1).$$

The user should again be allowed to type two more numbers.
2. If the first number typed is 2 the program should terminate. If the first number typed is not 0, 1, or 2, or if the second number is not between 0 and 20, the two values just typed should be rejected and new values requested.

11.4 Sorting

Many programming tasks require sorting (arranging) arrays according to some specified order. When lists of numbers are involved, this usually means arranging them according to size, from smallest to largest or from largest to smallest. For example, you may be required to produce a salary schedule in which salaries are printed from largest to smallest. When lists of names are involved, you may wish to arrange them in alphabetical order. In this section we'll describe the **bubble sort,** an algorithm that will take any array A(1), A(2), . . . , A(N) of numbers and rearrange them so that they are in ascending order—that is, so that

A(1) $\leq$ A(2) $\leq \cdots \leq$ A(N).

In Chapter 12 we'll show how algorithms used to sort arrays of numbers are easily modified to sort arrays whose entries are strings (for instance, names).

The bubble sort is not a very efficient sorting algorithm. However, it is reasonably easy to understand and for this reason serves as an excellent introduction to the topic of sorting. A more comprehensive treatment of this topic is included in Chapter 16. We demonstrate the bubble sort with a short array A containing only four values:

4 3 5 1

First, we compare the values in positions 1 and 2. If they are in the proper order (the first is less than or equal to the second), we leave them alone. If not, we interchange them:

4 3 5 1 becomes **3 4** 5 1.

Next we compare the values in positions 2 and 3 in the same manner:

3 **4 5** 1 remains 3 **4 5** 1.

Then we compare the values in positions 3 and 4:

3 4 **5** **1** becomes 3 4 **1** **5.**

The effect of these three comparisons was to move the largest value to the last position. This process is now repeated, except that this time the final comparison is omitted because the largest value is already in the last position:

3 **4** 1 5 remains **3** **4** 1 5.
3 **4** **1** 5 becomes 3 **1** **4** 5.

We repeat the process once more, this time noting that the final two comparisons are unnecessary because the correct numbers are already in the last two positions:

3 **1** 4 5 becomes **1** **3** 4 5.

The array is now in the proper order.

To summarize, the array A contains four values, and we make three passes through the array.

On pass number 1, we compare A(I) with A(I + 1) for I = 1, 2, 3.
On pass number 2, we compare A(I) with A(I + 1) for I = 1, 2.
On pass number 3, we compare A(I) with A(I + 1) for I = 1.

If an array contains N values instead of 4, we make N − 1 passes through the array. In this case the following comparisons are made:

On pass number 1, compare A(I) with A(I + 1) for I = 1, 2, ..., N − 1.
On pass number 2, compare A(I) with A(I + 1) for I = 1, 2, ..., N − 2.
On pass number 3, compare A(I) with A(I + 1) for I = 1, 2, ..., N − 3.

.

.

.

On pass number N − 2, compare A(I) with A(I + 1) for I = 1, 2.
On pass number N − 1, compare A(I) with A(I + 1) for I = 1.

Note that on each pass through the array, one fewer comparison is made. N − 1 comparisons are made the first time (I = 1, 2, ..., N − 1), N − 2 the second (I = 1, 2, ..., N − 2), N − 3 the third, and so on.

In general, on the Jth pass through the array, N − J comparisons are made, one for each I = 1, 2, 3, ..., N − J. Since J, the pass number, takes on the successive values 1 through N − 1, all necessary comparisons can be accomplished with the nested FOR/NEXT loops.

```
FOR J=1 TO N-1
   FOR I=1 TO N-J
      .
      .
      .
   NEXT I
NEXT J
```

The actual method of comparison is as follows: if A(I) is greater than A(I + 1), we must interchange them. Using the *temporary* variable T, the three statements

```
LET T = A(I)
LET A(I) = A(I+1)
LET A(I+1) = T
```

accomplish this. If A(I) is not greater than A(I + 1), these three lines must be skipped. The flowchart in Figure 11.1 displays the process just described. The corresponding program segment, shown in Figure 11.2, can be used in any program to sort, in ascending order, any one-dimensional array A of N numbers.

Figure 11.1
Flowchart to perform a bubble sort.

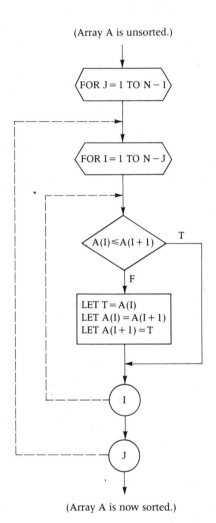

(Array A is unsorted.)

FOR J = 1 TO N − 1

FOR I = 1 TO N − J

A(I) ≤ A(I + 1)   T

F

LET T = A(I)
LET A(I) = A(I + 1)
LET A(I + 1) = T

I

J

(Array A is now sorted.)

Figure 11.2
Program segment to perform a bubble sort.

```
500 REM BUBBLE SORT TO ARRANGE THE N
510 REM TERMS OF ARRAY A IN ASCENDING ORDER
520 FOR J=1 TO N-1
530    FOR I=1 TO N-J
540       IF A(I)<=A(I+1) THEN 580
550       LET T=A(I)
560       LET A(I)=A(I+1)
570       LET A(I+1)=T
580    NEXT I
590 NEXT J
600 REM ARRAY A IS SORTED
```

If the comparisons are reversed, with line 540 being changed to

```
540    IF A(I)>=A(I+1) THEN 580
```

the program segment in Figure 11.2 will sort the array in descending rather than ascending order. This accounts for the name bubble sort—the smaller or lighter values are "bubbled" to the top.

Many applications requiring arrays to be sorted involve more than one array. For example, suppose C and P denote one-dimensional arrays with each pair C(I), P(I) giving an item code number and the price of the item. If the contents of these two arrays must be printed in a two-column report of item codes and prices, with the item codes appearing from smallest to largest, the list of pairs C(I),P(I) must be sorted so that the entries in C are in increasing order. This can be accomplished by modifying a bubble sort that sorts the array C. Simply insert lines that interchange P(I) and P(I + 1) whenever C(I) and C(I + 1) are interchanged. We illustrate with an example.

EXAMPLE 8

Several pairs of numbers are included in DATA lines. The first of each pair is a quality point average (QPA), and the second gives the number of students with this QPA. Write a program to produce a table with the two column headings QPA and FREQUENCY. The frequency counts in the second column are to appear in descending order.

Problem analysis

Two lists are given in the DATA lines. Let's use Q to denote the QPAs and F to denote the frequency counts. The following algorithm shows the three subtasks that must be performed.

a. Read arrays Q and F.
b. Sort the two arrays so that the frequencies appear in descending order.
c. Print the two arrays as a two-column table.

To code step (a), we must remember that the lists are presented in DATA lines as pairs of numbers. Thus, we will read values for Q(I) and F(I) for I = 1, 2, and so on, until all pairs have been read. Let's use the dummy pair 0, 0 as an EOD tag.

To code step (b), we will use a bubble sort to sort array F in descending order. However, since a pair Q(I), F(I) must not be separated, we will interchange Q values whenever the corresponding F values are interchanged.

The program

```
100 REM READ ARRAYS Q AND F
110 DIM Q(50),F(50)
120 FOR I=1 TO 50
130    READ Q(I),F(I)
140    IF (Q(I)=0) AND (F(I)=0) THEN 180
150 NEXT I
160 PRINT "I CAN ONLY HANDLE 49 PAIRS"
170 STOP
180 LET N=I-1
190 REM SORT ARRAYS Q AND F ACCORDING
200 REM TO DECREASING F VALUES
210 FOR J=1 TO N-1
220    FOR I=1 TO N-J
230       IF F(I)>=F(I+1) THEN 300
240       LET T=F(I)
250       LET F(I)=F(I+1)
260       LET F(I+1)=T
270       LET T=Q(I)
280       LET Q(I)=Q(I+1)
290       LET Q(I+1)=T
300    NEXT I
310 NEXT J
320 REM PRINT COLUMN HEADINGS AND TABLE VALUES
330 PRINT "QPA","FREQUENCY"
340 PRINT
350 FOR I=1 TO N
360    PRINT Q(I),F(I)
370 NEXT I
500 DATA 4.00,2,3.75,16,3.40,41,3.20,38,3.00,92
510 DATA 2.75,162,2.30,352,2.00,280,1.70,81,1.50,27
998 DATA 0,0
999 END
RUN
```

QPA	FREQUENCY
2.3	352
2.	280
2.75	162
3.	92
1.7	81
3.4	41
3.2	38
1.5	27
3.75	16
4.	2

```
READY
```

Lines 270–290 were inserted in the bubble sort to interchange Q values whenever the corresponding F values were interchanged.

11.5 Problems

Write a program to perform each task specified in Problems 1–14.

1. Print, in ascending order, any five input values L(1), L(2), L(3), L(4), and L(5). Your program should process many such sets of five integers during a single run. Test your program with the following input data.

5	4	3	2	1
5	1	2	3	4
−1	−2	−3	−4	−5
2	1	4	3	5
15	19	14	18	10
1	2	3	4	5

2. Modify your program for Problem 1 so that each group of five integers is printed in descending order. (Only one line needs to be changed.)
3. Print a single list of all 30 input values given in Problem 1. The numbers are to be printed from smallest to largest.
4. Any list of numbers typed at the terminal is to be printed in ascending order. The value 9999, when typed, is to indicate that the entire list has been entered.
5. In carrying out a bubble sort to sort an array A, several passes are made through A and on each pass several comparisons of A(I) and A(I + 1) are made to determine whether the values of A(I) and A(I + 1) should be swapped. If, on any one pass, no swaps are made—that is, if all of the pairs A(I),A(I + 1) are already in the desired order—you can be sure that the sorting is complete. Use this fact to write an improved version of the bubble sort. You will need a counter K that counts the number of swaps made on any one pass through the array. After each pass is complete, simply check to see if K = 0. If it is, the sort is complete. If not, set K = 0 and continue.
6. A list of numbers is to be read to obtain a two-column printout with the column headings ORIGINAL LIST and SORTED LIST. The first column is to contain the list values in the order in which they are read, and the second column is to contain the same values printed from largest to smallest. Use the following algorithm.

   a. Input the list values into identical arrays A and B.
   b. Sort array A into descending order.
   c. Print the table as described.

   Try your program using the following DATA lines.

   ```
   500 DATA 80, 70, 40, 90, 95, 38, 85, 42, 60, 70
   510 DATA 40, 60, 70, 20, 18, 87, 23, 78, 85, 23
   998 DATA 9999
   ```

7. Several numbers, ranging from 0 to 100, are to be read and stored in two arrays A and B. A is to contain those numbers that are less than 50, and the others are to be stored in array B. Arrays A and B are then to be sorted in descending order and printed side by side with the column headings LESS THAN 50 and 50 OR MORE. Test your program, using the input data shown in Problem 6.
8. Read an array L and sort it in ascending order. Then create a new array M containing the same values as L but with no repetitions. For example, if L(1) = 7, L(2) = L(3) = 8, and L(4) = L(5) = L(6) = 9, then the array M is to have M(1) = 7, M(2) = 8, and M(3) = 9. Print both arrays. Run your program using the DATA lines shown in Problem 6.
9. Read an array L and sort it in ascending order. Then modify L by deleting all values appearing more than once. For example, if L(1) = 7, L(2) = L(3) = 8, and L(4) = L(5) = L(6) = 9, then the new array is to have L(1) = 7, L(2) = 8, and L(3) = 9. Run your program using the DATA lines shown in Problem 6.
10. A study of the Tidy Corporation's annual reports for the years 1972–1980 yielded the following statistics.

Year	Gross sales (in thousands)	Earnings per share
1972	19,500	.27
1973	18,350	−.40
1974	18,400	−.12
1975	18,000	−.84
1976	18,900	.65
1977	20,350	.78
1978	24,850	1.05
1979	24,300	.68
1980	27,250	.88

Include the second and third columns of this table in DATA lines for a program to print two columns with the same headings as those shown. However, the Earnings-per-Share figures are to appear in ascending order. (Use the method described in Example 8.)

11. Include all three columns given for the Tidy Corporation (Problem 10) in DATA lines for a program to produce a three-column table with the same headings. However, the Gross Sales figures are to appear in descending order.

12. Following is the weekly inventory report of a sewing-supply wholesaler.

Item	Batches on hand Monday	Batches sold during week	Cost per batch	Sales price per batch
Bobbins	220	105	8.20	10.98
Buttons	550	320	5.50	6.95
Needles—1	450	295	2.74	3.55
Needles—2	200	102	7.25	9.49
Pins	720	375	4.29	5.89
Thimbles	178	82	6.22	7.59
Thread—A	980	525	4.71	5.99
Thread—B	1424	718	7.42	9.89

Include the five columns of this report in DATA lines by using one DATA statement for each item. Use the line numbers 800, 810, 820, . . . , 870. Your program is to produce a three-column report showing, for each item, the number of batches on hand at the end of the week, and the income generated by that item. However, the income column is to appear in descending order.

13. Using the inventory report shown in Problem 12, produce a five-column report showing the item names, the cost per batch, the sales price per batch, the dollar markup per batch, and the percent markup per batch. The figures in the last column should appear in descending order. (The percentages in the fifth column are given by (M/C)∗100, where M denotes the markup and C denotes the cost.)

14. N pairs of numbers are to be read so that the first of each pair is in array A and the second in array B. Sort the pairs A(I), B(I) so that A(1) ≤ A(2) ≤ ⋯ ≤ A(N) and also so that B(I) ≤ B(I + 1) whenever A(I) = A(I + 1). Print the modified array in two adjacent columns with the headings LIST A and LIST B. *Hint:* If A(I) > A(I + 1), a swap is necessary; if A(I) < A(I + 1), no swap is necessary; otherwise—that is, if A(I) = A(I + 1)—swap only if B(I) > B(I + 1).

11.6 Two-dimensional arrays

Data to be processed by the computer are often presented in tabular form. For example, you may wish to write a program to analyze the following data, which summarize the responses of college students to a hypothetical opinion poll concerning the abolition of grades.

Class	In favor of abolishing grades	Not in favor of abolishing grades	No opinion
Freshmen	207	93	41
Sophomores	165	110	33
Juniors	93	87	15
Seniors	51	65	8

If you wanted to determine the number of sophomores who were polled, you would add the three entries in the second row; to determine the percentage of sophomores polled who are not in favor of abolishing grades, the entry 110 would be divided by this sum. Many such calculations may be desired, and the computer is ideally suited for such tasks. What is needed is a convenient way to present these data to the computer. First, we will introduce some terminology to make it easier to refer to such tables of values.

A **two-dimensional array** is a collection of items arranged in a rectangular fashion. That is, there is a first (horizontal) row, a second row, and so on, and a first (vertical) column, a second column, and so on. An array with m rows and n columns is called an *m-by-n array* (also written *m × n array*). Thus the opinion-poll data are presented as a 4-by-3 array.

A particular item in an array is specified simply by giving its row number and column number. For example, the item in the third row and second column of the opinion-poll table is 87. By convention, when specifying an item in an array, we give the row number first. Hence, in the opinion-poll table, 33 is in the 2,3 position and 51 is in the 4,1 position. In mathematical notation we could write

$$P_{1,1} = 207, \quad P_{1,2} = 93, \quad P_{1,3} = 41$$

to indicate the values in the first row of our table. Since the BASIC character set does not include subscripts, this notation is changed as it was for one-dimensional arrays. Thus, the values in the opinion-poll table would be written as follows:

P(1,1) = 207	P(1,2) = 93	P(1,3) = 41
P(2,1) = 165	P(2,2) = 110	P(2,3) = 33
P(3,1) = 93	P(3,2) = 87	P(3,3) = 15
P(4,1) = 51	P(4,2) = 65	P(4,3) = 8

We say that P is the *name* of the array, that P(1,1), P(1,2), . . . are *doubly subscripted* variables, and that the numbers enclosed in parentheses are the *subscripts* of P. The symbol P(I,J) is read "P sub I comma J" or simply "P sub IJ."

The 4-by-3 array P can be visualized as follows:

		(Column)	
P	1	2	3
1	207	93	41
2	165	110	33
3	93	87	15
4	51	65	8

(Row)

This schematic displays the array name P, the row number for each item, and the column numbers.

The value of a doubly subscripted variable—that is, an array entry—is referenced in a program just as values of singly subscripted variables are referenced. The subscripts can be integer constants, variables, or expressions. For example, the FOR/NEXT loop

```
FOR J=1 TO 3
   LET P(1,J)=5*J
NEXT J
```

assigns the values 5, 10, and 15 to the first row P(1,1),P(1,2),P(1,3), of P. Similarly,

```
LET K=1
FOR I=1 TO 4
    LET P(I,K)=P(I,K)+6
NEXT I
```

adds 6 to each entry in the first column P(1,1),P(2,1),P(3,1),P(4,1) of P.

EXAMPLE 9. Here is a program segment to read the opinion-poll data into an array P.

```
100 REM READ VALUES FOR THE 4-BY-3 ARRAY P
110 FOR I=1 TO 4
120     REM READ VALUES FOR THE ITH ROW OF P
130     FOR J=1 TO 3
140         READ P(I,J)
150     NEXT J
160 NEXT I
500 DATA 207,93,41
510 DATA 165,110,33
520 DATA 93,87,15
530 DATA 51,65,8
```

When the first FOR statement (line 110) is executed, I is assigned the initial value 1. The J-loop then reads the first three data values 207, 93, and 41 for the variables P(1,1),P(1,2), and P(1,3), respectively. That is, when I = 1, values are read into the first row of P. Similarly, when I = 2, values are read into the second row, P(2,1),P(2,2),P(2,3), of P, and so on until all 12 values have been assigned to P.

Remark 1

The data do not have to be given in four lines as shown here. The single line

```
500 DATA 207, 93, 41, 165, 110, 33, 93, 87, 15, 51, 65, 8
```

could replace lines 500 through 530. The order in which they appear is all that matters.

Remark 2

The following five lines are used to assign values to P.

```
FOR I=1 TO 4
   FOR J=1 TO 3
       READ P(I,J)
   NEXT J
NEXT I
```

Some BASIC systems allow you to accomplish the same thing with a single statement called a MAT (matrix) statement. (**Matrix** is another name for an array of values.) Proper use of MAT statements can shorten your programs and make them easier to understand. The MAT statements are described in Chapter 17.

EXAMPLE 10. Let's use the program segment of Example 9 in a program to count the number of students in each class who participated in the opinion-poll survey.

Problem analysis

The following algorithm describes one way to carry out the specified task.

a. Read the opinion-poll data into array P. (Done in Example 9.)
b. Determine and print how many students in each class participated in the survey.

Since all three entries in any one row of P correspond to students in one of the four classes, the task in step (b) is to add the three entries in each row of P and print these four sums. Let's use S(1) to denote the sum of the entries in the first row, and similarly S(2), S(3), and S(4) for the other three row sums. These sums can be determined as follows.

```
LET S(1)=P(1,1)+P(1,2)+P(1,3)
LET S(2)=P(2,1)+P(2,2)+P(2,3)
LET S(3)=P(3,1)+P(3,2)+P(3,3)
LET S(4)=P(4,1)+P(4,2)+P(4,3)
```

However, note that S(I), for I = 1,2,3, and 4, is obtained by summing P(I,J) for J = 1,2, and 3. This is exactly the order of subscripts determined by the nested FOR/NEXT loops.

```
FOR I=1 TO 4
   FOR J=1 TO 3
      .
      .
      .
   NEXT J
NEXT I
```

The following program can now be written. Lines 100–160, which carry out step (a) of the algorithm, are simply the program segment shown in Example 9. To this we add lines 170–320, which represent one way to carry out step (b) of the algorithm.

The program

```
100 REM READ VALUES FOR THE 4-BY-3 ARRAY P
110 FOR I=1 TO 4
120    REM READ VALUES FOR THE ITH ROW OF P
130    FOR J=1 TO 3
140       READ P(I,J)
150    NEXT J
160 NEXT I
170 REM DETERMINE AND PRINT THE ROW SUMS OF P
180 PRINT "PARTICIPATION IN SURVEY BY CLASS."
190 PRINT "--------------------------------"
200 FOR I=1 TO 4
210    LET S(I)=0
220 NEXT I
230 FOR I=1 TO 4
240    FOR J=1 TO 3
250       LET S(I)=S(I)+P(I,J)
260    NEXT J
270    IF (I=1) THEN PRINT "FRESHMEN",
280    IF (I=2) THEN PRINT "SOPHOMORES",
```

```
290    IF (I=3) THEN PRINT "JUNIORS",
300    IF (I=4) THEN PRINT "SENIORS",
310    PRINT S(I)
320 NEXT I
500 DATA 207,93,41
510 DATA 165,110,33
520 DATA 93,87,15
530 DATA 51,65,8
999 END
RUN

PARTICIPATION IN SURVEY BY CLASS.
-----------------------------------
FRESHMEN        341
SOPHOMORES      308
JUNIORS         195
SENIORS         124
READY
```

Remark

This program could have been written using only one pair of nested FOR/NEXT loops by inserting appropriate lines in the program segment

```
100 REM READ VALUES FOR THE 4-BY-3 ARRAY P
110 FOR I=1 TO 4
120    REM READ VALUES FOR THE ITH ROW OF P
130    FOR J=1 TO 3
140       READ P(I,J)
150    NEXT J
160 NEXT I
```

that was used to carry out step (a) of the algorithm. Specifically, inserting the line

```
115 LET S(I)=0
```

serves to initialize the counters S(1),S(2),S(3), and S(4). Also, if the line

```
145 LET S(I)=S(I)+P(I,J)
```

is included, the required row sums S(1), S(2), S(3), and S(4) will be calculated. The lines that print the caption

```
PARTICIPATION IN SURVEY BY CLASS.
-----------------------------------
```

can be placed anywhere before line 110 and, finally, the lines that print the counts S(I) with the identifying labels can be placed just after S(I) is determined—that is, between lines 150 and 160.

Although these changes result in a shorter program, it is not necessarily better. In the program as given each of the two subtasks (steps (a) and (b)) in the algorithm occupies its own part of the program. (The REM statements in lines 100 and 170 identify these program segments.) That the resulting program may not be the shortest possible is of little consequence. The longer program obtained by segmenting is easier to read and certainly easier to modify, should that be required. The axiom "the shorter the better" is not always valid in programming.

When a subscripted variable such as B(1,1) is used in a program, the largest subscript allowed is 10. However, just as for singly subscripted variables, the DIM statement may be used to specify larger subscripts. For example, if A is to be an array with as many as 50 rows and 20 columns, then the statement

```
DIM A(50,20)
```

would be used. Both one- and two-dimensional arrays may be dimensioned with the same DIM statement.

```
10 DIM Z(15),M(25,30),A(20),N(100,45)
```

is a proper DIM statement; it reserves 15 memory locations for the one-dimensional array Z, $25 \times 30 = 750$ locations for the two-dimensional array M, 20 locations for the array A, and $100 \times 45 = 4500$ locations for the array N.

Many programming applications involve rearranging the entries in arrays. We saw one such situation in Section 11.4 where the entries in a one-dimensional array were rearranged to yield an array whose entries were in increasing or decreasing order. We conclude this chapter with two examples illustrating the rearrangement of entries in two-dimensional arrays.

EXAMPLE 11. Here is a program segment to interchange rows K and L of an N-by-N array A.

```
200 FOR J=1 TO N
210    LET T=A(K,J)
220    LET A(K,J)=A(L,J)
230    LET A(L,J)=T
240 NEXT J
```

When J = 1, the three statements in the range of the loop interchange A(K,1) and A(L,1), the first entries in the Kth and Lth rows of A. When J = 2, the second entries A(K,2) and A(L,2) are interchanged. Similar statements apply for J = 3, 4, . . . , N.

EXAMPLE 12. Here is a self-explanatory program.

```
100 DIM A(4,4)
110 REM READ VALUES FOR ARRAY A, ROW BY ROW
120 FOR I=1 TO 4
130    FOR J=1 TO 4
140       READ A(I,J)
150    NEXT J
160 NEXT I
170 REM FIND THE ROW NUMBER K OF THE ROW OF A
180 REM WITH THE LARGEST FIRST VALUE A(K,1)
190 LET K=1
```

```
200 FOR I=2 TO 4
210    IF A(I,1)>A(K,1) THEN LET K=I
220 NEXT I
230 REM INTERCHANGE ROW K AND ROW 1
240 FOR J=1 TO 4
250    LET T=A(K,J)
260    LET A(K,J)=A(1,J)
270    LET A(1,J)=T
280 NEXT J
290 REM PRINT THE MODIFIED ARRAY A, ROW BY ROW
300 FOR I=1 TO 4
310    FOR J=1 TO 4
320       PRINT A(I,J);
330    NEXT J
340    PRINT
350 NEXT I
500 DATA 22.25,21.75,28.63,29.84
510 DATA 61.20,55.40,59.55,62.33
520 DATA 33.35,42.78,39.25,48.62
530 DATA 44.45,43.25,27.62,39.00
999 END
RUN

 61.20    55.40    59.55    62.33
 22.25    21.75    28.63    29.84
 33.35    42.78    39.25    48.62
 44.45    43.25    27.62    39.00
READY
```

11.7 Problems

1. What will be printed when each program is run?

a.
```
100 FOR I=1 TO 4
110    FOR J=1 TO 4
120       LET M(I,J)=I*J
130    NEXT J
140 NEXT I
150 FOR K=1 TO 4
160    PRINT M(K,K);
170 NEXT K
180 END
```

b.
```
100 FOR I=1 TO 3
110    FOR J=1 TO 2
120       READ A(I,J)
130       LET B(J,I)=A(I,J)
140    NEXT J
150 NEXT I
160 PRINT B(2,1);B(2,2);B(2,3)
170 DATA 1,2,3,4,5,6,7,8,9
180 END
```

c.
```
100 FOR K=1 TO 3
110    FOR L=1 TO K
120       READ S(K,L)
130       LET S(L,K)=S(K,L)
140    NEXT L
150 NEXT K
160 FOR N=1 TO 3
170    PRINT S(N,2);
180 NEXT N
190 DATA 1,1,1,2,2,2,3,3,3
200 END
```

d.
```
110 READ X,Y
120 FOR J=1 TO X
130    FOR K=1 TO Y-J
140       READ M(J,K)
150       PRINT M(J,K)-K;
160    NEXT K
170    PRINT
180 NEXT J
190 DATA 2,3,9,3,6,8,2,4,3,1
200 END
```

```
e. 100 DIM M(4,4)
   110 FOR I=1 TO 4
   120    FOR J=1 TO 4
   130       IF I>J THEN LET M(I,J)=0 ELSE LET M(I,J)=1
   140       PRINT M(I,J);
   150    NEXT J
   160    PRINT
   170 NEXT I
   180 END
```

```
f. 110 FOR X=1 TO 3
   120    FOR Y=1 TO 4
   130       READ A(X,Y)
   135       LET B(X,Y)=A(X,Y)
   140       IF (X+Y)/2=INT((X+Y)/2) THEN LET B(X,Y)=0
   150       PRINT B(X,Y);
   160    NEXT Y
   170    RESTORE
   180    PRINT
   190 NEXT X
   200 DATA 2,8,7,3,4,6,9
   210 END
```

2. Find and correct the errors in the following program segments. You are to assume that values have already been assigned to the 5-by-5 array A.

```
a. 200 REM PRINT THE SUM S        b. 200 REM INTERCHANGE THE ROWS
   210 REM OF EACH ROW OF A          210 REM AND COLUMNS OF A
   220 LET S=0                       220 FOR I=1 TO 5
   230 FOR I=1 TO 5                   230    FOR J=1 TO 5
   240    FOR J=1 TO 5                240       LET T=A(I,J)
   250       LET S=S+A(I,J)          250       LET A(I,J)=A(J,I)
   260    NEXT J                      260       LET A(J,I)=T
   270    PRINT S                     270    NEXT J
   280 NEXT I                         280 NEXT I
```

Write a program to perform each task specified in Problems 3–20.

3. Read 16 values into the 4 × 4 array M. The array M is then to be printed. In addition, the four column sums are to be printed below their respective columns.
4. Repeat Problem 3 for an N × N array M in which N can be any integer up to 6. (Use the TAB function so that columns will line up.)
5. Read 16 values into the 4 × 4 array M. Then print the array. Row sums are to be printed to the right of their respective rows and column sums below their respective columns.
6. Repeat Problem 5 for an N × N array M in which N can be any number up to 6. (Use the TAB function.)
7. Values are to be read into an N × N array A. Then the sum of the entries in the upper-left to lower-right diagonal of A is to be printed. This sum is called the *trace* of the array (matrix) A. (N is to be input before the array values are read. You may assume that N will never exceed 6.)
8. Values are to be read into an N × N array A. The product of the entries in the upper-left to lower-right diagonal of A is to be printed. (Assume N ≤ 6.)
9. The *transpose* B of an N × N array A is the N × N array whose rows are the columns of A in the same order. Read the entries of A from DATA lines, and print the transpose B. (You may assume that N will be less than 6.)
10. The *sum* S of two N × N arrays A and B is the N × N array whose entries are the sums of the corresponding entries of A and B. Read A and B from DATA lines, and print the arrays A, B, and S. (You may assume that N will be less than 6.)
11. Read values into a 3 × 6 array B. The computer is then to perform the following tasks:
    a. Create and print a one-dimensional array whose Ith position contains the average of the 6 elements in the Ith row of B.
    b. Create and print another 3 × 6 array Z whose values are the values of B reduced by the average of all elements in B.

12. Create the following 5 × 5 array N:

```
  0   1   1   1   1
 -1   0   1   1   1
 -1  -1   0   1   1
 -1  -1  -1   0   1
 -1  -1  -1  -1   0
```

The values N(I,J) are to be determined during program execution without using READ or INPUT statements. The array N should be printed as it appears above. (*Hint:* The value to be assigned to N(I,J) can be determined by comparing I with J.)

13. Read values into a 5-by-3 array N. Then print the subscripts corresponding to the largest entry in N. If this largest value appears in N more than once, more than one pair of subscripts must be printed. Use the following algorithm.
   a. Read values for array N.
   b. Determine M, the largest number in array N.
   c. Print those subscripts I,J for which N(I,J) = M.

14. Read values into a 5-by-3 array N. Print the row of N with the smallest first entry. If this smallest value is the first entry in more than one row, print only the first of these rows. Then, interchange this row with the first row and print the modified array N. Use the following algorithm.
   a. Read values for array N.
   b. Find the first K such that row K has the smallest first entry.
   c. Print row K.
   d. Interchange rows 1 and K.
   e. Print the modified array N.

15. Read values into a 5-by-3 array A. Rearrange the rows of A so that their first entries are in ascending order. Print the modified array, row by row. (Use a bubble sort to place the first-column entries A(1,1), A(2,1), A(3,1), A(4,1), A(5,1) in ascending order. However, instead of swapping A(I,1) and A(I + 1,1) whenever they are out of order, you must interchange all of row I with row I + 1.)

16. Modify your program for Problem 15 to handle M-by-N arrays rather than just 5-by-3 arrays.

17. Read N pairs of numbers into an N-by-2 array A. Sort these pairs (that is, the rows of A) so that the first column entries are in ascending order and also so that A(I,2) ≤ A(I + 1,2) whenever A(I,1) = A(I + 1,1). (Use a bubble sort that will place the first-column entries A(1,1), A(2,1), . . . , A(N,1) in ascending order with the following modification. If A(I,1) > A(I + 1,1), swap rows I and I + 1; if A(I,1) < A(I + 1,1), no swap is necessary; otherwise—that is, if A(I,1) = A(I + 1,1)—swap only if A(1,2) > A(I + 1,2).)

18. An N × N array of numbers is called a *magic square* if the sums of each row, each column, and each diagonal are all equal. Test any N × N array in which N will never exceed 10. Values for N and array values should be input. Be sure to print out and identify all row, column, and diagonal sums, the array itself, and a message indicating whether or not the array is a magic square. Try your program on the following arrays.

```
a. 11  10   4  23  17          b.    4  139  161   26  174  147
   18  12   6   5  24              85  166  107  188   93   12
   25  19  13   7   1              98  152  138    3  103  157
    2  21  20  14   8             179   17   84  165  184   22
    9   3  22  16  15             183   21   13  175   89  170
                                  102  156  148   94    8  143
```

19. Five numbers are to be input to produce a five-column table as follows. The first column is to contain the five numbers in the order they are input. The second column is to contain the four differences of successive values in the first column. For example, if the first column contains 2 4 8 9 3, the second column will contain 2 4 1 -6. In the same way, each of columns 3 through 5 is to contain the differences of successive values in the column before it. Thus, if the values 1, 5, 9, 6, 12 are input, the output should be

```
 1    4    0   -7   23
 5    4   -7   16
 9   -3    9
 6    6
12
```

In the following suggested algorithm, K denotes a 5-by-5 array.
a. Input the first column of K.
b. Generate the remaining four columns of K as specified in the problem statement.
c. Print the table as specified.

20. N numbers are to be input to produce a table of differences as described in Problem 19. Assume that N is an integer from 2 to 10.

11.8 Review true-or-false quiz

1. Dimension statements may appear anywhere in a program as long as they appear before the arrays being dimensioned are used.   T F
2. The two programming lines

    ```
    100 DIM A(25)
    110 LET A=0
    ```

    will assign the value 0 to all 25 positions in the array A.   T F
3. If in an array Z the only locations to be used are Z(8), Z(9), Z(10), Z(11), and Z(12), there is no need to dimension Z since only five locations are needed.   T F
4. Once array L is assigned values in a program, the statement PRINT L is sufficient to cause the entire array to be printed.   T F
5. The programming line 50 LET A(I + 1) = 7 could never cause an error message to be printed.   T F
6. If a noninteger subscript is encountered during program execution, an error message will be printed and the program run will terminate.   T F
7. The statement LET G = 5 may appear in a program that contains the statement DIM G(100).   T F
8. Array values may be assigned by LET statements.   T F
9. Since two-dimensional arrays make use of two subscripts, they must be used in nested loops.   T F
10. If both one- and two-dimensional arrays are to be used in a program, two DIM statements must be used.   T F
11. The bubble sort is always used to arrange the terms of a list in ascending order.   T F
12. A FOR/NEXT loop can be used to read values from DATA lines only if a count of how many values are to be read is included.   T F

Processing String Data

The applications of strings encountered thus far have been limited. You have seen how string values can be assigned to string variables by LET, INPUT, and READ statements, how the contents of string variables can be printed, and how strings can be compared in relational expressions to determine if they are equal or not equal. In this chapter the topic of string variables is expanded. You will see how strings can be compared by using any of the relational operators =, <>, <, <=, >, and >= (Section 12.1), and how lists of strings can be processed by using subscripted string variables (Section 12.3).

BASIC also includes special string functions and string operations to assist you in many programming tasks involving string data. You will see how these string functions and operations can be used to examine the individual characters in a string and to build new strings from old ones. String functions and operations are described in Sections 12.5–12.9.

12.1 Strings in relational expressions

You will recall that strings can be compared for equality in IF statements. The following program reviews how BASIC tests for equality.

EXAMPLE 1

```
10 PRINT "TYPE FINI TO END THIS PROGRAM"
20 INPUT A$
30    IF A$="FINI" THEN 60
40    PRINT A$
50 GO TO 20
60 PRINT "ADIOS"
70 END
```

```
                    RUN

                    TYPE FINI TO END THIS PROGRAM
                    ? HELLO
                    HELLO
                    ? GOODBYE
                    GOODBYE
                    ? "   FINI"
                       FINI
                    ? FINI
                    ADIOS
                    READY
```

Remark 1   Recall that for two strings to be equal, they must be identical. Thus, "   FINI" is not equal to "FINI", since the first begins with blanks and the second does not.

Remark 2   When strings appear in relational expressions ("FINI" in line 30), quotation marks must be used.

BASIC allows strings to be compared by using any of the relational operators $=$, $<>$, $<$, $<=$, $>$, and $>=$. Thus, M\$ $<$ A\$ is an admissible relational expression. But to understand when one string is less than another string, you should have some knowledge of the method used to store a string in memory. Whenever a program requires the use of a string, each character of the string is assigned a numerical value, called its **numeric code.** It is these numerical values that are compared. As one would expect, the numeric code for the letter A is smaller than that for B, the numeric code for B is smaller than that for C, and so on. But it is not only letters that can be compared; each BASIC character has its own unique numeric code so that any two characters may be compared. One BASIC character is less than a second character if the numeric code of the first is less than the numeric code of the second.

Unfortunately, computer systems differ in their numeric codes. The *ordering* or *collating sequence* of the BASIC character set as given by the American Standard Code of Information Interchange (ASCII) is presented in Table 12.1. In what follows, this ordering sequence is assumed.

Using this ASCII ordering sequence, we can write the following.

"G" $<$ "P" since $71 < 80$.
"4" $<$ "Y" since $52 < 89$.
"\$" $<$ "↑" since $36 < 94$.
"8" $<$ "?" since $56 < 63$.

If strings containing more than one character are to be compared, they are compared character by character beginning at the left. Strings consisting only of letters of the alphabet are ordered just as they would appear in a dictionary.

TABLE 12.1   ASCII numeric codes for the BASIC character set.

Character	Numeric code	Character	Numeric code	Character	Numeric code
(blank)	32	5	53	J	74
!	33	6	54	K	75
"	34	7	55	L	76
#	35	8	56	M	77
$	36	9	57	N	78
%	37	:	58	O	79
&	38	;	59	P	80
'	39	<	60	Q	81
(	40	=	61	R	82
)	41	>	62	S	83
*	42	?	63	T	84
+	43	@	64	U	85
,	44	A	65	V	86
–	45	B	66	W	87
.	46	C	67	X	88
/	47	D	68	Y	89
0	48	E	69	Z	90
1	49	F	70	[	91
2	50	G	71	\	92
3	51	H	72	]	93
4	52	I	73	↑	94

EXAMPLE 2. Here are some relational expressions with their truth values.

Relational expression	Truth value
"AMA" > "AM"	True
"XYZW" > "XYZZE"	False
"1234" <= "1234"	True
"13N" > "14A"	False
"M24" <= "M31"	True
"P1" < "M394"	False
"BEAL TOM" < "BEALS TOM"	True

In the last expression, the fifth character in "BEAL TOM" is the blank character (ASCII code 32), whereas the fifth character in "BEALS TOM" is S (ASCII code 83). Since 32 < 83, the relational expression is true.

Caution

If your system does not use the ASCII collating sequence, you may find that the numeric code used for the blank character is larger than the code for S. If so, your computer will determine "BEAL TOM" < "BEALS TOM" as false.

EXAMPLE 3. Here is a program to print those words appearing in a data list that begin with the letter "B".

```
100 READ W$
110    IF W$="END OF LIST" THEN 999
120    IF (W$>="B") AND (W$<"C") THEN PRINT W$,
130 GO TO 100
500 DATA WHITE,BLACK,YELLOW,RED,BLUE,ORANGE,GREEN,PURPLE
510 DATA PINK,GRAY,MAGENTA,BEIGE,BROWN,VIOLET,LIME,AVOCADO
998 DATA "END OF LIST"
999 END
```

```
        RUN

        BLACK          BLUE          BEIGE          BROWN
        READY
```

A word from the data list is read into W$ and is immediately compared with the EOD tag "END OF LIST". (This EOD tag is not a member of the list being searched.) If W$<"B" it is not printed since its first letter must be an A. Similarly, if W$> = "C", it is rejected because its first letter must be C, D, E, . . . , or Z.

12.2 Problems

1. What will be printed when each program is run?
   a. ```
       10 FOR I=1 TO 3
       20   READ A$,B$
       30   IF A$<=B$ THEN PRINT A$
       40 NEXT I
       50 DATA A,AA,M,MO,M,KANT
       60 END
       ```
   b.  ```
       10 FOR J=1 TO 3
       20     READ C$,D$
       30     IF C$>D$ THEN LET C$=D$
       40     PRINT C$,D$
       50 NEXT J
       60 DATA CAT,DOG,"7","9",MAN,BEAST
       70 END
       ```
   c. ```
       10 LET M$="MIDDLE"
       20   READ A$
       30   IF A$="*" THEN STOP
       40   IF (A$>M$) AND (A$<"ZZZ") THEN LET A$="LAST"
       50   PRINT A$
       60 GO TO 20
       70 DATA HARRY, ALICE, PAUL, ROSE,"*"
       80 END
       ```

Write programs to perform each task specified in Problems 2–8.

2. A list of numbers appears in DATA lines. The user should be allowed to issue any of the following commands: LIST, to print the list of numbers; SUM, to print the sum of the numbers; AVERAGE, to print the average of the numbers; DONE, to terminate the run. After each command other than DONE is carried out, the user should be allowed to issue another command.
3. A list of English words is presented in DATA lines. Print those that begin with the letter G.
4. A list of English words is presented in DATA lines. Print those that begin with a letter from D to M, and then print a message telling how many words were printed and how many were in the given list.
5. A list of English words is presented in DATA lines. Print those whose first two letters are "TO".
6. For any string typed at the terminal, the computer is to print "THE FIRST CHARACTER IS A LETTER" or "THE FIRST CHARACTER IS NOT A LETTER", whichever message is correct. A user should be allowed to type many strings during a single program run, and the program should halt when "DONE" is typed.
7. A list of English words is presented in DATA lines. If any one of the words begins with the letter Y, all words beginning with the letter Y should be printed. However, if no word begins with the letter Y, the entire list should be printed.
8. A list of English words is presented in DATA lines. A user should be allowed to type any two words to obtain a listing of all words alphabetically between them. The program should halt when both input words are the same.
       ```

12.3 Subscripted string variables

BASIC allows you to use arrays to process lists of strings, such as names, rather than just lists of numbers. The symbols A\$, B\$, . . . , Z\$ are used as the names of arrays whose entries are strings.

The entries in string arrays are referenced just as entries in numerical arrays are referenced. Thus, if A\$ denotes a one-dimensional array, the subscripted variable A\$(7) denotes the seventh entry in A\$. If J = 7, then A\$(J) also denotes the seventh entry.

EXAMPLE 4. Here is a program to read ten names into an array A\$ and then search this array for any names typed at the terminal. The program will terminate when the word "DONE" is typed.

```
100 REM READ NAMES INTO THE ARRAY A$
110 FOR I=1 TO 10
120     READ A$(I)
130 NEXT I
140 REM SEARCH A$ FOR ANY NAME TYPED AT THE TERMINAL
150 PRINT "TYPE NAMES EXACTLY AS FOLLOWS"
160 PRINT "FIRST NAME (SINGLE SPACE) LAST NAME"
170 PRINT "TYPE 'DONE' WHEN FINISHED"
180 INPUT N$
190 IF N$="DONE" THEN 999
200 FOR I=1 TO 10
210     IF N$<>A$(I) THEN 240
220     PRINT N$;" IS IN THE LIST."
230     GO TO 180
240 NEXT I
250 PRINT N$;" IS NOT IN THE LIST."
260 GO TO 180
500 DATA ABRAHAM LINCOLN, ANDREW JOHNSON
510 DATA ULYSSES GRANT, RUTHERFORD HAYES
520 DATA JAMES GARFIELD, CHESTER ARTHUR
530 DATA GROVER CLEVELAND, BENJAMIN HARRISON
540 DATA WILLIAM MCKINLEY, THEODORE ROOSEVELT
999 END
RUN

TYPE NAMES EXACTLY AS FOLLOWS
FIRST NAME (SINGLE SPACE) LAST NAME
TYPE 'DONE' WHEN FINISHED
? LINCOLN
LINCOLN IS NOT IN THE LIST.
? ABRAHAM LINCOLN
ABRAHAM LINCOLN IS IN THE LIST.
? DONE
READY
```

EXAMPLE 5

Let's write a program to help a chemistry student learn the abbreviations for 12 of the basic elements in the periodic table. The computer is to type the element name, and the student is to respond with the correct abbreviation. If the abbreviation is wrong, the message INCORRECT should be printed with the correct abbreviation before the student goes on to the next element.

Problem analysis

Let's use the following variable names.

E$(I) = the Ith basic element in the periodic table.
A$(I) = the abbreviation of the Ith element.
  B$ = the abbreviation the student will type.

The arrays E$ and A$ will be read from DATA lines that will contain the elements and their standard abbreviations. Then, the element names will be printed one at a time in a FOR/NEXT loop. After each E$(I)—that is, each element—is printed, the student will type an abbreviation for the element, which will be assigned to B$. B$ will then be compared with A$(I). If they are equal, the next E$(I) will appear. If not, the message will be printed according to the problem description. The following algorithm also determines a count of the number of correct answers.

Algorithm

a. Print a message to the user describing what the program does.
b. Initialize T = 0 (counts number of wrong answers).
c. Read the elements and abbreviations into arrays E$ and A$, respectively.
d. Print the element names one by one, asking for the appropriate abbreviation. If the answer is incorrect, add 1 to T and print the correct abbreviation before going on to the next element.
e. Print the student's score (12 − T), and stop.

The program

```
100 PRINT "THIS PROGRAM WILL PRINT THE NAMES OF 12"
110 PRINT "ELEMENTS FROM THE PERIODIC TABLE. YOU ARE"
120 PRINT "TO RESPOND WITH THE CORRECT ABBREVIATIONS."
130 PRINT
140 REM T COUNTS THE NUMBER OF WRONG ANSWERS
150 LET T=0
160 REM READ ELEMENTS AND ABBREVIATIONS INTO ARRAYS E$ AND A$
170 DIM E$(12),A$(12)
180 FOR I=1 TO 12
190    READ E$(I),A$(I)
200 NEXT I
210 REM PRINT THE ELEMENTS ONE BY ONE AND WAIT
220 REM FOR AN ABBREVIATION TO BE INPUT
230 FOR I=1 TO 12
240    PRINT E$(I);
250    INPUT B$
260    IF B$=A$(I) THEN 290
270    PRINT "INCORRECT",A$(I)
280    LET T=T+1
290 NEXT I
300 PRINT
310 PRINT "YOUR SCORE IS"; 12-T;"CORRECT OUT OF 12"
```

```
500 DATA ALUMINUM,AL,GOLD,AU,SILVER,AG
510 DATA BORON,B,BROMINE,BR,CARBON,C
520 DATA COPPER,CU,CALCIUM,CA,COBALT,CO
530 DATA CHROMIUM,CR,CHLORINE,CL,HYDROGEN,H
999 END
RUN

THIS PROGRAM WILL PRINT THE NAMES OF 12
ELEMENTS FROM THE PERIODIC TABLE. YOU ARE
TO RESPOND WITH THE CORRECT ABBREVIATIONS.

ALUMINUM? AL
GOLD? GO
INCORRECT          AU
SILVER? AG
BORON? B
BROMINE? BR
CARBON? C
COPPER? CU
CALCIUM? CAL
INCORRECT          CA
COBALT? CO
CHROMIUM? CR
CHLORINE? CHL
INCORRECT          CL
HYDROGEN? H

YOUR SCORE IS 9 CORRECT OUT OF 12
READY
```

It is often necessary to arrange lists of strings in some specified order (for example, lists of names in alphabetical order). The bubble sort algorithm shown in Section 11.4 can also be used with lists of strings. The only change needed is to replace the numerical-variable names with string-variable names.

EXAMPLE 6. Here is a program to alphabetize any list of words typed at the terminal. The list is to be terminated by typing FINI.

```
100 REM BUBBLE SORT AS APPLIED TO STRINGS
110 DIM A$(50)
120 PRINT "ENTER YOUR LIST. TYPE FINI TO END."
130 FOR I=1 TO 50
140    INPUT A$(I)
150    IF A$(I)="FINI" THEN 190
160 NEXT I
170 PRINT "I CAN ONLY HANDLE 49 WORDS"
180 STOP
190 LET N=I-1
```

```
200 REM ALPHABETIZE THE N WORD ARRAY A$
210 FOR J=1 TO N-1
220    FOR I=1 TO N-J
230       IF A$(I)<=A$(I+1) THEN 270
240       LET T$=A$(I)
250       LET A$(I)=A$(I+1)
260       LET A$(I+1)=T$
270    NEXT I
280 NEXT J
290 REM PRINT THE ALPHABETIZED LIST
300 PRINT
310 PRINT "THE ALPHABETIZED LIST"
320 FOR I=1 TO N
330    PRINT A$(I)
340 NEXT I
999 END
RUN

ENTER YOUR LIST. TYPE FINI TO END.
? LINCOLN
? JOHNSON
? GRANT
? HAYES
? GARFIELD
? FINI

THE ALPHABETIZED LIST
GARFIELD
GRANT
HAYES
JOHNSON
LINCOLN
READY
```

Note that the temporary variable in lines 240 and 260 is T$ and not T. *Strings* must be assigned to string variables and *numbers* to numerical variables.

12.4 Problems

1. What will be printed when each program is run?

   a.
   ```
   10 FOR I=1 TO 3
   20    READ M$(I)
   30 NEXT I
   40 FOR J=3 TO 1 STEP -1
   50    IF M$(J)<="ROBERTS" THEN PRINT M$(J)
   60 NEXT J
   70 DATA ALBERT,ZIP,ROBERT
   80 END
   ```

   b.
   ```
   10 FOR J=1 TO 4
   20    READ X$
   30    IF X$="HAT" THEN RESTORE ELSE LET A$(J)=X$
   40 NEXT J
   50 FOR J=1 TO 3
   60    PRINT A$(J);
   70 NEXT J
   80 DATA AB,MAN,CAT,HAT
   90 END
   ```

```
c. 10 FOR J=1 TO 4
   20    READ F$(J),L$(J)
   30 NEXT J
   40 FOR I=4 TO 1 STEP -1
   50    PRINT L$(I);",";F$(I)
   60 NEXT I
   70 DATA JOHN,CASH,ELTON,JOHN
   80 DATA JOHN,DENVER,JOHN,PAYCHECK
   90 END
```

Write a program to perform each task specified in Problems 2–12.

2. A list of names in the form "Last, First" is presented in DATA lines. A user should be allowed to issue any of the following commands: LIST, to print the list in the order given in the DATA lines; SORTLIST, to print the list in alphabetical order; and DONE, to terminate the run. After any command other than DONE, the user should be allowed to issue another command.

3. Last year's sales report of the J. T. Pencil Company reads as follows.

January	$32,350	July	$22,000
February	$16,440	August	$43,500
March	$18,624	September	$51,400
April	$26,100	October	$29,000
May	$30,500	November	$20,100
June	$28,600	December	$27,500

Produce a two-column report with the headings MONTH and SALES. Sales figures are to appear in descending order. Include the given data in DATA lines with the months JANUARY through DECEMBER appearing first and the 12 sales figures following.

4. Compute the semester averages for all students in a psychology class. A separate DATA line should be used for each student and should contain the student's name and five grades. A typical DATA line might read

```
700 DATA "LINCOLN JOHN",72,79,88,97,90
```

The output should be in tabular form, with the two column headings STUDENT and SEMESTER AVERAGE. Semester averages are to appear in descending order.

5. Modify Problem 4 so that the table is printed with the students' names in alphabetical order.

6. Modify Problem 4 as follows. A letter grade should be given according to the following table.

Average	Grade
90–100	A
80–89	B
70–79	C
60–69	D
Below 60	E

The five strings A, B, C, D, and E should be read into an array N$. The output should be in tabular form with the two column headings STUDENT and LETTER GRADE. (No sorting is required for this problem.)

7. Allow a user to create an array L$ of words as follows. The computer is to request (INPUT statement) that a word be typed. If the word has not already been typed, it should be added to the array; if it has, then it should be ignored. In either case the user should then be allowed to enter another word. However, if the user types the word LIST, the array L$ created to that point should be printed and another request made. If the user types END, the program run should terminate.

8. A list of N names appears in DATA lines ("Last,First"). Separate the names into three arrays. The first array is to contain all names A through K, the second all names L through Q, and the third all names R through Z. The three arrays are to be printed one under the other with the three headings A–K, L–Q, and R–Z.

9. Allow the user to input the names of the residents of the town of Plymouth who attended the June Town Meeting. The names are to be entered in the order in which the people arrived at the meeting. After each name the voting precinct of that resident is to be typed. (There are four precincts in Plymouth.) A typical entry will therefore be ALDEN PRISCILLA, 3. When the user types DONE,0 the program should print four lists according to precinct.

10. Using the following table, determine the batting average and slugging percentage for each player. In the table, 1B indicates a single, 2B a double, 3B a triple, HR a homerun, and AB the number of times a player has been at bat. (The table is to be presented in DATA lines, one for each player.)

$$\text{batting average} = \frac{\text{number of hits}}{\text{AB}} \qquad \text{slugging percentage} = \frac{\text{total bases}}{\text{AB}}$$

Player	1B	2B	3B	HR	AB
Gomez	100	22	1	14	444
Boyd	68	20	0	3	301
Jackson	83	15	8	7	395
O'Neil	68	22	1	8	365
Struik	65	11	3	5	310
McDuffy	54	11	4	0	256
Vertullo	78	18	1	15	418
Ryan	25	1	1	0	104
Torgeson	49	15	0	11	301
Johnson	54	5	2	0	246

Print two tables. The first should list the players in alphabetical order, with their batting averages and slugging percentages in two adjacent columns. The second table should list the players with their batting averages and slugging percentages but in order of decreasing batting average.

11. A list of names is presented in DATA lines. A typical DATA statement might be

```
500 DATA STAN,MUSIAL,GEORGE,RUTH
```

The user should be allowed to issue any of the following commands: LIST, to print the names in the order given in the DATA lines (each line of the output is to contain a first name and a last name separated by one blank space); PRINTSORT, to print the names in alphabetical order (DOM DIMAGGIO would appear before JOE DIMAGGIO); END, to terminate the run.

12. Write a program to produce each of the following designs. When needed, the strings "A", "B", "C", . . . , "G" are to be read from DATA lines.

```
a. A                          b. ABCDEFG
   BB                            BCDEFG
   CCC                           CDEFG
   DDDD                          DEFG
   EEEEE                         EFG
   FFFFFF                        FG
                                 G
```

```
c. A A A A                    d. CCCCCCCC
    B B B                        C
    C C C C                      C
     D D D                       C
    E E E                        CCCCCCCC
```

```
e.    A                       f.     A
     B B                            BBB
    C   C                          CCCCC
    D   D                          DDDDDD
    E       E  (Use TAB function.)  EEEEEEEEE  (Use TAB function.)
```

12.5 String functions

Four of the most useful **string functions** are described in this section. The first determines the length of a string, and the other three are used to examine individual characters or groups of characters in a string.

The STRING function LEN

The value of LEN(A$) is the number of characters in the string A$. For this reason it is called the LENGTH function.

EXAMPLE 7

```
10 LET Z$="JOHN AND MARY"
20 LET A=LEN(Z$)
30 PRINT A
40 END
RUN

 13
READY
```

As always, blanks contained in quoted strings are counted as characters.

EXAMPLE 8. Here is a program to print only those strings that contain exactly three characters.

```
10 FOR I=1 TO 6
20    READ X$
30     IF LEN(X$)=3 THEN PRINT X$
40 NEXT I
50 DATA "THE","I DO","ONE","OLD ","THREE","127"
60 END
RUN

THE
ONE
127
READY
```

Note that "I DO" has four characters—three letters and an embedded blank. Similarly, "OLD " has a trailing blank character.

The STRING function LEFT$

The value of LEFT$(A$,N) is the string consisting of the first N characters of A$. (Some systems use a **substring qualifier** A$(I:J) to indicate the substring in the Ith through the Jth positions of A$. On such systems use A$(1:N) instead of LEFT$(A$,N).)

EXAMPLE 9

```
10 LET Y$="SEVEN"
20 FOR N=1 TO LEN(Y$)
30    PRINT LEFT$(Y$,N)
40 NEXT N
50 END
RUN

S
SE
SEV
SEVE
SEVEN
READY
```

(On systems using the substring qualifier, use 30 PRINT Y$(1:N) in place of line 30.)

EXAMPLE 10. Here is a program to print only those words that begin with whatever prefix is input by a user.

```
100 PRINT "TYPE A PREFIX";
110 INPUT P$
120 PRINT
130 FOR K=1 TO 10
140    READ A$
150    IF LEFT$(A$,LEN(P$))=P$ THEN PRINT A$
160 NEXT K
170 DATA ENABLE,ENACT,ENGAGE,ENSURE,ENDORSE
180 DATA OBCLUDE,OBDURATE,OBJECT,REACT,RECISION
190 END
RUN

TYPE A PREFIX? OB

OBCLUDE
OBDURATE
OBJECT
READY
```

(On systems using the substring qualifier, LEFT$(A$,LEN(P$)) would be replaced by A$(1:LEN(P$)).)

The STRING function RIGHT$

The value of RIGHT$(A$,N) is the string consisting of all characters in A$ from the Nth character on. (*Caution:* Some systems use RIGHT$(A$,N) to denote the string consisting of the last N characters of A$.)

EXAMPLE 11

```
10 LET Y$="SEVEN"
20 FOR N=1 TO LEN(Y$)
30    PRINT RIGHT$(Y$,N)
40 NEXT N
50 END

SEVEN
EVEN
VEN
EN
N
READY
```

(On systems using the substring qualifier, use 30 PRINT Y$(N:LEN(Y$)) in place of line 30.)

The STRING function MID(dle)$

The value of MID$(A$,I,J) is the string of J characters from A$ beginning with the Ith character of A$.

EXAMPLE 12

```
10 LET Y$="ABCD"
20 FOR I=1 TO LEN(Y$)
30    PRINT MID$(Y$,I,1)
40 NEXT I
50 END
RUN

A
B
C
D
READY
```

(On systems using the substring qualifier, use 30 PRINT Y$(I:I).)

EXAMPLE 13. Here is a program to count the number of As in a string A$ of any length.

```
100 LET C=0
110 INPUT A$
120 FOR I=1 TO LEN(A$)
130    IF MID$(A$,I,1)="A" THEN LET C=C+1
140 NEXT I
150 PRINT "NUMBER OF A'S IS";C
160 END
RUN

? ABACADABRA
NUMBER OF A'S IS 5
READY
```

(On systems using the substring qualifier, use 130 IF A$(I:I) = "A" THEN LET C = C + 1.)

The string functions LEN, LEFT$, RIGHT$, and MID$ can also be used with arrays whose entries are strings. For example, if L$ has been dimensioned as a string array, then

LEN(L$(I))	gives the number of characters in the string L$(I).
LEFT$(L$(I),3)	gives the 3-character string consisting of the first three characters in L$(I). (The corresponding substring qualifier is L$(I)(1:3).)
RIGHT$(L$(I),5)	gives the string consisting of all characters in L$(I) from the fifth character on. (The corresponding substring qualifier is L$(I)(5:LEN(L$(I)).)
MID$(L$(I),M,N)	gives the string of N characters in L$(I) beginning with the Mth character. (The corresponding substring qualifier is L$(I)(M:M + N − 1).)

We conclude this section with an example illustrating the use of string functions with arrays.

EXAMPLE 14. A list of ten words appears in DATA lines. Print those containing the 4-letter sequence TION followed by those containing the 2-letter sequence IS.

Problem analysis   Let's begin with the following simple algorithm.

a. Read the 10 words into an array L$.
b. For I = 1 to 10, print L$(I) if L$(I) contains TION.
c. For I = 1 to 10, print L$(I) if L$(I) contains IS.
d. Stop.

Step (a) is easily coded:

```
100 REM READ 10 WORDS INTO ARRAY L$
110 DIM L$(10)
```

```
120 FOR I=1 TO 10
130    READ L$(I)
140 NEXT I
```

Writing a program segment to carry out step (b) requires that we compare the successive 4-character sequences in L$(I) with the string TION. For example, if L$(I) = "EXHIBITIONIST", we can compare the string TION with EXHI, XHIB, HIBI, and so on. The first of these 4-character sequences is given by MID$(L$(I),1,4), the second by MID$(L$(I),2,4), the third by MID$(L$(I),3,4), and so on. Since LEN(L$(I)) denotes the number of characters in L$(I), the last 4-character sequence in L$(I) is given by MID$(L$(I),LEN(L$(I))-3,4). Thus, to determine if L$(I) contains TION, we can compare TION with MID$(L$(I),J,4) for J = 1,2, . . . , LEN(L$(I))-3. If a match is found, L$(I) should be printed and no further comparisons made. Lines 150 to 260 of the following program use this method to carry out step (b) of the algorithm.

A similar analysis applies to step (c) whose code is shown in lines 270 to 390 of the program.

The program

```
100 REM ***** READ 10 WORDS INTO ARRAY L$ *****
110 DIM L$(10)
120 FOR I=1 TO 10
130    READ L$(I)
140 NEXT I
150 REM ***** PRINT WORDS IN L$ THAT CONTAIN "TION"
160 PRINT "WORDS CONTAINING TION"
170 PRINT
180 FOR I=1 TO 10
190    FOR J=1 TO LEN(L$(I))-3
200       IF MID$(L$(I),J,4)="TION" THEN 240
210    NEXT J
220    REM L$(I) DOES NOT CONTAIN "TION"
230    GO TO 260
240    REM L$(I) CONTAINS "TION"
250    PRINT L$(I)
260 NEXT I
270 REM ***** PRINT WORDS IN L$ THAT CONTAIN "IS"
280 PRINT
290 PRINT "WORDS CONTAINING IS"
300 PRINT
310 FOR I=1 TO 10
320    FOR J=1 TO LEN(L$(I))-1
330       IF MID$(L$(I),J,2)="IS" THEN 370
340    NEXT J
350    REM L$(I) DOES NOT CONTAIN "IS"
360    GO TO 390
370    REM L$(I) CONTAINS "IS"
380    PRINT L$(I)
390 NEXT I
400 PRINT
500 DATA EXHIBITIONIST,DUPLICATION,DISARM,HATEFUL,LISTEN
510 DATA MULTIPLICATION,PARIS,PREDICTION,ISOLATION,MISER
999 END
```

```
RUN

WORDS CONTAINING TION

EXHIBITIONIST
DUPLICATION
MULTIPLICATION
PREDICTION
ISOLATION

WORDS CONTAINING IS

EXHIBITIONIST
DISARM
LISTEN
PARIS
ISOLATION
MISER

READY
```

Remark 1   On systems using the substring qualifier, replace MID$(L$(I),J,4) by L$(I)(J:J+3) in line 200, and MID$(L$(I),J,2) by L$(I)(J:J+1) in line 330.

Remark 2   Since TION most often occurs at the end of a word, the program could be made slightly more efficient by examining the 4-character sequences in L$(I) from the last to the first. The single change

```
190 FOR J=LEN(L$(I))-3 TO 1 STEP -1
```

accomplishes this.

12.6 Combining strings (concatenation)

The **concatenation operator +** allows you to combine two or more strings into a single string. (Some systems use the & and some use a comma instead of +.) Thus, the statement

```
LET X$="PARA"+"MEDIC"
```

assigns the string "PARAMEDIC" to the variable X$. Similarly, if A$ = "PARA" and B$ = "MEDIC" the statement

```
LET X$=A$+B$
```

does exactly the same thing.

EXAMPLE 15. Here is a program to illustrate the concatenation operator.

```
10 LET X$="BIOLOGY"
20 LET Y$="ELECTRONICS"
30 LET Z$=LEFT$(X$,3)+RIGHT$(Y$,8)
40 PRINT Z$
50 END
RUN

BIONICS
READY
```

(On systems using the substring qualifier, use 30 LET Z$ = X$(1:3) + Y$(8:LEN(Y$)).)

Using only the functions LEFT$ and RIGHT$, we could have caused BIONICS to be printed at the terminal, but we could not have assigned the string "BIONICS" to the variable Z$.

EXAMPLE 16. Here is a program to interchange the first and last names given in the string "EMILY DICKINSON".

```
100 LET A$="EMILY DICKINSON"
110 PRINT A$
120 REM FIND THE POSITION I OF THE BLANK IN A$
130 FOR I=1 TO LEN(A$)
140    IF MID$(A$,I,1)=" " THEN 160
150 NEXT I
160 REM STORE THE FIRST NAME IN F$ AND THE LAST NAME IN L$
170 LET F$=LEFT$(A$,I-1)
180 LET L$=RIGHT$(A$,I+1)
190 LET A$=L$+", "+F$
200 PRINT A$
210 END
RUN

EMILY DICKINSON
DICKINSON, EMILY
READY
```

(On systems using the substring qualifier, use A$(I:I) in line 140, A$(1:I-1) in line 170, and A$(I + 1:LEN(A$)) in line 180.)

Remark

The technique illustrated in this example has two immediate applications: it gives you additional control over the precise form of your printed output, and it allows you to alphabetize a list of names, even if first names are given first (simply interchange first and last names and then use a standard sorting algorithm to alphabetize your list).

EXAMPLE 17. Here is a program to assign the contents of A$ to B$, but in reverse order. Thus, if A$ = "AMNZ", then B$ will contain "ZNMA".

```
100 LET A$="RORRIM"
110 LET B$=""
120 REM USING THE CONCATENATION OPERATOR
130 REM "ADD" EACH OF THE CHARACTERS OF A$ TO B$
140 FOR I=LEN(A$) TO 1 STEP -1
170    LET B$=B$+MID$(A$,I,1)
180 NEXT I
190 PRINT A$;" IN REVERSE ORDER IS ";B$
200 END
RUN

RORRIM IN REVERSE ORDER IS MIRROR
READY
```

The string constant " " appearing in line 110 denotes a string containing no characters—not even the nonprinting blank character. Thus, the statement LET B$ = " " ensures that we will enter the FOR/NEXT loop that appends letters to B$ with nothing in B$.

Remark 1

The MID$ function allows you to print a given string in reverse order. The concatenation operator is what allows you to assign the new string to B$.

Remark 2

A string containing no characters is called the null (empty) string; its length is zero. Thus, if B$ = " ", then LEN(B$) = 0. The program shown in this example illustrates the principal reason that programming languages such as BASIC allow the null string. When you wish to determine a numerical sum by adding a list of numbers, you begin with a sum of zero; when you wish to build a new string by concatenating a list of characters or strings, you begin with the empty string.

12.7 Problems

1. What will be printed when each program is run?
   (For systems that use LEFT$, RIGHT$, and MID$.)
   a.
   ```
   10 LET A$="CYBERNETIC"
   20 PRINT LEFT$(A$,LEN(A$)/2)
   30 END
   ```

   b.
   ```
   10 LET B$="A TO Z"
   20 PRINT RIGHT$(B$,6);" TO ";LEFT$(B$,1)
   30 END
   ```

   c.
   ```
   10 LET A$="CONSTRUCTION"
   20 LET B$="SULTAN OF SWAT"
   30 LET C$=LEFT$(A$,3)+LEFT$(B$,5)+RIGHT$(A$,9)
   40 PRINT C$
   50 END
   ```

   d.
   ```
   10 LET A$="BIOLOGY"
   20 LET B$="PHYSICS"
   30 LET C$=LEFT$(A$,3)
   40 FOR I=1 TO LEN(B$)
   50    LET C$=C$+MID$(B$,I,1)
   60 NEXT I
   70 PRINT C$
   80 END
   ```

2. What will be printed when each program is run?
(For systems that use the substring qualifier.)

a.
```
10 LET A$="CYBERNETIC"
20 PRINT A$(1:LEN(A$)/2)
30 END
```

b.
```
10 LET B$="A TO Z"
20 PRINT B$(6:6);" TO ";B$(1:1)
30 END
```

c.
```
10 LET A$="CONSTRUCTION"
20 LET B$="SULTAN OF SWAT"
30 LET C$=A$(1:3)+B$(1:5)+A$(9:LEN(A$))
40 PRINT C$
50 END
```

d.
```
10 LET A$="BIOLOGY"
20 LET B$="PHYSICS"
30 LET C$=A$(1:3)
40 FOR I=1 TO LEN(B$)
50    LET C$=C$+B$(I:I)
60 NEXT I
70 PRINT C$
80 END
```

3. Write a single program statement to perform each of the following tasks.
a. Print the first character of A$.
b. Print the second character of A$.
c. Print the last character of A$.
d. Print the first three characters of A$.
e. Print the last three characters of A$.
f. Print the first and last characters of A$.
g. Transfer control to line 70 if A$ and B$ have the same number of characters.
h. Transfer control to line 95 if the first character of A$ equals the last character of A$.
i. Transfer control to line 160 if the first two characters of A$ are the same.
j. Assign the first N characters of A$ to B$.

4. Write a single program statement to perform each of the following tasks.
a. A$ is a two-letter string. Interchange these letters to obtain the string B$.
b. Interchange the first two characters in S$ to obtain T$.
c. Create a string F$ consisting of the first three characters of G$ and the last three characters of H$.
d. Transfer control to line 150 if the first character of A$, the second character of B$, and the third character of C$, spell "YES".

Write a program for each task specified in Problems 5–15. Do not use arrays.

5. Any five-character string input at the terminal is to be printed in reverse order. If the string does not contain exactly five characters, nothing is to be printed. A user should be allowed to try many strings, and the program should halt when the user types "DONE".

6. Any string input at the terminal is to be printed in reverse order. The program should halt only when the user types "DONE".

7. All strings appearing in DATA lines are to be examined to determine and print those that begin with whatever letter is input at the terminal. A user is to be allowed to try different letters during a single run.

8. Two five-letter words are to be input at the terminal. They are to be compared, letter by letter. If two corresponding letters are different, a dollar sign should be printed. Otherwise, the letter should be printed. For example, if "CANDY" and "CHIDE" are input, the output should be C$$D$.

9. Two words are to be input to obtain a listing of those letters in the second word that are also in the first. For example, if "STRING" and "HARNESS" are typed, the output should be RNSS, since these four letters in the second word HARNESS are also in the first.

10. A string containing two words separated by a comma is to be input. The two words are to be printed in reverse order without the comma. For example, if "GARVEY, STEVE" is typed, the output should be STEVE GARVEY.

11. Read a list of names from DATA lines. Each name is in the following form: last name, comma, first name, space, middle initial, period (BUNKER,ARCHIE Q.). The computer is then to print the names with first name first (ARCHIE Q. BUNKER). Each full name is to be read into a single string variable.

12. Input a string, and change all occurrences of the letter Y to the letter M.

13. Read a list of words from DATA lines to determine the average number of letters per word.

14. Read a list of words from DATA lines, and print out only those words with exactly N letters. N is to be input by the user, who should be allowed to try several different values for N during a single program run.

15. Read a list of strings appearing in DATA lines to determine how many times a particular letter or other character appears in this list. The letter or character is to be input by a user, who should be allowed to try several different characters during the same run. The program run should terminate whenever the user types the word END.

Write a program for each task specified in Problems 16–18. Use arrays if they help.

16. A program is to contain the following DATA lines.

```
800 DATA 9
810 DATA "MARIAN EVANS","JAMES PAYN","JOSEPH CONRAD"
820 DATA "EMILY DICKINSON","HENRY THOREAU","JOHN PAYNE"
830 DATA "JOHN FOX","MARY FREEMAN","GEORGE ELIOT"
```

The names are to be read twice. On the first pass, only those names with a last name beginning with a letter from A to M are to be printed. The remaining names are to be printed in the second pass.

17. Alphabetize the list of names given in Problem 16. Use the following algorithm.
   a. Read the names into an array A$.
   b. Create a new array B$ containing the names in A$ but with last names first.
   c. Sort B$ into alphabetical order. When a swap is made in B$, make the corresponding swap in A$.
   d. Print array A$.

18. English prose can be written in DATA lines by representing each line of text as a string occupying a single DATA line. When this is done, the last DATA line should contain a dummy value such as "END OF TEXT" as an EOD tag.

```
500 DATA "WHEN IN THE COURSE OF HUMAN EVENTS, IT BECOMES"
501 DATA "NECESSARY FOR ONE PEOPLE TO DISSOLVE THE POLITICAL"
             .
             .
             .
998 DATA "END OF TEXT"
```

You may have to restrict the length of the strings appearing in the DATA lines if your system restricts the length of strings that can be assigned to string variables. Write a program to read any such text into an array L$ to determine some or all of the following statistics.
   a. A count of the number of words of text.
   b. A count of the number of N-letter words for N = 1,2,3, ...
   c. A two-column table giving each word used and its frequency. The column of words should be in alphabetical order.
   d. A total count of the number of articles and conjunctions used. For this you should create a list of articles and conjunctions and determine how many of the words are in this list. (Be sure you include *a, an, the, and, but, however, or, nor*.)

12.8 Conversion between characters and their numeric codes

In this section we illustrate the functions **ORD** and **CHR$,** which are defined as follows.

The **ORD** function converts any character in the BASIC character set to its numeric code. Thus, if the ASCII collating sequence is used, ORD("B") = 66 and ORD(" + ") = 43. The ORD function is illustrated in Example 18.

The **CHR$** function converts any valid numeric code to its corresponding character. Thus, if ASCII codes are used, CHR$(66) = "B" and CHR$(43) = " + ". The CHR$ function is illustrated in Example 19.

The ORD and CHR$ functions are inverses of each other. If N denotes a valid numeric code and if A$ denotes a single BASIC character, then

$$ORD(CHR\$(N))=N \quad and \quad CHR\$(ORD(A\$))=A\$$$

EXAMPLE 18. Here is a program to print the ordering sequence used by any BASIC system.

The characters whose numeric codes are desired are included in DATA lines. The final DATA value "END" is used as an end of data marker. To conserve paper, we use a FOR/NEXT loop to print the ordering sequence in tabular form.

```
100 REM PROGRAM TO PRINT ORDERING SEQUENCE
105 REM USED BY ANY BASIC SYSTEM
110 REM
120 REM ASSIGN OUTPUT FORMATS
130 LET F$="   CHAR   CODE   CHAR   CODE   CHAR   CODE"
140 LET H$="      #    ##"
150 REM
160 REM PRINT COLUMN HEADINGS
170 PRINT USING F$
180 REM
190 REM PRINT TABLE VALUES
200 PRINT
210 FOR I=1 TO 3
220    READ A$
230    IF A$="END" THEN 999
240    PRINT USING H$,A$,ORD(A$);
250 NEXT I
260 GO TO 200
500 DATA A,B,C,D,E,F,G,H,I,J,K,L,M
510 DATA N,O,P,Q,R,S,T,U,V,W,X,Y,Z
520 DATA "0","1","2","3","4","5","6","7","8","9"
530 DATA ":",";","<",">","=","?","!","#","$"
540 DATA "&","'","(",")","*","+",",","-",".","/"
550 DATA " ","↑",END
999 END
RUN
```

CHAR	CODE	CHAR	CODE	CHAR	CODE
A	65	B	66	C	67
D	68	E	69	F	70
G	71	H	72	I	73
J	74	K	75	L	76
M	77	N	78	O	79
P	80	Q	81	R	82
S	83	T	84	U	85
V	86	W	87	X	88
Y	89	Z	90	0	48
1	49	2	50	3	51
4	52	5	53	6	54
7	55	8	56	9	57
:	58	;	59	<	60
>	62	=	61	?	63
!	33	#	35	$	36
&	38	'	39	(	40
)	41	*	42	+	43
,	44	−	45	.	46
/	47		32	↑	94

```
READY
```

EXAMPLE 19. This example illustrates the CHR$ function.

```
10 PRINT "THE SEQUENCE OF CHARACTERS CORRESPONDING TO THE"
20 PRINT "NUMERIC CODES CONTAINED IN THE DATA LINES IS:"
30 PRINT
40 READ N
50    IF N=0 THEN 99
60    PRINT CHR$(N);
70 GO TO 40
80 DATA 42,42,42,72,79,87,68,89,42,42,42
90 DATA 0
99 END
RUN

THE SEQUENCE OF CHARACTERS CORRESPONDING TO THE
NUMERIC CODES CONTAINED IN THE DATA LINES IS:

***HOWDY***
READY
```

12.9 Conversion between numerical strings and numerical values

The STRING function STR$

This function converts a numerical value to a string. For example, the programming line

```
25 LET A$=STR$(234)
```

assigns the string "234" to A$.

EXAMPLE 20

```
10 LET A=15.37
20 LET B=10
30 PRINT STR$(A);"+";STR$(B);"=";STR$(A+B)
40 END
RUN

15.37+10=25.37
READY
```

Observe that no blank spaces appear in the output as they would if line 30 were changed to
30 PRINT A;" + ";B;" = ";A+B.

An alternate form of the STRING function is

STR$(**n,f**)

where **n** denotes any numerical expression and **f** denotes any format specification (as used with the PRINT USING statement.) If the expression STR$(**n,f**) appears in a PRINT statement, the value of the numerical expression **n** will be printed according to the format specification **f**.

EXAMPLE 21

```
10 LET A=24.3675
20 LET B$=STR$(A,INTEREST IS ##.## DOLLARS.)
30 PRINT B$
40 END
RUN

INTEREST IS 24.37 DOLLARS.
READY
```

The VALUE function VAL

The VALUE function reverses the process just described for STR$; that is, it converts a string to its numerical value. For example, the programming line

```
120 LET A=VAL("537.2")
```

will assign the numerical value 537.2 to A. In an expression VAL(**s**), the value of **s** must be a string whose contents form a valid number.

EXAMPLE 22

```
10 READ A$,B$
20 LET C$=STR$(VAL(A$)+VAL(B$))
30 PRINT A$;"+";B$;"=";C$
40 DATA "123","456"
50 END
RUN

123+456=579
READY
```

12.10 Problems

1. What will be printed when each program is run?

   a. ```
   10 FOR I=5 TO 15 STEP 2
   20   PRINT STR$(I);
   30 NEXT I
   40 END
   ```

   b. ```
   10 REM W=NUMBER OF WINS
   20 REM G=NUMBER OF GAMES PLAYED
   30 LET W=42
   40 LET G=63
   50 LET B$=STR$(W,## WINS )
   60 LET C$=STR$(G-W,AND ## LOSSES )
   70 LET D$=STR$(W/G,GIVES A WINNING PERCENTAGE OF .###.)
   80 PRINT B$;C$;D$
   90 END
   ```

```
c. 10 LET A$="31"
   20 LET B$="31"
   30 PRINT A$;"+";B$;"=";
   40 PRINT VAL(A$)+VAL(B$)
   50 END

d. 10 LET L$="E"
   20 LET N=ORD(L$)-ORD("A")+1
   30 PRINT L$;N
   40 END

e. 10 LET D$="7"
   20 LET N=ORD(D$)-ORD("0")
   30 PRINT D$;N
   40 END
```

Use string functions to write a program for each task specified in Problems 2–6.

2. Produce the following output (exactly as shown.)

a. 987654	b. 987654	c. 1 1 1 1 1
98765	87654	2 2 2 2
9876	7654	3 3 3 3 3
987	654	4 4 4 4
98	54	5 5 5 5 5
9	4	

3. For any string input at the terminal, two columns are to be printed. The first column is to contain the characters in the string and the second their numeric codes.

4. Input any decimal, and print the sequence of digits without the decimal point. For example, if 764.38 is input, the output should be 7 6 4 3 8.

5. Repeat Problem 4 with no spaces separating the digits printed.

6. Input two positive integers A and B for which A < B. The program should print the decimal expansion of A/B to N places where N is also input during execution. No spaces are to separate the decimal digits being printed.

12.11 Review true-or-false quiz

1. It now makes sense to use the condition A<"B" in an IF statement.   T   F

2. The ASCII numeric codes given in Table 12.1 are used by all BASIC systems as the numeric codes assigned to the BASIC character set.   T   F

3. If A$ denotes any string, then A$ = CHR$(ORD(A$)).   T   F

4. If A is any number, LEN(A) will give the number of digits in A.   T   F

5. If LEN(X$) = LEN(Y$), then X$ = Y$.   T   F

6. LEN("GO TO")<>LEN("GOTO").   T   F

7. LEN(X$ + Y$) = LEN(X$) + LEN(Y$).   T   F

(For systems using LEFT$, RIGHT$, MID$)

8. B$ = LEFT$(B$,LEN(B$)).   T   F

9. Although it may be convenient to use the functions LEFT$ and RIGHT$, they are not necessary. The function MID$ can always be used in their place.   T   F

10. If X$ = "MADAM", then MID$(X$,3,3) has the value "D".   T   F

(For systems using the substring qualifier.)

11. B$=B$(1:LEN(B$))   T   F

12. If Y$="SEVEN", then Y$(3:3) has the value "V".   T   F

13. If A$="CYBER72", then A$(6:2) has the value "72".   T   F

13

Data Files

Although DATA statements provide the means for presenting large quantities of data to the computer, situations do arise in which they prove to be inadequate. For example, it may happen that the output values of one program are required as the input values of another program, or even of several other programs. For this reason BASIC allows for input data to come from a source external to the program (other than a terminal keyboard), and for the output to be stored on some peripheral device for later use. This is accomplished by the use of files.

A *BASIC* **file** is a named collection of related data that can be referenced by a BASIC program.

The BASIC statements used for file processing are all of one of the following four types.

1. Statements in which you establish a communication link between a program and any files to be used as input or output files. The files named in such statements are said to have been "opened."
2. Statements to read information from a file or write information to a file.
3. Statements to position a file at its beginning.
4. Statements to "close" a file—that is, to terminate any communication between a program and a file.

The files considered in this text are called sequential files because their contents are ordered in sequence; that is, there is a first entry, a second entry, a third, and so on. Thus, it makes sense to talk about statements to position a file at its beginning. Associated with each sequential file is a conceptual pointer. If the file is used as an input file, the pointer is positioned at the next input value; if it is used as an output file, the pointer is positioned just after the most recent output value.

227

Methods for creating and reading files and the BASIC statements needed to perform these tasks are described in this chapter. You should be forewarned, however, that BASIC systems vary in the form of the statements used to manipulate files. Although the file statements for your system may closely resemble those described in this chapter, you should consult your BASIC manual for the precise forms required. In what follows, we have not attempted to point out all of the differences in how BASIC systems handle files. Our objective is to indicate those applications for which files are appropriate and to illustrate those programming techniques that can be used for file processing on any system. Only major differences in BASIC systems are discussed.

13.1 The INPUT# and PRINT# statements (BCD files)

Let's assume that a file named SCORES contains the following six lines. (The use of the term "lines" as it applies to files will be explained shortly.)

```
NICKLAUS
206
MILLER
208
WATSON
205
```

In Example 1 we show how a BASIC program can access the data contained in this file, and in Example 2 we show how the file SCORES can be created.

EXAMPLE 1. Here are two programs that use the data contained in the file SCORES.

Program A	Program B
10 OPEN "SCORES" FOR INPUT AS FILE 1	10 FILE#1="SCORES"
20 LET N=1	20 LET N=1
30 INPUT#1,A$	30 INPUT#1,A$
40 INPUT#1,S	40 INPUT#1,S
50 PRINT A$,S	50 PRINT A$,S
60 LET N=N+1	60 LET N=N+1
70 IF N<=3 THEN 30	70 IF N<=3 THEN 30
80 END	80 END
RUN	RUN
NICKLAUS 206	NICKLAUS 206
MILLER 208	MILLER 208
WATSON 205	WATSON 205
READY	READY

In each program, line 10 specifies SCORES as the name of the file to be used. In addition, line 10 assigns the integer 1 as the **file designator** (also called the **file ordinal**) for this file. The file designator must be an unsigned integer. Whenever the file is used in the program, it is referenced by its designator and not by its name. As shown in lines 30 and 40, this is accomplished by using INPUT#1 instead of INPUT.

Each time the INPUT# statements at lines 30 and 40 are executed, values for A$ and S are input from the file SCORES. Line 50 prints these two values as shown in the output.

Remark 1   The keywords FOR INPUT in the OPEN statement are required only on some BASIC systems.

Remark 2   If your system uses the FILE# statement shown in Program B, you may be required to type a system command such as GET,SCORES before you type the RUN command. Your BASIC manual will show the precise form that you must use.

EXAMPLE 2. Here are two programs that can be used to create the file SCORES.[1]

PUTS DATA IN   *Program A*   *Program B*

```
10 OPEN "SCORES" FOR OUTPUT AS FILE 2     10 FILE#2="SCORES"
20     INPUT A$,S                          20     INPUT A$,S
30     IF A$="XXX" THEN 70                  30     IF A$="XXX" THEN 70
40     PRINT#2,A$                           40     PRINT#2,A$
50     PRINT#2,S                            50     PRINT#2,S
60 GO TO 20                                 60 GO TO 20
70 CLOSE 2                                  70 RESTORE#2
80 END                                      80 END
RUN                                         RUN

? NICKLAUS,206                              ? NICKLAUS,206
? MILLER,208                                ? MILLER,208
? WATSON,205                                ? WATSON,205
? XXX,0                                     ? XXX,0
READY                                       READY
```

In each program, line 10 designates a file with ordinal 2 and name SCORES. (The keywords FOR OUTPUT in the OPEN statement are required only on some BASIC systems.)

Each time the INPUT statement in line 20 is executed, we type a name and a score as shown in the computer printout.

The PRINT# statements at line 40 and 50 cause the output to be transmitted to file 2 (that is, to the file SCORES), rather than to the terminal printer or video display.

In Program A, the statement CLOSE 2 in line 70 terminates any communication between the program and the file SCORES. In addition, it ensures that the file SCORES will be saved for later use. Any files used in a program should be "closed" before the run terminates.

In Program B, the statement RESTORE#2 in line 70 "restores" the file pointer to the beginning of the file before program execution terminates. The reasons for including this final RESTORE# statement differ for different systems. Although not always required, it is a good (and safe) policy to restore all files with the RESTORE# statement just before the program run terminates.

Remark 1   Quotation marks are not printed on files. Thus, the statement PRINT#2,"NICKLAUS" prints NICKLAUS on file 2, and not "NICKLAUS".

---

[1] Some BASIC systems also allow you to create input files simply by typing their contents at your terminal keyboard. Such files are called *terminal files* and are described in Appendix B.

Remark 2   If your system uses the FILE# statement, you may have to type a command such as SAVE,SCORES or REPLACE,SCORES if you wish to preserve the data file for later use. Your BASIC manual will show the precise form that you must use.

In the preceding example, each time either of the statements PRINT#2,A$ or PRINT#2,S is executed a single value is "printed" on the file SCORES. In addition, the computer "prints" a special **end-of-line mark** after this value, as indicated in the following schematic representation of the six values stored on the file.

| NICKLAUS | v | 206 | v | MILLER | v | 208 | v | WATSON | v | 205 | v | $\cdot\ \cdot\ \cdot$ |

(v denotes the end-of-line mark.)

It is customary to visualize this file as containing the six distinct lines

```
NICKLAUS
206
MILLER
208
WATSON
205
```

If you write a program that uses this file as an input file, you should use INPUT# statements that are consistent with such a data structure; that is, each INPUT# statement should input a value for a single variable: a string variable if the next input value is a string and a numerical variable if it is a number.

When using the PRINT# statement to create a file that will be used as an input file, some care must be taken. In particular, if a single PRINT# statement is used to transmit two or more values to a file (that is, if two or more values are to be printed on one line of the file), they must be printed with separating commas. Thus, to print the values of the variables A$ and S on one line of file #2 you would use the statement

```
PRINT#2,A$;",";S
```

and not

```
PRINT#2,A$;S    or    PRINT#2,A$,S
```

That is, the comma must actually be "printed" on the file. When the file is used later as an input file, the computer recognizes the comma as separating two distinct input values.

If you modify the program shown in Example 2 by replacing the lines

```
40 PRINT#2,A$
50 PRINT#2,S
```

by the single line

```
40 PRINT#2,A$;",";S
```

the output file SCORES would consist of three distinct lines as follows.

```
NICKLAUS,206
MILLER,208
WATSON,205
```

Any program that uses this file as an input file should use INPUT# statements that are consistent with this data structure. The statement INPUT#2,A$,S would be appropriate.

Note the use of semicolons in the statement

```
PRINT#2,A$;",";S
```

When using a PRINT# statement to direct the output to a file that will be used later as an input file, the usual practice is to use semicolons, and not commas, to separate any variables and constants included in a PRINT# statement. On some BASIC systems you *must* use semicolons.

Caution: If a string containing a comma is output to a file, and if the file is used later as an input file, the computer will not recognize the comma as part of the string. Rather, it will recognize it as separating two distinct input values. For example, the programming lines

```
50 LET X$="NICKLAUS,JACK"
60 PRINT#1,X$
```

will create one line of a file containing

```
NICKLAUS,JACK
```

But, the information contained in this line cannot be read with the statement INPUT#1,X$ even though it was created with the statement PRINT#1,X$. You would have to use a statement such as INPUT#1,X$,Y$ so that NICKLAUS would be assigned to X$ and JACK to Y$. The safest policy when directing output to a file is to avoid strings that contain commas. (If you are familiar with the string functions described in Chapter 12, you can use a special character (such as #) to denote a comma. Then, when strings are input from the file, the individual characters can be examined to determine if the symbol used to denote a comma is present.)

EXAMPLE 3. Here are two programs to create a short file and then read it.

Program A

```
10 OPEN "INV35" FOR OUTPUT AS FILE 5
20    LET A$="NEEDLES"
30    LET M=4300
40    LET N=.62
50    PRINT#5,A$;",";M;",";N
60 CLOSE 5
65 OPEN "INV35" FOR INPUT AS FILE 5
70    INPUT#5,B$,X,Y
80    PRINT B$;X;Y
90 CLOSE 5
99 END
RUN

NEEDLES 4300   .62
READY
```

Program B

```
10 FILE#5="INV35"
20    LET A$="NEEDLES"
30    LET M=4300
40    LET N=.62
50    PRINT#5,A$;",";M;",";N
60 RESTORE#5
70    INPUT#5,B$,X,Y
80    PRINT B$;X;Y
90 RESTORE #5
99 END
RUN

NEEDLES 4300   .62
READY
```

In each program, line 10 designates the ordinal number 5 for the file INV35, line 50 prints the values of A$, M, and N on one line of this file, with a comma between successive output values.

In Program A, line 60 terminates the communication between the program and the file INV35 that was established in line 10. Line 65 reestablishes this communication except that INV35 is now used as an input file. (The OPEN statement automatically positions the file pointer at the beginning of the file.)

In Program B, line 60 "restores" the file pointer to the beginning of the file.

In each program, line 70 inputs three values from INV35 and assigns them to B$, X, and Y. Line 80 prints these values as shown in the output.

Each file used as an input file contains a special **end-of-file mark** following its last datum. This end-of-file mark serves two purposes.

1. While reading data from a file, the end-of-file mark will be sensed by the computer. Any attempt to read information beyond this end-of-file mark will result in an error diagnostic and program execution will terminate.

2. Most BASIC systems allow you to include a statement in your program that will transfer control to any line number you specify if the end-of-file mark has been sensed. On some systems, you can write

```
200 IF END#1 THEN 240
```

to transfer control to line 240 if the end-of-file mark has been sensed. On other systems, you must use the equivalent statement

```
200 NODATA#1,240
```

Your BASIC manual will show the precise form that you must use. In the following example, we illustrate how such an *end-of-file statement* can be used to determine whether or not more data are available for input.

EXAMPLE 4

Each line of a file named BIRTHS contains a name and a birthdate in the form

name, month, day, year

where *name* denotes a string, and *month*, *day*, and *year* denote integers.

The following program segment reads and prints the information contained in the file. We assume that the file BIRTHS has been opened as an input file with ordinal 1.

```
200 IF END#1 THEN 240
210     INPUT#1,N$,M,D,Y
220     PRINT N$,M;"/";D;"/";Y
230 GO TO 200
240 REM CONTENTS OF FILE#1 HAVE BEEN DISPLAYED
```

Line 200 checks whether more data are available on file 1. If the end-of-file mark has not been reached, the *end-of-file specifier* END#1 is *false* and no transfer is made to line 240. Lines 210 and 220 read and print one line of the file and line 230 transfers control back to line 200. This looping continues until the last line on file 1 has been read and printed. When this happens the end-of-file specifier END#1 is *true;* that is, the end-of-file mark has been sensed. The IF statement then transfers control out of the loop to line 240.

Remark 1

On systems that use the NODATA# statement to detect the end of a file, you would simply replace line 200 by

```
200 NODATA#1,240
```

Remark 2

Using an end-of-file statement as in line 200 obviates the need to use an EOD tag as the last entry in a file or a data count as the first entry.

The contents of a file created by a BASIC program using the PRINT# statement are stored as a sequence of BCD (*binary coded decimal*) characters. This means that a numerical value such as 38 is stored as two separate codes, one for 3 and one for 8, and not as the binary-number representation (100110) of the number 38. Similarly, the information "SAM 31.7" is stored as a sequence of eight code numbers, one for each of the characters "S", "A", "M", " ", "3", "1", ".", and "7". Such files are referred to as BCD files or *text* files: text because their contents are stored as a sequence of characters.

As illustrated in this section, the PRINT# statement is used to create BCD files and the INPUT# statement is used to read them. In Section 13.3 we will describe the WRITE# and READ# statements that many BASIC systems provide for creating and reading *binary* files— that is, files in which numbers are stored using the binary number representations that the computer uses for processing numerical values.

As noted at the outset of this chapter, the files considered in this text are called *sequential files* because their contents are ordered in sequence; that is, there is a first entry, a second entry, a third, and so on. When reading from or writing to a sequential file, the following rules apply.

1. Data in a sequential file must be accessed in order. Thus, to read a particular entry in the file, all entries preceding it must be read first, even though they may not be needed.

2. If an existing sequential file is to be modified, either by changing a value in the file or by adding a value to the end of the file, you must create a new copy of the entire file containing whatever changes are desired. The modification of existing files is referred to as *file maintenance* and is the subject of Section 13.5.

13.2 Problems

1. Here is a program to create a BCD file GRADES.

```
100 FILE#1="GRADES"
110    READ A$,N1,N2
120     IF A$="X" THEN 150
130     PRINT#1,A$;",";N1;",";N2
140 GO TO 110
150 RESTORE#1
160 DATA JOAN,80,90
170 DATA SAM,100,80
180 DATA GREG,80,40
190 DATA MARY,70,30
200 DATA MARK,50,90
210 DATA X,0,0
220 END
```

What is printed by each program in parts (a) and (b)?

a.
```
10 FILE#1="GRADES"
20 IF END#1 THEN 60
30    INPUT#1,B$,A,B
40     IF A>B THEN PRINT B$
50 GO TO 20
60 RESTORE#1
70 END
```

b.
```
10 FILE#3="GRADES"
20 LET P$="PASS"
30 LET F$="FAIL"
40 IF END#3 THEN 90
50    INPUT#3,N$,X,Y
60    LET A=(X+2*Y)/3
70     IF A>65 THEN PRINT N$,P$ ELSE PRINT N$,F$
80 GO TO 40
90 RESTORE#3
99 END
```

2. Here is a program to create a BCD file COMM.

```
100 OPEN "COMM" FOR OUTPUT AS FILE 1
110    READ N$,S,Q
120     IF N$="XXX" THEN 150
130     PRINT#1,N$;",";S;",";Q
140 GO TO 110
150 CLOSE 1
160 DATA J.D.SLOANE,13000,10000
170 DATA R.M.PETERS,5000,5000
180 DATA A.B.CARTER,7400,5000
190 DATA I.O.ULSTER,12000,10000
200 DATA XXX,0,0
210 END
```

What is printed by each program in parts (a) and (b)?

a.
```
10 OPEN "COMM" FOR INPUT AS FILE 1
20 IF END#1 THEN 90
30    INPUT#1,N$,S,Q
40     IF S<=Q THEN 20
50    PRINT N$
60    PRINT "EXCESS: ";S-Q
70    PRINT
80 GO TO 20
90 CLOSE 1
99 END
```

```
b. 10 OPEN "COMM" FOR INPUT AS FILE 2
   20 IF END#2 THEN 90
   30    LET C=0
   40    INPUT#2,A$,X,Y
   50    IF S>Q THEN LET C=.10*(S-Q)
   60    LET W=265+C
   70    PRINT A$,W
   80 GO TO 20
   90 CLOSE 2
   99 END
```

3. Create a BCD file named INFO containing the following information about employees of the Libel Insurance Company. The file INFO is to be used as an input file in Problems 4–8 (1 and 2 denote male and female, respectively).

ID	Sex	Age	Years of service	Annual salary
2735	1	47	13	20,200.00
2980	2	33	6	14,300.00
3865	2	41	15	23,900.00
4222	1	22	2	11,400.00
4740	1	59	7	19,200.00
5200	2	25	3	13,000.00
5803	1	33	13	21,500.00
7242	2	28	4	13,400.00
7341	1	68	30	25,500.00
8004	1	35	6	14,300.00
9327	2	21	3	9,200.00

Problems 4–8 refer to the file INFO created in Problem 3.

4. Print a five-column report with a title and appropriate column headings displaying the employee information contained in the file INFO. (The sex column is to contain MALE or FEMALE, and not 1 or 2.)

5. Print two reports showing the employee information contained in INFO by sex. Each report is to be titled and is to have four appropriately labeled columns.

6. Print a two-column report showing ID numbers and annual salaries of all employees whose annual salary exceeds $15,000.00. In addition to printing column headings, be sure the report has an appropriate title.

7. Print a two-column report as described in Problem 6 for all employees whose annual salaries exceed the average annual salary of all Libel employees. Following the report, display the total annual salary earned by these employees. The title of the report should include the average salary of all Libel employees.

8. Print a report showing the ID numbers, years of service, and salaries of all employees who have been with the firm for more than 5 years.

9. A wholesaler's inventory yields the following information for each item on hand:

Item code	Item type	Units on hand	Average cost per unit	Sale price per unit
ITEM 1	A	20500	1.55	1.95
ITEM 2	A	54000	0.59	0.74
ITEM 3	B	8250	3.40	4.10
ITEM 4	B	4000	5.23	6.75
ITEM 5	A	15000	0.60	0.75
ITEM 6	A	10500	1.05	1.35
ITEM 7	B	6000	7.45	9.89
ITEM 8	B	7500	5.10	5.43
ITEM 9	B	15500	3.10	4.10

Create a BCD file INVTRY containing these inventory data.

Problems 10–12 refer to the file INVTRY created in Problem 9.

10. Print a five-column report displaying exactly the information in INVTRY.
11. Print two separate reports, the first displaying the given information for type-A items and the second for type-B items.
12. Print a five-column report showing the item code, the number of units on hand, and the total cost, total sales price, and total income these units represent (income = sales − cost). The report is to be concluded with a message showing the total cost, total sales price, and total income represented by the entire inventory.

13.3 The READ# and WRITE# statements (binary files)

A second type of BASIC file—one that must be created by a BASIC program—is called a **binary file.** This means that each number contained in the file appears in a form that corresponds exactly to the binary representation of the number in the computer's memory unit. For this reason, programs using binary files will execute more quickly than programs using BCD files; the computer must translate numerical values in BCD files to their binary form before any calculations can take place. A disadvantage of using binary files is that they should not be listed at the terminal; since numerical values are stored in binary form, the printout will not be readable.

To create a binary file under program control, you use the WRITE# statement instead of the PRINT# statement. To read a binary file, you use the READ# statement instead of the INPUT# statement. The awkward "comma" situation encountered with the PRINT# and INPUT# statements does not occur when you use binary files.

EXAMPLE 5. Here is a program to create a short binary file.

```
10 FILE#2="DATA"
20    INPUT X,Y
30    IF X=9999 THEN 60
40    WRITE#2,X,Y
50 GO TO 20
60 RESTORE#2
70 END
RUN

? 2,3
? 4,8
? 5,18
? 9999,0
READY
```

Line 40 "writes" two values on file #2—the two values typed in response to the INPUT statement at line 20. When X = 9999, after the fourth pair of values is entered, the program terminates with no output values being displayed at the terminal.

Remark

In this section we use the FILE# statement to "open" all files, the RESTORE# statement to restore all file pointers just before program termination, and the END# specifier to detect the end of a file. The corresponding OPEN, CLOSE, and NODATA statements are described in Section 13.1.

EXAMPLE 6. Here is a program to examine the contents of the binary file DATA created by the program in Example 5.

```
10 FILE#1="DATA"
20 IF END#1 THEN 60
30    READ#1,A,B
40    PRINT A;B
50 GO TO 20
60 RESTORE#1
70 END
RUN

 2   3
 4   8
 5  18
READY
```

Line 30 reads two values from file #1, and line 40 prints them at the terminal. This process is continued until the end-of-file is reached.

This example illustrates that files created with the WRITE# statement (binary files) must be read with the READ# statement, just as files created at the terminal or with the PRINT# statement (BCD files) must be read with the INPUT# statement.

In Example 7, we create a binary file and in Example 8 we show a program that uses this file as an input file. Using the output file of one program as an input file for another program is a common use of files.

EXAMPLE 7. Here is a program to create a binary file STAT containing the name and the number of field goals, field goal attempts, free throws, and free-throw attempts for any number of basketball players.

```
100 REM PROGRAM TO CREATE A BINARY FILE STAT
110 REM CONTAINING BASKETBALL STATISTICS
120 REM   N$ = PLAYER'S NAME
130 REM    B = NUMBER OF FIELD GOALS
140 REM   B1 = NUMBER OF FIELD GOAL ATTEMPTS
150 REM    F = NUMBER OF FREE THROWS
160 REM   F1 = NUMBER OF FREE THROW ATTEMPTS
170 FILE#3="STAT"
180 PRINT "AFTER EACH ? ENTER A PLAYER'S NAME,AND"
190 PRINT "THE NUMBER OF FIELD GOALS, FIELD GOAL ATTEMPTS,"
200 PRINT "FREE THROWS,AND FREE THROW ATTEMPTS."
210 PRINT "TYPE X,0,0,0,0 TO STOP."
220 PRINT
230 INPUT N$,B,B1,F,F1
240    IF N$="X" THEN 270
250    WRITE#3,N$,B,B1,F,F1
260 GO TO 230
270 RESTORE#3
500 END
RUN
```

```
          AFTER EACH ? ENTER A PLAYER'S NAME,AND
          THE NUMBER OF FIELD GOALS, FIELD GOAL ATTEMPTS,
          FREE THROWS,AND FREE THROW ATTEMPTS.
          TYPE X,0,0,0,0 TO STOP.

          ? HANSON,18,42,12,17
          ? JOHNSON,6,15,5,12
          ? WHITE,22,45,8,14
          ? ANDERSON,35,74,18,25
          ? DONATO,12,33,5,9
          ? DALEY,9,21,8,11
          ? X,0,0,0,0

          READY
```

When the program is executed, no output will be printed but the statistics for each of the seven players will be written on the file STAT. To test such a program, you would insert program statements to cause some or all of the output to be printed. Once you are convinced that the program is correct, delete these lines.

Remark

Although we cannot "see" the file, we know that it was written by a WRITE# statement that writes a string and four numerical values each time it is executed. Thus, the file can be visualized as a sequence of lines of the form

string   number   number   number   number

It should be read by READ# statements that are consistent with such a data structure.

EXAMPLE 8. Here is a program to read the statistical data on the binary file STAT and produce three tables. The first prints the data included on STAT and, in addition, the field goal and free-throw percentages for each player. The last line is a complete set of statistics for the team. The second lists those players whose field goal percentage is less than the team's average and the third those players whose free-throw percentage is less than the team's average.

The program

```
100 REM PROGRAM TO PRINT THREE TABLES
105 REM OF BASKETBALL STATISTICS
110 REM
120 REM THE FOLLOWING VARIABLE NAMES ARE
125 REM ASSOCIATED WITH AN INDIVIDUAL PLAYER
130 REM      N$ = PLAYER'S NAME
140 REM       B = NUMBER OF FIELD GOALS
150 REM      B1 = NUMBER OF FIELD GOAL ATTEMPTS
160 REM       F = NUMBER OF FREE THROWS
170 REM      F1 = NUMBER OF FREE THROW ATTEMPTS
180 REM
190 REM THE FOLLOWING VARIABLE NAMES ARE
195 REM ASSOCIATED WITH THE TEAM
200 REM      T1 = NUMBER OF FIELD GOALS
210 REM      T2 = NUMBER OF FIELD GOAL ATTEMPTS
220 REM      T3 = NUMBER OF FREE THROWS
230 REM      T4 = NUMBER OF FREE THROW ATTEMPTS
240 REM
```

```
250 FILE#4="STAT"
260 REM ***** INITIALIZE COUNTERS T1,T2,T3,T4 *****
270 LET T1=0
280 LET T2=0
290 LET T3=0
300 LET T4=0
310 REM ***** ASSIGN OUTPUT FORMATS *****
320 LET H$="  PLAYER      FG  FGA   PCT    FT  FTA   PCT"
330 LET F$="######## ### ###  .### ### ###  .###"
340 REM ***** PRINT FIRST TABLE *****
350 PRINT USING H$
360 PRINT
370 IF END#4 THEN 450
380     READ#4,N$,B,B1,F,F1
390     PRINT USING F$,N$,B,B1,B/B1,F,F1,F/F1
400     LET T1=T1+B
410     LET T2=T2+B1
420     LET T3=T3+F
430     LET T4=T4+F1
440 GO TO 370
450 PRINT USING F$,"TEAM",T1,T2,T1/T2,T3,T4,T3/T4
460 PRINT
470 REM ***** PRINT SECOND TABLE *****
480 PRINT "PLAYERS WHOSE FIELD GOAL PERCENTAGE"
485 PRINT "IS LESS THAN TEAM AVERAGE."
490 RESTORE#4
500 IF END#4 THEN 540
510     READ#4,N$,B,B1,F,F1
520     IF B/B1<T1/T2 THEN PRINT N$
530 GO TO 500
540 PRINT
550 REM ***** PRINT THIRD TABLE *****
560 PRINT "PLAYERS WHOSE FREE THROW PERCENTAGE"
565 PRINT "IS LESS THAN TEAM AVERAGE."
570 RESTORE#4
580 IF END#4 THEN 620
590     READ#4,N$,B,B1,F,F1
600     IF F/F1<T3/T4 THEN PRINT N$
610 GO TO 580
620 RESTORE#4
999 END
RUN
```

PLAYER	FG	FGA	PCT	FT	FTA	PCT
HANSON	18	42	.429	12	17	.706
JOHNSON	6	15	.400	5	12	.417
WHITE	22	45	.489	8	14	.571
MARCOTT	14	30	.467	5	9	.556
ANDERSON	35	74	.473	18	25	.720
DONATO	12	33	.364	5	9	.556
DALEY	9	21	.429	8	11	.727
TEAM	116	260	.446	61	97	.629

```
PLAYERS WHOSE FIELD GOAL PERCENTAGE
IS LESS THAN TEAM AVERAGE.
HANSON
JOHNSON
DONATO
DALEY

PLAYERS WHOSE FREE THROW PERCENTAGE
IS LESS THAN TEAM AVERAGE.
JOHNSON
WHITE
MARCOTT
DONATO
READY
```

Remark   The RESTORE# statements at lines 490 and 570 allow the data on file STAT to be read a second and third time.

13.4 Problems

1. Below are two programs to create binary files ABC1 and ABC2.

Program to create file ABC1

```
100 FILE#1="ABC1"
110    READ A,B$,C
120    IF C=0 THEN 210
130    WRITE#1,A,B$,C
140 GO TO 110
150 DATA 1,JOAN,78
160 DATA 2,SAM,75
170 DATA 3,GREG,86
180 DATA 4,ALICE,81
190 DATA 5,MARK,93
200 DATA 6,X,0
210 RESTORE#1
220 END
```

Program to create file ABC2

```
100 FILE#2="ABC2"
110    READ M$,S
120    IF M$="Y" THEN 210
130    WRITE#2,M$,S
140 GO TO 110
150 DATA SAL,64
160 DATA JILL,72
170 DATA JACK,88
180 DATA JANE,95
190 DATA PETE,79
200 DATA Y,0
210 RESTORE#2
220 END
```

What will be printed when each program in parts (a) through (d) is run?

a.
```
100 FILE#1="ABC1"
110 IF END#1 THEN 150
120    READ#1,K,J$,L
130    PRINT J$,L
140 GO TO 110
150 RESTORE#1
160 END
```

b.
```
100 FILE#2="ABC2"
110 READ#2,B$,K
120 LET A=K
130 IF END#2 THEN 170
140    READ#2,A$,K
150    IF K>A THEN LET A=K
160 GO TO 130
170 PRINT A
180 RESTORE#2
190 END
```

c.
```
100 FILE#1="ABC1"
110 FILE#2="ABC2"
120 READ#1,N,A$,X
130 READ#2,B$,Y
140 LET S=X+Y
150 LET W=1
160 IF END#1 THEN 230
170    READ#1,N,A$,X
180    READ#2,B$,Y
```

```
190     IF S>X+Y THEN 160
200     LET S=X+Y
210     LET W=N
220 GO TO 160
230 PRINT "FIRST PLACE---TEAM";W
240 RESTORE#1
250 RESTORE#2
260 END
```

d.
```
100 FILE#1="ABC1"
110 FILE#2="ABC2"
120 LET I=1
130     READ#1,N,A$,S
140     READ#2,B$,L
150     IF I/2<> INT(I/2) THEN PRINT A$,S ELSE PRINT B$,L
160     LET I=I+1
170 IF I<=5 THEN 130
180 RESTORE#1
190 RESTORE#2
200     READ#1,N,A$,S
210     READ#2,B$,L
220     IF I/2<>INT(I/2) THEN PRINT A$,S ELSE PRINT B$,L
230     LET I=I+1
240 IF I<=10 THEN 200
250 RESTORE#1
260 RESTORE#2
270 END
```

2. Write a program to create a binary file SALES that includes the following information:

Employee name	Base salary	Quota	Commission rate	Sales
ALLISON	$350	$7,000	5%	$10,900
SCOLLINS	400	9,000	5.5%	7,600
GRACIA	390	6,500	6%	9,700
HOWSE	425	3,500	5%	10,200
REYNIA	450	7,500	4.7%	7,100
SHEA	400	2,100	5%	4,250
FREEMAN	375	4,000	4%	3,500
FISKE	425	8,500	5.5%	11,400
ALMON	450	7,400	6.5%	8,500
BRENNAN	475	9,300	5.2%	4,200

The file SALES is to be used as an input file in Problems 3–7.

Problems 3–7 refer to the file SALES created in Problem 2.

3. Print a five-column report with column headings displaying exactly the information in the file SALES.
4. Print two lists, the first containing the names of those salespersons whose sales have exceeded their quotas, and the second the names of those whose sales have not.
5. Print a four-column report showing each employee's name, base salary, commission, and total earnings. A salesperson receives a commission only on those sales that exceed the quota.
6. Print a two-column report showing the names and total earnings of those salespersons whose total earnings exceed the average total earnings of the entire sales staff.
7. Calculate the total amount of commissions paid to all salespersons during the time period.

8. The following table describes an investor's stock portfolio.

Name of stock	Number of shares	Last week's closing price	Current week's closing price
STERLING DRUG	800	16.50	16.125
DATA GENERAL	500	56.25	57.50
OWEN ILLINOIS	1200	22.50	21.50
MATTEL INC	1000	10.75	11.125
ABBOTT LAB	2000	33.75	34.75
FED NATL MTG	2500	17.75	17.25
IC GEN	250	43.125	43.625
ALO SYSTEMS	550	18.50	18.25

Write a program to create a binary file DATA that contains this information. Now prepare reports as follows. Each report is to have a title, and each column is to be labeled.
a. A printed report displaying precisely the information contained in the file DATA.
b. A five-column report, with the first four columns as in part (a) and a fifth column showing the percentage increase or decrease for each security.
c. A four-column report showing the stock name, the equity at the close of business last week, the equity this week, and the dollar change in equity. The report should be concluded with a message showing the total net gain or loss for the week.

13.5 File maintenance

Updating existing data files is a common programming application. In this section we give two examples illustrating this practice. The first involves updating a short simplified inventory file originally created as a BCD file, and the second involves updating a short binary file. However, it should be remarked that, in practice, data files usually are not short and require rather complicated programs to maintain them. Our objective is simply to show that file maintenance is possible. A complete discussion of the many techniques used in file-maintenance programs is beyond the scope of an introductory text such as this one.

EXAMPLE 9

A *BCD* file named INVTRY contains the following data.

```
A10010,2000
A10011,4450
C22960,1060
D40240,2300
X99220,500
X99221,650
Y88000,1050
Y88001,400
```

The first entry in each line denotes an item code, and the second entry gives the quantity on hand. Our task is to write a program to allow a user to update INVTRY to reflect all transactions since the last update.

Problem analysis

Let's assume that the user must specify, for each item to be changed, the item code, the number of units shipped since the last update, and the number of units received since the last update. Thus, the user will come to the terminal armed with a list such as the following.

Item Code	Shipped	Received
A10010	1200	1000
A10011	1000	550
D40240	1800	2000
Y88000	300	0

A person carrying out this task by hand might proceed as follows.

a. Read an item code.
b. Search the file INVTRY for this code, and change the units-on-hand figure as required.
c. If more changes are to be made, go to step (a).
d. Have the updated copy of INVTRY typed.

This algorithm is not suitable for a BASIC program. Step (b) says to change a *single* number appearing on the file INVTRY, and this cannot be done when using sequential files. We will first input the data from INVTRY into arrays (subscripted variables) and then make the necessary changes in these arrays. After this has been done for each item requiring a change, step (d) will involve creating a new copy of INVTRY by using the PRINT# statement. Before rewriting this algorithm in a form suitable for a BASIC program, let's choose variable names.

C\$ = the array of item codes from file INVTRY.
Q = the corresponding array of quantities from INVTRY.
N = the number of lines in the file INVTRY.
X\$ = the item code to be typed.
S = the quantity shipped.
R = the quantity received.

In the following algorithm we require the user to type END after all changes have been made.

The algorithm

a. Input arrays C\$ and Q from the file INVTRY.
b. Enter an item code X\$.
c. If X\$ = END, make a new copy of INVTRY and stop.
d. Find I such that C\$(I) = X\$. If X\$ is not in the list, go to step (b).
e. Enter the quantities S and R corresponding to item X\$.
f. Let Q(I) = Q(I) + R − S, and go to step (b).

The following flowchart describes this algorithm in sufficient detail to be coded directly to a BASIC program.

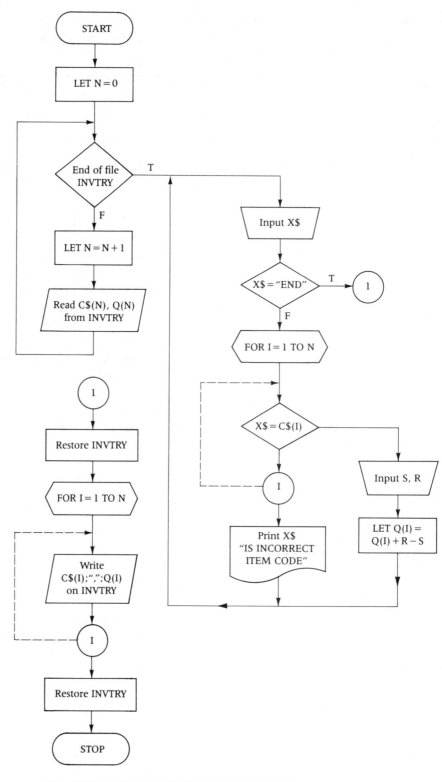

The program

```
100 REM INVENTORY UPDATE PROGRAM
110 REM    C$ = ARRAY OF ITEM CODES FROM FILE INVTRY
120 REM    Q  = ARRAY OF QUANTITIES FROM FILE INVTRY
130 REM    N  = NUMBER OF LINES IN FILE INVTRY
140 REM    X$ = ITEM CODE TO BE INPUT
150 REM    S  = QUANTITY SHIPPED (OF ITEM X$)
160 REM    R  = QUANTITY RECEIVED (OF ITEM X$)
```

```
170 FILE#1="INVTRY"
180 REM ***** INPUT ARRAYS C$ AND Q FROM FILE 1 *****
190 DIM C$(50),Q(50)
200 LET N=0
210 IF END#1 THEN 250
220     LET N=N+1
230     INPUT#1,C$(N),Q(N)
240 GO TO 210
250 REM ***** UPDATE ARRAYS C$ AND Q *****
260     PRINT
270     PRINT "ITEM CODE";
280     INPUT X$
290     IF X$="END" THEN 430
300     REM ***** SEARCH ARRAY C$ FOR ITEM X$ *****
310     FOR I=1 TO N
320         IF C$(I)=X$ THEN 360
330     NEXT I
340     PRINT X$;" IS NOT A CORRECT ITEM CODE"
350 GO TO 260
360     REM ***** ENTER S AND R TO UPDATE Q(I) *****
370     PRINT "UNITS SHIPPED";
380     INPUT S
390     PRINT "UNITS RECEIVED";
400     INPUT R
410     LET Q(I)=Q(I)+R-S
420 GO TO 260
430 REM ***** UPDATE THE FILE INVTRY *****
440 RESTORE#1
450 FOR I=1 TO N
460     PRINT#1,C$(I);",";Q(I)
470 NEXT I
480 PRINT "INVTRY IS UPDATED"
490 RESTORE#1
999 END
RUN
ITEM CODE? A10010
UNITS SHIPPED? 1200
UNITS RECEIVED? 1000

ITEM CODE? A10011
UNITS SHIPPED? 1000
UNITS RECEIVED? 550

ITEM CODE? D40240
UNITS SHIPPED? 1800
UNITS RECEIVED? 2000

ITEM CODE? Y88000
UNITS SHIPPED? 300
UNITS RECEIVED? 0

ITEM CODE? END
INVTRY IS UPDATED
READY
```

Remark 1

Although this program creates an updated file INVTRY, we cannot "see" it. The only printed output is the message INVTRY IS UPDATED. To get a printed copy of the current contents of INVTRY, we could use a short program such as the following.

```
100 REM DISPLAY THE CONTENTS OF INVTRY
110 FILE#1="INVTRY"
120 PRINT "ITEM CODE","UNITS ON HAND"
130 IF END#1 THEN 170
140    INPUT#1,X$,Q
150    PRINT X$,Q
160 GO TO 130
170 RESTORE#1
180 END
RUN

ITEM CODE        UNITS ON HAND
A10010              1800
A10011              4000
C22960              1060
D40240              2500
X99220              500
X99221              650
Y88000              750
Y88001              400
READY
```

Remark 2

If file INVTRY is a binary file rather than a BCD file, simply replace lines 230 and 460 by

```
230 READ#1,C$(N),Q(N)
460 WRITE#1,C$(I),Q(I)
```

We conclude this chapter with an example of a program that updates an existing *binary* file.

EXAMPLE 10

The ID numbers and names of all employees of the Land Foundry Company are stored on the binary file EMPLOY. The file begins with a count of the number of employees, and a typical line is

```
23501   AHEARN JOHN F.
```

Let's write a program to allow a user to add new employees to this binary file.

Problem analysis

As explained earlier, you cannot add data to a previously created sequential file. You must make a complete new copy of the file being sure to add any new data to this copy before it is closed (or restored).

For the problem at hand we will read all ID numbers and names from the binary file EMPLOY into arrays, add any new names and ID numbers to these arrays, and then use the arrays to create a new updated copy of EMPLOY.

To allow us to write a concise algorithm describing this process, we will use the following variable names.

L   = the array of ID numbers.
N$ = the corresponding array of names.
C   = number of employees. (As stated in the problem statement, this is the first value on the file.)
E$ = the name of a new employee to be added to the file.
I   = the ID number assigned to the employee E$.

The algorithm

a. Read the count C from the file EMPLOY.
b. Read the ID numbers and names into arrays L and N$.
c. Input an ID number I and name E$ (an ID of 0 will end the input session).
d. If I = 0, make a new copy of EMPLOY and stop.
e. If I is already in array L, print an appropriate message and go to step (c).
f. Add 1 to C, I to array L, and E$ to array N$.
g. Go to step (c).

The program

```
100 REM PROGRAM TO UPDATE THE FILE "EMPLOY"
110 FILE#1="EMPLOY"
120 REM ***** READ THE ARRAYS L AND N$ FROM FILE#1 *****
130 REM C COUNTS THE NUMBER OF EMPLOYEES INCLUDED
140 DIM L(100),N$(100)
150 READ#1,C
160 FOR K=1 TO C
170    READ#1,L(K),N$(K)
180 NEXT K
190 PRINT "AFTER EACH ? TYPE AN ID AND NAME AS FOLLOWS."
200 PRINT "ID, LAST (SPACE) FIRST (SPACE) MIDDLE INITIAL"
210 PRINT "(TYPE 0,X TO END THIS SESSION.)"
220 PRINT
230    INPUT I,E$
240    IF I=0 THEN 360
250    REM ***** SEARCH ARRAY L FOR THE ID NUMBER I *****
260    FOR K=1 TO C
270       IF I=L(K) THEN 340
280    NEXT K
290    REM ***** ADD I AND E$ TO THE ARRAYS L AND N$
300    LET C=C+1
310    LET L(C)=I
320    LET N$(C)=E$
330 GO TO 220
340    PRINT "THE ID";I;"IS ASSIGNED TO ";N$(K)
350 GO TO 220
360 REM ***** UPDATE FILE#1 *****
370 RESTORE#1
380 WRITE#1,C
390 FOR K=1 TO C
400    WRITE#1,L(K),N$(K)
410 NEXT K
420 RESTORE#1
```

```
430 PRINT "FILE EMPLOY IS UPDATED"
990 END
RUN

AFTER EACH ? TYPE AN ID AND NAME AS FOLLOWS.
ID, LAST (SPACE) FIRST (SPACE) MIDDLE INITIAL
(TYPE 0,X TO END THIS SESSION.)

? 63334, MANN HEATHER A

? 23501, JACKSON SUSAN A
THE ID 23501 IS ASSIGNED TO AHEARN JOHN F

? 33501, JACKSON SUSAN A

? 0,X
FILE EMPLOY IS UPDATED
READY
```

Remark 1   The following short program reads and displays the current contents of the binary file EMPLOY.

```
100 FILE#1="EMPLOY"
110 PRINT "ID NUMBER","EMPLOYEE'S NAME"
120 READ#1,C
130 FOR K=1 TO C
140    READ#1,I,E$
150    PRINT I,E$
160 NEXT K
170 RESTORE#1
180 END
RUN

ID NUMBER       EMPLOYEE'S NAME

  23501         AHEARN JOHN F
  53241         ANDERSON ALBERT G
  15653         SIMPSON DONALD C
  37671         HENDRIX SAMUEL D
  49313         POST EDWARD L
  44446         MURRAY HAROLD N
  83817         CONNORS FRANK J
  23786         SILVA JOSE R
  23619         SEMPLE ALBERT J
  63334         MANN HEATHER A
  33501         JACKSON SUSAN A
READY
```

Remark 2

If the file EMPLOY is a BCD file rather than a binary file, simply replace lines 150, 170, 380, and 400 by

```
150 INPUT#1,C
170 INPUT#1,L(K),N$(K)
380 PRINT#1,C
400 PRINT#1,L(K);",";N$(K)
```

13.6 Problems

Problems 1–4 refer to the file EMPLOY maintained by the Hollis Investment Corporation. The contents of EMPLOY are as follows.

Name	Age	Years of service	Monthly salary
Murray George	53	21	2100.00
Ritchie Albert	41	13	1850.00
Galvin Fred	62	35	2475.00
Cummings Barbara	37	16	1675.00
Gieseler Norma	41	20	2200.00
Hughes Bette	52	18	2050.00
Meland Ralph	29	5	1550.00
Tibeau Frances	30	7	1340.00

1. Create the file EMPLOY as described in Section 13.1 or Section 13.3. Your program that creates this file should conclude with a program segment that reads and displays the contents of the file.
2. Print a report showing the names and yearly salaries of all Hollis employees. Salaries are to be listed from largest to smallest.
3. Print a report as in Problem 2 with the names in alphabetical order.
4. The employers of Hollis have negotiated a 5% across-the-board salary increase. Update the file EMPLOY to reflect this increase.

Problems 5–8 refer to the following product survey.

A manufacturing company sends a package consisting of eight new products to each of ten families and asks each family to rate each product on the following scale.

$$0 = \text{poor} \quad 1 = \text{fair} \quad 2 = \text{good} \quad 3 = \text{very good} \quad 4 = \text{excellent}$$

Here are the results in tabular form.

```
                    Family number
                 |1 2 3 4 5 6 7 8 9 10
                 ---------------------
               1 |0 1 1 2 1 2 2 1 0 1
               2 |2 3 3 0 3 2 2 3 4 1
               3 |1 3 4 4 4 1 4 2 3 2
               4 |3 4 2 4 3 1 3 4 2 4
Product number 5 |0 1 3 2 2 2 1 3 0 1
               6 |4 4 4 3 2 1 4 4 1 1
               7 |1 3 1 3 2 4 1 4 3 4
               8 |2 2 3 4 2 2 3 4 2 3
```

5. Create a file RATE containing the information in this table. Then use this file to print a two-column report showing the product numbers and the average rating for each product.
6. Use the file RATE to print a report as in Problem 5. However, the average ratings are to appear from smallest to largest.

7. Use the file RATE to print a two-column report as follows. The first column is to give the product numbers receiving at least six ratings of 3 or better. The second column is to give the number of these ratings obtained.

8. An error in the transcription of the numbers in the survey is discovered. The correct results for Families 1 and 7 are as follows:

Family 1	3 2 4 2 2 4 1 3
Family 7	2 3 4 4 2 4 3 2

Update the file RATE to include these corrected values.

Problems 9–11 refer to the following files maintained by the Sevard Company.

	File SST				File WEEKLY	
Employee ID	Year-to-date income	Hourly rate			Employee ID	This week's hours
24168	12442.40	7.35			24168	40
13725	17250.13	11.41			13725	36
34104	10425.00	6.50			34104	32
28636	11474.25	6.75			28636	40
35777	15450.35	10.45			35777	40
15742	14452.00	10.05			15742	30

9. A Social Security tax deduction of 6.65% is taken on the first $29,700 earned by an employee. Once this amount is reached, no further deduction is made. Using the files SST and WEEKLY, produce a report giving the ID number, the current week's gross pay, and this week's Social Security deduction for each employee.

10. Modify the program written for Problem 9 to update the year-to-date income in the file SST.

11. Using the files SST and WEEKLY, print a list of the ID numbers of all employees who have satisfied the Social Security tax requirement for the current year. With each ID number printed, give the year-to-date income figure.

12. The file NAMES contains a list of names. Write a program to allow a user to issue any of the following commands: LIST, to list the names at the terminal; ADD, to add a name to the list; DELETE, to delete a name from the list; ALPHA, to alphabetize the list of names; DONE, to update the file NAMES and terminate the run. After each command other than DONE is carried out, the user should be allowed to issue another command. (You should be able to use your program to create the file NAMES as well as to update an existing file.)

13. A file GRADE contains the following information.

```
2
Edwards       75    93
Lebak         91    65
Myers         41    83
Nolan         89    51
Post          78    63
Sovenson      56    87
Block         82    82
```

The two numbers following each name represent grades, and the first value—the number 2—tells how many grades have previously been recorded on the file for each student. Write a program to allow a user to enter any of the following commands.

LIST:	to obtain a printout of the current contents of the file GRADE.
AVERAGE:	to obtain a listing of student names and averages.
ADD:	to add an additional grade for each student. (Each student's name should be printed to allow the user to enter the next grade.)
DONE:	to terminate the run. When this command is issued, an updated file GRADE should be created.

14. Write a program to create a file PRIME that contains all prime numbers less than 10,000. The file PRIME is to be used in Problems 15–17.

Problems 15–17 refer to the file PRIME created in Problem 14.

15. Input a positive integer N≥2. Determine all prime factors of N and also the sum of these factors. (Use the file PRIME.)
16. Input a positive integer N≥2. Determine the prime factorization of N. If N = 90 the output should be

    2 3 3 5

    If N = 13 the output should be

    13 IS PRIME

    (Use the file PRIME.)
17. Update PRIME to include all prime numbers less than 20,000. (To do this, calculate only those primes between 10,000 and 20,000.)

13.7 Review true-or-false quiz

1. At most two files can be referenced in a program—one for input data and one for output data.   T   F
2. If a program uses a file as an input file, then the program cannot also use this file as an output file.   T   F
3. Input data to a program cannot be read from a file and also from DATA lines. These two methods of supplying input data are incompatible.   T   F
4. BCD is an acronym for the expression *binary coded data*.   T   F
5. A number stored on a BCD file is stored as a sequence of codes, with each code representing a single character.   T   F
6. A number stored on a binary file is stored in a form that corresponds exactly to the way the computer stores the number in its memory unit.   T   F
7. The contents of a binary file are easily examined using the LIST command.   T   F
8. The END# specifier (NODATA statement, on some systems) obviates the need to use an EOD-tag as the last entry or a count as the first entry in a data file.   T   F

Subroutines

In Chapter 7 you saw that, when a function is needed in a program, it is sufficient to define the function once in a DEF statement. The function may then be referenced as many times as necessary. Very often you will find that the same *sequence* of instructions is needed in two or more places within a program. BASIC also allows you to include this sequence of instructions just once in a program, even though it is to be used in several different parts of the program. Such a sequence of instructions is called a **subroutine.** In this chapter the GOSUB and RETURN statements, which allow you to write and use BASIC subroutines, are described and illustrated.

Some, but not all, BASIC systems allow you to construct user-defined functions whose definitions cannot be made in a single DEF statement. Such functions are called *multi-line functions* and are described in Section 14.3.

14.1 The GOSUB and RETURN statements

The GOSUB statement is used to transfer control to a subroutine, and the RETURN statement is used to transfer control back from the subroutine. A BASIC subroutine is any sequence of BASIC programming lines to carry out a specific task. It *must* contain at least one RETURN statement. Here is a subroutine to print a row of dashes.

```
500 REM ***SUBROUTINE TO PRINT 40 DASHES***
510 FOR I=1 TO 40
520    PRINT "-";
530 NEXT I
540 PRINT
550 RETURN
```

Program control is transferred to this subroutine each time the statement GOSUB 500 is encountered during program execution. For example, in a program containing this subroutine, the three lines

```
200 GOSUB 500
210 PRINT "TODAY'S STARTING LINE-UP"
220 GOSUB 500
230 (next statement)
```

will cause the printout

```
-----------------------------------------------
TODAY'S STARTING LINE-UP
-----------------------------------------------
```

Line 200 transfers control to line 500 (the subroutine) and a row of dashes is printed. The RETURN statement in line 550 then transfers control back to line 210, the first line following the GOSUB statement just used. When line 220 is encountered, control again passes to the subroutine and another row of dashes is printed. This time the RETURN statement transfers control back to line 230.

EXAMPLE 1. Here is a program to print the average of any two input values and also the average of their squares.

```
100 PRINT "ENTER TWO NUMBERS";
110 INPUT A,B
120 GOSUB 300
130 LET A=A*A
140 LET B=B*B
150 PRINT "SQUARES ARE:";A;B
160 GOSUB 300
170 STOP
300 REM ***SUBROUTINE TO PRINT THE AVERAGE OF A AND B***
310 LET M=(A+B)/2
320 PRINT "THEIR AVERAGE IS";M
330 RETURN
999 END
RUN

ENTER TWO NUMBERS? 3,4
THEIR AVERAGE IS 3.5
SQUARES ARE: 9  16
THEIR AVERAGE IS 12.5
READY
```

The subroutine consists of lines 300–330. Line 120 transfers control to line 300, and 3.5, the average of 3 and 4, is printed. The RETURN statement then transfers control back to line 130, the line following the GOSUB statement just used. Lines 130 and 140 assign the squares (9 and 16) to A and B, and line 150 prints these squares. When line 160 is encountered, a second transfer is made to the subroutine and 12.5, the average of 9 and 16, is printed. This time the RETURN statement transfers control back to line 170, which, in this program, terminates execution. Following is a schematic representation of the action described.

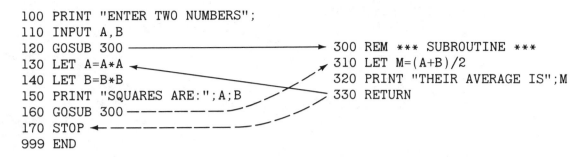

Remark 1

The program segment on the left is referred to as the **main program** or the **calling program,** and we say that the main program "calls" the subroutine.

Remark 2

The STOP statement (line 170) is used to ensure that the subroutine is entered only under the control of a GOSUB statement.

Remark 3

The GOSUB statement differs from the GO TO statement in that it causes the computer to "remember" which statement to execute next when it encounters a RETURN statement. As described, this is the statement immediately following the GOSUB statement used to "call" the subroutine.

Remark 4

Note that we used M (for mean) and not A (for average), in the subroutine. If line 310 is changed to

```
310 LET A=(A+B)/2
```

the original value of A will be destroyed during the first subroutine "call" and incorrect results will be printed. Thus, when writing subroutines you must make sure that the variable names you use do not conflict with variable names used in other parts of the program for different purposes.

The general forms of the GOSUB and RETURN statements are as follows.

ln$_1$ **GOSUB ln**$_2$ (**ln**$_2$ is the line number of the first statement of the subroutine.)

ln RETURN

Line **ln**$_1$ transfers control to line **ln**$_2$, and program execution continues as usual. When the first RETURN statement is encountered, control transfers back to the line following line **ln**$_1$.

A subroutine may be called from within another subroutine. Following is a schematic representation of a program that does this. The action of the program is indicated by the arrows labeled a, b, c, and d.

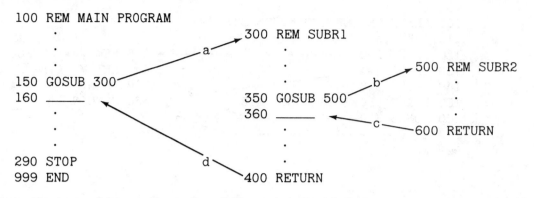

EXAMPLE 2. Here is a program to print a short report for each employee whose name and annual salary are included in DATA lines.

Two subroutines are used. The first prints the report for one employee. The second simply prints a row of dashes and is "called" by the first subroutine.

The main program

```
100 REM MAIN PROGRAM
110 REM N$=EMPLOYEE'S NAME
120 REM  A=ANNUAL SALARY OF N$
130 READ N$,A
140    IF N$="END-OF-DATA" THEN 999
150    REM PRINT ANNUAL AND WEEKLY SALARIES
160    PRINT
180    GOSUB 300
190 GO TO 130
900 DATA "S.J.BRYANT",18500
910 DATA "T.S.ENDICOTT",25700
998 DATA "END-OF-DATA",0
999 END
```

The first subroutine

```
300 REM ***PRINT SHORT SALARY REPORT***
310 REM   W=WEEKLY SALARY
320 GOSUB 500
330 LET W=A/52
340 LET W=INT(W*100+0.5)/100
350 PRINT "EMPLOYEE NAME: ";N$
360 PRINT "ANNUAL SALARY:";A
370 PRINT "WEEKLY SALARY:";W
380 GOSUB 500
390 RETURN
```

The second subroutine

```
500 REM ***SUBROUTINE DASHES***
510 FOR I=1 TO 40
520    PRINT "-";
530 NEXT I
540 PRINT
550 RETURN
```

For the given DATA lines (900–998), this program produces the following printout.

```
------------------------------------------
EMPLOYEE NAME: S.J.BRYANT
ANNUAL SALARY: 18500
WEEKLY SALARY: 355.77
------------------------------------------


------------------------------------------
EMPLOYEE NAME: T.S.ENDICOTT
ANNUAL SALARY: 25700
WEEKLY SALARY: 494.23
------------------------------------------
```

Remark

Programming applications calling for long printed reports are not uncommon. If confronted with such a programming task you will do well to examine the requirements carefully to see if the long report really consists of several short reports that are to be repeated several times. Such short reports are often ideal candidates for subroutines.

In the preceding chapters we have attempted to stress the importance of segmenting programming tasks into smaller, more manageable subtasks. A program can often be made more readable if such subtasks are performed by subroutines, even though they may be referenced in only one programming line. An instance of this practice is the subroutine used in the preceding example to print a salary report for one employee. Note that it is referenced only in line 180 of the main program.

Following are some comments on the use of subroutines.

1. The first line (or lines) of a subroutine should describe the task being performed.
2. A subroutine must contain one or more RETURN statements.
3. A subroutine must be entered only by using a GOSUB statement. You should use a STOP statement as the last line of your main program to avoid inadvertently entering a subroutine.
4. A subroutine should be used if it will make your program easier to read and understand.
5. A subroutine can contain a GOSUB statement transferring control to another subroutine. However, a subroutine should not call itself.

We conclude this section with two examples illustrating the use of subroutines. The first is an application to economics and the second concerns the manipulation of whole numbers.

EXAMPLE 3

An airline charter service estimates that ticket sales of $1000 are required to break even on a certain excursion. It thus makes the following offer to an interested organization. If ten people sign up, the cost will be $100 per person. However, for each additional person, the cost per person will be reduced by $3.00. Produce a table showing the cost per customer and the profit to the airline for N = 10, 11, 12, . . . , 30 customers. In addition, a message is to be printed giving the number of customers that will maximize the profit for the airline. Column headings, underlined by a row of dashes, are to be used, and a row of dashes is to precede and follow the final message.

Problem analysis

Let's use the following variable names.

N = number of people who sign up for the excursion (N will be between 10 and 30, inclusive).
C = cost per person (if N people sign up, C = 130 − 3N).
P = profit to the airline (if N people sign up, P = NC − 1000).
N1 = number of people yielding a maximum profit to the airline.
P1 = maximum profit to the airline (initially, P1 = 0).

Producing a table of values with column headings is not new to us. We can use the statement

```
PRINT "NO. OF PEOPLE","COST/PERSON","AIRLINE PROFIT"
```

to print the column headings and a FOR/NEXT loop initiated with FOR N = 10 TO 30 to produce the table values. However, if we wish our columns to be centered under the column headings, the TAB function or a PRINT USING statement must be used. We will use the TAB function:

```
PRINT TAB(5);N;TAB(19);C;TAB(36);P
```

According to the problem statement, three rows of dashes are to be printed. Rather than write the loop that does this three times, we will use a subroutine.

```
500 REM SUBR TO PRINT A ROW OF DASHES
510 FOR I=1 TO 46
520    PRINT "-";
530 NEXT I
540 PRINT
550 RETURN
```

Finally, the number N1 of customers that yields a maximum profit P1 to the airline must be determined. Each time a new profit P is computed, it will be compared with P1, the largest profit obtained to that point. If P is larger, we will let P1 = P and N1 = N. If not, N1 and P1 will not be changed. To keep our main program as uncluttered as possible, we also do this in a subroutine.

```
600 REM SUBR TO RECORD THE NUMBER N1 OF CUSTOMERS
610 REM YIELDING THE MAXIMUM PROFIT P1
620 IF P<=P1 THEN 650
630 LET P1=P
640 LET N1=N
650 RETURN
```

The program

```
100 REM PROGRAM TO PRINT A TABLE OF AIRLINE EXCURSION RATES
110 REM AND DETERMINE THE MAXIMUM PROFIT TO THE AIRLINE
120 LET P1=0
130 PRINT "NO. OF PEOPLE","COST/PERSON","AIRLINE PROFIT"
140 GOSUB 500
150 REM COMPUTE AND PRINT THE TABLE VALUES
```

```
160 FOR N=10 TO 30
170    LET C=130-3*N
180    LET P=N*C-1000
190    PRINT TAB(5);N;TAB(19);C;TAB(36);P
200    GOSUB 600
210 NEXT N
220 GOSUB 500
230 PRINT N1;"CUSTOMERS YIELD MAX PROFIT OF";P1;"DOLLARS."
240 GOSUB 500
250 STOP
500 REM SUBR TO PRINT A ROW OF DASHES
510 FOR I=1 TO 46
520    PRINT "-";
530 NEXT I
540 PRINT
550 RETURN
600 REM SUBR TO RECORD THE NUMBER N1 OF CUSTOMERS
610 REM YIELDING THE MAXIMUM PROFIT P1
620 IF P<=P1 THEN 650
630 LET P1=P
640 LET N1=N
650 RETURN
999 END
RUN
```

```
NO. OF PEOPLE   COST/PERSON     AIRLINE PROFIT
----------------------------------------------------
       10           100             0
       11            97            67
       12            94           128
       13            91           183
       14            88           232
       15            85           275
       16            82           312
       17            79           343
       18            76           368
       19            73           387
       20            70           400
       21            67           407
       22            64           408
       23            61           403
       24            58           392
       25            55           375
       26            52           352
       27            49           323
       28            46           288
       29            43           247
       30            40           200
----------------------------------------------------
 22 CUSTOMERS YIELD MAX PROFIT OF 408 DOLLARS.
----------------------------------------------------

READY
```

EXAMPLE 4

Let's write a program to do whole-number arithmetic. For any four positive integers A, B, C, and D typed at the terminal, we will find two integers X and Y for which

$$A/B + C/D = X/Y$$

and X/Y is reduced to lowest terms. The output will be printed as displayed. For example, if 3, 4, 5, and 6 are typed, the output will be

$$3/4 + 5/6 = 19/12.$$

Problem analysis

This is a familiar problem, and the approach we will take is the same as that used in elementary school arithmetic.

1. The least common denominator (LCD) E of B and D will be found.
2. A/B and C/D will be changed to equivalent fractions P/E and Q/E. This will give A/B + C/D = (P + Q)/E.
3. The quotient (P + Q)/E will be reduced to lowest terms X/Y.

This approach serves to *segment* the original task into three more manageable subtasks.

1. There are many ways to find the LCD of two numbers B and D. The method we will use says that the LCD of B and D is B · D/F, where F is the greatest common factor of B and D. For example, the LCD of 3 and 5 is 3 · 5/1 = 15; the LCD of 6 and 9 is 6 · 9/3 = 18; the LCD of 15 and 25 is 15 · 25/5 = 75.

The algorithm we employ to find the greatest common factor F of B and D uses the fact that F must be an integer between 1 and the smaller of B and D inclusive. For example, the greatest common factor of 3 and 8 must be between 1 and 3; the greatest common factor of 12 and 18 must be between 1 and 12. To find F exactly, it is necessary only to check all the integers from 1 to the smaller of B and D. The largest such integer that is a factor of both B and D is the greatest common factor F. The following flowchart segment describes a good procedure for this. After calculating F, we can write E, the LCD of B and D, as E = B · D/F.

(B and D are any positive integers)

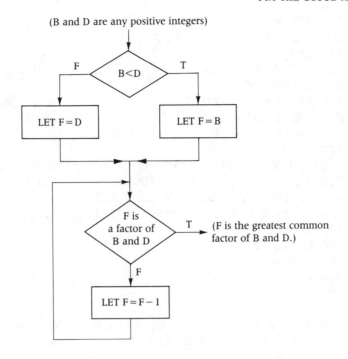

(F is the greatest common factor of B and D.)

2. We must find P and Q such that

$$A/B = P/E \quad \text{and} \quad C/D = Q/E.$$

Solving for P and Q, we obtain

$$P = A \cdot (E \div B);$$
$$Q = C \cdot (E \div D).$$

The sum A/B + C/D is now (P + Q)/E.

3. (P + Q)/E must now be reduced to obtain X/Y. To do this, we find the greatest common factor of P + Q and E and divide it into P + Q to get X and into E to get Y. But we already have a method for doing so from Part (1). If we let B = P + Q and D = E, and use the flowchart to get F, we can write

$$X = (P + Q)/F \quad \text{and} \quad Y = E/F.$$

Notice that the same sequence of steps (the calculation of the greatest common factor) must be used in two different parts of the program. This presents an excellent opportunity to use a subroutine.

The program

```
100 PRINT "ENTER FOUR POSITIVE INTEGERS A,B,C,AND D"
110 PRINT "FOR THE TWO FRACTIONS A/B AND C/D."
120 INPUT A,B,C,D
130 REM CALCULATE THE LEAST COMMON DENOMINATOR E
140 GOSUB 300
150 LET E=B*D/F
160 REM FIND P AND Q WITH P/E=A/B, Q/E=C/D
170 LET P=A*(E/B)
180 LET Q=C*(E/D)
```

```
190 REM REDUCE (P+Q)/E TO LOWEST TERMS X/Y
200 REM AND PRINT RESULTS
210 LET B=P+Q
220 LET D=E
230 GOSUB 300
240 LET X=(P+Q)/F
250 LET Y=E/F
260 PRINT A;"/";B;"+";C;"/";D;"=";X;"/";Y
270 STOP
300 REM SUBROUTINE FINDS GREATEST COMMON FACTOR
310 REM OF B AND D AND STORES RESULT IN F
320 IF B<D THEN LET F=B ELSE LET F=D
330 IF (B/F=INT(B/F)) AND (D/F=INT(D/F)) THEN 360
340    LET F=F-1
350 GO TO 330
360 RETURN
999 END
RUN

ENTER FOUR POSITIVE INTEGERS A,B,C,AND D
FOR THE TWO FRACTIONS A/B AND C/D.
? 3,4,5,6
 3 / 4 + 5 / 6 = 19 / 12
READY
```

14.2 Problems

1. What will be printed when each program is run?

   a.
   ```
   100 FOR I=1 TO 3
   110    READ X,Y
   120    GOSUB 300
   130 NEXT I
   140 STOP
   300 PRINT I;X;Y;X+Y
   310 RETURN
   500 DATA 3,5,8
   510 DATA 6,-2,1
   999 END
   ```

   b.
   ```
   110 LET A=5
   120 LET B=3
   130 IF A<B THEN 150
   140 GOSUB 200
   150 GOSUB 300
   160 GO TO 999
   200 PRINT A-B
   210 RETURN
   300 PRINT B-A
   400 RETURN
   999 END
   ```

   c.
   ```
   100 FOR I=1 TO 4
   110    GOSUB 200
   120    PRINT S
   130 NEXT I
   140 STOP
   200 LET S=0
   210 FOR J=1 TO I
   220    LET S=S+J
   230 NEXT J
   240 RETURN
   999 END
   ```

   d.
   ```
   110 LET M=5
   120 GOSUB 300
   130 PRINT M
   140 STOP
   300 LET M=M+1
   310 GOSUB 400
   320 RETURN
   400 LET M=(M+1)*(M+1)↑2
   410 RETURN
   999 END
   ```

2. Write a program to print all numbers in a data list and then print them again, this time in ascending order. Assume that the first datum is a count of how many numbers are included. Use the following algorithm.

   a. Read the count N and the array A.
   b. Print A.
   c. Sort A into ascending order.
   d. Print the sorted array A and stop.

Since the list must be printed twice, use a subroutine for this task. Also, to keep the main program as simple as possible, do the sorting in a subroutine. Use the given algorithm to guide your choice of REM statements.

3. A data list contains many sets of scores S1,S2, and S3. The three values 0, 0, 0 are used to terminate the data list. Write a program to print a four-column report as follows. The three scores are to be printed in the first three columns, and the fourth is to contain the larger of the two values (S1 + S2 + S3)/3 and (S1 + S2 + 2 * S3)/4. Use a subroutine to process S1, S2, and S3 to obtain the larger of these two "averages." The subroutine is to contain no print statements. (Subscripted variables are not required.)

4. A list of numbers is to be processed to obtain a two-column printout. The first column is to contain the numbers in the order given, and the second is to contain a count of how many numbers in the list are strictly less than the number appearing in the first column. Write a program to allow a user to input any list of numbers to obtain the printout described. Use the following algorithm.

   a. Input the array A.
   b. For each number A(I) in the list, determine the count C(I) of how many numbers are less than A(I).
   c. Print the arrays A and C side by side.

Use a subroutine to carry out step (b). Choose REM statements so that your program is easy to understand. (You are not to assume that the numbers will be typed in increasing order.)

5. Write a program for the following game. There are two players, player A and player B, who alternate in choosing a whole number from 1 to 5. (Players should lose their turns if the choice is not between 1 and 5.) Although the players are not aware of it, each number chosen is assigned a point value according to the following table.

Number chosen	Point value
1	3
2	2
3	2
4	1
5	2

The first player to accumulate a total of 15 points wins. Messages should be printed to indicate whose turn it is and, of course, who the winner is when the game is over. The point value for the number chosen by a player is to be determined in a subroutine.

6. An apple orchard occupying one acre of land now contains 25 apple trees, and each tree yields 450 apples per season. For each new tree planted, the yield per tree will be reduced by 10 apples per season. How many additional trees should be planted so that the total yield is as large as possible? Produce a table showing the yield per tree and the total yield if N = 1, 2, 3, . . . , 25 additional trees are planted. Use column headings underlined by a row of dashes, and also separate the message, telling how many additional trees to plant, from the table by a row of dashes.

7. An organization can charter a ship for a harbor cruise for $9.75 a ticket provided that at least 200 people agree to go. However, the ship's owner agrees to reduce the cost per ticket by 25¢ for each additional 10 people signing up. Thus, if 220 people sign up, the cost per person will be $9.25. Write a program to determine the maximum revenue the ship's owner can receive if the ship's capacity is 400 people. In addition, prepare a table showing the cost per person and the total amount paid for N = 200, 210, 220, . . . , 400 people. Use column headings underlined by a row of dashes. The maximum revenue the ship's owner can receive should be printed following the table and separated from it by a row of dashes.

8. A merchant must pay the fixed price of $1.00 a yard for a certain fabric. From experience it is known that 1000 yards will be sold each month if the material is sold at cost and also that each 10-cent increase in price will mean that 50 fewer yards will be sold each month. Write a program to produce a table showing the merchant's profit for each selling price from $1.00 to $3.00 in increments of 10¢. In addition, a message giving the selling price that will maximize the profit is to be printed. Column headings underlined with a row of dashes are to be used, and a row of dashes is to separate the table from the final message.

9. Write a program to allow a user to create an array L as follows. The user is allowed to input as many numbers X as desired. When a value for X is entered, the following is to happen.

a. If X = 0, the entire array created to that point is to be printed and the program is to halt.

b. If X is negative, the array to that point is to be printed and the user is to be allowed to enter another number.

c. If X is positive and not already in the array, it should be added to L and the user is to be allowed to enter another number. (Note that the very first positive value typed will be placed in L(1).)

d. If X is already in the array L, the index I for which L(I) = X is to be printed and the user is to enter another number.

A subroutine is to be used to search the array L for the value X. The subroutine is to have no GO TO statements, is not to print anything, and is not to be used to add X to the array.

10. Write a subroutine to determine the digits of a positive integer K, and store these digits in a list whose name is also K. Using this subroutine, write a program to print the digits of the integer K as a sequence, to print this sequence in the reverse order, and finally to print the positive integer determined by reversing the digits of the original number. For example, if K = 347, the output should be as follows.

$$
\begin{array}{ccc}
3 & 4 & 7 \\
7 & 4 & 3 \\
743 & &
\end{array}
$$

11. Consider the following three print statements.

```
320 PRINT "XXX---XXX---XXX---XXX"
420 PRINT "---XXX---XXX---XXX"
520 PRINT "XXXXXXXXXXXXXXXXXXXXX"
```

In what follows, XXX---XXX---XXX---XXX is referred to as the pattern of line 320, and similarly for lines 420 and 520.

a. Write three subroutines: the first to print the pattern of line 320 L times, the second to print the pattern of line 420 M times, and the third to print the pattern of line 520 N times.

b. Write a calling program to allow a user to input values for L, M, and N so that L + M + N lines will be printed: L lines of the first pattern, M of the second, and N of the third.

c. Write a second program to allow a user to input seven integers A(1), B(1), A(2), B(2), A(3), B(3), and C. A(1), A(2), and A(3) are to be the integers 1, 2, or 3. The computer is then to print

pattern number A(1) on B(1) successive lines;
pattern number A(2) on B(2) successive lines;
pattern number A(3) on B(3) successive lines.

This entire process is to be repeated C times.

d. Alter the patterns specified in lines 320, 420, and 520. (Note: The process described in this problem is not unlike the method used to design intricate patterns in weaving.)

12. n! (read "n factorial") is defined as the product

$$
n! = n \cdot (n - 1) \cdot (n - 2) \cdots 3 \cdot 2 \cdot 1
$$

if n is a positive integer and as 1 if n = 0. Write a subroutine to evaluate n! for any nonnegative integer n and then a simple calling program so that the subroutine can be tested.

13. The binomial coefficient

$$
\binom{n}{r} = \frac{n!}{(n - r)!\, r!}
$$

occurs in many different contexts. Here it is assumed that n and r are integers such that $0 \leq r \leq n$.

a. Using the factorial subroutine of Problem 12 write a subroutine to evaluate $\binom{n}{r}$ for any integers n and r. Write a simple calling program to test this subroutine. Run it for large values of n and explain what went wrong.

b. Write a subroutine to correctly evaluate $\binom{n}{r}$ for large values of n. (You must not use the factorial subroutine.)

14. Use the subroutine of Problem 13(b) to do the following.

  a. Evaluate the sum

$$S = \binom{N}{0} + \binom{N}{1} + \binom{N}{2} + \cdots + \binom{N}{N}$$

  b. For each integer N from 0 to 10, the N + 1 values

$$\binom{N}{0}, \binom{N}{1}, \binom{N}{2}, \cdots, \binom{N}{N}$$

  are to be printed on a line. Use TAB(6*I + 1) to print the Ith of these N + 1 values.

  c. Print the following values. N is input during program execution.

$$\binom{1}{0}, \binom{2}{1}, \binom{3}{2}, \cdots, \binom{N}{N-1}$$

  d. Print the following values.

$$\binom{2}{0}, \binom{3}{1}, \binom{4}{2}, \cdots, \binom{N}{N-2}$$

14.3 Multi-line functions

The user-defined functions discussed in Section 7.3 may be referred to as single-line functions, since they must be completely defined by only one program statement. Some BASIC systems allow you to write multi-line functions by using the DEF and FNEND (end of function) statements.

EXAMPLE 5. Here is a program to print the smaller of any two numbers entered at the terminal.

```
100 DEF FNS(X,Y)
110     IF X<=Y THEN LET FNS=X
120     IF X>Y THEN LET FNS=Y
130 FNEND
140 PRINT "ENTER TWO NUMBERS";
150 INPUT A,B
160 LET S=FNS(A,B)
170 PRINT "SMALLER IS",S
180 END
RUN

ENTER TWO NUMBERS? 7,3
SMALLER IS      3
READY
```

Execution of this program begins at line 140. Lines 100–130 serve to define the function FNS but cause no action until the function is referenced in line 160. When the function reference FNS(A,B) in line 160 is encountered, A and B supply values for the variables X and Y appearing in the function definition and the lines between the DEF and FNEND statements are executed. These two lines assign the smaller of X and Y (equivalently of A and B) to FNS. This value, FNS, is the value of the expression FNS(A,B) in line 160.

Remark 1   Line 160 shows that the multi-line function FNS is referenced in exactly the same way that single-line functions are referenced.

Remark 2   You may have noticed that we could have defined FNS as follows.

```
100 DEF FNS(X,Y)
110    IF X<=Y THEN LET FNS=X ELSE LET FNS=Y
120 FNEND
```

Although only one statement is needed between the DEF and FNEND statements, the function FNS cannot be defined as a single-line function. The purpose of single-line functions is to assign a name to a *numerical expression* so that the expression can be referenced by name. A multi-line function can be used to assign a name to any BASIC *statement* or group of statements.

Remark 3   As shown in lines 110 and 120, a value must be assigned to the function name FNS before the FNEND statement is encountered.

EXAMPLE 6

Let's write a program for the following game. Two players alternate in typing a whole number from 1 to 5. The computer assigns a point value (unknown to the players) for each number typed according to the following table.

Number chosen	Point value
1	3
2	2
3	2
4	1
.5	2
any other	0

The first player to accumulate a total of 15 points or more wins.

Problem analysis   The input and output values for this program are as follows.

Input: A sequence of numbers, alternately typed by the two players.
Output: The scores of the two players when one of them has a score of 15 or more.

An algorithm for this task is not difficult if we leave out the details. In the algorithm we use the following variable names.

A = Accumulated score of first player.
B = Accumulated score of second player.
X = The most recent input value.

The algorithm
a. Initialize A and B to 0.
b. Input the first player's selection X.
c. Add the point value of X to A.
d. If A> = 15, print the results and stop.
e. Input the second player's selection X.
f. Add the point value of X to B.
g. If B> = 15, print the results and stop.
h. Go to step (b).

In coding this algorithm, only steps (c) and (f) may be troublesome. Since the point value of X is the same whether X is typed by the first player (step (b)) or the second (step (e)), we can use the following multi-line function FNS to obtain the point value FNS(X) for X.

```
DEF FNS(X)
    LET FNS=0
    IF X=1 THEN LET FNS=3
    IF (X=2) OR (X=3) OR (X=5) THEN LET FNS=2
    IF X=4 THEN LET FNS=1
FNEND
```

The required program can now be coded directly from the algorithm.

The program
```
100 REM THE FUNCTION FNS DETERMINES THE POINT VALUE
110 REM OF ANY NUMBER X
120 DEF FNS(X)
130    LET FNS=0
140    IF X=1 THEN LET FNS=3
150    IF (X=2) OR (X=3) OR (X=5) THEN LET FNS=2
160    IF X=4 THEN FNS=1
170 FNEND
180 REM----PROGRAM EXECUTION BEGINS HERE----
190 PRINT "*****GAME FOR TWO PLAYERS*****"
200 PRINT "PLAYERS ALTERNATE IN CHOOSING ONE OF"
205 PRINT "THE NUMBERS 1,2,3,4,AND 5."
210 PRINT "THESE NUMBERS HAVE CODED POINT VALUES."
220 PRINT "THE FIRST PLAYER TO ACCUMULATE"
225 PRINT "AT LEAST 15 POINTS WINS."
230 PRINT "NUMBERS OTHER THAN 1,2,3,4,AND 5"
235 PRINT "HAVE THE POINT VALUE 0."
240 REM     A=ACCUMULATED SCORE FOR FIRST PLAYER
250 REM     B=ACCUMULATED SCORE FOR SECOND PLAYER
260 LET A=0
270 LET B=0
280 PRINT "FIRST PLAYER'S TURN";
290    INPUT X
300    LET A=A+FNS(X)
310    IF A>=15 THEN 370
320 PRINT "SECOND PLAYER'S TURN";
330    INPUT X
340    LET B=B+FNS(X)
350    IF B>=15 THEN 370
360 GO TO 280
370 REM GAME IS OVER-PRINT THE RESULTS
380 PRINT
```

```
390 PRINT "FIRST PLAYER'S SCORE",A
400 PRINT "SECOND PLAYER'S SCORE",B
410 IF A>=15 THEN PRINT "FIRST"; ELSE PRINT "SECOND";
420 PRINT " PLAYER WINS"
430 END
```

Remark

An interesting variation of this game is to have two players play many games until one of the players can figure out exactly what point values correspond to the numbers 1, 2, 3, 4, and 5. If you choose to use the program in this way, you might modify it so that the point values from the numbers 1, 2, 3, 4, and 5 are easily changed.

Here are some rules governing the use of multi-line functions.

1. The variables used in the DEF statement are called "dummy" variables (X and Y in Example 5 and X in Example 6). They may be used elsewhere in the program for some other purpose with no conflict arising.

2. Variables other than the "dummy" variables may be used between the DEF and FNEND statements. Unlike the "dummy" variables, such a variable has the same meaning wherever it may appear in the program. The usual practice while writing functions is to use only variable names that are not used elsewhere in the program (dummy variables are an exception to this practice).

3. The function name must be assigned a value before the FNEND statement is encountered.

4. The function name can appear on the left of the equal sign in a LET statement but not on the right.

5. The only way the program statements in a function definition can be executed is by referencing the function. A GO TO or IF statement must not transfer control from outside a function definition to a line in the definition. Similarly, a GO TO or IF statement appearing in a function definition must not transfer control to a statement outside the function definition.

6. Functions are defined near the beginning of a program before they are referenced.

14.4 Problems

What will be printed when the programs in Problems 1 and 2 are run?

```
1. 100 DEF FNM(X,Y)
   110     IF X<Y THEN LET FNM=Y
   120     IF X>=Y THEN LET FNM=X
   130 FNEND
   140 READ A
   150     READ B
   160     IF B=9999 THEN 190
   170     LET A=FNM(A,B)
   180 GO TO 150
   190 PRINT A
   200 DATA 3,5,1,7,4,9,2,999
   210 END
```

2.
```
100 DEF FNA(X,Y)=SQR(X↑2+Y↑2)
110 DEF FNB(X,Y)=X+Y
120 DEF FNC(X,Y)
130    IF FNA(X,Y)<FNB(X,Y) THEN LET FNC=FNA(X,Y)
140    IF FNA(X,Y)>=FNB(X,Y) THEN LET FNC=FNB(X,Y)
150 FNEND
160 FOR I=1 TO 3
170    READ A,B
180    PRINT FNC(A,B)
190 NEXT I
200 DATA 1,1,3,4,5,12
210 END
```

3. Write a multi-line function FNS(X) to give -1 if X has a negative value, 1 if X has a positive value, and 0 if X is zero.

Write a program to perform each task specified in Problems 4–11.

4. Input the three numbers A, B, and C from the quadratic equation $Ax^2 + Bx + C = 0$. If the equation has no real roots, print a message to that effect. If it has real roots, print the larger of the two roots. Use a multi-line function to determine the larger root.

5. Produce a two-column table in which the first column contains the values of X and the second contains the maximum of sin X, cos X, and tan X ($X = 0, 0.1, 0.2, \ldots, 1.5$). Use a multi-line function to determine this maximum value.

6. Produce a table of values for the function whose value is $1 - x^2$ for $0 \leqslant x < 1$ and $1 - (x - 2)^2$ for $1 \leqslant x \leqslant 2$. The function values are to be determined by a multi-line function.

7. Determine the gross salary for an H-hour week if the hourly wage is D dollars and if time-and-a-half is earned for all hours worked over 32. The gross salary is to be found by a multi-line function.

8. Use a multi-line function to determine the least common multiple of any two positive integers typed at the terminal.

14.5 Review true-or-false quiz

1. A program need not contain the same number of GOSUB statements as RETURN statements.   T F

2. The GOSUB statement is really unnecessary, since the GO TO statement will accomplish the same thing.   T F

3. A STOP statement must appear on the line that immediately precedes the first line of each subroutine.   T F

4. If one subroutine calls a second subroutine, the first must appear in the program before the second.   T F

5. If a variable appears both in a subroutine and in the main program, it can be assigned any value in the subroutine without changing its value in the main program.   T F

6. Subroutines should be used only when a group of statements is to be performed more than once.   T F

7. Before a subroutine call is made, care must be taken to ensure that variables appearing in the subroutine are assigned their proper values.   T F

8. When defining a multi-line function, you must assign a value to the function name before the FNEND statement is encountered.   T F

9. Any variable appearing between the DEF and FNEND statements of a function definition can appear elsewhere in the program for any purpose whatever.   T F

15

Random Numbers and Their Application

If a coin is tossed several times, a sequence such as HTTHTHHHTTH, where H denotes a head and T a tail, is obtained. We call this a **randomly generated sequence** because each letter is the result of an experiment (tossing a coin) and could not have been determined without actually performing the experiment. Similarly, if a die (a cube with faces numbered 1 through 6) is rolled several times, a randomly generated sequence such as 5315264342 is obtained. The numbers in such a randomly generated sequence are called **random numbers.**

BASIC contains a built-in function called RND used to generate sequences of numbers that have the appearance of being randomly generated. Although these numbers are called random numbers, they are more accurately referred to as **pseudo-random numbers** because the RND function does not perform an experiment such as tossing a coin to produce a number; rather, it uses an algorithm carefully designed to generate sequences of numbers that emulate random sequences. This ability to generate such sequences makes it possible for us to use the computer in many new and interesting ways. Using "random-number generators," people have written computer programs to simulate the growth of a forest, to determine the best location for elevators in a proposed skyscraper, to assist social scientists in their statistical studies, to simulate game playing, and to perform many other tasks.

15.1 The RND function

The RND function is used somewhat differently than the other BASIC functions. If the expression RND(X) appears in a program, its value will be a number from 0 up to, but not including, 1:

    0 ≤ RND(X) < 1.

The particular value assumed by RND(X) is unpredictable. It will appear to have been selected randomly from the numbers between 0 and 1.

EXAMPLE 1. Here is a program to generate and print eight random numbers lying between 0 and 1.

```
100 LET X=1
110 FOR I=1 TO 8
120    PRINT RND(X)
130 NEXT I
140 END
RUN

1.78311E-2
.597702
.986238
.526585
.302629
.619982
.899148
.184081
READY
```

Observe that each time line 120 is executed a different number is printed even though the same expression RND(X) is used.

The value of X in RND(X) has different meanings on different systems; in Example 1, we used X = 1. Your system may allow or even require you to use RND(0), RND(−1), or some other form of the RND function. On some systems, RND(X) will produce different random sequences for different values of X. Experiment! The BASIC standard specifies that the abbreviated form RND be used; we will adhere to this latter form in what follows.

EXAMPLE 2. Here is a program to generate 1000 random numbers between 0 and 1 and determine how many are in the interval from 0.3 to 0.4.

```
10 LET C=0
20 FOR I=1 TO 1000
30    LET R=RND
40    IF (R>0.3) AND (R<0.4) THEN LET C=C+1
50 NEXT I
60 PRINT "OF 1000 NUMBERS GENERATED,"
70 PRINT C;"WERE BETWEEN 0.3 AND 0.4."
80 END
RUN

OF 1000 NUMBERS GENERATED,
 104 WERE BETWEEN 0.3 AND 0.4.
READY
```

Each time line 30 is executed, RND takes on a different value, which is then assigned to R. The IF statement at line 40 determines whether R lies in the specified interval. In this example it was necessary to assign the value of RND to a temporary variable R so that the comparisons could be made. If we had written

```
40 IF (RND>0.3) AND (RND<0.4) THEN LET C=C+1
```

the two occurrences of RND would have different values, which is not what was wanted in this situation.

The numbers generated by the RND function are nearly uniformly distributed between 0 and 1. For example, if many numbers are generated, approximately as many will be less than .5 as greater than .5, approximately twice as many will be between 0 and 2/3 as between 2/3 and 1, approximately 1/100th of the numbers will be between .37 and .38, and so on. The examples throughout the rest of this chapter illustrate how this property of random-number sequences can be put to use by a programmer.

EXAMPLE 3. Let's write a program to simulate tossing a coin 20 times. An H is to be printed each time a head occurs and a T each time a tail occurs.

Problem analysis

Since RND will be less than .5 approximately half the time, let's say that a head is tossed whenever RND is less than .5. The following program is then immediate.

```
10 FOR I=1 TO 20
20    IF RND<.5 THEN PRINT "H"; ELSE PRINT "T";
30 NEXT I
40 END
RUN

HHTHTTTHTTHTHTHHHTTH
READY
```

Remark

If you wish to simulate tossing a bent coin that produces a head twice as often as a tail, you could say that a head is the result whenever RND < .66667. Thus, one change in line 20 allows the same program to work in this case.

Normally, if a program containing RND is run a second time, exactly the same sequence of random numbers is generated and used. Although this result can be useful during the debugging process, it does not reflect what actually happens in real-life situations. The BASIC statement **RANDOMIZE** is designed to cause different and unpredictable sequences to be generated each time a program is run.[1] Its form is

ln RANDOMIZE

as illustrated in the following program.

---

[1] Some systems do not allow the RANDOMIZE statement but do provide the means for causing different sequences of random numbers to be generated. The BASIC manual for your system will describe how to do this.

EXAMPLE 4. Here are two "runs" of a program using RANDOMIZE.

```
100 RANDOMIZE
110 FOR I=1 TO 5
120    PRINT RND
130 NEXT I
140 END
RUN

 .182351
 .400231
 .909222
 .612347
 .338525
READY
RUN

 .621112
 .121235
 6.71728E-2
 .425276
 .882146
READY
```

We conclude this section with an example of how the RND function can be used to simulate a real-life situation.

EXAMPLE 5

A professional softball player has a lifetime batting average of .365. Assuming she will come to bat four times in each of her next 100 games, estimate in how many games she will go hitless, have one hit, have two hits, have three hits, and have four hits.

Problem analysis

To simulate one time at bat, we will generate a number RND and concede a hit if RND<0.365. For any one game we will compare four such numbers with 0.365. If in a particular game K hits are made (0≤K≤4), we will record this by adding 1 to the counter C(K + 1). Thus, C(1) counts the number of hitless games, C(2) the games in which one hit is made, and so on.

The flowchart

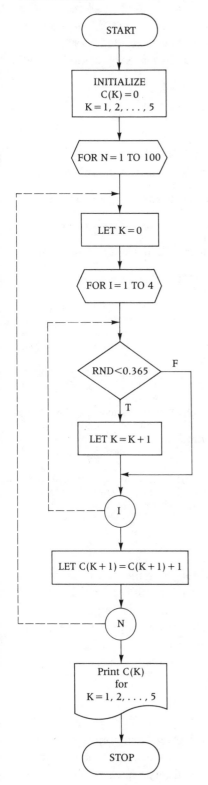

The program

```
100 REM INITIALIZE COUNTERS TO ZERO
110 FOR K=1 TO 5
120    LET C(K)=0
130 NEXT K
140 REM N LOOP COUNTS THE NUMBER OF GAMES
150 FOR N=1 TO 100
160    REM I LOOP DETERMINES NUMBER K OF HITS IN ONE GAME
170    LET K=0
180    FOR I=1 TO 4
190       IF RND<0.365 THEN LET K=K+1
200    NEXT I
210    LET C(K+1)=C(K+1)+1
220 NEXT N
230 PRINT "HITS PER GAME","FREQUENCY"
240 PRINT
250 FOR K=1 TO 5
260    PRINT TAB(6);K-1;TAB(18);C(K)
270 NEXT K
280 END
RUN

HITS PER GAME   FREQUENCY

      0             16
      1             39
      2             35
      3              9
      4              1
READY
```

Remark

In this example, we concede a hit if the condition RND<0.365 in line 190 is true. If we change this condition to RND<=0.365, essentially the same results will occur; it is extremely unlikely that RND will ever take on the exact value 0.365. In fact, if C denotes any constant, it is extremely unlikely that RND will take on the exact value C. But, even if it does, it will happen so rarely that no significant change in the simulation being carried out will occur.

15.2 Problems

Write a program to perform each task specified in Problems 1–10.

1. Print approximately one-fourth of all values appearing in DATA lines. A decision to print or not to print should be made as the number is read.
2. Print approximately 1% of all integers from 1000 to 9999, inclusive. They are to be selected randomly.
3. Simulate tossing two coins 100 times. The output should be a count of the number of times each of the possible outcomes HH, HT, TH, and TT occurs.
4. Simulate tossing three coins ten times. The output should be a list of ten terms such as HHH, HTH, HHT, and so on.
5. Simulate tossing K coins N times. The output should be a list of N terms in which each term is a sequence of K Hs and Ts. N and K are to be input.
6. A game between players A and B is played as follows. A coin is tossed three times or until a head comes up, whichever occurs first. As soon as a head comes up, player A collects $1 from player B. If no head comes up on any of the three tosses, player B collects $6 from player A. In either case, the game is over. Your program is to simulate this game 1000 times to help decide whether A or B has the advantage, or if it is a fair game.
7. Generate an array L of 1000 random numbers between 0 and 1. Using L, determine an array C as follows. C(1) is a count of how many entries of L are between 0 and .1, C(2) a count of those between .1 and .2, and so on. The array C should then be printed.
8. Create an array B of approximately 20 different integers from 1 to 100. The integers are to be chosen randomly. B should be printed, but only after it has been completely determined.
9. Read 20 different names into an array L$. Create and print an array R$ containing approximately 10 different names selected randomly from L$. Do not print R$ until after it has been completely determined.
10. The first three hitters in the Bears' batting order have lifetime batting averages of .257, .289, and .324, respectively. Simulate their first trip to the plate for the next 100 games, and tabulate the number of games in which they produce zero, one, two, and three hits.

15.3 Random integers

Many computer applications require generating random *integers* rather than just random numbers between 0 and 1. For example, suppose a manufacturer estimates that a proposed new product will sell at the rate of 10 to 20 units each week and wants a program to simulate sales figures over an extended period of time. To write such a program, you must be able to generate random integers from 10 to 20 to represent the estimated weekly sales. To do this, you can multiply RND, which is between 0 and 1, by 11 (the number of integers from 10 to 20) to obtain

$$0 \leq 11*\text{RND} < 11.$$

If many numbers are obtained using 11*RND, they will be nearly uniformly distributed between 0 and 11. This means that the value of INT(11*RND) will be one of the integers 0, 1, 2, ..., 10. Thus, if you add 10 to this expression, you will get an integer from 10 to 20:

$$10 \leq \text{INT}(11*\text{RND}) + 10 \leq 20.$$

The important thing here is that integers generated in this manner will appear to have been chosen randomly from the set of integers {10, 11, 12, ..., 20}.

In general, if A and B are integers with A < B,

$$INT((B - A + 1)*RND)$$

will generate an integer from 0 to B − A. (Note that B − A + 1 gives the number of integers between A and B, inclusive.) Thus, adding A to this expression, we obtain

$$INT((B - A + 1)*RND) + A$$

whose value is an integer chosen randomly from the set {A, A + 1, A + 2, . . . , B}.

EXAMPLE 6. Let's write a program to generate 20 numbers randomly selected from the set {1, 2, 3, 4, 5}.

Problem analysis

From the preceding discussion we know that the expression INT(5*RND) will be an integer from 0 to 4. Thus, INT(5*RND) + 1 will be an integer from 1 to 5, as required.

```
10 FOR I=1 TO 20
20     PRINT INT(5*RND)+1;
30 NEXT I
40 END
RUN

 1  2  5  1  5  5  4  3  5  3  3  4  2  4  2  2  1  5  4  1
READY
```

EXAMPLE 7. Let's write a program to generate 20 numbers randomly selected from the set {100, 101, 102, . . . , 199}.

Problem analysis

The technique used in Example 6 is also applicable here. Since INT(100*RND) is an integer from 0 to 99, we must add 100 to obtain an integer from the specified set. Thus, the program required is that of Example 6 with line 20 changed to

```
20 PRINT INT(100*RND) + 100
```

EXAMPLE 8

If a pair of dice is rolled, the sum of the top faces is an integer from 2 to 12. Let's write a program to simulate rolling a pair of dice 1000 times and determine a count of how many times each of the possible sums occurs.

Problem analysis

It is not enough simply to generate numbers from 2 to 12 using the expression INT(11*RND) + 2. Doing this, each of the 11 numbers would have approximately an equal chance of occurring, but anyone who has rolled dice knows that this is not what actually happens. To obtain realistic results, we should try to simulate what *actually* takes place.

When a single die is rolled, a random number from 1 to 6 is obtained. We can simulate this rolling of a single die by using the expression INT(6*RND) + 1. Thus, for the task at hand, two such numbers should be generated and added to obtain our number from 2 to 12. The following flowchart describes the required program. In the flowchart, S denotes the sum obtained from one roll of the two dice, and C(S), for S = 2 to 12, is a count of how many times a sum of S occurred.

The flowchart

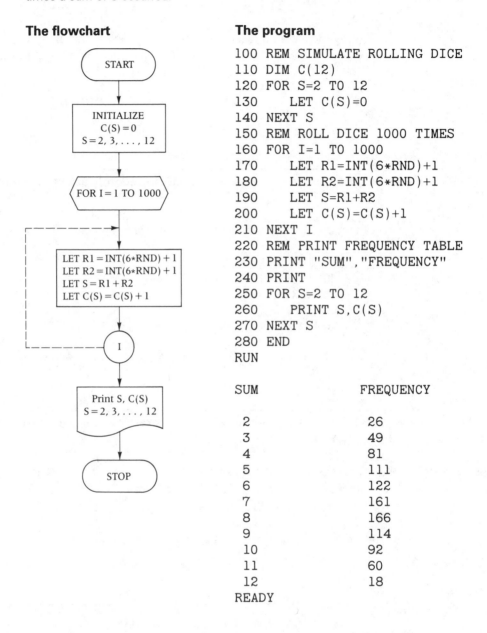

The program

```
100 REM SIMULATE ROLLING DICE
110 DIM C(12)
120 FOR S=2 TO 12
130    LET C(S)=0
140 NEXT S
150 REM ROLL DICE 1000 TIMES
160 FOR I=1 TO 1000
170    LET R1=INT(6*RND)+1
180    LET R2=INT(6*RND)+1
190    LET S=R1+R2
200    LET C(S)=C(S)+1
210 NEXT I
220 REM PRINT FREQUENCY TABLE
230 PRINT "SUM","FREQUENCY"
240 PRINT
250 FOR S=2 TO 12
260    PRINT S,C(S)
270 NEXT S
280 END
RUN
```

SUM	FREQUENCY
2	26
3	49
4	81
5	111
6	122
7	161
8	166
9	114
10	92
11	60
12	18

READY

15.4 Simulation

The speed of modern computing machines, together with their ability to generate rather good random sequences, allows us to approach many problems in ways not previously possible. The simulation of future events based on data obtained by observing the results of similar or related previous events is now a common computer application. Example 5 of Section 15.1, concerning the estimation of a ball player's future performance, is one illustration of the simulation of a real-life situation. In this section we give two examples showing how this technique may be used in a business setting.

EXAMPLE 9

A retail store will soon handle a new product. A preliminary market survey indicates that between 500 and 1000 units will be sold each month. (The survey is no more specific than this.) Write a program to simulate sales for the first six months. The retail store management is to be allowed to experiment by specifying the periodic (monthly) inventory purchase.

Problem analysis

The problem statement does not specify the nature of the output. Let's agree to print a table showing the following items.

P = monthly inventory purchase (to be input).
M = the month (1, 2, . . . , 6).
B = quantity on hand at the beginning of the month.
S = estimated sales (500–1000) for one month.
E = quantity on hand at the end of a month (initially 0).

For each month we must generate a random integer S from 500 to 1000. There are 501 integers to choose from (501 = 1000 − 500 + 1). Thus, we can use the expression

    INT(501*RND) + 500

to select an integer randomly from 500 to 1000.

As soon as the monthly inventory purchase P is input, we can calculate the following amounts:

Quantity on hand at beginning of month: $B = E + P$.
Estimated sales for one month: $S = INT(501*RND) + 500$.
Quantity on hand at end of month: $E = B - S$ if $B > S$; otherwise, $E = 0$.

The program

```
100 REM NEW PRODUCT SIMULATION
110 REM    P=MONTHLY INVENTORY PURCHASE
120 REM    M=MONTH (1,2,...,6)
130 REM    B=ON HAND-BEGINNING OF MONTH
140 REM    S=SALES FOR ONE MONTH (500-1000)
150 REM    E=ON HAND-END OF MONTH
160 PRINT "MONTHLY INVENTORY PURCHASE";
170 INPUT P
180 PRINT
190 PRINT "MONTH","ON HAND AT","ESTIMATED","ON HAND AT"
195 PRINT ,"START OF MONTH","SALES","END OF MONTH"
200 PRINT
210 LET E=0
220 FOR M=1 TO 6
230    LET B=E+P
240    LET S=INT(501*RND)+500
250    IF B>S THEN LET E=B-S ELSE LET E=0
260    PRINT M,B,S,E
270 NEXT M
280 END
RUN
```

```
            MONTHLY INVENTORY PURCHASE? 1000

    MONTH        ON HAND AT        ESTIMATED     ON HAND AT
                 START OF MONTH    SALES         END OF MONTH

      1             1000            533            467
      2             1467            699            768
      3             1768            953            815
      4             1815            589           1226
      5             2226            906           1320
      6             2320            939           1381
    READY
```

EXAMPLE 10

The owner of a drive-in theater is planning a $5.00-per-car special for Tuesday nights. Previous experience indicates that between 150 and 200 cars enter the theater on Tuesdays and that the number of people arriving in each car varies from one to five. Approximately one-half of the cars have two passengers, approximately one-fourth have four, and the remaining one-fourth have either one, three, or five passengers, with each of these last three counts being equally likely. Experience also indicates that a special of the type being planned will result in a 30% to 50% increase in the number of cars arriving on any one night. Assuming that the regular admission price is $2.50 per person, simulate the admissions for the next five Tuesdays to compare the revenue under the special price with what would be taken in at the regular price.

Problem analysis

The problem statement does not specify the precise form of the output. Let's agree to produce a five-column printout showing the following values for each of the five Tuesdays.

N1 = the number of cars under the regular admission price.
C = the total number of passengers in the N1 cars.
R1 = the total revenue represented by these C people (R1 = C*2.50).
N2 = the number of cars under the special admission price.
R2 = the total revenue represented by these N2 cars (R2 = N2*5).

The specification of "what" is to be printed leads us directly to the following algorithm.

The algorithm

a. Choose N1 (a random integer from 150 to 200).
b. Determine the total number C of passengers in the N1 cars.
c. Multiply 2.50 by C to obtain the revenue R1.
d. Increase N1 by from 30% to 50% to obtain N2.
e. Multiply 5.00 by N2 to obtain the revenue R2.
f. Print the values N1, C, R1, N2, R2 on one line.
g. Go to step (a) until five lines have been printed.

Steps (a), (c), (e), and (f) can each be accomplished with one programming line, whereas step (g) simply involves setting up a FOR/NEXT loop.

Step (b) is more complicated. To determine the count C, we must determine the number of people in each of the N1 cars and add these N1 numbers together. Since one-half of the cars have two passengers, we will generate a random number R between 0 and 1 and add 2 to C if R $\leq$ .5. Similarly, since approximately one-fourth of the cars have four passengers, we will add 4 to C if $1/2 < R < 3/4$. However, if R $\geq$ 3/4, we must select a number from the set {1, 3, 5} and add it to C. You may check that the BASIC expression

```
2*INT(3*RND) + 1
```

has a value from the set {1, 3, 5} and that each of these three numbers is equally likely to occur. The following program segment shows one way to carry out the method just described for finding the count C.

```
LET C=0
FOR I=1 TO N1
   LET R=RND
   IF R<=0.5 THEN LET C=C+2
   IF (0.5<R) AND (R<0.75) THEN LET C=C+4
   IF R>=0.75 THEN LET C=C+2*INT(3*RND)+1
NEXT I
```

Step (d) requires that we generate a number from 30 to 50 to represent the percentage by which N1 must be increased to obtain N2. Letting P denote this percentage, step (d) can be accomplished as follows.

```
LET P = INT(21*RND) + 30
LET N2 = N1 + (P/100)*N1
LET N2 = INT(N2 + .5)
```

The third line rounds N2 to a whole number since it is a count.

The program

```
100 PRINT "                    DRIVE-IN SIMULATION"
110 PRINT
120 PRINT "REGULAR ADMISSION - $2.50 PER PERSON"
130 PRINT "SPECIAL ADMISSION - $5.00 PER CAR"
140 PRINT
150 LET A$="   REGULAR ADMISSION          SPECIAL ADMISSION "
154 LET B$="--------------------------    -------------------"
158 LET C$="NUMBER   NO. OF   REVENUE    NUMBER    REVENUE"
162 LET D$="OF CARS  PEOPLE              OF CARS"
166 LET E$="  ###       ###     ####.##      ###     ####.##"
170 PRINT USING A$
174 PRINT USING B$
176 PRINT USING C$
178 PRINT USING D$
180 PRINT
190 REM SIMULATE ADMISSIONS FOR FIVE TUESDAYS
200 FOR T=1 TO 5
210    REM N1 = NUMBER OF CARS AT REGULAR ADMISSION PRICE
220    LET N1=INT(51*RND)+150
230    REM C = TOTAL NUMBER OF OCCUPANTS OF THE N1 CARS
240    LET C=0
250    FOR I=1 TO N1
260       LET R=RND
```

```
270          IF R<=0.5 THEN LET C=C+2
280          IF (0.5<R) AND (R<0.75) THEN LET C=C+4
290          IF R>=0.75 THEN LET C=C+2*INT(3*RND)+1
300      NEXT I
310      REM R1 = REVENUE REPRESENTED BY THE C CUSTOMERS
320      LET R1=C*2.50
330      REM N2 = NUMBER OF CARS AT SPECIAL ADMISSION PRICE
340      LET P=INT(21*RND)+30
350      LET N2=N1+(P/100)*N1
360      LET N2=INT(N2+.5)
370      REM R2 = REVENUE REPRESENTED BY THE N2 CARS
380      LET R2=N2*5.00
390      REM PRINT ONE ROW OF THE REPORT
400      PRINT USING E$,N1,C,R1,N2,R2
410  NEXT T
420  END
RUN


               DRIVE-IN SIMULATION


REGULAR ADMISSION - $2.50 PER PERSON
SPECIAL ADMISSION - $5.00 PER CAR
```

REGULAR ADMISSION			SPECIAL ADMISSION	
NUMBER OF CARS	NO. OF PEOPLE	REVENUE	NUMBER OF CARS	REVENUE
153	395	987.50	211	1005.00
197	538	1345.00	288	1440.00
197	539	1347.50	292	1460.00
167	450	1125.00	235	1175.00
196	554	1385.00	257	1285.00

```
READY
```

15.5 Problems

1. Write BASIC statements to print the following.
   a. A nonnegative random number (not necessarily an integer) less than 4.
   b. A random number less than 11 but not less than 5.
   c. A random number less than 3 but not less than -5.
   d. A random integer between 6 and 12, inclusive.
   e. A random number from the set $\{0, 2, 4, 6, 8\}$.
   f. A random number from the set $\{1, 3, 5, 7, 9\}$.
2. Which of these relational expressions are always true? Which are always false? Which may be true or false?
   a. RND>=0
   b. 4*RND<=4
   c. INT(7*RND)<=6
   d. INT(2*RND+4)<6
   e. RND<=RND
   f. INT(RND)<=RND
   g. RND+1>RND
   h. RND+RND=2*RND
3. What values can be assumed by each of the following expressions? For each expression, tell whether the possible values are all equally likely to occur.
   a. INT(2*RND+1)
   b. 3*INT(RND)
   c. INT(5*RND)-2
   d. INT(2*RND+1)+INT(2*RND+1)
   e. INT(6*RND+1)+INT(6*RND+1)
   f. INT(3*RND+1)*(INT(3*RND)+1)

4. If two coins are tossed, two heads, two tails, or one of each may result. The following program was written to simulate tossing two coins a total of 20 times. If it is run, the output will not reflect what would happen if the coins were actually tossed. Explain why, and then write a correct program.

```
100 FOR I=1 TO 20
110    LET R=INT(3*RND)
120    IF R=0 THEN PRINT "TWO HEADS"
130    IF R=1 THEN PRINT "TWO TAILS"
140    IF R=2 THEN PRINT "ONE OF EACH"
150 NEXT I
160 END
```

Write a program to perform each task specified in Problems 5–16.

5. Print a sequence of 20 letters that are selected randomly from the word RANDOM.

6. Randomly select and print an integer from 1 to 100 and then another from the remaining 99.

7. Create an array B of exactly 20 different integers from 1 to 100. The integers are to be chosen randomly. The array should be printed, but only after it is completely determined.

8. Read 20 different names into an array L$. Write programs to do the following.
   a. Create and print an array R$ containing approximately 10 different names selected randomly from L$.
   b. Randomly select one name from L$, and then randomly select another from the remaining 19 names.
   c. Randomly select exactly 10 different names from L$.

9. Starting with $D(1) = 1, D(2) = 2, D(3) = 3, \ldots, D(52) = 52$, rearrange the terms of D as follows: select an integer K from 1 to 52 and swap $D(K)$ with $D(52)$, select K from 1 to 51 and swap $D(K)$ with $D(51)$, select K from 1 to 50 and swap $D(K)$ with $D(50)$, and so on. The last step in this process is to select K from 1 to 2 and swap $D(K)$ with $D(2)$. Then print the entries of D in four columns, each containing 13 numbers. Explain in what sense your program shuffles a standard bridge deck and deals one hand in bridge.

10. Print 20 sets of three integers D, L, and F with $0 \leq D < 360, 5 \leq L \leq 15$, and $1 \leq F \leq 4$. (*Note:* If we interpret D as a direction and L as a length, we can create a design using these numbers as follows. Starting at a point on our paper, we draw a line of length L in the direction given by D. At the end of this line segment we draw one of four figures as specified by F. Using the end of this first line segment as our starting point, we repeat the process using the second of our 20 triples D, L, F. This process illustrates, in a very elementary way, what some people refer to as random art.)

11. A retail store will soon carry a new product. A preliminary market analysis indicates that between 300 and 500 units will be sold each week. (The survey is no more specific than this.) Assuming that each unit costs the store $1.89, write a program to simulate sales for the next 16 weeks. The store management is to be allowed to specify the selling price to obtain a printout showing the week, the estimated sales in number of units, the total revenue, the income (revenue − cost), and the cumulative income. The user should be allowed to try many different selling prices during a single program run.

12. Juanita Fernandes is offered the opportunity to transfer to another sales territory. She is informed that, for each month of the past year, sales in the territory were between $18,000 and $30,000, with sales of $25,000 or more being twice as likely as sales under $25,000. A 4% commission is paid on all sales up to $25,000 and 8% on all sales above that figure. Simulate the next six months' sales, and print the monthly sales and commission to give Juanita some information on which to base her decision to accept or reject the transfer.

13. The IDA Production Company will employ 185 people to work on the production of a new product. It is estimated that each person can complete between 85 and 95 units each working day. Previous experience shows that the absentee rate is between 0% and 15% on Mondays and Fridays and between 0% and 7% on the other days. Simulate the production for one week. The results of this simulation are to be printed in four columns showing the day of the week, the number of workers present, the number of units produced, and the average number produced per worker.

14. Jones and Kelley are to have a duel at 20 paces. At this distance Jones will hit the target on the average of two shots in every five and Kelley will hit one in every three. Kelley shoots first. Who has the best chance of surviving? Use a FOR/NEXT loop to run the program 20 times and print the results.

15. (Drunkard's Walk) A poor soul, considerably intoxicated, stands in the middle of a 10-foot-long bridge that spans a river. The inebriate staggers along, either toward the left bank or toward the right, but fortunately cannot fall off the bridge. Assuming that each step taken is exactly one foot long, how many steps will be taken before the drunkard reaches either bank of the river?

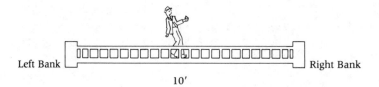

Left Bank   Right Bank

10'

It must be assumed that it is just as likely that a step will be toward the left bank as toward the right. You must do three things.
a. Find how many steps are taken in getting off the bridge.
b. Tell which bank is reached.
c. Let the drunkard go out for several nights and arrive at the same point (the center) on the bridge. Find, on the average, how many steps it takes to get off the bridge.

16. (Two-Dimensional Random Walk) This is a two-dimensional variation of the "Drunkard's Walk" described in Problem 15. The streets in a small town are laid out as in the following diagram. Each vertical line and each horizontal line denotes a street. At the intersection labelled T is a tavern and in the tavern is a drunkard. The drunkard's home is at the intersection labelled H. A fence encloses the entire town except for the two gates labelled G1 and G2.

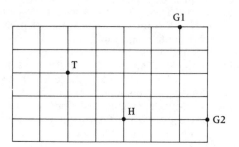

The drunk leaves the tavern and proceeds in a direction chosen randomly. After walking one block, the drunkard becomes confused and continues on in a new direction (which may be the same) chosen randomly. Proceeding in this manner the drunkard will eventually arrive at home H, or will leave town by way of gate G1 or gate G2.

Write a program to simulate this random walk. For each walk, the computer is to tell whether the drunkard reached home or left town. It is also to tell how many blocks were walked and how many times the drunkard returned to the tavern before arriving home or leaving town. (*Suggestion:* Label the intersections by using pairs of numbers (I,J) for I = 1 to 6 and J = 1 to 8. (Note that in the diagram there are 6 streets running east-west and 8 running north-south.) The starting position for each walk will then be (3,3).)

17. Two knights begin at diagonally opposite corners of a chessboard and travel randomly about the board but always making legitimate knight moves. (The knight moves either one step forward or backward and then two steps to the right or left or else two steps forward or backward and one step to the right or left.) Calculate the number of moves before one knight captures the other. However you number the squares, each knight's move should be printed as it is taken.

18. A single trip for a knight is defined as follows. The knight starts in one corner of a chessboard and randomly makes N knight moves to arrive at one of the 64 squares of the chessboard. (See Problem 17 for a description of an admissible knight move.) Write a program to simulate 1000 such trips for a knight to determine counts of how many times each square was reached at the end of a trip. These counts should be presented as an 8-by-8 table displaying the counts for the 64 squares. A value for N is to be supplied by a user who is allowed to obtain such a frequency table for many values of N during a single program run.

19. SIM is a game in which two players take turns drawing lines between any two of the six dots numbered 1 through 6 in the following diagram.

Lines drawn by the first player are colored red, and those drawn by the second player are colored blue. The loser is the first player to complete a triangle with three of these six dots as vertices. For example, if the second player draws a line (blue) between dots 2 and 4, 6 and 4, and 2 and 6, this player has completed a blue triangle and hence loses. Write a program in which the computer is the second player. The computer is to record all moves and announce the end of each game with a message stating who won. (*Hint:* Use a 6-by-6 array H(I,J) to record the moves. If the first player types 3, 5 to indicate that a red line is drawn between these two dots, set H(3,5) = H(5, 3) = 1. If the computer picks 2, 6 (to be done randomly), then set H(2, 6) = H(6, 2) = 2. Note that a triangle of one color has been completed when there are three different numbers I, J, K for which H(I,J) = H(J,K) = H(K,I).)

15.6 A statistical application

Programmers are often confronted with tasks that simply cannot be programmed to run within a specified time limit. When this happens, it is not always necessary to abandon the task. It may be that satisfactory results can be obtained by doing only part of the job. The following example, which illustrates one such situation, makes use of the statistical fact that the average of a large collection of numbers can be estimated by taking the average of only a fraction of the numbers, provided that the numbers picked are chosen randomly.

EXAMPLE 11

A researcher has compiled two lists A and B of 1000 measurements each. For each pair of measurements, one from list A and one from list B, a lengthy series of calculations (which is known to take 0.1 second of computer time) must be performed to determine a value V. In addition, the average of all such numbers V is to be found. Write a program to assist the researcher in this task. The program must take no longer than 30 minutes of computer time. (Computer time is very valuable.)

Problem analysis

On the surface this appears to be a simple programming task. For each pair A(I), B(J) we simply determine V, add this V to a sum accumulator S (S = S + V), and finally divide S by the number of Vs added. However, let's estimate how long such a program would take. Since each list contains 1000 entries, there are 1000 times 1000 or 1,000,000 (one million) pairs A(I), B(J) to be treated. For each pair we must determine V, which takes 0.1 second. Thus, it will take 1,000,000/10 = 100,000 (one hundred thousand) seconds, or nearly 28 hours, to determine all such Vs—which is considerably more than the 30 minutes allowed.

About the only way out of this dilemma is to treat only a fraction of the million pairs A(I), B(J) and use their average as an estimate of the actual average desired. Determining V for 1 out of every 100 pairs will take approximately .28 hour, which is under 17 minutes. So that the average obtained will be a reliable estimate of the average of all Vs, we must choose these pairs randomly. To do so, we will generate I, J in a nested FOR/NEXT loop and determine V for the pair A(I), B(J) only if RND < .01.

In the following flowchart, which describes the program, N is a count of how many pairs were "chosen" and S denotes the sum of the corresponding V values.

The flowchart

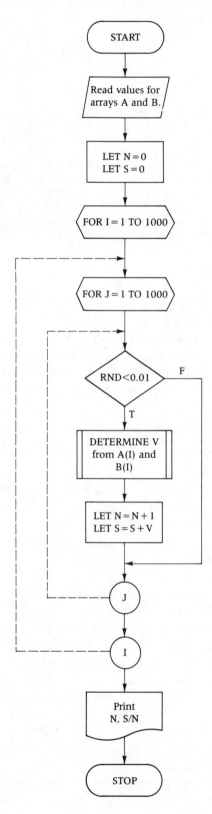

Remark

The flowchart symbol

is used to denote a predefined process. In this example, the predefined process is the lengthy sequence of calculations that determine V. Most often, predefined processes are written as subroutines.

15.7 Monte Carlo

The speed of modern computing machines, together with their ability to generate rather good random sequences, allows us to approach many problems in ways not previously possible. The following example illustrates one such method, called the **Monte Carlo Method.** When you complete the example, you should have little difficulty in explaining why this name is applied to the technique involved.

EXAMPLE 12

Consider the following figure of a circle inscribed in a square.

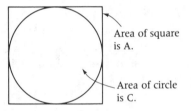

Area of square is A.

Area of circle is C.

If darts are randomly tossed at this figure and tosses landing outside the square are ignored, we can expect the number of darts falling within the circle to be related to the number falling on the entire square as the area C of the circle is related to the area A of the square. We will use this observation to approximate the area C of a circle of radius 1.

Problem analysis

Let's suppose that N darts have landed on the square and that M of these are in the circle. Then, as noted in the problem statement, we will have the approximation

$$M/N \doteq C/A,$$

or, solving for C,

$$C \doteq M \times A/N.$$

The more darts thrown (randomly), the better we can expect this approximation to be. The problem, then, is to simulate this activity, keeping an accurate count of M and N. To simplify this task, let's place our figure on a coordinate system with its origin at the center of the circle as shown in the following diagram.

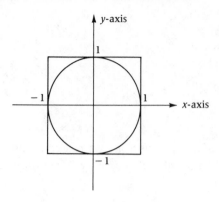

A point (x,y) will lie in the square if both x and y lie between -1 and $+1$. Such a point will lie within the circle if

$$x^2 + y^2 < 1.$$

To simulate tossing a single dart, we randomly generate two numbers x and y between -1 and $+1$. The following algorithm describes this process for N = 10,000 tosses.

    a. Let M = 0. (M counts the darts falling within the circle.)
    b. For N = 1 to 10000, do the following:
           Generate x and y between -1 and 1.
           If $x^2 + y^2 < 1$, add 1 to M.
    c. Print M × A/N (approximate area of the circle).
    d. Stop.

Since 2*RND − 1 gives a random number between -1 and $+1$, and since the area A of the square is 4, the following program is immediate.

```
100 LET M=0
110 FOR N=1 TO 10000
120    LET X=2*RND-1
130    LET Y=2*RND-1
140    IF X↑2+Y↑2<1 THEN LET M=M+1
150 NEXT N
160 PRINT "AREA IS";4*M/10000
170 END
RUN

AREA IS 3.132
READY
```

Remark

Since we know that the area of a circle of radius 1 is π (approximately 3.1416), we see that the result is accurate to one decimal place. To obtain greater accuracy, we would take more than 10,000 points. If RND were a true random number generator—i.e., if it actually performed an experiment such as tossing coins to generate numbers—we could expect to obtain any degree of accuracy desired by taking N large enough. The fact that it is not a true random number generator places a limit on the accuracy obtainable.

15.8 Modular arithmetic and random numbers

The realization that the use of random numbers in computer programs makes possible new and promising applications of the computer brought about an intensive search for ways to generate sequences of numbers possessing the attributes of random sequences. In this section, we describe a method for generating such sequences that has its basis in modular arithmetic. The method is one of the very first tried and is probably still the most widely used.

To illustrate, let us start with 33 as the first number in a sequence to be generated. To obtain the second number in the sequence, we multiply the first by 33 to obtain $33 \cdot 33 = 1089$; however, we will keep only the last two digits, 89, of this product. To obtain the third number, multiply the second by 33 to obtain $89*33 = 2937$ and again keep only the 37. (To keep the last two digits of any product, divide the product by 100 to obtain a quotient and a remainder; the remainder will be the last two digits. Thus, if $89*33 = 2937$ is divided by 100 the quotient is 29 and the remainder is 37 as desired. When we divide the product by 100 and keep only the remainder, we say we are multiplying modulo 100; 100 is called the modulus.) Continuing to multiply each new number obtained by 33 modulo 100, we get

$$33*33 = 89 \bmod 100$$
$$89*33 = 37 \bmod 100$$
$$37*33 = 21 \bmod 100$$
$$\cdot$$
$$\cdot$$
$$\cdot$$

The first 20 integers in the sequence so generated are

33, 89, 37, 21, 93, 69, 77, 41, 53, 49, 17, 61, 13, 29, 57, 81, 73, 9, 97, 1.

Although these numbers were not randomly generated (we know exactly how they were produced), they are rather uniformly distributed between 0 and 100. For example, the interval 0 to 25 contains five integers as do the intervals 25 to 50, 50 to 75, and 75 to 100. If we want numbers between 0 and 1, we can simply divide each of these twenty numbers by 100, the modulus, to obtain

.33, .89, .37, .21, .93, .69, .77, .41, .53, .49, .17, .61, .13, .29, .57, .81, .73, .09, .97, .01.

The process just described can be generalized by using numbers other than 33 and 100. In the following description of this procedure, S is used to denote the starting value and M to denote that multiplication is to be done modulo M. The product of two integers A and B modulo M is the remainder R obtained upon division of the product AB by M and is given by

$$R = A*B - M*INT(A*B/M).$$

Algorithm to generate sequences of numbers between 0 and 1

a. Assign values to M and S.
b. Let A = S.
c. Replace A with A*S modulo M.
d. A/M is the next number.
e. Go to Step (c) if another number is desired.

If M and S are chosen appropriately, the numbers generated will have many of the attributes of random numbers. The program that follows uses $M = 2^{27} = 134,217,728$ and $S = 5^9 = 1,953,125$, and the first 100 numbers generated are printed. A nested FOR/NEXT loop is used to print the output in five easily read columns.

```
100 LET M=134217728
110 LET S=1953125
120 LET A=S
130 FOR I=1 TO 20
140    FOR J=1 TO 5
150       LET A=A*S-M*INT(A*S/M)
160       PRINT A/M,
170    NEXT J
180    PRINT
190 NEXT I
200 END
RUN
```

.70943	.257827	.400745	.62517	.981427
.185363	.870218	.621112	.124809	6.27842E-2
.337099	.947539	.592915	.888228	.918056
.161427	.757541	4.89928E-2	.159934	.892505
.463627	.344976	.406942	.929196	.708945
.637107	.292836	.929551	.448788	.120792
.358115	.757185	.525653	.224344	.792201
.44222	.723934	.132426	.300629	.767218
.949606	.934484	9.72372E-2	.478121	.534915
.779967	.498923	.947894	.787949	.314953
.766037	.063589	.351397	.295223	.130359
.599345	.773146	.733931	.193787	.176778
.338585	.181512	.39269	.909332	.556717
.048375	.515124	.923405	.447031	.546351
.317964	2.03578E-2	.376684	.156732	.653963
.789149	.385196	.894504	.403706	.254774
.676639	.019278	.280298	.151697	.236821
.371235	.759049	.822296	.575478	.332057

READY

Whether the numbers generated using these values for M and S emulate random numbers is of course a very relevant question. Problem 5 of Section 15.9 describes a useful statistical test for making this evaluation.

To assist you in making promising choices for M and S, we state the following guidelines that, experience has shown, increase the likelihood that "good" random sequences will be obtained.[2]

---

[2]*Random Numbers*, by Robert E. Smith, is an excellent and inexpensive monograph on random-number generators and the statistical tests used for measuring their goodness. It is available from Control Data Corporation, Minneapolis, Minnesota.

1. M should be large. (For a variety of reasons, powers of 2 are popular.)
2. M and S should have no common factors. (We used 2^{27} and 5^9 for these values.)
3. S should not be too small in comparison to M.

The method described in this section is called the **power residual method:** "power" because successive powers of a single number S are used and "residual" because the numbers used are residues (remainders) upon division by a fixed number M. In all likelihood, the RND function provided with your BASIC system will generate random numbers using a method not unlike the power residual method.

15.9 Problems

Write a program for each task specified in Problems 1–6.

1. A principle of statistics tells us that the mean (average) of a large collection of numbers can be approximated by taking the mean of only some of the numbers, provided that the numbers selected are chosen randomly. Generate a one-dimensional array L containing 500 numbers (any numbers will do), and print the mean M of these 500 numbers. To test the stated principle of statistics, randomly select approximately 30 numbers from L and print their mean. Use a FOR/NEXT loop to repeat this process 20 times. The 20 means obtained should cluster about M.

2. Numbers generated by using RND are uniformly distributed between 0 and 1. In many applications, a different distribution of random numbers is desired. The following subroutine will generate random numbers R that lie between 0 and 1, but that are not uniformly distributed.

```
500 LET S=0
510 FOR I=1 TO 10
520     LET S=S+RND
530 NEXT I
540 LET R=S/10
550 RETURN
```

  a. Include this subroutine in a program that generates 500 random numbers R and prints a frequency table showing counts of how many of the 500 numbers are in each of the intervals 0-.1, .1-.2, . . . , .9-1.

  b. Explain the output produced by your program.

  c. Modify the given subroutine so that it averages N numbers generated by RND instead of 10. Repeat part (a) using the modified subroutine. Arrange things so that a user can specify several different values for N during a single program run. The program should halt when the user types a value for N that is less than 1 or that is not an integer.

3. Use the subroutine given in Problem 2 in a program that generates 500 random integers in the range 1–30. The results are to be printed as a two-column frequency table showing how many times each of the integers from 1 to 30 was generated.

4. Generate "random" numbers by the power residual method. Your program should have the following features.

  a. M, S, and the number N of values to be generated are to be supplied by the user.

  b. The numbers generated are to be placed in an array L.

  c. A frequency table should be printed showing counts of how many of the N numbers are in each of the intervals 0-.1, .1-.2, . . . , .9-1.

  d. After the frequency table has been printed the user should be allowed to issue any of the following commands.

     LIST,K to "see" the first K numbers in L.
     LISTSOME,K to see every Kth number in L.
     NEW,1 to try new numbers M, S, and N.

However, if the second input value is 0, the program should halt.

5. Let L be an array of N numbers between 0 and 1. Using the array L determine an array C as follows: C(1) is a count of how many entries of L are between 0 and .1, C(2) a count of those between .1 and .2, and so on. If L emulates a random sequence, we can expect each C(J) to be approximately E = N/10. In statistics, the value

$$X = \frac{(C(1) - E)^2}{E} + \frac{(C(2) - E)^2}{E} + \cdots + \frac{(C(10) - E)^2}{E}$$

is called the chi-square statistic for C. If it is small, it means that the C(J) do not differ drastically from the expected value E. For the present situation, statistics tells us that, if X ⩾ 16.92, we can be 95% confident that L does not emulate a random sequence. Thus, unless X < 16.92, we should reject L as a potential random sequence. Assuming that N and the list C are known, write a subroutine to compute and print the chi-square statistic X. (*Note:* If C gives a count of numbers in intervals other than (0,.1), (.1,.2), and so on, a critical value other than 16.92 must be used. The test described here is called a Chi-Square Goodness of Fit Test and is described in most introductory statistics books.)

6. Let a function $y = f(x)$ have positive values for all x between A and B as in the following diagram.

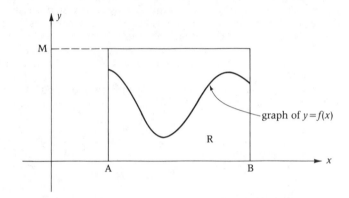

A point (x, y) with A < x < B will lie in the region R if 0 < y < $f(x)$. If M is a number such that $f(x) \leq M$ for all such x, the area of the rectangle of height M shown in the diagram is M*(B − A). Use the Monte Carlo Method to approximate the area R. Try your program for the following cases.
a. $y = 1 - x^3$, A = 0, B = 1
b. $y = \sin(x)$, A = 0, B = $\pi/2$
c. $y = \sin(x)/x$, A = 0, B = 1

15.10 Review true-or-false quiz

1. The RND function generates sequences of numbers using a well-defined algorithm.   T   F
2. If 100 numbers are generated by the statement LET R = RND, then approximately one-half of these numbers will be less than 50.   T   F
3. With equal likelihood the expression INT(2*RND) will have the value 0 or 1.   T   F
4. With equal likelihood the expression INT(3*RND + 2*RND + 1) will have one of the values 1, 2, 3, 4, or 5.   T   F
5. Let L$ be an array of 100 different names. If we wish to select exactly 20 of these names randomly, we can generate 100 random numbers between 0 and 1 and select the Ith name in the array L$ if the Ith number generated is less than 0.2.   T   F
6. A certain experiment has two possible outcomes, Outcome 1 and Outcome 2. To simulate this experiment on the computer, we can generate a number R = RND and specify that Outcome 1 occurs if R is less than .5 and Outcome 2 occurs otherwise.   T   F
7. RND/RND = 1.   T   F
8. Although the RND function can be used to generate negative numbers, this is almost never done.   T   F

9. If BASIC did not have an RND function, it would be a simple matter to include in any program a subroutine that would perform its role.   T   F

10. The value of the expression INT(17*RND) + 1 is an integer between 1 and 17, inclusive.   T   F

11. The value of the expression INT(5*RND) + 5 is an integer between 5 and 10, inclusive.   T   F

16

Sorting and Searching

Many computer applications require sorting data according to some specified order. The most obvious of these concern programming tasks to produce printed reports with columns of figures appearing in ascending or descending order, or columns of names appearing in alphabetical order. Less obvious, but equally important, applications of sorting concern programming tasks that require searching given collections of data for specified values. In this text, we have considered several examples that involved searching lists of numbers or lists of strings, and, in each case, a sequential search was performed; that is, the value being sought was compared with the successive list entries, starting with the first, until a match was found. If nothing is known about how the list entries are ordered, then this method is as good as any. However, lists whose entries are sorted according to some specified order can be searched much more efficiently.

For the reasons cited, much attention has been given to the problem of sorting and many different sorting algorithms have been developed. The *bubble sort* algorithm described in Section 11.4 is but one of these. Although this algorithm can be used for many of the applications encountered by beginning programmers, it is very inefficient and not suitable for a great many programming tasks. In this chapter, we will describe some of the techniques used to write efficient sorting algorithms. In addition, we will present a very efficient search algorithm. (A comprehensive treatment of all topics covered in this chapter, and many more, can be found in the text *Sorting and Searching*, by Donald Knuth.[1])

---

[1]*The Art of Computer Programming, Vol. 3: Sorting and Searching*, by Donald E. Knuth (Addison-Wesley, Reading, Mass., 1973).

16.1 Insertion sort

The sorting algorithm described in this section is called an *insertion sort* and is somewhat more efficient than the bubble sort (about twice as fast). Although it is not one of the most efficient sorting algorithms, it is easy to understand and will help us describe an algorithm that is very efficient.

Suppose the list A(1), A(2), . . . , A(N) is to be sorted in ascending order. We start with a list containing only the one entry A(1). Then we compare the next term A(2) with A(1) and these are swapped if necessary to give a list with the two entries

$$A(1), A(2)$$

in the proper order. Next A(3) is compared with A(2) and, if necessary, with A(1) to determine where it should be inserted. We illustrate with the following list:

3 2 5 4 1

Start with a single entry list:	3
Insert the 2 before the 3:	2, 3
Place 5 after the 3:	2, 3, 5
Insert 4 between 3 and 5:	2, 3, 4, 5
Insert 1 before the 2:	1, 2, 3, 4, 5

Let us examine this process of insertion more carefully. Suppose the items

$$A(1), A(2), A(3), \ldots, A(I)$$

are in order and A(I + 1) is to be inserted in its proper place. Temporarily assigning the value of A(I + 1) to the variable T, we proceed as follows.

If $T \geq A(I)$	no swap is necessary and no further comparisons are required.
If $T < A(I)$	let A(I + 1) = A(I). (This moves A(I) one position to the right.) Note that T "remembers" the original value of A(I + 1).
If $T \geq A(I - 1)$	let A(I) = T and the insertion is complete.
If $T < A(I - 1)$	let A(I) = A(I - 1). (This moves A(I - 1) one position to the right.) T still remembers the original value of A(I + 1).

.
.
.

(Continue this process until T, the original value of A(I + 1), has been inserted in its proper place.)

In the following algorithm, which describes this process, J takes on the successive values I, I-1, I-2, and so on, until J<1 or T≥A(J), whichever occurs first. If J<1 occurs, T is placed in A(1). If T≥A(J) occurs, T is placed in its proper position A(J+1).

a. Let J=I and T=A(I+1) (to compare A(J) with T).
b. If J<1 or T≥A(J), go to step (e).
c. Let A(J+1)=A(J) (moves A(J) one position to the right).

Figure 16.1
Flowchart to sort array A by
the insertion method.

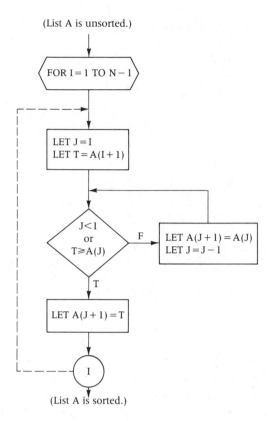

(List A is unsorted.)

FOR I = 1 TO N − 1

LET J = I
LET T = A(I + 1)

J < 1
or
T ≥ A(J)

F   LET A(J + 1) = A(J)
LET J = J − 1

T

LET A(J + 1) = T

I

(List A is sorted.)

d. Let J = J − 1 and repeat step (b).
e. Let A(J + 1) = T. (The insertion is complete.)

To sort a list A(1), A(2), . . . , A(N), this procedure must be repeated for each value of I from 1 to N − 1. The flowchart in Figure 16.1 describes this process. The following subroutine is written directly from this flowchart. It can be used in any program to sort an array A of N numbers into ascending order.

```
500 REM SUBR TO PERFORM AN INSERTION SORT
510 FOR I=1 TO N-1
520     LET J=I
530     LET T=A(I+1)
540     IF J<1 THEN 590
550     IF T>=A(J) THEN 590
560         LET A(J+1)=A(J)
570         LET J=J-1
580     GO TO 540
590     LET A(J+1)=T
600 NEXT I
610 RETURN
```

Remark 1

If a list of N strings (for instance, names) is to be alphabetized, simply use A$ and T$ rather than A and T.

Remark 2

If the array A must be sorted into descending order, simply change the comparison T ≥ A(J) in line 550 to T ≤ A(J).

Remark 3   Note that we use two IF statements (lines 540 and 550) to code the decision diamond

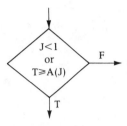

This was done to avoid a possible subscript error on systems that do not allow subscripts less than 1. If you use the compound condition

```
(J<1) OR (T>=A(J))
```

the comparison $T> = A(J)$ is meaningless, if $J<1$.

Remark 4   The insertion sort is very fast for lists that are "almost" in order. Can you see why?

Although the insertion sort is not one of the most efficient sorting algorithms, it is ideally suited for sorting lists that are to be entered by using a slow input device such as your terminal keyboard. If you input your unsorted list directly into A(1),A(2), and so on, the computer will have adequate time to insert the last value you entered in its proper position while you are preparing to type the next input value.

16.2 Shell's method (SHELLSORT)

A principal reason for the inefficiency of the bubble sort is that it moves array entries at most one position at a time. (Recall that in the bubble sort all comparisons involve adjacent array entries A(I) and A(I + 1) which are swapped if they are out of order.) The insertion sort improves slightly on this technique, but not much. For example, consider the following list.

$$4 \quad 2 \quad 3 \quad 1 \quad 7 \quad 8 \quad 9$$

Either of the two methods will make numerous comparisons and swaps to sort this list, even though only one swap is actually needed. Certainly, no sorting algorithm should be expected to recognize this one swap. However, the example does suggest that we might do better than the two methods presented. The key is to allow comparisons and swaps between list entries that are not next to each other. The method we now describe is called *Shell's method.*[2]

The idea behind Shell's method is to precede the insertion algorithm by a process that moves the "smaller" values to the left and the "larger" values to the right more quickly. To illustrate the method, we'll sort the following list.

$$7 \quad 1 \quad 6 \quad 3 \quad 4 \quad 2$$

First imagine the list divided into two parts, and make the comparison indicated.

[2]"A High-Speed Sorting Procedure," by Donald L. Shell, *Communications of the ACM,* **2** (July 1959), pp. 30–32.

Thus, 7 and 3 will be swapped, 1 and 4 will not, and 6 and 2 will. This gives us a new list:

3 1 2 7 4 6

Note that these three comparisons resulted in moving the "small" values 2 and 3 to the left and the "large" values 6 and 7 to the right, each by more than one position.

Dividing the original list of six entries into two parts led us to compare entries three positions apart. Similarly, we can compare entries that are two positions apart and make the following comparisons.

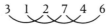

Note that 2 is compared with 3 and swapped. Then 4 is compared with 3, which was moved to the third position. But this is just an application of the insertion method applied to the list

3 2 4.

Similarly, comparing 7 with 1 and 6 with 7 is the same as using the insertion method for the list

1 7 6.

These comparisons leave us with

2 1 3 6 4 7.

The final step is to compare entries one position apart. But this is the insertion method applied to the list of all six terms, so we know the list will be sorted.

Let's summarize the process just used to sort a list of length 6.

A(1), A(2), A(3), A(4), A(5), A(6)

First, the list was rearranged so that entries three positions apart were in order—that is, each of the following two-element lists was sorted.

A(1), A(4)
A(2), A(5)
A(3), A(6)

Next, the list obtained was rearranged so that entries two positions apart were in order—that is, each of the following three-element lists was sorted.

A(1), A(3), A(5)
A(2), A(4), A(6)

Finally, the list was rearranged so that entries one position apart were in order, which resulted in a completely sorted list.

The important thing for you to note is that each of these partial sorts used the insertion method.

We now describe Shell's method for sorting an array A of length N.

a. Select an integer S from 1 to N/2.
b. Sort the array A so that entries S positions apart are in order.
c. If S = 1, stop. The array is sorted.
d. Pick a new and smaller S (S ≥ 1), and go to Step (b).

For the list with six entries the values S = 3, S = 2, and S = 1 were chosen. Of course, the successive values S = 3, 2, 1 are not always to be used. The sequence of S values that yields the fastest sort is not known. The most common practice is to use the successive S values INT(N/2),INT(N/4),INT(N/8), and so on, until a value S<1 is reached. The flowchart in Figure 16.2 displays the steps in the algorithm for these S values. The only part of this flowchart that may be difficult to code is the box corresponding to step (b) of the written algorithm. To accomplish this, each of the following lists must be sorted.

$$A(1), A(1 + S), A(1 + 2S), A(1 + 3S), \ldots$$
$$A(2), A(2 + S), A(2 + 2S), A(2 + 3S), \ldots$$
$$\vdots$$
$$A(S), A(S + S), A(S + 2S), A(S + 3S), \ldots$$

As indicated in the worked-out example, a modification of the insertion algorithm is used.

The flowchart in Figure 16.3, which sorts the list

$$A(K), A(K + S), A(K + 2S), \ldots$$

is identical to the insertion-algorithm flowchart (Figure 16.1) except that it uses increments of S rather than increments of 1. In particular, a value T being inserted in its proper place is

Figure 16.2
Flowchart to sort array A by Shell's method.

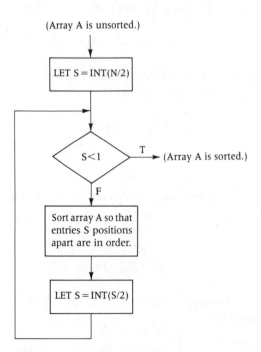

(Array A is unsorted.)

LET S = INT(N/2)

S<1 — T → (Array A is sorted.)

F

Sort array A so that entries S positions apart are in order.

LET S = INT(S/2)

Figure 16.3
Flowchart to sort the list
A(K), A(K+S), A(K+2S),
A(K+3S), ...

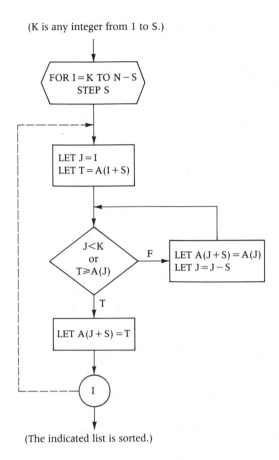

(K is any integer from 1 to S.)

(The indicated list is sorted.)

compared with A(J) for J = I, I − S, I − 2S, and so on, until J<K or T≥A(J), whichever occurs first. To sort all of the lists indicated above, we must carry out the process shown in Figure 16.3 for K = 1,2,3, . . . , S.

The following subroutine, SHELLSORT, is now easily coded from the flowcharts in Figures 16.2 and 16.3. The subroutine can be used in any program to sort a list of N numbers into ascending order. It is very fast.

```
500 REM SUBROUTINE SHELLSORT
510 LET S=INT(N/2)
520 IF S<1 THEN RETURN
530    REM SORT ARRAY A SO THAT ENTRIES
540    REM S POSITIONS APART ARE IN ORDER
550    FOR K=1 TO S
560       FOR I=K TO N-S STEP S
570          LET J=I
580          LET T=A(I+S)
590          IF J<K THEN 640
600          IF T>=A(J) THEN 640
610             LET A(J+S)=A(J)
620             LET J=J-S
630          GO TO 590
640          LET A(J+S)=T
650       NEXT I
660    NEXT K
670    LET S=INT(S/2)
680 GO TO 520
```

Remark 1   If a list of N strings is to be alphabetized, simply use A$ and T$ rather than A and T.

Remark 2   If the array A must be sorted into descending order, simply change the comparison T≥A(J) in line 600 to T≤A(J).

16.3 Binary search

Suppose an array A of length N has been sorted in ascending order. The first step in a "binary" search for a specified value V is to compare V with the "middle" term A(M). When this is done, one of three things will happen.

V = A(M), in which case V is found.
V < A(M), in which case V is in the left half of the list, if at all.
V > A(M), in which case V is in the right half of the list, if at all.

Thus, if V is not found by these comparisons, the search may be confined to a list half the length of the original list. The next step would be to compare V with the "middle" term of this smaller list. If this "middle" term is V, the search is complete. If not, the number of terms to be considered is again halved. Continuing in this manner, we could search the entire list very quickly. We illustrate by searching the following list of 13 numbers for the value V = 67.

28   31   39   43   48   52   **60**   62   67   73   77   86   89

V = 67 is compared with the middle term, 60. Since it is larger, only the last six terms need be considered.

62   67   **73**   77   86   89

This shorter list has two "middle" terms. When this happens, let's agree to use the leftmost of these. Thus, V = 67 is compared with 73. Since it is smaller, the search is confined to the two values

62   67.

These final two values are both "middle" terms, so 62 is used. V = 67 is larger than 62, which leaves only the term 67. This final comparison results in a match, and V = 67 is found.

Note that V was compared with just four "middle" terms. In the same manner a search for any value V can be completed by comparing V with at most four such "middle" terms. If none of these four values is V, it must be concluded that V is not in the list. Using this method on any list with fewer than 2^N terms, we will either find V by comparing it with at most N "middle" terms or be sure that V is not in the list. Thus, a list with $1023 = 2^{10} - 1$ terms requires 10 or fewer steps to find V or to conclude that it is not present. In contrast, a sequential search of a list with 1023 terms requires 1023/2 comparisons, on the average, to do the same thing.

As simple as a binary search may appear, care must be taken to state the algorithm precisely so that it can be programmed (coded) without bugs. Perhaps the safest way to do this is to use two variables, say L and R (for left and right), to store the leftmost and rightmost positions yet to be searched. Thus, at the outset the position of the middle term is M = INT((1 + N)/2), L = 1, and R = N. If V<A(M), only the terms in positions L through M − 1 need be considered, so R will be replaced by M − 1. Similarly, if V>A(M), L will be replaced by M + 1. The position of the next middle term is M = INT((L + R)/2). If L≤R, the comparison of V with A(M) must be repeated. However, if L>R, no more comparisons are required and we must conclude that V is not in the list. The flowchart shown in Figure 16.4 displays an algorithm for carrying out this process.

This flowchart can be coded to give the following subroutine to search an array A of N numbers, whose entries are in ascending order.

```
700 REM BINARY SEARCH SUBROUTINE
710 REM TO SEARCH ARRAY A FOR THE VALUE V
720 REM M=0 DENOTES THAT V IS NOT IN ARRAY A
730 REM OTHERWISE A(M)=V
740 LET M=INT((1+N)/2)
750 LET L=1
760 LET R=N
770 IF (V=A(M)) OR (L>R) THEN 810
780    IF V<A(M) THEN LET R=M-1 ELSE LET L=M+1
790    LET M=INT((L+R)/2)
800 GO TO 770
810 IF (L>R) THEN LET M=0
820 RETURN
```

Remark 1   If an alphabetized list of words, such as names, is to be searched for a given name, simply use A$ and V$ rather than A and V.

Figure 16.4
Binary-search algorithm.

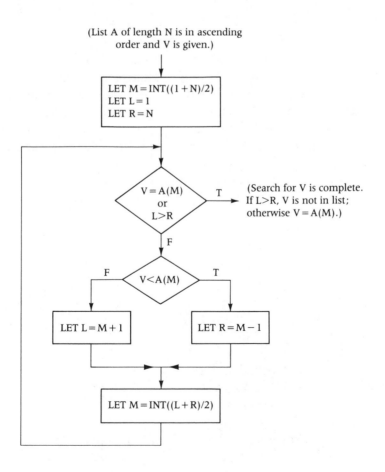

(List A of length N is in ascending order and V is given.)

LET M = INT((1 + N)/2)
LET L = 1
LET R = N

V = A(M) or L>R   T → (Search for V is complete. If L>R, V is not in list; otherwise V = A(M).)

F

V<A(M)

F   T

LET L = M + 1   LET R = M − 1

LET M = INT((L + R)/2)

Remark 2   If the array A is in descending order, change the condition $V < A(M)$ in line 780 to $V > A(M)$.

Remark 3   If you know that the entries in a list are in ascending order, but know nothing else about the list, then the binary-search algorithm is the fastest search algorithm available to you.

16.4 External sorting—the merge sort

The bubble sort, insertion sort, and Shellsort algorithms are instances of **internal-sorting algorithms.** This term is used to indicate that all of the data being sorted are stored in the computer's main memory at the same time. If the data to be sorted do not fit into memory, the usual practice is to sort them in parts, store these parts as files by using one or more secondary storage devices (tape units or disk units), and then merge these files into a single sorted file. This process is called **external sorting**—the data to be sorted are stored on external storage devices, and are never stored in their entirety in the computer's main memory.

In this section we describe one of the many methods used to merge sorted files into a single sorted file. We illustrate the method by showing how two lists of numbers

$$A_1 \leqslant A_2 \leqslant A_3 \leqslant \cdots \leqslant A_m$$

and

$$B_1 \leqslant B_2 \leqslant B_3 \leqslant \cdots \leqslant B_n$$

can be merged into a single list

$$C_1 \leqslant C_2 \leqslant C_3 \leqslant \cdots \leqslant C_{m+n}$$

First, we compare A_1 with B_1 and store the smaller as C_1. Suppose B_1 is smaller. Then $C_1 = B_1$ and we compare A_1 with B_2. If this time A_1 is smaller, then $C_2 = A_1$ and we compare A_2 with B_2. (If it happens that two values being compared are equal, we will assign the A entry to list C.) We continue in this manner until all terms in one of the two lists have been stored as C entries. The remaining terms in the other list are then placed in the C list as they appear. This process is called a *merge-sort* process since two sorted lists are *merged* into a single *sorted* list.

Applying this merge-sort method to the lists

    A = 3 4 6 8 9 10 13
    B = 5 8 8

we obtain

$$
\begin{aligned}
C_1 &= 3 && \text{since } 3 \leqslant 5 \\
C_2 &= 4 && \text{since } 4 \leqslant 5 \\
C_3 &= 5 && \text{since } 6 > 5 \\
C_4 &= 6 && \text{since } 6 \leqslant 8 \\
C_5 &= 8 && \text{since } 8 \leqslant 8 \\
C_6 &= 8 && \text{since } 9 > 8 \\
C_7 &= 8 && \text{since } 9 > 8 \\
C_8 &= 9 \\
C_9 &= 10 && \text{since all of list B has been stored in C.} \\
C_{10} &= 13
\end{aligned}
$$

If two lists, stored as File 1 and File 2, are to be merged into File 3, the same method can be used. The following algorithm shows one way to do this. In the algorithm, A and B denote single values read from File 1 and File 2, respectively.

Merge algorithm (to merge File 1 and File 2 into File 3)

Either File 1 or File 2 may be empty. If the entries of Files 1 and 2 are in ascending order, the entries of File 3 will be in ascending order.

a. If File 1 is empty, go to step (e). Otherwise, read A from File 1.
b. If File 2 is empty, go to step (f). Otherwise, read B from File 2.
c. If A≤B, then
      write A on File 3.
      If File 1 is out of data, write B on File 3 and go to step (e).
      Read A from File 1.
    Else (if A>B)
      write B on File 3.
      If file 2 is out of data, go to step (f).
      Read B from File 2.
d. Repeat step (c).
e. Copy the rest of File 2 onto File 3 and stop.
f. Copy A and the rest of File 1 onto File 3 and stop.

To help in following the action of this algorithm, we display the steps in the flowchart shown in Figure 16.5. Note that each flowchart symbol to read a value from a file is preceded by an end-of-file test. You will recall that such a test can be coded in BASIC by using an end-of-file statement. For example the flowchart segment

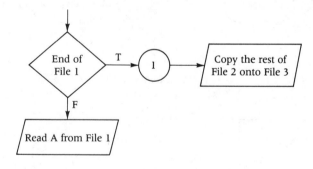

can be coded as

```
IF END#1 THEN 320
READ#1,A
```

or as

```
NODATA#1,320
READ#1,A
```

where 320 is the first line number of a program segment that copies the remaining data in File 2 onto File 3.

Figure 16.5
Flowchart to merge
File 1 and File 2
into File 3.

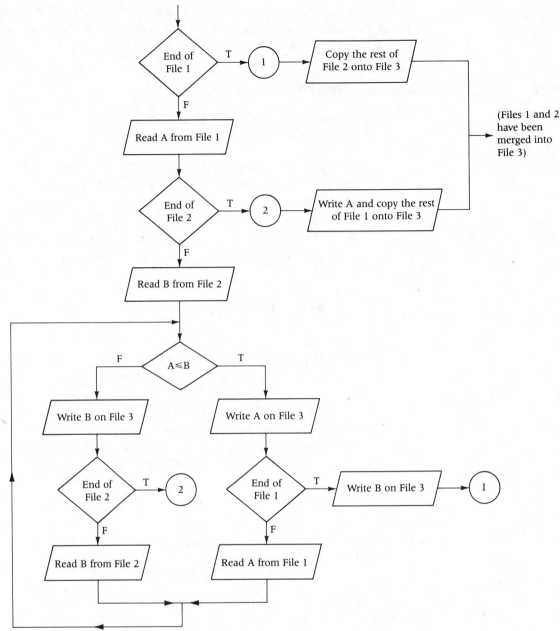

The merge-sort program shown in Figure 16.6 was written directly from this merge-sort algorithm.

The method described for merging two files into a single file can be generalized to allow more than two files to be merged. The following algorithm and corresponding subroutine show one way to do this.

Figure 16.6
Merge-Sort program for the
algorithm displayed in
Figure 16.5.

```
100 REM PROGRAM TO MERGE FILES 1 AND 2 INTO FILE 3
110 REM FILE 3 WILL BE IN ASCENDING ORDER IF
115 REM FILES 1 AND 2 ARE IN ASCENDING ORDER
120 REM     A DENOTES A VALUE READ FROM FILE 1
130 REM     B DENOTES A VALUE READ FROM FILE 2
140 FILE#1="DATA1"
150 FILE#2="DATA2"
160 FILE#3="DATA3"
170 IF END#1 THEN 320
180 INPUT#1,A
190 IF END#2 THEN 370
200 INPUT#2,B
210 REM ***** WRITE THE SMALLER OF A AND B ON FILE 3 *****
220 IF A<=B THEN 270
230    PRINT#3,B
240    IF END#2 THEN 370
250    INPUT#2,B
260 GO TO 220
270    PRINT#3,A
280    IF END#1 THEN 310
290    INPUT#1,A
300 GO TO 220
310 PRINT#3,B
320 REM ***** COPY THE REST OF FILE 2 ONTO FILE 3 *****
330 IF END#2 THEN 420
340    INPUT#2,B
350    PRINT#3,B
360 GO TO 330
370 REM *** COPY A AND THE REST OF FILE 1 ONTO FILE 3 ***
380    PRINT#3,A
390    IF END#1 THEN 420
400    INPUT#1,A
410 GO TO 380
420 REM ***** MERGE IS COMPLETE *****
430 RESTORE#1
440 RESTORE#2
450 RESTORE#3
460 END
```

Merge algorithm (to merge K files, numbered 1 through K, into a single file, numbered L)

One or more of the K files to be merged may be empty files. If the entries in each of files 1 through K are in ascending order, the entries in File L will be in ascending order.

a. Read the first entries of Files 1 through K into A(1), A(2), . . . , A(K). If file number I is empty, assign the "large" number 1E30 to A(I).

b. Find J such that A(J) is the smallest of A(1), A(2), . . . , A(K).

c. If A(J) = 1E30, stop; the merge is complete.

d. Write A(J) onto File L and read another value for A(J) from File J. But if the end of File J is encountered, assign 1E30 to A(J).

e. Go to Step (b).

Figure 16.7
Subroutine to merge Files 1
through K into File L.

```
100 REM ****** SUBROUTINE MERGE-SORT ******
110 REM THIS SUBROUTINE MERGES INPUT FILES 1
115 REM THROUGH K INTO FILE L (L>K)
120 REM
130 REM IF THE INPUT FILES ARE SORTED IN ASCENDING ORDER,
140 REM FILE L WILL ALSO BE SORTED IN ASCENDING ORDER.
150 REM
160 REM THE SUBROUTINE ASSUMES THAT ALL FILES
165 REM WERE OPENED IN THE MAIN PROGRAM AND THAT
170 REM THEY WILL BE CLOSED OR RESTORED THERE.
180 REM
190 REM FOR I=1 TO K, A(I) DENOTES A VALUE READ FROM FILE I
200 REM ARRAY A MUST BE DIMENSIONED IN THE MAIN PROGRAM
210 REM
220 REM READ FIRST ENTRIES OF INPUT FILES INTO
230 REM ARRAY A. SET A(I)=1E30 IF FILE I IS EMPTY.
240 FOR I=1 TO K
250    IF END#I THEN LET A(I)=1E30 ELSE INPUT#I,A(I)
260 NEXT I
270 REM ***** FIND J SUCH THAT A(J) IS LEAST *****
280    LET J=1
290    FOR I=2 TO K
300       IF A(I)<A(J) THEN LET J=I
310    NEXT I
320    REM ***** TEST FOR MERGE COMPLETION *****
330    IF A(J)=1E30 THEN 380
340    REM *** WRITE A(J) ON FILE L AND GET NEXT A(J) ***
350    PRINT#L,A(J)
360    IF END#J THEN LET A(J)=1E30 ELSE READ#J,A(J)
370 GO TO 280
380 REM ***** MERGE IS COMPLETE *****
390 RETURN
```

16.5 Problems

Write a program to perform each task specified in Problems 1–15. The subroutines presented in this chapter may be used where appropriate. Be sure to use the top-down approach.

1. Read an array L of integers from DATA lines, and then create two arrays A and B as follows. A is to contain the odd integers appearing in L, and B the even integers. A and B are to be sorted in ascending order before being printed.

2. Read a list of positive integers into an array L and then create arrays L1 and L2 with L1 containing those values that exceed the average of all input values and with L2 containing the others. Sort L1 and L2 in descending order and print them as adjacent columns with the headings LIST1 and LIST2.

3. Read a list of positive integers into an array L and then create arrays L1 and L2 as follows. L1 is to contain those integers that exceed the *median* of the input list and L2 is to contain the others. L1 and L2 are to be printed as adjacent columns and each column is to appear in ascending order. (The median of a list of numbers $a_1 \le a_2 \le a_3 \cdots \le a_n$ is the middle term if n is odd and the average of the two "middle" terms if n is even.) (*Remark:* Only the array L needs to be sorted.)

4. Read an array L, and sort it in ascending order. L is then to be modified by deleting all values appearing more than once. For example, if L(1) = 7, L(2) = L(3) = 8, and L(4) = L(5) = L(6) = 9, then the new array is to have L(1) = 7, L(2) = 8, and L(3) = 9. Run your program for the DATA values 19, 23, 2, 7, 23, 23, −1, −1, 7, 7, −9.

5. N pairs of numbers are to be read from DATA lines so that the first of each pair is in array A and the second in array B. Sort the pairs A(I),B(I) so that $A(1) \leq A(2) \leq \cdots \leq A(N)$. (If two entries in the array A are swapped, the corresponding entries in B must also be swapped.) Print the modified arrays with the first column containing the entries of A and the second containing the corresponding B values.

6. Read an N-by-2 array M from DATA lines. M(I,1) and M(I,2) should be read by the same READ statement. Sort this array so that

$$M(1,1) \leq M(2,1) \leq M(3,1) \leq \cdots \leq M(N,1).$$

(If M(I,1) and M(J,1) are swapped, so must M(I,2) and M(J,2) be swapped.) Print the modified array M as a table with N rows and 2 columns.

7. Each of several DATA lines contains three numbers: the first is the ID number of a person, the second gives the annual salary of this person, and the third is a 1 if the person is in management and a 2 otherwise. Produce three tables as follows. Table 1 is to contain three columns for these three values; however, the rows must be ordered according to increasing ID numbers. Table 2 is to contain two columns showing the ID numbers and salaries of management personnel. Its rows are to be ordered so that salaries appear in decreasing order. Table 3 is to contain the same information for nonmanagement personnel. (No assumption is to be made about ID numbers except that they are all different.)

8. Read arrays A and B as in Problem 5. Sort the pairs A(I),B(I) so that $A(1) \leq A(2) \leq \cdots \leq A(N)$ and also so that $B(I) \leq B(I + 1)$ whenever $A(I) = A(I + 1)$. Print the modified arrays in two columns.

9. Read an N-by-2 array M as in Problem 6. Sort M so that $M(1,1) \leq M(2,1) \leq \cdots \leq M(N,1)$ and also so that $M(I,2) \leq M(I + 1,2)$ whenever $M(I,1) = M(I + 1,1)$. Write an algorithm to perform this sort, and include it as a subroutine in your program. Note that this is essentially a dictionary-type ordering. If the two pairs M(I,1),M(I,2) and M(J,1),M(J,2) are not the same, the first will precede the second if $M(I,1)<M(J,1)$ or if $M(I,1) = M(J,1)$ and $M(I,2) < M(J,2)$.

10. Create an array A of 1000 terms with

$$A(I) = I^2 - I + 1.$$

Search this array for each of the following ten numbers (they are to appear in DATA lines).

$$\begin{array}{ccccc} 205663 & 676507 & 3131 & 225 & 62751 \\ 810901 & 202951 & 164212 & 678153 & 723351 \end{array}$$

As each number is read, it is to be printed along with the I value indicating its position in the array. If it is not in the array, an appropriate message should be printed. Use a binary search. (A need not be sorted; it is in order.)

11. Create the array A as in Problem 10. Then search A for each of the 1000 values

$$V = J^4 - J^2 + 1 - 1E6*INT((J^4 - J^2 + 1)/1E6),$$

where $J = 1, 2, \ldots, 1000$. For each V found in the array, print the J that gave it, the position M in the array A at which V is stored, the value V being sought, and the value of A(M). These last two values should be the same. Values of V not found should cause nothing to be printed. (Use a binary search. A sequential search will take too long. Try it and see.)

12. Create an array A of 1000 terms with

$$A(I) = I^5 - 2001*INT(I^5/2001).$$

Sort this array using a Shellsort and also using a bubble sort. There will be a noticeable difference in time.

13. Two input lists of positive integers, each appearing in ascending order, are to be read into arrays L1 and L2. The two arrays are then to be merged into a single array L whose entries are also in ascending order. L is to be printed, five numbers to the line.

14. Two input lists of positive integers, each appearing in ascending order, are to be read into arrays L1 and L2. The contents of these two arrays are then to be printed as a single column, from smallest to largest. The arrays L1 and L2 are not to be merged into a single array.

15. Two lists of English words are presented in DATA lines. The word END terminates both lists. The two lists are to be alphabetized and printed in two columns. Then the lists are to be merged into one alphabetized list, and this list is to be printed using as little space as possible while yet preserving the identity of the words. Two subroutines are to be used: one to sort a list and the other to merge two previously sorted lists into a single sorted list.

16.6 Review true-or-false quiz

1. An array must be sorted in ascending order before a sequential search may be made.   T   F
2. It is desirable to use sorting algorithms that compare and swap only adjacent entries, for such algorithms will not only be easier to understand but will generally be very efficient.   T   F
3. The idea behind the insertion sort is to build a list by starting with one value and then placing each successive value in its proper position relative to all values included to that point.   T   F
4. The idea of the Shellsort is to use the insertion method on shorter and shorter lists.   T   F
5. One reason the Shellsort is efficient is that "small" values are moved to the left by more than one position at a time.   T   F
6. A binary search can be made only on lists that are sorted.   T   F
7. Each step in a binary search for a value V involves comparing V with an array entry A(M) to determine if V = A(M), V < A(M), or V > A(M). At most 15 such steps are required to determine if a value V is included in an array of length 30,000.   T   F
8. Algorithms used to sort data that are stored in a computer's main memory are called *internal-sorting algorithms*.   T   F
9. The expressions *external-sorting* and *merging* are synonymous.   T   F
10. External-sorting algorithms can be used to sort data that will not fit in the computer's main memory.   T   F
11. External-sorting procedures often utilize internal-sorting algorithms.   T   F

17

Matrices

A two-dimensional array is normally thought of as a rectangular array having rows and columns. For example, a 2-by-3 array B with entries $B(1,1)=5$, $B(1,2)=3$, $B(1,3)=4$, $B(2,1)=6$, $B(2,2)=7$, and $B(2,3)=9$ would be visualized as the rectangular array of numbers

$$\begin{bmatrix} 5 & 3 & 4 \\ 6 & 7 & 9 \end{bmatrix}$$

having two rows and three columns. A one-dimensional array (list) A with entries $A(1) = 4$, $A(2) = 8$, $A(3) = 2$, and $A(4) = 1$ can also be thought of as a rectangular array

$$\begin{bmatrix} 4 \\ 8 \\ 2 \\ 1 \end{bmatrix}$$

that has four rows and one column.

We define a **matrix** to be any rectangular array of numbers. (The plural of *matrix* is *matrices*.) Thus, both one- and two-dimensional arrays are matrices. Because matrices have proven to be a useful aid in the solution of a variety of problems, the most common mathematical operations on matrices have been included in extended versions of BASIC. This chapter will describe and illustrate the BASIC statements used to perform matrix operations.

17.1 Assigning values to a matrix: the MAT READ and MAT INPUT statements

The MAT READ and MAT INPUT statements are used to assign values to matrices. The clarity and conciseness with which a program can be written using these two statements are evident in the following examples.

EXAMPLE 1. Here is a program to read six numbers into a 2-by-3 matrix B and print the matrix B.

For purposes of comparison the program is written in two ways: on the left with subscripted variables and on the right with BASIC matrix statements.

```
10 FOR I=1 TO 2              10 DIM B(2,3)
20    FOR J=1 TO 3           20 MAT READ B
30        READ B(I,J)        30 MAT PRINT B;
40        PRINT B(I,J);      40 DATA 5,3,4,6,7,9
50    NEXT J                 50 END
60    PRINT                  RUN
70 NEXT I
80 DATA 5,3,4,6,7,9           5  3  4
90 END
RUN                           6  7  9
                             READY
    5  3  4

    6  7  9
READY
```

The programming lines

```
10 DIM B(2,3)
20 MAT READ B
```

cause the computer to read six values from DATA lines. These values are assigned to the matrix B by rows; that is, B(1,1), B(1,2), B(1,3) will be read first, and then B(2,1), B(2,2), B(2,3) will be read. The MAT PRINT statement (line 30) is described in the next section.

Matrices should be dimensioned. If they are not, BASIC assumes that they are 10-by-10 arrays (11-by-11 where zero subscripts are used). Thus, if the DIM statement in Example 1 were omitted, the attempt to read more than the six values presented in the DATA lines would result in an OUT OF DATA message, and the run would terminate.

If your system uses zero subscripts, you can normally change this with the statement

ln OPTION BASE 1

or some similar statement as described in your BASIC manual. In what follows, the assumption is that the smallest subscript is 1.

EXAMPLE 2. Here is a program to assign values to a matrix during program execution.

```
10 DIM B(2,3)
20 MAT INPUT B
30 MAT PRINT B;
40 END
RUN

? 5,3,4
? 6,7,9
 5  3  4

 6  7  9
READY
```

In response to the question mark, you must type the proper number of values to fill the first row of the matrix (matrices are always assigned by row) and then type ®. Another question mark will appear. The process should be repeated until the matrix, as defined, has been completely assigned. Only then will program execution continue.

More than one matrix may appear in a MAT READ or MAT INPUT statement.

EXAMPLE 3

```
10 DIM C(3,4),D(2,2)
20 MAT READ C,D
30 DATA 8,7,6,5,4,3,2,1
40 DATA 8,7,6,5,4,3,2,1
50 END
```

Two matrices C and D are dimensioned in line 10. Line 20 instructs the computer to read the two matrices C and D. C is read completely before D is read to give

$$C = \begin{bmatrix} 8 & 7 & 6 & 5 \\ 4 & 3 & 2 & 1 \\ 8 & 7 & 6 & 5 \end{bmatrix} \qquad D = \begin{bmatrix} 4 & 3 \\ 2 & 1 \end{bmatrix}$$

The general forms of the MAT READ and MAT INPUT statements are

ln MAT READ **a,b,c, . . .**

ln MAT INPUT **a,b,c, . . .**

where **a,b,c, . . .** denote matrices.

17.2 The MAT PRINT statement

This statement is used to print matrices. The programming line

    30 MAT PRINT B;

in Example 1 caused the matrix B to be printed by rows, the semicolon after B indicates that B should be printed using the packed format. One line is automatically skipped between each row of the matrix. If line 30 had been

    30 MAT PRINT B,

the matrix would again be printed by rows, but only one number would appear in each print zone, as shown in the next example.

EXAMPLE 4

```
10 DIM B(2,3)
20 MAT READ B
30 MAT PRINT B;
40 MAT PRINT B,
50 DATA 5,3,4,6,7,9
60 END
RUN
 5   3   4

 6   7   9

 5              3              4

 6              7              9
READY
```

If no punctuation follows the matrix in a MAT PRINT statement, the comma is assumed.

More than one matrix may appear in a MAT PRINT statement.

EXAMPLE 5

```
10 DIM C(3,4),D(2,2)
20 MAT READ C,D
25 MAT PRINT C,D;
30 DATA 8,7,6,5,4,3,2,1
40 DATA 8,7,6,5,4,3,2,1
50 END
RUN
```

8	7	6	5
4	3	2	1
8	7	6	5

```
 4   3

 2   1
READY
```

Matrix C is printed first according to its format, followed by matrix D according to its format.

The general form of the MAT PRINT statement is

ln MAT PRINT **azbzcz...**

where **a,b,c, ...** denote matrices and **z** is either a comma or a semicolon. The second matrix is printed under the first, the third under the second, and so on.

17.3 One-dimensional matrices

When we are using matrix operations, a one-dimensional array is regarded as a matrix with one column. Thus, the two dimension statements DIM A(5) and DIM A(5,1) are equivalent. If an array A with five elements is to be regarded as having one row with five entries, it must be dimensioned with DIM A(1,5).

EXAMPLE 6. Here are two programs that yield the same results.

```
10 FOR I=1 TO 5          10 DIM A(1,5)
20    READ A(I)          20 MAT READ A
30    PRINT A(I);        30 MAT PRINT A;
40 NEXT I                40 DATA 3,1,6,5,4
50 DATA 3,1,6,5,4        50 END
60 END                   RUN
RUN
                          3   1   6   5   4
 3   1   6   5   4       READY
READY
```

EXAMPLE 7

```
10 DIM M(4)
20 MAT READ M
30 MAT PRINT M
40 DATA 4,3,2,1
50 END
RUN
 4

 3

 2

 1
READY
```

17.4 Matrix operations

BASIC allows the standard matrix operations of addition, subtraction, multiplication, and scalar multiplication. These operations are defined as follows.

Addition (Subtraction):   The sum (difference) of two matrices A and B is formed by adding (taking the difference of) the corresponding entries in A and B. The matrices must have the same dimensions.

Scalar Multiplication: The product cA, where c denotes a scalar (number) and A a matrix, is formed by multiplying each entry in A by c.

Multiplication: The product C = A × B of the row and column matrices

$$A = [a \quad b \quad c] \qquad B = \begin{bmatrix} x \\ y \\ z \end{bmatrix}$$

is the 1-by-1 matrix

$$C = [ax + by + cz].$$

For example,

$$[1 \quad 2 \quad 4] \times \begin{bmatrix} 1 \\ 3 \\ 4 \end{bmatrix} = [1 \cdot 1 + 2 \cdot 3 + 4 \cdot 4] = [23]$$

$$[3 \quad 2] \times \begin{bmatrix} 1 \\ 5 \end{bmatrix} = [3 \cdot 1 + 2 \cdot 5] = [13]$$

Note that the number of columns of A must equal the number of rows of B. To find the product A × B of matrices other than row-and-column matrices, we consider the rows of A as row matrices and the columns of B as column matrices. Then, the entry in the Ith row and Jth column of A × B is found by taking the product of the Ith row of A and the Jth column of B as described above. The product matrix A × B will have the same number of rows as A and the same number of columns as B. For example,

$$\begin{bmatrix} 2 & 3 & 1 \\ 4 & 1 & 2 \end{bmatrix} \times \begin{bmatrix} 1 & 2 \\ 3 & 4 \\ 1 & 5 \end{bmatrix} = \begin{bmatrix} 2 \cdot 1 + 3 \cdot 3 + 1 \cdot 1 & 2 \cdot 2 + 3 \cdot 4 + 1 \cdot 5 \\ 4 \cdot 1 + 1 \cdot 3 + 2 \cdot 1 & 4 \cdot 2 + 1 \cdot 4 + 2 \cdot 5 \end{bmatrix} = \begin{bmatrix} 12 & 21 \\ 9 & 22 \end{bmatrix}$$

The BASIC statements to perform these operations are as follows.

```
MAT S=A+B
MAT D=A−B
MAT S=(C)*A
MAT P=D*E
```

Matrices A and B must have the same dimensions so that A + B and A − B can be calculated. Also, so that the product P = D*E will be defined, the number of columns of D must equal the number of rows of E.

EXAMPLE 8. Here is a program to compute and print A + B, 2B, and A*B for the following matrices A and B.

$$A = \begin{bmatrix} 2 & 3 & 4 \\ 6 & 7 & 7 \\ 4 & 4 & 3 \end{bmatrix} \qquad B = \begin{bmatrix} 1 & 2 & 1 \\ 1 & 2 & 1 \\ 1 & 0 & 0 \end{bmatrix}$$

```
100 DIM A(3,3),B(3,3),C(3,3)
110 MAT READ A,B
120 MAT C=A+B
130 PRINT "THE MATRIX A+B"
140 PRINT
150 MAT PRINT C;
160 MAT C=(2)*B
170 PRINT "THE MATRIX 2*B"
180 PRINT
190 MAT PRINT C;
200 MAT C=A*B
210 PRINT "THE MATRIX A*B"
220 PRINT
230 MAT PRINT C;
240 DATA 2,3,4,6,7,7,4,4,3
250 DATA 1,2,1,1,2,1,1,0,0
260 END
RUN

THE MATRIX A+B

 3  5  5

 7  9  8

 5  4  3
```

```
          THE MATRIX 2*B

           2   4   2

           2   4   2

           2   0   0


          THE MATRIX A*B

           9   10   5

          20   26   13

          11   16   8
          READY
```

Remark 1   The matrix C that is to be calculated must be dimensioned to the exact size in a DIM statement.

Remark 2   Line 160 is typical of assignment statements that multiply a matrix by a scalar. Note that the scalar (2 in this case) is enclosed in parentheses. The statement is MAT C = (2)*B, not MAT C = 2*B. The scalar may be any numerical expression, but it must be enclosed in parentheses.

Remark 3   Matrix operations must be performed in assignment statements as shown in lines 120, 160, and 200. Statements such as MAT PRINT A + B are not allowed.

EXAMPLE 9

A plumbing-supply company has developed the following data over the past quarter.

	April	May	June
Income	20,415	22,355	33,451
Expenses	19,041	20,851	26,152

Write a program to compute the monthly profit for these three months and also the amount that should be put aside for tax purposes if the tax rate is 18% on all profits.

Problem analysis   Let's read the income into a 1-by-3 matrix I and the expenses into another 1-by-3 matrix E. Then the profit for each month is given by the entries in the matrix P = I − E and the taxes are given in the matrix T = .18P.

The program

```
100 REM PROFIT AND TAX COMPUTATION FOR ONE QUARTER
110 DIM I(1,3),E(1,3),P(1,3),T(1,3)
120 MAT READ I,E
130 MAT P=I-E
140 MAT T=(.18)*P
150 READ A$,B$,C$
160 PRINT ,A$,B$,C$
165 PRINT
170 PRINT "PROFIT",
180 MAT PRINT P,
190 PRINT "TAXES",
200 MAT PRINT T,
500 DATA 20415,22355,33451
510 DATA 19041,20851,26152
520 DATA APRIL,MAY,JUNE
999 END
RUN
```

	APRIL	MAY	JUNE
PROFIT	1374	1504	7299
TAXES	247.32	270.72	1313.82
READY			

The matrix expressions that may be evaluated in matrix-assignment statements are very limited compared with the freedom allowed in forming BASIC expressions with LET statements. At most one operation may be performed in a single matrix-assignment statement. Statements such as

```
MAT X=MAT Y+Z-(3)*W
```

are not allowed. Furthermore, a matrix may not be used as an operand in a statement assigning values to the same matrix. Thus, statements such as

```
MAT A=A+B
MAT A=(2)*A
```

are not allowed.

17.5 Matrix functions

Certain matrix functions are included in the BASIC language.

The CON function

The statement

```
10 MAT D=CON(4,7)
```

will generate a 4-by-7 matrix D, all of whose entries are 1s.

The ZER function

The statement

    20 MAT E=ZER(5,6)

will generate a 5-by-6 matrix E, all of whose entries are 0s. The ZER function is useful when initializing all values of an array to 0.

The IDN function

The statement

    30 MAT F=IDN(3,3)

will generate the 3-by-3 identity matrix (1s in the upper-left to lower-right diagonal and 0s elsewhere). The product of the N-by-N identity matrix and any other N-by-N matrix A is A.

The arguments in these three functions need not be positive integer constants; they may be any BASIC numerical expressions. As illustrated in the following example, they can be used to assign dimensions to matrices other than those given in DIM statements.

EXAMPLE 10. Here is an illustration of the CON, ZER, and IDN functions.

```
100 DIM C(20,20),Z(20,20),I(20,20)
110 INPUT A,B
120 MAT C=CON(A,B)
130 MAT Z=ZER(B,A)
140 MAT I=IDN(A+B,A+B)
150 MAT PRINT C;Z;I;
160 END
RUN

? 3,2

  1  1

  1  1

  1  1

  0  0  0

  0  0  0

  1  0  0  0  0

  0  1  0  0  0

  0  0  1  0  0

  0  0  0  1  0

  0  0  0  0  1
READY
```

Remark

The matrices C, Z, and I are initially dimensioned as 20-by-20 arrays in line 100. They are redimensioned in lines 120, 130, and 140 using the functions CON, ZER, IDN. If values other than 3 and 2 are input, this program will print matrices of different dimensions. The only restriction is that you cannot redimension a matrix so that it requires more memory locations (the product of its dimensions) than those reserved in the initial DIM statement (20 × 20 = 400 in this example).

BASIC contains the matrix functions **TRN** and **INV** to determine the *transpose* and *inverse*, respectively, of a matrix A. The transpose is the matrix whose rows are the columns of A. Thus, the transpose of

$$\begin{bmatrix} 1 & 2 \\ 3 & 4 \\ 5 & 6 \end{bmatrix} \quad \text{is} \quad \begin{bmatrix} 1 & 3 & 5 \\ 2 & 4 & 6 \end{bmatrix}.$$

The inverse of a matrix A is the matrix B for which A*B = B*A = I, the identity matrix. Only certain square matrices (same number of rows as columns) can have inverses. You may check that

$$\begin{bmatrix} 1 & 1 \\ 0 & 1 \end{bmatrix} \times \begin{bmatrix} 1 & -1 \\ 0 & 1 \end{bmatrix} = \begin{bmatrix} 1 & -1 \\ 0 & 1 \end{bmatrix} \times \begin{bmatrix} 1 & 1 \\ 0 & 1 \end{bmatrix} = \begin{bmatrix} 1 & 0 \\ 0 & 1 \end{bmatrix}$$

so that the inverse of

$$\begin{bmatrix} 1 & 1 \\ 0 & 1 \end{bmatrix} \quad \text{is} \quad \begin{bmatrix} 1 & -1 \\ 0 & 1 \end{bmatrix}$$

The functions TRN and INV are used in assignment statements as follows.

ln MAT **a** = TRN(**b**)
ln MAT **a** = INV(**b**)

where **a** and **b** denote different matrices.

The function TRN can sometimes be used to enhance the output of a program. For example, suppose that a 4-by-6 matrix A is to be printed. The statement

```
MAT PRINT A,
```

cannot be used, since A has six columns; at most five values will be printed on a line. If the statement

```
MAT PRINT A;
```

is used, the six columns may not "line up" because of the packed format. However, if the two statements

```
MAT T=TRN(A)
MAT PRINT T,
```

are used, there are only four columns to be printed and the difficulty vanishes.

Neither the inverse nor the transpose of a matrix may be calculated in place. Hence, statements such as

```
100 MAT B = D*INV(C)
200 MAT M = TRN(A) + E
```

are not allowed.

EXAMPLE 11. Here is a program to read and print a 3-by-3 matrix C and then to calculate and print both the inverse of C and the product of C and its inverse.

```
100 DIM A(3,3),B(3,3),C(3,3)
110 MAT READ C
120 PRINT "MATRIX C"
130 PRINT
140 MAT PRINT C
150 MAT B=INV(C)
160 PRINT "INVERSE OF C"
170 PRINT
180 MAT PRINT B
190 MAT A=C*B
200 PRINT "MATRIX C TIMES INVERSE OF MATRIX C"
210 PRINT
220 MAT PRINT A
230 DATA 1,2,3,9,8,7,-2,5,-7
240 END
RUN

MATRIX C

 1              2              3

 9              8              7

-2              5             -7

INVERSE OF C

-.478947        .152632       -5.26316E-2

 .257895       -5.26316E-3     .105263

 .321053       -4.73684E-2    -5.26316E-2

MATRIX C TIMES INVERSE OF MATRIX C

 1.             0             -1.24345E-14

 0              1.             3.55271E-15

-4.44089E-16   -3.55271E-15    1
READY
```

EXAMPLE 12

Write a program to solve the following linear system for x, y, z, and w.

$$
\begin{aligned}
x + y + z + w &= 2 \\
x + 2y - z + w &= 3 \\
2x + 3y + z - 2w &= 0 \\
x + y + 2z - 2w &= 1
\end{aligned}
$$

Problem analysis

Observing how matrix multiplication is performed, we can rewrite this system of equations in matrix form as follows.

$$
\begin{bmatrix}
1 & 1 & 1 & 1 \\
1 & 2 & -1 & 1 \\
2 & 3 & 1 & -2 \\
1 & 1 & 2 & -2
\end{bmatrix}
\times
\begin{bmatrix}
x \\ y \\ z \\ w
\end{bmatrix}
=
\begin{bmatrix}
2 \\ 3 \\ 0 \\ 1
\end{bmatrix}
$$

Let A denote the indicated 4-by-4 matrix, and let C denote the 4-by-1 matrix on the right-hand side. This matrix equation can then be written as follows.

$$
A \times
\begin{bmatrix}
x \\ y \\ z \\ w
\end{bmatrix}
= C
$$

Now suppose A has the inverse B. (If it does not, this method doesn't work. However, if this system of equations has precisely one solution, which is the case in many applications, A will have an inverse.) Then, since B × A = I, the identity matrix, we can multiply both sides of the matrix equation by B to obtain the following.

$$
\begin{bmatrix}
x \\ y \\ z \\ w
\end{bmatrix}
= B \times C
$$

The values for x, y, z, and w are thus the four entries obtained when the product B × C is performed. This analysis suggests the following simple algorithm.

Algorithm

a. Assign values to the 4-by-4 matrix A and the 4-by-1 matrix C from the given system of equations.
b. Calculate the inverse B of A and the product P = B×C.
c. Print the product P, which will display the values x, y, z, and w satisfying the given equations.

The following program clearly shows the power of the matrix operations. It would be a challenging task to write a program to solve such equations without using matrix operations.

The program

```
100 DIM A(4,4),B(4,4),C(4,1),P(4,1)
110 MAT READ A,C
120 MAT B=INV(A)
130 MAT P=B*C
140 MAT PRINT P
500 DATA 1,1,1,1
510 DATA 1,2,-1,1
520 DATA 2,3,1,-2
530 DATA 1,1,2,-2
540 DATA 2,3,0,1
999 END
RUN

-36

 23

 11

  4
READY
```

17.6 Problems

1. What will be printed when each program is run?

a.
```
10 DIM A(4,1)
20 MAT READ A
30 MAT PRINT A;
40 DATA 2,4,6,8,1,3,5
50 END
```

b.
```
10 MAT D=CON(3,3)
20 FOR I=1 TO 3
30    LET D(I,2)=D(I,2)+4
40 NEXT I
50 MAT PRINT D;
60 END
```

c.
```
10 DIM H(4,4),I(8,8)
20 MAT I=IDN(4,4)
30 FOR J=1 TO 4
40    MAT H=(J)*I
50 NEXT J
60 MAT PRINT H;
70 END
```

d.
```
10 DIM A(4,3)
20 FOR I=1 TO 4
30    FOR J=1 TO 3
40       LET A(I,J)=I+J
50    NEXT J
60 NEXT I
70 MAT PRINT A;
80 END
```

e.
```
10 DIM A(5,5)
20 MAT A=ZER(5,5)
30 FOR K=1 TO 5
40    READ A(K,K)
50 NEXT K
60 MAT PRINT A;
70 DATA 7,9,1,3,5
80 END
```

f.
```
10 DIM M(8,8)
20 MAT M=ZER(5,5)
30 FOR I=1 TO 5
40    LET M(I,I)=M(I,I)+I
50 NEXT I
60 MAT PRINT M;
70 END
```

2. Each of the following programs contains at least one error. Make corrections to ensure that all programs will run to completion.

a.
```
10 DIM A(8,1),B(8,1)
20 MAT READ A
30 MAT B=4*A
40 MAT PRINT B
50 DATA 4,3,2,1,3,5,7,9
60 END
```

b.
```
10 DIM M(2,2),D(2,2)
20 MAT M=CON(2,2)
30 MAT D=(M+M)+M
40 MAT PRINT D
50 END
```

```
c. 10 DIM A(2,3),B(3,2),C(2,2)     d. 10 DIM A(2,3),B(2,3)
   20 MAT READ A,B                    20 MAT READ A,B
   30 LET C=A*B                       30 MAT PRINT A+B
   40 MAT PRINT C                     40 DATA 2,4,6,5,7,9
   50 DATA 3,1,7,2,6,3                50 DATA 3,5,8,2,7,3
   60 DATA 5,9,1,8,-3,0               60 END
   70 END
```

Write a program to perform each task specified in Problems 3–20.

3. Read a 2-by-3 matrix A from DATA lines, and print both A and the transpose of A.

4. Read a 2-by-3 matrix A from DATA lines to determine its transpose B and the product A*B of A and its transpose. Print the three matrices A, B, and A*B.

5. Read two 3-by-2 matrices from DATA lines, and print the two matrices, the sum of the two matrices, and the transpose of this sum.

6. Input nine values for the 3-by-3 matrix A. Then print the matrices A and $A^2 = A*A$.

7. Print the cube $A^3 = A*A*A$ of any 3-by-3 matrix A whose entries are input at the terminal.

8. Read a 3-by-3 matrix A from DATA lines, and then print the matrices A, A^2, A^3, ..., A^N where N is a positive integer input at the terminal. Try your program for the value N = 6 and the matrix

$$A = \begin{bmatrix} .2 & .4 & .4 \\ .01 & .02 & .97 \\ .8 & .05 & .15 \end{bmatrix}$$

9. Often when we are using the computer to manipulate matrices whose entries are integers, we generate matrices with entries that are not actually integers as desired but are very close to integers. For instance (see Example 11), the product of a matrix and its inverse, which should be the identity matrix, often has entries very close to 0 and 1 that should actually be 0 or 1. Write a subroutine to convert all such matrices to their correct integer form.

10. DATA line 500 contains the current salaries of the eight employees of a small business. Line 510 contains the individual merit increases to be given to each employee. In addition, each person is to receive a cost-of-living adjustment of 2.5% of the current salary. Calculate and print the new salaries using only the matrix statements.

11. Last year's budgets for the seven departments in a retail store appear in DATA lines. Because of inflation, it is decided to increase each budget by 3.4%. Using only matrix statements, print the new budgets and also the total amount that must be budgeted for all seven departments.

12. A list of allowable medical-insurance claims for the preceding year is given in DATA lines. Because of a $50-deductible clause, each claim is to be reduced by $50. The amount actually paid on each claim is 80% of this reduced amount. Using only matrix statements, print the amount paid on each claim and the total amount paid.

13. An investment club owns shares in seven different companies. The first seven figures in the following DATA lines give the number of shares owned, and the second seven figures give the respective current values of these seven stocks.

```
300 DATA 100,275,350,65,840,975,355
310 DATA 37.50,12.125,42.75,87.375,125.25,8.75,34.375
```

Using only matrix statements, print the total paper value of this stock portfolio.

14. Write a program to print the transpose of the sum of two M-by-N matrices A and B.

15. Given two N-by-N matrices A and B, write a program to print the following.
   a. $(A + B)^2$ and $A^2 + 2AB + B^2$
   b. $A^2 - B^2$ and $(A + B)(A - B)$
   c. AB and BA

16. Write a program to print the two 4-by-3 matrices A and B side by side rather than one underneath the other. You may assume that both matrices contain integers of no more than four digits.

17. A square matrix A with positive entries is called a regular stochastic matrix if the sum of the entries in each row is 1. For example,

$$\begin{bmatrix} .1 & .9 \\ .6 & .4 \end{bmatrix} \quad \text{and} \quad \begin{bmatrix} .2 & .4 & .4 \\ .01 & .02 & .97 \\ .8 & .05 & .15 \end{bmatrix}$$

are regular stochastic matrices. For such a matrix A, it is known that the successive powers $A, A^2, A^3, \ldots$ approach a matrix T all of whose rows are identical. Write a program to approximate T for any regular stochastic matrix A read from DATA lines. (A user should be allowed to input an error tolerance E. The matrix A^k to be used as an approximation for T is to be the first power A^k whose entries differ from the corresponding entries of A^{k-1} by less than E.)

18. Using the method of Example 12, write a program to solve linear systems of five equations in five unknowns.

19. Write a program to solve linear systems of N equations in N unknowns. You may assume that N will be 2, 3, 4, 5, or 6. Allow a user to type a value for N and then type in the coefficients.

20. A matrix that has only one column is also called a vector. If the vector $\begin{bmatrix} x \\ y \end{bmatrix}$ is rotated through an angle of θ degrees, its image $\begin{bmatrix} x' \\ y' \end{bmatrix}$ is given by

$$x' = x \cos \theta - y \sin \theta$$
$$y' = x \sin \theta + y \cos \theta$$

or in matrix form

$$\begin{bmatrix} x' \\ y' \end{bmatrix} = \begin{bmatrix} \cos \theta & -\sin \theta \\ \sin \theta & \cos \theta \end{bmatrix} \begin{bmatrix} x \\ y \end{bmatrix}$$

Write a program to print the image of a vector when the vector and the angle are typed at the terminal.

17.7 Review true-or-false quiz

1. Once a matrix B has been read from DATA lines, the entries of B may not be changed during program execution.   T   F

2. In BASIC, *one-dimensional arrays* are considered to be *matrices* having one column.   T   F

3. If a program contains the statement DIM A(10,10), the matrix A can be given different dimensions by using the CON, ZER, or IDN functions.   T   F

4. If an 8-by-8 matrix B has been dimensioned in a DIM statement, it may be redimensioned during program execution only if both dimensions are kept less than or equal to 8.   T   F

5. In some programs it may be necessary to dimension a matrix more than once by using more than one DIM statement.   T   F

6. The statement MAT A = A + C is not allowed.   T   F

7. If A and B are both M-by-N matrices, their sum will be printed by the statement MAT PRINT A + B.   T   F

8. Matrices must be assigned values by using matrix statements.   T   F

9. The statement MAT B = A*INV(C) is not allowed.   T   F

10. The two statements MAT A = (3)*B and MAT A = B + B + B are equivalent.   T   F

Appendix A:
A Typical Session at the
Computer Terminal

During a typical session at the computer terminal, you should be able to perform the following tasks.

1. Establish communication between the terminal and the time-sharing system (log-in).
2. Save your program for later use.
3. Retrieve and run a program that was previously saved.
4. Modify a saved program.
5. Break communication between the terminal and the time-sharing system (log-off).

In this appendix, the system commands that allow you to carry out these tasks are described.

A.1 The log-in procedure

The log-in procedure differs from system to system. Normally, you will need a **password** and a **user number.** With these in hand, you should follow the log-in procedure described in the User's Guide for your BASIC system.

Following is the printout generated during a log-in to a typical time-sharing system. The underlined characters are printed by the computer.

(The time-sharing system identifies itself.)

```
USER NUMBER: ABC652          (The user number ABC652 is typed.)
PASSWORD:                    (The password is typed but not displayed at the terminal.)
SYSTEM: BASIC                (The BASIC language is selected.)
NEW OR OLD: NEW              (A new program will be typed.)
NEW FILE NAME: PROG2         (The name PROG2 is chosen.)
READY                        (The log-in procedure is complete.)
```

You may now type in your program or any system command. For example, after READY is printed, you may proceed as follows (underlined characters are printed by the computer).

```
READY
100 LET S=13*2+9
110 PRINT S
120 END
RUN

 35
READY
LIST

100 LET S=13*2+9
110 PRINT S
120 END
READY
```

A.2 Saving your program

A file created under the NEW command is called a **local** or **temporary file.** It continues to exist only as long as you are logged into the system. To preserve such a file for later use, you may issue the SAVE command.

```
SAVE          (You type this.)
READY         (Printed by the computer.)
```

The SAVE command creates a permanent copy of the current local file. This permanent copy is called a **permanent file,** for it will continue to exist even after you log off the system.

The following printout shows how you can type in two programs and create a permanent copy of each of them (underlined characters are printed by the computer).

```
NEW                       (Indicates that a new program will be typed.)
NEW FILE NAME--PROG1      (You name the program PROG1.)
READY                     (The local file PROG1 is empty.)
(Type your first program.)
    .
    .
    .
SAVE                      (Save PROG1 as a permanent file.)
READY                     (PROG1 also exists as the local file.)
```

```
NEW                            (Indicates that a new program will be typed.)
NEW FILE NAME--PROG2           (You name the program PROG2.)
READY                          (The new local file PROG2 is empty.)
(Type your second program.)
         .
         .
         .
SAVE                           (Save PROG2 as a permanent file.)
READY                          (PROG2 also exists as the local file.)
```

If you now log-off the system, the permanent files PROG1 and PROG2 will not be lost and can be used again at another time.

A.3 Retrieving a permanent file

Let's assume that the files PROG1 and PROG2 have been made permanent by the SAVE command. If at a later session you wish to run these programs, you may proceed as follows (underlined characters are printed by the computer).

```
(log-in)
         .
         .
         .
NEW OR OLD: OLD                (A previously saved file is wanted.)
OLD FILE NAME--PROG1           (Request PROG1.)
READY                          (PROG1 is now the local file.)

RUN
         .
         .
         .
    (PROG1 will be executed.)
         .
         .
         .
READY

LIST
         .
         .
         .
    (PROG1 will be listed.)
         .
         .
         .
READY

OLD                            (Type OLD to request another permanent file.)
OLD FILE NAME--PROG2           (Request PROG2.)
READY                          (PROG2 is now the local file.)
```

At this point, the files PROG1 and PROG2 continue to exist as permanent files. They can be retrieved as local files by issuing the OLD command, and, as local files, they can be executed or listed using the commands RUN and LIST. They can also be modified as described in the next section.

A.4 Modifying a permanent file

It is often the case that a program is saved before it is completely debugged. Let's assume that a permanent file named POWER2 contains such a program. To modify POWER2, you must first use the OLD command to retrieve it as the local file. Having done this, you can modify the local file POWER2 just as you could when creating it under the NEW command. After making the necessary modifications, you may replace the permanent copy of POWER2 with the modified version by typing

    REPLACE

The modified version is now the permanent file and can be retrieved at any subsequent session at the terminal.

The following printout illustrates what has just been described (underlined characters are printed by the computer).

    OLD   (Request a permanent file.)
    OLD FILE NAME--POWER2
    READY   (POWER2 is now the local file.)

    LIST

    100 LET A=5   (Contents of POWER2.)
    110 LET B=A↑2
    120 PRINT B
    130 END
    READY

    100 LET A=7   (Change line 100.)
    LIST

    100 LET A=7   (Updated POWER2.)
    110 LET B=A↑2
    120 PRINT B
    130 END
    READY

    REPLACE
    READY   (Updated version of POWER2 is now permanent.)

    RUN   (The local file POWER2 is executed.)
     49
    READY

If in this example you type SAVE instead of REPLACE, the system will print a message such as

    FILE EXISTS or POWER2 ALREADY PERMANENT

and will leave the permanent file POWER2 unchanged. If you really mean to replace the old version with the new one, you must type REPLACE. However, if you wish to preserve the permanent file POWER2 and also save the modified version that now exists as the local file POWER2, you must first rename the local file. This can be accomplished by typing

    RENAME, POWER3

where POWER3 is chosen as the new name for the local file. (You should consult the User's Guide for your system to find the precise form of the RENAME command.)

Having renamed the local file as POWER3, and assuming that you had not previously saved a file under that name, you may type the command SAVE to create a permanent copy of POWER3.

A.5 Log-off procedure

Before you log off, be sure that all permanent files no longer needed are excised from permanent storage. Each BASIC system that allows you to SAVE programs also allows you to remove them from permanent storage. On some systems the command

    UNSAVE PROG7

will remove PROG7 from permanent storage, whereas another system may require that you type

    PURGE, PROG7

The precise form to be used will be described in the User's Guide for your system. Normally, a listing of all your permanent files can be obtained with the system command CATALOG.

To break the communication link between your terminal and the time-sharing system, type

    BYE

Should this command not log you off of your system, consult your User's Guide.

IMPORTANT: At this time turn your terminal off.

Appendix B:
Terminal Files

Section 13.1 describes how you can write BASIC programs to create data files that will be used as input files to programs. Some, but not all, BASIC systems allow you to create data files simply by typing their contents at your terminal keyboard just as you would type a program. We illustrate with two examples.

EXAMPLE 1

To create a file containing the names NICKLAUS, MILLER, and WATSON with their respective scores 206, 208, and 205, you can type the following.

```
10,NICKLAUS,206
20,MILLER,208
30,WATSON,205
```

The numbers 10, 20, and 30 are line numbers, just as in an ordinary BASIC program. They are necessary when you enter a file at your terminal keyboard. If you omit the line numbers and begin your data entry by typing

```
NICKLAUS,206
```

the computer will attempt to interpret NICKLAUS as a system command and will print a diagnostic message indicating that NICKLAUS is not an admissible system command.

Next, you would save this file just as you save your BASIC programs. In the following program we assume that the file has been saved with the name SCORES.

```
10 FILE#1="SCORES"
20 IF END#1 THEN 60
30    INPUT#1,K,A$,S
40    PRINT A$,S
50 GO TO 20
60 END
RUN

NICKLAUS          206
MILLER            208
WATSON            205
READY
```

Line 20 transfers program control to the END statement if the end of file #1 has been reached. (The END# specifier is described in Section 13.1.)

The INPUT# statement in line 30 inputs three values from the file SCORES that are assigned to K, A$, and S. Note that the line numbers (10, 20, and 30) in the data file are assigned to the variable K but that K is not used in the program for any other purpose. The INPUT# statement does not make a distinction between line numbers and your data; all values in the file are treated as data.

EXAMPLE 2

To create a file containing the values 5,3,7,9,7,8,4,6, and 5, in that order, you can type the following:

```
10,  5,  3,  7
20,  9,  7,  8
30,  4,  6,  5
```

As in Example 1, the numbers 10, 20, and 30 are line numbers. They are required when creating a file at your terminal keyboard even if only numbers are to be stored on the file. If you type

```
5,  3,  7
9,  7,  8
4,  6,  5
```

the computer will "think" that you have three lines, numbered 5, 9, and 4, and will store these lines, in order, as follows:

```
4,  6,  5
5,  3,  7
9,  7,  8
```

This is not the order we specified.

In the following program we assume that the file has been saved with the name DATA3.

```
10 FILE#1="DATA3"
20 IF END#1 THEN 80
30    INPUT#1,K,A,B,C
40    PRINT "RATINGS:";A;B;C
50    PRINT "AVERAGE:";(A+B+C)/3
60    PRINT
70 GO TO 20
80 END
RUN

RATINGS:   5   3   7
AVERAGE:   5

RATINGS:   9   7   8
AVERAGE:   8

RATINGS:   4   6   5
AVERAGE:   5

READY
```

Appendix C:
Answers to
Selected Problems

Section 1.3

1. T   **2.** F   **3.** F   **4.** T   **5.** F   **6.** F   **7.** F   **8.** F   **9.** F   **10.** F   **11.** T   **12.** F

Section 2.3

1. 5% discount
2. Decide whether the discount is applicable.
3. 693.50
4. 250.00
5. 80.00 and 0, 128.00 and 0, 176.00 and 48.00, 206.00 and 78.00
6. 4 dollars
7. 6 dollars per hour
8. Step (c) is used to determine if there is any overtime. G denotes gross pay. B denotes pay for overtime hours.
9. 21
10. 1 1
  2 2
  3 6
  4 24
  5 120
  6 720
11. 55
12. 2,4,7,8,14,28,64

13. Variable names:

NAME	= name of an item
COST	= fixed cost for the item NAME
PRICE	= sale price for the item NAME
QTY	= number of units of NAME sold
GROSS	= gross sales for the item NAME
INCOME	= income from the item NAME

Algorithm:

a. Print column headings as specified.

b. Read NAME and values for COST, PRICE, and QTY, for one item.

c. Assign the value of the product QTY × PRICE to GROSS.

d. Multiply QTY times (PRICE-COST) to obtain a value for INCOME.

e. Enter NAME and the values GROSS and INCOME under the appropriate column headings.

f. Return to step (b) until the report is complete.

15. Variables:

CORP	= corporation name
SHARES	= number of shares
PRICE	= current price for one share
EARN	= earnings for one share
EQTY	= equity represented by all shares of corporation CORP
PE	= price/earnings ratio for one share

Algorithm:

a. Print column headings as specified.

b. Read CORP and values for SHARES, PRICE, and EARN.

c. Assign the value of the product SHARES × PRICE to EQTY.

d. Divide PRICE by EARN to obtain a value for PE.

e. Enter CORP and the values SHARES, EARN, EQTY, and PE under the appropriate column headings.

f. Return to step (b) until the report is complete.

17. a. Start with SUM = 0 and COUNT = 0.

b. Add the number on the top card to SUM and add 1 to COUNT.

c. Remove the top card and return to step (b) until all cards have been processed.

d. Divide SUM by COUNT to obtain the average AV and proceed to step (e) with the original stack of cards in hand.

e. If the number on the top card exceeds AV, write the letter G on the card; otherwise write the letter L.

f. Remove the top card and return to step (e) until all cards have been examined.

18. a. Depress the CLEAR key.

b. Insert your ID card into reader as shown.

c. Enter your four-digit code and depress ENTER.

d. Enter amount of check (2500 or 5000) and depress ENTER.

e. Place check in punch unit, blank side toward you.

f. Remove check when READY light comes on.

Section 2.4

1. F   **2.** F   **3.** T   **4.** F   **5.** F   **6.** F   **7.** T

Section 3.4

1. a. 17   b. 33   c. −2   d. −6   e. −15   f. system dependent: −9 or 9   g. 17
h. 9   i. 0.25   j. −9   k. 64   l. 3

2. a. 3.5   b. 5   c. 0.75   d. 0.75   e. 10   f. 25   g. 4.5   h. 1.6667   i. 10
j. 3   k. −8   l. −8

3. a, c, d, e, f, g, and j are not admissible.

4. a. admissible; −12.3

b. admissible; 4

c. 4*(−3); −12

d. admissible; 10

e. admissible; system dependent: 12 or −12

f. 5E1; 50

g. admissible; 9

h. admissible; system dependent: 9 or −9

i. 7/(−14); −0.5

    j. admissible; − 5
    k. admissible; 4.5
    l. admissible; system dependent: − 3 or undefined

5. a. 0.06*P   b. 5*X+5*Y   c. A↑2+B↑2   d. 6/(5*A)
    e. A/B+C/D   f. (A+B)/(C+D)   g. A*X↑2+B*X+C
    h. (B↑2−4*A*C)↑0.5   i. (X↑2+4*X*Y)/(X+2*Y)

6. a. X+1+Y   b. A↑2−B↑2   c. A↑3+A↑2*B+A   d. A*B/C
    e. A/B/C   f. X↑4+X↑3*D+X↑2*C+X*B+A   g. P↑Q↑R
    h. 1/A/B/C/D

Section 3.8

1. a.   110 LET M=7   b.   120 LET B=B+7
    c.   130 LET H=2*H   d.   140 LET C2=(A−B)/2
    e.   150 LET A=(1+R)↑10   f.   160 LET X=X−2*Y
    g.   170 LET C$="COST"   h.   180 LET A$="DOE,JANE"
    i.   190 LET Q$=P$ j.   200 LET S$="*****"

2. a.   50 LET X=(A+B)*C   b.   correct
    c.   100 LET R=M−N   d.   correct
    e.   15 LET X1=2+3*X   f.   100 LET S=A+B
    g.   correct   h.   40 LET Y=4*10↑0.5
    i.   5 PRINT "SUMMING PROGRAM"   j.   correct
    k.   70 LET A$="DISCOUNT"   l.   35 LET B$="B+B+B"
    m.   40 LET A$="AREA"   n.   correct
    o.   correct   p.   correct
    q.   60 LET M$="MONTHLY RENT"   r.   correct

3. a.   12   b.   AMOUNT=   108
    c.   −2   d.   5
    e.   −1   f.   LIST PRICE   45
    g.   BOBBY LOVES   DISCOUNT   4.5
       MARY   SELLING PRICE   40.5

4. a.

	A	B	C
100	1	—	—
110	1	2	—
120	1	2	1
130	1	2	3
140	4	2	3
150	4	5	3
160	4	5	2
170	4	20	2
180	2	20	2
190	2	20	11

b.

	N	Output
100	1	
110	1	1
120	2	
130	2	2
140	6	
150	6	6
160	42	
170	42	42

c.

	X	Y	Z	Output
100	0	—	—	
110	0	7	—	
120	0	7	7	
130	0	7	7	7
140	7	7	7	
150	7	343	7	
160	7	343	7	343

5. a.

	S	A	Output
100	0	—	
110	0	25	
120	25	25	
130	25	25	25
140	50	25	
150	50	25	50
160	25	25	
170	25	25	25

b.

	X	Y	Output
100	1.5	—	
110	1.5	0.6	
120	1.5	0.6	0.6
130	−1.5	0.6	
140	−1.5	0.6	−1.5
150	−1.5	0.6	0.6

c.

	N	C	S	G	P	Output	
100	130	—	—	—	—		
110	130	3	—	—	—		
150	130	3	3.6	—	—		
160	130	3	3.6	468	—		
170	130	3	3.6	468	78		
180	130	3	3.6	468	78	SALES	468
190	130	3	3.6	468	78	PROFIT	78

d.

	A	P	Output
100	—	—	NTH POWERS OF 7
110	7	—	
120	7	7	
130	7	49	
140	7	49	FOR N = 2 49
150	7	343	
160	7	343	FOR N = 3 343
170	7	2401	
180	7	2401	FOR N = 4 2401
190	7	2401	

Section 3.9

1. F   **2.** T   **3.** T   **4.** F   **5.** F   **6.** F   **7.** T   **8.** T   **9.** F   **10.** T   **11.** F
12. F   **13.** F   **14.** T

Section 4.7

1.
```
100 LET A=14
110 LET B=30
120 LET S=A+B
130 PRINT "SUM IS",S
140 END
```
Output: SUM IS   44

2.
```
100 LET X=5
120 LET Y=20
125 LET S=X+Y
130 PRINT "X+Y=",S
140 END
```
Output: X+Y=   25

3.
```
110 LET P=120
120 LET D=0.1*P
130 LET C=P-D
140 PRINT "DISCOUNT",D
150 PRINT "COST",C
160 END
```
Output: DISCOUNT   12
            COST   108

4.
```
100 LET L$="AVERAGE"
110 LET A=9
120 LET B=7
130 LET M=(A+B)/2
140 PRINT L$,M
150 END
```
Output: AVERAGE   8

5. Syntax: 30 LET D=23000
Programming: 40 LET R=.06
Syntax: 50 LET A=R*D
Output: ANSWER IS   1380

6. Programming: 50 LET A=(N1+N2)/2
Syntax: 60 PRINT "AVERAGE IS",A
Output: AVERAGE IS   19.5

7. Syntax and programming:
    40 LET T=0.05
Syntax:
    70 PRINT "TOTAL COST=",S
Output: TOTAL COST= 126

8. Syntax and programming: 60 LET X=-B/A
Output: SOLUTION IS -6.28571

9. Programming: 165 LET T=A
                180 LET B=T
Output: A =   5
           B =   8
           A =   8
           B =   5

10. Syntax: quotes missing in lines 170 and 190
Programming: 185 LET T=V*R
Output: TAX ON FIRST CAR IS   297
          TAX ON SECOND CAR IS   376.2

Section 4.8

1. T   **2.** F   **3.** T   **4.** F   **5.** T   **6.** T   **7.** F   **8.** T   **9.** T   **10.** F

Section 5.2

1. 120 LET A=100*(1.06)↑X

5. 120 LET A=X/19.2

9. 120 LET A=(4*X/3.14159)↑0.5

3. 120 LET A=X+0.045*X

7. 120 LET A=X/(52*40)

Section 5.4

1. a

	Output:		b.	Output:		c.	Output:		d.	Output:
	1			A B C			1 1			5
	1			B A C			2 2			−1
	2			C A B			3 6			4
	3			A C B			4 24			−2
	5			B C A			5 120			3
	8			C B A			·			·
	·			·			·			·
	·			·			·			·
	·									

2. a. 60 GO TO 40

   c. 40 LET T=0.08*X.

      Change line number 50 to 25.

   b. 40 LET D=B−A. Interchange lines 50 and 60.

   d. 50 LET R=N↑(1/2)

      80 GO TO 50

Section 5.5

1. T   **2.** F   **3.** T   **4.** F   **5.** F   **6.** F   **7.** T   **8.** T   **9.** F

Section 6.4

1. a. T   b. T   c. F   d. T   e. F   f. T   g. F   h. F   i. T   j. F   k. F   l. F

2. a. (A−B)*(A+B) is not a relational expression. Error message.

   b. The comma will cause an error message.

   c. 2<Y<4 is not an admissible relational expression. Error message.

   d. If A<B, control is transferred to line 70. Infinite loop.

   e. Line 51 will be executed next whether or not X<X−B.

   f. Improper use of IF statement. Error message.

   g. NOT (K/3) is not an admissible logical expression. Error message.

   h. (A OR B) is not an admissible logical expression. Error message.

   i. If J ≠ K, control is transferred to line 40. Infinite loop.

   j. K=4 OR 7 is not an admissible logical expression. Error message.

3. a. Change line 60 to 60 IF N<=15 THEN 40.

   b. Delete line 150.

4. a. −1   b. 5   c. 14   d. 3   e. 5   f. 52

                 1.75   THAT'S ALL

5. a.
```
10 INPUT N
20 IF N>=50 THEN LET N=N/2
30 IF N<25 THEN LET N=N/2
40 PRINT N
50 END
```

b.
```
30 IF A>0 THEN LET S=20
```
Delete lines 40 and 50.

c.
```
10 INPUT X,Y
20 IF (X<=0) OR (Y<=0) THEN 10
30 LET S=X+Y
40 PRINT S
50 END
```

d.
```
10 INPUT A,B
20 IF A<=B THEN 60
30 LET T=A
40 LET A=B
50 LET B=T
60 PRINT "SMALLEST IS",A
70 PRINT "LARGEST IS",B
80 END
```

Section 6.10

1. T   **2.** T   **3.** F   **4.** F   **5.** T   **6.** F   **7.** T   **8.** T   **9.** F   **10.** F   **11.** T
12. T   **13.** F   **14.** T   **15.** F

Section 7.2

1. a. 9   b. 6   c. 18   d. 26   e. −43   f. 2.4   g. 1200   h. 4   i. 3
2. a. 4   b. 5   c. 6   d. −4   e. 2865   f. 2860   g. 2900   h. 3000   i. 2864.714
3. a.

0	8
1	8
2	6
3	2
4	4

b.

1.1	1
1.21	1
1.331	1
1.4641	1

c.

13.99	13.99
13.993	13.99
13.996	14.
13.999	14.

d.

3
7
9
21

4. a. `10 LET X=INT(10*X+0.5)/10`   c. `30 LET X=INT(1000*X+0.5)/1000`
e. `50 LET X=1000*INT(X/1000+0.5)`

Section 7.4

1. a. Programming error: `50 LET V=FNZ(X)`
b. Programming error: `20 DEF FNS(X)=X↑2`
c. Syntax error: use FNC for FCN
d. Syntax error: `40 LET J=FNC(I,FND(I))`

2. a.

0	3
1	4
2	5
3	6

b.

50
60
70
80

3. a.   `10 DEF FNF(C)=9/5*C+32`   b.   `20 DEF FNC(F)=5/9*(F−32)`
c.   `30 DEF FNM(F)=F/5280`   d.   `40 DEF FNM(K)=K/1.6093`
e.   `50 DEF FNK(M)=1.6093*M`   f.   `60 DEF FNA(X,Y)=(X+Y)/2`
g.   `70 DEF FNS(D,T)=D/T`   h.   `80 DEF FNS(X,Y)=X−Y/100*X`
i.   `90 DEF FNC(X,Y)=X/15*Y/100`
j.   `200 DEF FNH(A,B)=SQR(A↑2+B↑2)`
k.   `210 DEF FNA(R)=3.14159*R↑2`
l.   `220 DEF FNV(R)=4/3*3.14159*R↑3`
m.   `230 DEF FNS(A)=SIN(3.14159/180*A)`

Section 7.5

1. T   **2.** F   **3.** T   **4.** F   **5.** F   **6.** T   **7.** F   **8.** T   **9.** T   **10.** T   **11.** F
12. F   **13.** T

Section 8.4

1. a. `BASEBALL'S HALL OF FAME     COOPERSTOWN,N.Y.          U.S.A.`
b.

0	5	10	15	20
25	30	35	FINI	

c. `5 TIMES 8 = 40`
d. `HAPPY`
`        HAPPY`
`                HOLIDAY`
e. `1 3 5 7`
`2 4 6 8`
f. `IF A= 5 A+2= 7`
`IF A= 10 A+2= 12`
`IF A= 15 A+2= 17`

2. a. `10 PRINT X;"/";Y;"=";X/Y`   c. `30 PRINT "X-";Y;"=";-X`
   e. `50 PRINT "DEPT.NO.";Y+Y+X`
3. a. `145 PRINT`   b. `120 PRINT "7";`   c. Prints TEAFORTWO
   `150 PRINT X;`
   `160 LET X=X+1`

Section 8.6

1. a. ```
   0
    -1
     -2
      -3
       -4
   THAT'S ENOUGH
   ```
   b. ```
   7777777
         7
         7
         7
         7
         7
         7
   ```

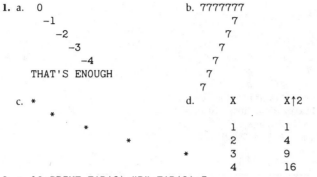

   c. ```
   *
     *
       *
         *
           *
   ```
   d. ```
        X        X↑2

        1        1
        2        4
        3        9
        4        16
   ```

2. a. `10 PRINT TAB(6);"B";TAB(9);3`
   b. `20 PRINT X;TAB(19);0.04*X;TAB(37);0.06*X;TAB(55);0.08*X`
   c. `90 PRINT 0;TAB(15);0;TAB(29);0;TAB(43);0;TAB(57);0;TAB(71);0`
   d. `25 PRINT TAB((72-N)/2);"...name..."` where N = number of characters in name

Section 8.8

1. a. ```
   1/8=12.5 CENTS
   3/8=37.5 CENTS
   5/8=62.5 CENTS
   7/8=87.5 CENTS
   ```
   b. ```
   TIME 1 A= 0.00
   TIME 2 A= 0.01
   TIME 3 A= 0.01
   ```
   c. ```
   123456789
      23.60
      23.6
   ```
   d. ```
   RIVERBOAT
            BOATSWAIN
   ```
   e. `POPEYE`
   f. ```
   BOBBY LOVES JUDITH
   JUDI LOVES BOB
   ```

---

# Section 8.9

**1.** F    **2.** T    **3.** F    **4.** T    **5.** F    **6.** T    **7.** F

---

# Section 9.2

**1.** a. 4        b. 6        c. CATWOMAN        d. 7
        7           4                              3
        1                                          18
                                                   4

**2.** a. Change line 30 to 30 DATA 1,A
   b. Replace Y in lines 10 and 20 by Y$.
      Replace ; in line 10 by ,.
   c. Replace HELLO in line 20 by "HELLO".
   d. Change line 50 to 50 DATA "DOOLEY,TOM".
   ```

3. a. 140 READ X
    150 LET S=S+X

    b. 130 READ A
    160 IF N<=4 THEN 130

    c. 105 LET N=0
    107 LET S=0
    130 LET N=N+1
    150 GO TO 110

    d. 160 IF X=999 THEN 190
    170 LET S=S+X
    180 GO TO 140
    190 PRINT S
    200 GO TO 130

Section 9.5

1. a. 9
    3
    5

    b. 3
    5
    3
    5

    c. ROBINHEAD

    d. ALLEN 40
    ALLEN 40

2. a. Delete lines 150 and 160.

    b. Insert REM in lines 110 and 120
    135 RESTORE
    160 IF I>4 THEN 130

Section 9.6

1. T **2.** F **3.** F **4.** F **5.** T **6.** T **7.** F **8.** F **9.** T **10.** T **11.** F
12. T **13.** T **14.** F **15.** F **16.** T

Section 10.4

1. a. 4
    5
    6

    b. 5
    1
    −3

    c. TIMES THROUGH LOOP = 2
    3

    d. +++///

    e. LOOP

    f. 6
    4

    g. 2 9
    5 3

    h. 5 2
    −9 −6

2. a. Syntax error: 50 NEXT N

    b. Programming error: 25 LET C=0
    Delete line 40.

    c. Programming error:
    40 READ Y
    50 LET S=S+Y
    65 PRINT "SUM IS";S

    d. Programming error:
    Step S is admissible but the step value
    cannot be changed within the loop.
    30 LET S=0
    40 FOR N=1 TO 5
    50 LET S=S+N
    60 PRINT S

Section 10.7

1. a. 2
    3
    2
    3
    2
    3

    b. 13 16 11 14

    c. 1 1 1 1 1
    2 2 2 2 2
    3 3 3 3 3

    d. 2 3 4 5
    3 4 5
    4 5
    5

    e. 108

    f.
```
       *
      ***
     *****
    *******
   *********
    *******
     *****
      ***
       *
```

2. a. Syntax error: interchange lines 50 and 60.

    b. Programming error: include STEP -1 in lines 20 and 30.

    c. Programming error: 30 IF I>=J THEN 50

    d. Programming error: 30 IF R<=C THEN 60

Section 10.8

1. F   **2.** T   **3.** T   **4.** F   **5.** T   **6.** F   **7.** T   **8.** F   **9.** T   **10.** F   **11.** T

Section 11.3

1. a. 5   b. 3 1 5   c. 8   d. 8   8
          4   3   3

2. a. DIM statement needed.   b. Values of L(6) through L(10) are lost.
   c. 425 LET S=L(1)
      430 FOR J=2 TO N
      440 IF S<L(J) THEN LET S=L(J)

Section 11.7

1. a. 1 4 9 16   b. 2 4 6
   c. 1 1 2   d. 8 1
                                5

   e. 1 1 1 1   f. 0 8 0 3
      0 1 1 1   2 0 7 0
      0 0 1 1   0 8 0 3
      0 0 0 1

2. a. Interchange lines 220 and 230.
   b. 230 FOR J=I+1 TO 5

Section 11.8

1. T   **2.** F   **3.** F   **4.** F   **5.** F   **6.** F   **7.** T   **8.** T   **9.** F   **10.** F   **11.** F   **12.** F

Section 12.2

1. a. A   b. CAT   DOG
      M   7   9
                       BEAST   BEAST
   c.   HARRY
        ALICE
        LAST
        LAST

Section 12.4

1. a. ROBERT   b. ABMANCAT   c. PAYCHECK,JOHN
      ALBERT   DENVER,JOHN
                                          JOHN,ELTON
                                          CASH,JOHN

Section 12.7

1. a. CYBER   b. Z TO A   c. CONSULTATION   d. BIOPHYSICS
2. Same answers as Problem 1.
3. a. 10 PRINT LEFT$(A$,1)   or   10 PRINT A$(1:1)
   b. 15 PRINT MID$(A$,2,1)   or   15 PRINT A$(2:2)
   c. 20 PRINT RIGHT$(A$,LEN(A$))   or   20 PRINT A$(LEN(A$):LEN(A$))
   d. 25 PRINT LEFT$(A$,3)   or   25 PRINT A$(1:3)
   e. 30 PRINT RIGHT$(A$,LEN(A$)-2)   or   30 PRINT A$(LEN(A$)-2:LEN(A$))
   f. 35 PRINT LEFT$(A$,1);RIGHT$(A$,LEN(A$))   or
        PRINT A$(1:1);A$(LEN(A$):LEN(A$))
   g. 40 IF LEN(A$)=LEN(B$) THEN 70
   h. 45 IF LEFT$(A$,1)=RIGHT$(A$,LEN(A$)) THEN 95   or
        IF A$(1:1)=A$(LEN(A$):LEN(A$)) THEN 95

```
        i. 50 IF LEFT$(A$,1)=MID$(A$,2,1) THEN 160    or
              IF A$(1:1)=A$(2:2) THEN 160
        j. 55 LET B$=LEFT$(A$,N)    or    LET B$=A$(1:N)
     4. a. 10 LET B$=RIGHT$(A$,2)+LEFT$(A$,1)    or    LET B$=A$(2:2)+A$(1:1)
        b. 15 LET T$=MID$(S$,2,1)+LEFT$(S$,1)+RIGHT$(S$,3)    or
              LET T$=S$(2:2)+S$(1:1)+S$(3:LEN(S$))
        c. 20 LET F$=LEFT$(G$,3)+RIGHT$(H$,LEN(H$)-2)    or
              LET F$=G$(1:3)+H$(LEN(H$)-2:LEN(H$))
        d. 25 IF LEFT$(A$,1)+MID$(B$,2,1)+MID$(C$,3,1)="YES" THEN 150    or
              IF A$(1:1)+B$(2:2)+C$(3:3)="YES" THEN 150
```

Section 12.10

1. a. 579111315   b. 42 WINS AND 21 LOSSES GIVES A WINNING PERCENTAGE OF .667
c. 31+31=62   d. E 5   e. 7 7

Section 12.11

1. F   **2.** F   **3.** F   **4.** F   **5.** F   **6.** T   **7.** T   **8.** T   **9.** T   **10.** F   **11.** T
12. T   **13.** F

Section 13.2

1. a.
```
   SAM
   GREG
   MARY
```
b.
```
   JOAN      PASS
   SAM       PASS
   GREG      FAIL
   MARY      FAIL
   MARK      PASS
```

2. a.
```
   J.D.SLOANE
   EXCESS: 3000

   A.B.CARTER
   EXCESS: 2400

   I.O.ULSTER
   EXCESS: 2000
```
b.
```
   J.D.SLOANE      565
   R.M.PETERS      265
   A.B.CARTER      505
   I.O.ULSTER      465
```

Section 13.4

1. a.
```
   JOAN      78
   SAM       75
   GREG      86
   ALICE     81
   MARK      93
```
b. 95   c. FIRST PLACE----TEAM 4

d.
```
   JOAN      78
   JILL      72
   GREG      86
   JANE      95
   MARK      93
   SAL       64
   SAM       75
   JACK      88
   ALICE     81
   PETE      79
```

Section 13.7

1. F   **2.** F   **3.** F   **4.** F   **5.** T   **6.** T   **7.** F   **8.** T

Section 14.2

1. a.
```
1   3   5    8
2   8   6   14
3  -2   1   -1
```
b.
```
 2
-2
```
c.
```
 1
 3
 6
10
```
d. 343

Section 14.4

1. 9
   5
  13

2. 1.41421

Section 14.5

1. T   **2.** F   **3.** F   **4.** F   **5.** F   **6.** F   **7.** T   **8.** T   **9.** F

Section 15.5

1. a. `10 PRINT 4*RND`   b. `20 PRINT 6*RND+5`
    c. `30 PRINT 8*RND-5`   d. `40 PRINT INT(7*RND)+6`
    e. `50 PRINT 2*INT(5*RND)`   f. `60 PRINT 2*INT(5*RND)+1`

2. a. T   b. T   c. T   d. T   e. either   f. T   g. T   h. either (but most likely false)

3. a. 1,2 (equally likely)   b. 0
    c. −2,−1,0,1,2 (equally likely)   d. 2,3,4 (3 about half the time; 2 and 4 each about one-fourth the time)
    e. 2,3,4, . . . , 12 (not equally likely—simulates rolling a pair of dice)
    f. 1,2,3,4,6,9 (not equally likely)

4. ONE OF EACH, TWO HEADS, and TWO TAILS will be printed about the same number of times. In practice, ONE OF EACH will occur about half the time.

Section 15.10

1. T   **2.** F   **3.** T   **4.** F   **5.** F   **6.** F   **7.** F   **8.** F   **9.** T   **10.** T   **11.** F

Section 16.6

1. F   **2.** F   **3.** T   **4.** F   **5.** T   **6.** T   **7.** T   **8.** T   **9.** F   **10.** T   **11.** T

Section 17.6

1. a.
```
2
4
6
8
```
b.
```
1 5 1
1 5 1
1 5 1
```
c.
```
4 0 0 0
0 4 0 0
0 0 4 0
0 0 0 4
```
d.
```
2 3 4
3 4 5
4 5 6
5 6 7
```
e.
```
7 0 0 0 0
0 9 0 0 0
0 0 1 0 0
0 0 0 3 0
0 0 0 0 5
```
f.
```
1 0 0 0 0
0 2 0 0 0
0 0 3 0 0
0 0 0 4 0
0 0 0 0 5
```

2. a. `30 MAT B=(4)*A`   b. `30 MAT D=(3)*M`
    c. `30 MAT C=A*B`   d. `15 DIM S(2,3)`
                                `30 MAT S=A+B`
                                `35 MAT PRINT S`

Section 17.7

1. F   **2.** T   **3.** T   **4.** F   **5.** F   **6.** T   **7.** F   **8.** F   **9.** T   **10.** F

Index

To the owner of this book:

We'd like to know as much about your experiences with *BASIC: An Introduction to Computer Programming, 2nd edition,* as you care to offer. Only through your comments and the comments of others can we learn how to make this book a better book for future readers.

1. Under what circumstances did you use this book?
   _____ As a student   _____ As an instructor
   _____ As a computer hobbyist _____ Other

2. Approximately, how much of the book did you actually use?
   _____ 1/4 _____ 1/2 _____ 3/4 _____ All

3. What did you like most about the book?

4. What did you like least about the book?

5. As you know, BASIC systems differ. Did you find the presentation of any of the BASIC statements to be especially troublesome to you? What changes do you feel will improve the book?

6. Other comments:

7. Optional:

Name and address: _____

_____

_____

_____

School: _____

Date: _____

Sincerely,
Robert J. Bent
George C. Sethares

_____
FOLD HERE

CUT PAGE OUT

FOLD HERE

NO POSTAGE
NECESSARY
IF MAILED
IN THE
UNITED STATES

BUSINESS REPLY MAIL
FIRST CLASS   PERMIT NO. 84   MONTEREY, CALIF.

POSTAGE WILL BE PAID BY ADDRESSEE

Robert J. Bent
George C. Sethares
BROOKS/COLE PUBLISHING COMPANY
MONTEREY, CA 93940